READING THE MEDIEVAL IN EARLY MODERN ENGLAND

In English literary and historical studies the border between the Middle Ages and the early modern period, and hence between medieval and early modern studies, has in recent years become increasingly permeable. The chapters in this volume, written by medievalists and early modernists, consider the ways in which medieval culture was read and reconstructed by writers and scholars in early modern England. It also addresses the reciprocal process: the way in which early modern England, while apparently suppressing the medieval past, was in fact shaped and constructed by it, albeit in ways that early modern thinkers had an interest in suppressing. The book deals with this process as it is played out in literature in particular, but also in visual culture, for example in mapping, and in material culture, as in the physical destruction of the medieval past in the early modern English landscape.

GORDON McMULLAN is Reader in English at King's College London and a general editor of Arden Early Modern Drama. He is the author of *The Politics of Unease in the Plays of John Fletcher* (1994) and the editor of the Arden edition of Shakespeare and Fletcher's *Henry VIII* (2000). His monograph, *Shakespeare and the Idea of Late Writing*, is forthcoming from Cambridge University Press.

DAVID MATTHEWS lectures in medieval literature at the University of Manchester. He is the author of *The Making of Middle English, 1765–1910* (1999) and the editor of *The Invention of Middle English: An Anthology of Sources* (2000). He is currently working on political verse of the thirteenth and fourteenth centuries.

READING THE MEDIEVAL IN EARLY MODERN ENGLAND

EDITED BY

GORDON McMULLAN

AND

DAVID MATTHEWS

CAMBRIDGE
UNIVERSITY PRESS

CAMBRIDGE UNIVERSITY PRESS
Cambridge, New York, Melbourne, Madrid, Cape Town, Singapore, São Paulo

Cambridge University Press
The Edinburgh Building, Cambridge CB2 8RU, UK

Published in the United States of America by Cambridge University Press, New York

www.cambridge.org
Information on this title: www.cambridge.org/9780521868433

© Cambridge University Press 2007

First published 2007

Printed in the United Kingdom at the University Press, Cambridge

A catalogue record for this publication is available from the British Library

ISBN 978-0-521-86843-3 hardback

Contents

Illustrations

vii

Contributors

PATRICIA BADIR, Associate Professor of English at the University of British Columbia, works on religious iconography and post-medieval devotional writing and has published on community identity in medieval and early modern drama. Her book, *The Maudlin Impression: Mary Magdalen and English Religious Writing, 1560–1700*, is forthcoming.

SARAH BECKWITH, Marcello Lotti Professor of English at Duke University, is a leading figure in the study of late medieval religious writing and of medieval drama. She is the author of *Signifying God: Social Relation and Symbolic Act in the York Corpus Christi Plays* (2001) and is currently working on a book on Shakespeare and the transformation of sacramental culture.

ANKE BERNAU is Lecturer in Medieval Literature and Culture at the University of Manchester. She co-edited *Medieval Virginities* with Ruth Evans and Sarah Salih (2003). Her cultural history, *Virginity*, will be published by Granta. She is currently working on a study of national foundation myths in the Middle Ages.

BERNHARD KLEIN is Reader in Literature at the University of Essex. He has written *Maps and the Writing of Space in Early Modern England and Ireland* (2001) and *On the Uses of History in Recent Irish Writing* (2007). He has also edited or co-edited several collections of essays, including most recently *Sea Changes: Historicizing the Ocean* (2004).

GORDON McMULLAN is Reader in English at King's College London and a general editor of Arden Early Modern Drama. *The Politics of Unease in the Plays of John Fletcher* was published in 1994 and his Arden edition of Shakespeare and Fletcher's *Henry VIII* in 2000 and he has edited or co-edited three collections of essays. His monograph, *Shakespeare and the Idea of Late Writing*, is forthcoming from Cambridge University Press.

DAVID MATTHEWS lectures in medieval literature at the University of Manchester. His *The Making of Middle English, 1765–1910* was published in 1999 and was followed by *The Invention of Middle English: An Anthology of Sources* in 2000. He is currently working on political verse of the thirteenth and fourteenth centuries.

LARRY SCANLON, Associate Professor of English at Rutgers University, is the author of *Narrative, Authority and Power: The Medieval Exemplum and the Chaucerian Tradition* (Cambridge University Press, 1994) as well as numerous articles on the *exemplum*, Gower, and medieval sexualities. He is a former editor of *Studies in the Age of Chaucer*.

CATHY SHRANK, Lecturer in English at the University of Sheffield, works on Renaissance humanism, identities, translation and the book as physical object. Her book, *Writing the Nation: Literature, Humanism and English Identities, 1530–1580* was published in 2004; an essay on *Coriolanus* was recently published in *Shakespeare Quarterly*; and an edition of Massinger's *The City Madam* is forthcoming in the Globe Quartos series.

JAMES SIMPSON, Professor of English at Harvard University, is the author of the recent *Reform and Cultural Revolution*, volume II (1350–1547) of the *Oxford English Literary History*. He has published extensively on Gower, on *Piers Plowman*, and on images and idolatry.

JENNIFER SUMMIT is Associate Professor of English at Stanford University. She works in both medieval and early modern literature, specifically on Chaucer, Spenser, Reformation culture and periodisation. Her book, *Lost Property: The Woman Writer and English Literary History, c. 1380–1589*, was published in 2000. She is currently working on a book on post-Reformation libraries and their construction of the medieval past.

STEPHANIE TRIGG is Associate Professor of English at the University of Melbourne and author of *Congenial Souls: Chaucer's Readers, Medieval to Postmodern* (2001). She is currently working on a cultural history of the Order of the Garter and on an interdisciplinary study of the representation of women's work in late medieval England.

DAVID WALLACE is Judith Rodin Professor of English at the University of Pennsylvania. His *Chaucerian Polity: Absolutist Lineages and Associational Form in England and Italy* was published in 1999. He is editor of the revisionary *Cambridge History of Medieval English Literature* (1999) and, with Carolyn Dinshaw, *The Cambridge Companion to Medieval Women's*

Writing (2003). His most recent book is *Premodern Places: Calais to Surinam, Chaucer to Aphra Behn* (2004).

DEANNE WILLIAMS is Associate Professor of English at York University, Toronto. She is the author of *The French Fetish from Chaucer to Shakespeare* (Cambridge University Press, 2004), which received the Roland H. Bainton Prize in 2005, and the co-editor of *Postcolonial Approaches to the European Middle Ages: Translating Cultures* (Cambridge University Press, 2004). Current projects include a study of Shakespearean medievalism and an edition of Greene's *Friar Bacon and Friar Bungay*.

Acknowledgements

Turning a set of essays – many though not all of which began life as conference papers – into book chapters is a slow and complex process and we are very grateful to everyone involved for their patience. We would like to thank the contributors in particular for staying with us through the inevitably long-drawn-out stages of collection, submission, revision and final version, and in particular for being prepared to rethink their individual essays in light of the others. We would like also to thank the anonymous readers for Cambridge University Press for arguing in favour of publication. Above all, we would like to thank Sarah Stanton both for supporting the project in the first place and for being so precise in outlining what she needed to make the material work not just as a collection of essays but as a book. She sets the standards, which must be a bit daunting, for commissioning editors everywhere, and her support for early-period criticism is invaluable.

We are grateful to two institutions – King's College London and the University of Newcastle, New South Wales – for providing both context and funding for the two conferences out of which this collection emerged. We are grateful too to those who took part in the two conferences, either by contributing papers or by chairing sessions or simply by being present, but who are not represented by an essay in this volume: in London, these include Julia Boffey, Helen Cooper, Janet Cowan, Ruth Evans, Simon Gaunt, Alexandra Gillespie, Robert Mills, Helen Moore, Miri Rubin, Paul Strohm and Louise Sylvester; in Newcastle, Hilary Carey, Louisa Connors, Hugh Craig, Elizabeth Keen, David Keyworth, Ruth Lunney, Jenna Mead, Sally Parkin, Thomas Prendergast, Juanita Feros Ruys, Jonathan Sawday and Lawrence Warner. We would like in particular to thank Peter Holbrook.

Gordon McMullan is especially grateful to the University of Newcastle, NSW, for awarding him a Research Visitorship for the summer (or, rather, winter) of 2003 which enabled him both to share the running of the second conference and to write the first draft of his essay. He is grateful to David for setting the whole thing up in the first place, and he would like to thank his then head of department, Ann Thompson (herself, of course, known for her work on Chaucer and Shakespeare), and other colleagues in the Department of English at King's – especially Clare Lees and the members of the Research Committee – for enthusing about, supporting, and helping to secure funds for the London conference. And he would like to thank the librarians of Sydney University Library and the British Library for their assistance.

David Matthews is grateful to the Research Management Committee of the University of Newcastle, which funded the conference and overcame the tyranny of distance with generous travel grants. He also wishes to thank Hugh Craig, Head of the School of Language and Media, for his support.

On a more personal level, we want also to thank the following for making the process fun (or as near to fun as running two conferences and editing a collection of essays are ever likely to be): Jeni Porter, John Potts, Rohan Mead and *As You Do*. And Mac wants in particular to thank Jonathan Sawday, Ruth Evans and Emily Wade for sharing a breathtaking few days' sailing in the Whitsundays after the Newcastle conference. Climbing into the dinghy off a pier straight out of the old cinema Bacardi adverts was one of life's perfect moments. If only all conferences concluded in such style.

DAVID MATTHEWS
GORDON McMULLAN

Abbreviations

BL	British Library
CUL	Cambridge University Library
DNB	Leslie Stephen and Sidney Lee (eds.), *Dictionary of National Biography*, 66 vols. (London, 1885–1901)
EETS, os	Early English Text Society, original series
EiC	*Essays in Criticism*
ELN	*English Language Notes*
Harl. MS	Harley Manuscript
JMEMS	*Journal of Medieval and Early Modern Studies*
MLR	*Modern Language Review*
ODNB	H. C. G. Matthews and Brian Harrison (eds.), *The Oxford Dictionary of National Biography*, 60 vols. (Oxford: Oxford University Press, 2004) and online edition, http://www.oxforddnb.com/2005–
OED	*Oxford English Dictionary*
PL	J.-P. Migne (ed.), *Patrologia Latina cursus completus . . . series Latina*, 221 vols. (Paris, 1844–65)
SAC	*Studies in the Age of Chaucer*
STC	A. W. Pollard and G. R. Redgrave, *A Short-Title Catalogue of Books Printed in England, Scotland, & Ireland . . .* (London: Bibliographical Society, 1926); 2nd edn, rev. and enl. Katherine A. Pantzer (London: Bibliographical Society, 1986)

Introduction: reading the medieval in early modern England

David Matthews and Gordon McMullan

I

The printed text of *The Two Noble Kinsmen*, a Shakespeare and Fletcher collaboration first performed in 1613 though not published until 1634, opens with a prologue noting the play's debt to Geoffrey Chaucer and *The Knight's Tale*, a debt expressed as a sense of responsibility to the poet of the medieval past:

> If we let fall the nobleness of this
> And the first sound this child hear be a hiss,
> How will it shake the bones of that good man
> And make him cry from under ground, 'Oh, fan
> From me the witless chaff of such a writer
> That blasts my bays and my famed works makes lighter
> Than Robin Hood!'[1]

Elaborating both on this responsibility and on the impossibility of reaching the same heights of poetic achievement as Chaucer, the writer of the prologue (who may be John Fletcher, though the 'we' seems to encompass both the playwrights and the acting company) pursues his modesty topos: to aspire to Chaucer's art involves a 'breathless swim / In . . . deep water' (24–5) and the audience is asked to hold out 'helping hands' while the playwrights 'tack about / And something do to save' themselves (26–7). The extended metaphor becomes so overblown that the effect is humorous; we know, as of course we are supposed to know, that Shakespeare and Fletcher are not really cowering under Chaucer's long shadow. For all the awe that he inspires, Chaucer is in the grave. *The Two Noble Kinsmen* may be only a 'child' of Chaucer's work, but this child lives and Chaucer does not.

By 1613, interest in Chaucer was in fact declining. As Ann Thompson notes, a cluster of Chaucer-inspired plays around 1599–1602 may reflect interest sparked by the two Chaucer editions of Thomas Speght (1598 and 1602), but thereafter the medieval poet's influence on drama declined markedly and Speght's 1602 edition was to be the last for more than a century.[2] The prologue, then, offers a nod to a poet whose influence is declining and the prospect of an unquiet Chaucer does not, finally, feel unduly daunting to the play's authors or to their interpellated audience: 'You shall hear / Scenes, though below his art, may yet appear / Worth two hours' travail. To his bones sweet sleep!' (27–9). Chaucer does not actually pronounce the speech of complaint the prologue puts in his mouth which is in any case contingent on the play failing in performance, something which the prologue, at its end, seems confident will not happen.

The spectre of Chaucer has nonetheless been raised and the play's indebtedness acknowledged. While the prologue moves from threatening the appearance of an inconvenient ghost from the medieval past to the exorcism of that ghost, it is still Chaucer's version of the story that lives 'constant to eternity'. By mentioning Chaucer at all, Fletcher (or whoever it is) raises the possibility both that the sleep of the spectral medieval past might not be as easy as he would wish and that the medieval continues not just to be read and received in his own day but also works to construct the ways in which it is read. The prologue might be playful, even lacking in the respect it professes, but it also acknowledges that, without its source, the play would not exist.

In this example of reading the medieval in early modern England, then, some of the ambivalences in the process of that reading can be seen. On the one hand the medieval past is, like Chaucer, safely in the grave and sweetly sleeping. But on the other, that past threatens both to speak from the grave to complain of shaken bones and to shape the way the present conceives it: medieval culture thus addresses attempts later made to adapt it and, behind the rhetorical construction of early modern superiority, it manages to insert a certain anxiousness into that later work. At the same time as it gestures toward the sense of rupture between medieval and early modern, the prologue to *The Two Noble Kinsmen* shows an anxiety about the legacy of the one for the other and the possibility of *continuity* between them. This legacy and its ramifications – the anxious attempts to suppress the early modern period's medieval heritage, the continuities that nevertheless make themselves felt, and the ways in which the early modern was in fact constructed by way of the medieval – form the subject of *Reading the Medieval in Early Modern England*.

II

In English literary and historical studies, the borderline between the Middle Ages and the period known, depending on the disciplinary or theoretical affiliations of the writer, either as 'the Renaissance' or as 'the Early Modern' has in recent years become increasingly – and, to some, unexpectedly – permeable.[3] There should, though, be nothing surprising about this as a development. As long ago as 1948, Wallace Ferguson argued that the period known as the 'Middle Ages' had been deliberately constructed as a time of obscurity and superstition, the dead past against which a self-consciously renascent culture needed to define itself.[4] More recently, Jacques Le Goff has consistently argued for the relative unimportance of 'the Renaissance' in any overarching framework of periodisation when compared with, on the one hand, the Middle Ages and, on the other, the Industrial Revolution. 'I ask only that the Renaissance be seen in proper proportion, as a brilliant but superficial interlude', says Le Goff provocatively, adding: 'In history there is no such thing as rebirth. There is only change, in this case camouflaged as a return to antiquity.' 'Renaissance' is thus not something that marks the end of the Middle Ages but is rather 'a recurrent feature of a very long period of time during which men were constantly seeking authority in the past, in a previous golden age'.[5] For Le Goff, in other words, the terms 'Medieval' and 'Renaissance' do not mark distinct, discrete time periods, but are, rather, interrelated – each, in its way, the product of the other.

Le Goff's views might seem extreme but they in fact have considerable value in focusing attention on the lack of equivalence between two terms usually considered consonant. It is fundamental to these terms that they be seen to refer to two completely different periods and to imply that they naturally arose from those periods. Yet both are early modern coinages, the one designed as derogatory suppression of a culture, the other as celebratory rebadging. As Ferguson argued at length in *The Renaissance in Historical Thought*, the terms have their own history and, though it seems now that they have existed for ever, he shows that the use of 'Renaissance' to refer to a general phase of European history did not commence until the nineteenth century. Yet despite the depth of the recognition in the late twentieth century of the inadequacy of the firm line drawn between 'Medieval' and 'Renaissance', this division, given its most famous expression by Jacob Burckhardt in the mid-nineteenth century, has proved remarkably persistent.[6] In separate but equally trenchant critiques of early modernists' historical assumptions published in the early 1990s, David Aers and Lee Patterson took aim not, as might be expected, at old historicists but at cutting-edge cultural materialists, attacking their 'presentist' orientation and their use of an imagined monolithic 'medieval' as a foil for their understanding of the early modern period as the birthplace of individualism.[7] This habit reflected the thoroughgoing opposition apparent in criticism in the 1980s – especially in Britain – between residually philological medieval studies and burgeoning French-theory-inspired modern studies. At the institutional level, this opposition unhelpfully and in a sense paradoxically, bearing in mind the cultural materialists' self-image as mould-breakers, entrenched an understanding of the medieval which in fact barely differed from the Burckhardtian vision of the previous century.

As James Simpson observes in his essay in this collection, '[s]trict periodisation, especially between medieval and early modern, always implies a choice to be made', a choice requiring certain exclusions or rejections. He continues:

The passion with which we reject one alternative necessarily determines the passion by which we choose another. They are forms of each other, determining, often unconsciously, the forms of the work we do, and committing us to repetitive rehearsal of a five-hundred-year historical agon. (29)

This collection of essays, we believe, marks a moment when there are at last signs that this agon may be nearing its end. Over the last few years, in English literary and historical studies at least, the troubled and increasingly porous border between the Middle Ages and the early modern period – and hence between Medieval and Early Modern Studies – has been under renewed and insistent challenge. Medievalists now range far into the sixteenth century as a matter of course – a tendency abundantly clear in the *Cambridge History of Medieval English Literature* edited by David Wallace (1999) – as well as in his *Premodern Places* (2004) – and in James Simpson's volume *Reform and Cultural Revolution* for the *Oxford English Literary History* (2002), each of which offers an overarching account of the 'Medieval' that reads the English Reformation as a more significant event for a modern understanding of medieval culture than some of the usual suspects – the end of the Wars of the Roses, say, or the Tudor accession.[8] Of course, chronology is not the only thing at stake here: much that has been traditionally considered the invention or discovery of the sixteenth or seventeenth centuries has been re-examined in the light of medieval precursors – perhaps most notably the hotly contested concept of the individual, directly addressed in the polemical reassessments of Patterson and Aers.

At the same time (and despite the resistance inherent in institutional structures), early modernists too have begun to reject the policing of strict boundaries between periods. The historiographical and theological debates initiated by such groundbreaking interventions as Eamon Duffy's *The Stripping of the Altars* – in which the notion that the Reformation in England created a clean break with Roman Catholicism is taken to task – or the essays of Berndt Hamm – who asks 'Why should the "Age" of the Reformation not be understood along with the Late Middle Ages as a stage in a larger era of cultural, institutional, intellectual and religious history?' – have set the proponents of continuity against those of caesura, enforcing a reassessment of the nature and impact of Reformation and prompting early modern literary scholars to rethink their understanding of the relationship between their period and its inheritance.[9]

This activity fits well with the established cross-period engagement of early drama specialists who, encouraged by the substantial materials on early performance history collated by the *Records of Early English Drama* (*REED*) project, have for a while now been emphasising the continuities rather than the differences between so-called 'Medieval' and 'Renaissance' or 'Early Modern' drama: books as distinct as Greg Walker's *Plays of Persuasion* (1991), Paul White's *Theatre and Reformation* (1993) and Scott McMillin and Sally-Beth MacLean's *The Queen's Men and their Plays* (1998) have made convincing claims about Reformation and post-Reformation theatrical practice which refuse to be limited by an unnecessary fixity of division between 'medieval' and 'early modern' drama.[10] The title of John Cox and David Scott Kastan's *New History of Early English Drama* (1997) and the name of the journal set up in collaboration with *REED* – *Early Theatre* – mark the developing emphasis on theatrical continuities over the last decade, as does the inclusion of the 'medieval' plays *Mankind* and *Everyman* in the forthcoming Arden Early Modern Drama series.[11]

This recognition is by no means confined to the field of early theatre studies. A string of recent publications – by SunHee Kim Gertz, Derek Pearsall, and Pearsall and Duncan Wu – has proposed continuities between Chaucer and Shakespeare or between Chaucer and Spenser.[12] And a range of recent books – by, *inter alia*, Helen Cooper, Benjamin Griffin and several of the contributors to the current collection, notably Cathy Shrank, Jennifer Summit and Deanne Williams – extends this sense of continuity and dependence by assessing textual phenomena from the fourteenth to the seventeenth centuries.[13] The influence of the New British History initiated by J. G. A. Pocock and others – and subsequently of the developing field of Archipelagic Studies – has similarly encouraged early modernists such as Andrew Hadfield and Philip Schwyzer to read the creation of national structures in terms of continuity rather than disjunction between the periods: they argue, despite the reluctance of many early modernists working in this area to look back further than the early sixteenth century, that the construction of English nationhood cannot be mapped through period parochialism.[14]

The implications of these reassessments of periodicity for the study of both the medieval and the early modern are abundantly clear. Early modernists have begun to acknowledge for the first time in a generation the importance of the late (and sometimes also the early) Middle Ages in the construction of post-Reformation understandings of literary tradition, nationhood and the self. Medievalists, equally, are beginning to grasp the importance of the re-reading in the sixteenth and seventeenth centuries of their period and of the impact this re-reading has had in shaping the modern vision of the medieval. And while the latter are, for institutional reasons, perhaps more eager than the former to embrace this development, both publishers' catalogues and recent conference programmes suggest a considerable pace of change. Seth Lerer's *Chaucer and His Readers* and Theresa Krier's collection *Refiguring Chaucer in the Renaissance*, for instance, are groundbreaking contributions to the emerging field.[15] Both focus specifically on Chaucer studies rather than on wider medieval culture, but the agendas of recent conferences suggest a broadening of interest beyond Chaucer: in 2004 alone, John Watkins's seminar on 'Shakespeare and the Middle Ages' at the Shakespeare Association of America conference, the three sessions organised by Sarah Kelen under the heading 'Renaissance Retrospection' at the International Medieval Congress at Kalamazoo, and the seminar entitled 'Medievalism in English Renaissance Literature' run by one of our contributors, Deanne Williams, for the MLA meeting in Philadelphia all suggest the currency of the topic. In 2006, the conference 'Renaissance Medievalisms' at Victoria College, University of Toronto sustains the theme.

Reading the Medieval in Early Modern England marks the emergence of this renewed recognition of the close relationship between the 'medieval' and the 'early modern' by exploring the full range of ways in which the Middle Ages were constructed and reconfigured in the early modern period. The essays in this collection are not only concerned, however, with the early modern re-reading of the medieval, a unidirectional move that might tend simply to reinscribe the old boundaries; they also, as we have begun to suggest, address the ways in which the early modern was constructed through or in negotiation with the medieval. Our contributors emphasise continuities, but they also acknowledge the inevitability of certain kinds of period boundary – when, for instance, Bernhard Klein notes a fundamental shift between medieval and early modern cartography – while also noting the ways in which the early modern, even as it marks its difference from the medieval, also acknowledges its fundamental dependence upon what preceded it. It will be immediately clear to readers that the term 'Reformation' is central to the concerns of this volume in a way that 'Renaissance', say, is not. This is perhaps best explained by way of Jennifer Summit's formulation: writing about Leland, she reads early modern English geography as 'the product less of Renaissance than of Reformation – less, that is, of a newly awakened, classicised self-consciousness than of an ongoing, politically driven struggle to redefine and contain the nation's own medieval past' (160). The construction of the nation is in fact central to the understanding we develop in this collection of the relationship between different versions of the past: we wish to argue that the early modern must be defined not in distinction from the medieval but through it, that the urge to periodise and the development of the concept of nationhood are wholly interpenetrated, and that the reading of the medieval in early modern England has in several ways bequeathed to us our understanding of both the medieval and the early modern.

III

This collection of essays had its origin in connected conferences run by the editors at King's College London in November 2002 and at the University of Newcastle, New South Wales, in August 2003. Three further essays were specially commissioned in order to complement and complete the set of essays that emerged from the conferences, and each contributor has revised his or her individual essay in light of the whole. The result, we believe, is an innovative and distinctive collection with an overall coherence and identity that emerges from the shared point of origin of the essays and the relationships developed between them. There are five sections, covering 'Period', 'Text', 'Nation', 'Geography' and 'Reformation', which engage with questions of periodisation, the technology of print, nationhood, visual and cartographic culture, and religion – sections which, we believe, build up a full account of the difference it makes to address medieval and early modern materials outside the usual period boundaries. The sections are interconnected: we expect readers will wish to dip in and read individual essays and we believe each essay in its way broaches the principal issues of the collection as a whole, but we think too that reading the essays consecutively builds a narrative that might not be wholly apparent from selective reading.

We begin with considerations of periodisation, initially through James Simpson's informal yet polemical reflections on the subject, for which he draws on his experiences researching and writing *Reform and Cultural Revolution*. His essay is, in a sense, a stock-taking in the wake of the publication of the book in which he describes the exhilaration provoked by writing a literary history that traverses the 1530s, a decade defined by the Act of Supremacy but decisive also in forming specific kinds of memory and ways of processing memory. Simpson argues that this decade initiated both the theme of the 'Middle Ages' and the methods we still use to study the centuries embraced by that term and he proposes breaking out of 'the binary, revolutionary logic that underlies the very notion of periodisation in the first place' in order to find ways for medievalists to address early modernists through historicising the alleged rupture between the periods and estranging both by '[r]epeated traversing of the medieval/early modern divide' (28, 30).

Extending Simpson's demonstration of the shortcomings of periodisation, Deanne Williams turns to a specific text – Robert Greene's play *Friar Bacon and Friar Bungay* – as a base from which to explore the self-consciousness of early modern writers as they engaged with and constructed ideas of the medieval past and to demonstrate the double reading made of that past as one of religious credulity yet nascent national consciousness. Using Paul de Man's idea of a 'rhetoric of temporality' as her model, Williams assesses the various ways in which the play deconstructs Elizabethan ways of understanding the past, noting for instance that the title character, Friar Bacon, is drawn in ways that seem both to reiterate a homogeneous, fixed conception of the medieval and at the same time to undermine any sense of 'a linear and compartmentalised vision of history' (47). By way, she argues, of a range of tropes – principally irony, melancholy and doubling – Greene rejects, even as he apparently sustains, an early modern vision of the medieval as magical and stable, reading it instead as a 'site of conflict' (48).

The printed word was of course a principal focus for conflict in the Reformation and the second section – on questions of the text – addresses certain issues of print culture as they become apparent through the examination of early modern editions of medieval texts. Larry Scanlon, extending the critique of periodisation begun by Simpson and Williams, offers a new account of the first edition of *Piers Plowman*, produced in three impressions in 1550 by the radical printer, Robert Crowley. This edition has usually been regarded as a Protestant misreading of an essentially medieval, Catholic text and, although Scanlon is by no means trying to deny the impact of Protestantism on Crowley's text of the poem, he argues that that Protestantism is expressed 'in terms that are primarily philosophical, poetic and political' and that any sectarianism *per se* in Crowley's *Piers* should be seen as 'occasional and secondary' (58). Crowley looks beyond Langland's

Catholicism, valuing the ideals of his poem and articulating continuities that are, for Scanlon, 'too subtle, too ambiguous and too complex to be subsumed under notions of appropriation or misrecognition' (58). Analysing Crowley's paratextual material, Scanlon finds in it only a minimal anti-Catholicism, turning instead to what he regards as the primary ideological purpose of the edition, that is, its commitment to vernacular literacy and the extension of the text to a wider audience which he will equip with the information necessary to understand the poem. In this respect, Crowley's most important ideological ambition coincides entirely with Langland's own, Catholic, advocacy of vernacular literacy.

Just as Langland was taken up in the context of Protestantism, so was Chaucer increasingly refashioned as a proto-Protestant in the sixteenth century. Like Scanlon, David Matthews is particularly interested in the paratexts of Tudor editions, focusing on the prefatory material and glosses in Thomas Speght's two editions of Chaucer. Speght is evidently dealing with a thoroughly medieval figure in Chaucer, but his project is also a modernising one which looks to dignify the poet and to direct interpretation for a late sixteenth-century readership. Speght draws Chaucer into line with the Reformation by portraying him as an ever more anticlerical poet. Like John Bale, who wants, in Cathy Shrank's words, 'to regulate and contain the interpretations of his readers', Speght produces a Chaucer who will overtly satisfy the likely ideological demands of Tudor readers (191). But no more than in the case of Crowley is Speght motivated simply by anti-Catholicism. There is another project at work, Matthews argues, one underpinned by a notion of continuity. Speght promotes the poet in his role as an adherent of the Lancastrian cause, a move which Matthews relates to Speght's own desire for advancement in the Tudor state via his dedication to Queen Elizabeth's minister, Robert Cecil. Speght's hints of a patronage relationship which would mirror that which he constructs between Chaucer and John of Gaunt offers a clear sense of ideological continuity between medieval and early modern.

A major site of both continuity and conflict across the centuries is the gradual development of English and British nationhood, particularly as expressed through contested myths of origin. Our third section provides three angles on the early modern engagement with, or evasion of, the medieval materials of emergent nationalism. Stephanie Trigg opens by re-assessing the sixteenth- and seventeenth-century appropriation of the foundational story of the Order of the Garter, examining the quest in early modern historiography for the imagined true origins of the Order's famous motto, *honi soit qui mal y pense*. This motto, Trigg argues, 'encapsulates the mixed inheritance of the medieval past for early modernity' (105). Early modern historians writing on the Order cannot reject the medieval because they are drawn to the continuity of national tradition that the Order represents; at the same time, they wish to impose their own critical judgements on the medieval past, producing the medieval period as a historical object worthy of study and dispute within antiquarian discourse. These early modern considerations, in turn, are appropriated in more recent and official histories of the Order which perpetuate certain foundational mythologies, reproducing the medieval narrative of feminised origins passed on to them by early modern writers only in order, again like the early modern writers, to displace those origins with the voice of masculine common sense and reason.

Like Trigg, Anke Bernau is concerned both with sixteenth-century chronicle history and its reuses of the medieval past and with the gendering of that history and that reuse, focusing on the sixteenth-century negotiation of Galfridian history. Again like Trigg, she assesses in particular the early modern displacement of feminised origins. As her exemplar, she recounts and describes the reception of the myth of Albina in early modern England, noting the particular challenges and opportunities offered to Elizabethan and Jacobean historiographers by a specifically female myth of origin. The myth, which was considered threatening in offering an alternative to, for instance, the tale of Brutus, was effectively suppressed, yet nevertheless retained an ability, alongside parallel myths such as that of Boudica, to unsettle and undermine the gendering of English/British nationalism. Such explorations of national origins through female figures, Bernau argues, 'allowed historiographers to articulate – however inadvertently – the ambiguities and fearful uncertainties of writing such histories' and opened up continuing uncertainties both about concepts of racial authenticity and about the possibility of clear, unified points of origin for the nation (117).

Extending the question of the representation of nationhood, Gordon McMullan examines the Jacobean theatre's engagement with the early British past. Responding to an observation made at the London conference by Clare Lees that too often current work crossing the boundaries between the medieval and the early modern focuses only on a narrow period covering the very late fifteenth and early sixteenth centuries, McMullan chooses to analyse the Jacobean theatrical representation of Anglo-Saxon and mythic British pasts and traces their relationship with – indeed their centrality to – the developing ideology of nationhood, arguing that individual plays with early settings form 'part of a larger theatrical project to interpret Elizabethan and Jacobean Britain through the reconstruction of a range of different pasts, especially medieval pasts' (120). He initially offers readings of two Jacobean plays with Anglo-Saxon settings – Brewer's *The Love-Sick King* and Middleton's *Hengist, King of Kent* – in order to demonstrate both that early English history is read on the Jacobean stage alongside the emergence of English colonial enterprise as reverse colonial history and that that reading is heavily inflected by sectarianism. He then returns to the subject-matter of Bernau's essay by reading Fletcher and Massinger's *The Sea Voyage* as a version of the Albina myth in order to demonstrate that the early modern stage, plotting the development of 'British' nationalism, re-read the medieval not only in plays with overt early English settings but also in the absence of such settings and thus to suggest the extent to which myths of origin pervade early modern dramatic representation in general.

Bernhard Klein's essay on early modern reworkings of medieval cartography also begins with myths of origin – in this case, those provided in *mappaemundi*, representing as they do an interest in religious 'truth' as much as in geographical accuracy – as he plots the development from medieval mapmaking to the early modern 'New Geography' initiated by Ortelius, Mercator and others. Like McMullan, Klein turns to the early modern stage – in particular to the protagonist of Marlowe's *Tamburlaine* – for a representation of the function of mapmaking in modelling changing constructions of the world and thus of the self and he notes that the transition to the 'disembodied, desacralised and entirely secular spaces' of early modern maps is by no means as complete and unproblematic as might be assumed (144). He takes Tamburlaine's attitude to cartography as his exemplar, noting the conqueror's role as a reader of maps: Tamburlaine defies the gods in part by redefining geography and by making the centre of the world a location of his own choosing, yet his cartographic language betrays his lack of confidence in the innovations he is forcefully championing. Just as, for all the desacralising violence of his assault on institutions, Tamburlaine is unable to remove all the traces of the spiritual in his remapping of the world, so the economy of the Reformation, 'push[ing] away from a feudal system of mutual obligations towards the open market', leaves tangible traces of what had preceded it (157). At the end of the play, 'the continued centrality of the body to all spatial imaginings is affirmed – even as that body is finally ejected – when the dying Tamburlaine collides with a world map' and the transition from body-centred medieval mapmaking to the desacralised space of early modern cartography is performed as the realisation even of the 'Scourge of God' that he is unable to stand outside the dislodging process he has himself initiated (157).

Jennifer Summit is also fascinated both by cartographic process and by the Reformation's inability fully to erase the traces of the Catholic/medieval past. She turns to Leland's *Itinerary*, a set of fragmentary notes towards a map of England that was never made but whose aims were later fulfilled, she argues, in Camden's *Britannia* and Speed's *Theatre of the Empire of Great Britain*, to show that the development of early modern geography is part 'of an ongoing, politically-driven struggle to redefine and contain the nation's own medieval past' (160). She shows that, while the aim of Reformation cartography and chorography might have been to empty 'the English landscape of its immediate history by replacing it with an illustrious, ancient past waiting to be "discovered"', in fact, as is clear from Leland, 'in the wake of the Reformation it was impossible to experience the English landscape without also confronting physical evidence of the medieval past and the violence that historical change inflicted on it' (160). In other words, '[w]hile Protestant propaganda cast the Reformation as an organic development within England, the English landscape suggested otherwise', offering ocular proof that England had not been 'discovered' but had been subject to a violent reshaping through which 'formerly sacred spaces [were] actively converted, like its inhabitants, to support new structures of belief and government', evidence of which is finessed through the language of natural process (160–1). She then reverses her focus, arguing that the displacement of the medieval past in representations of the English landscape initiated by Leland provided a 'template' for the displacement of the inhabitants of colonised countries, demonstrating that the past, far from disappearing, 'continued to exert a presence as palpable as the ruins it left behind' (176).

It is a marker of the pervasiveness of the concern with Reformation in this volume that Summit's essay, while clearly linked with Klein's in its engagement with cartographic and chorographic culture, also looks forward to Cathy Shrank's essay in the final section. Shrank is concerned to show the role of reformers as self-consciously forming a break with the medieval past yet being at the same time indebted to that past in ways they are not always comfortable recognising. John Bale, she writes, 'endeavours to differentiate his age from "that most blynde and ignoraunt tyme"', the Middle Ages; yet on the other hand, despite his drive for scholarly innovation, Bale and his work are rooted in medieval sources, traditions and genres (181). Chronicle, morality play and miracle play are essential to Bale, whose lifespan (1495–1563) makes him a transitional figure across the traditional boundaries between medieval and early modern: Shrank regards him 'as a Janus figure, looking back as much as forward' (181). We need to be wary, she concludes, of the rhetoric of novelty and difference promoted by reformist writers such as Bale who used the medium of print to shape an audience of like-minded readers, controlling material which would otherwise reveal affinities and continuities with the late medieval past.

Sarah Beckwith turns to the Shakespeare canon, and in particular to *Measure for Measure*, in order to focus on the transformations in penitential practice that occurred after the Reformation, the dramatic exploration of which, she argues, reveals the radical nature of Shakespeare's medievalism. 'From its original and pastoral purpose in the cure of souls', she argues, 'penance became . . . the means of the punishment and exposure of souls and bodies', a process which – paradoxically in the Reformation context – served to extend ecclesiastical authority (198). She uses Simon McBurney's 2004 National Theatre production of *Measure for Measure* to underline the play's role as a critique of this transformation in penitential practice, demonstrating that Shakespeare, in the figure of the Duke, reverses the standard Protestant theatrical deployment of the figure of the friar so that 'the combined anti-fraternalism and anti-theatricalism of the tradition works against the theatricality of the crown/dukedom/monarchy, rather than the theatricality of the church', exposing the problems inherent in the subsumption of church to monarch (201). Shakespeare, in Beckwith's reading, represents the impossibility of penitence in a society which lacks remorse and thus fails to acknowledge that 'confession is never exclusively about the self but always about an acknowledgement of the self in relation to others' (204).

Patricia Badir, in the collection's final essay, extends this engagement with the complexities of Reformation by exploring Protestant interest in the figure of the Magdalene, focusing in particular on the reuses of Magdalene imagery by Aemilia Lanyer and Nicholas Breton. She also notes a range of visual images of the Magdalene such as those of Tintoretto, Titian and Rogier van der Weyden which 'draw upon medieval iconography in which Christ, the Word, is figured as a book, and the Magdalene, in a rather bizarre moment of reflexivity, is the exemplary reader of her own story' (212). Badir argues 'that pre-Reformation treatments of Mary Magdalene are not exclusively eroticised manifestations of the corporeal piety of the late Middle Ages', turning to other early modern representations in order to show the importance of the medieval Magdalene (especially where form and narration are concerned) (215). Briefly alluded to in Lanyer's *Salve Deus Rex Judaeorum*, the Magdalene 'is also identifiable in other works by seventeenth-century Protestant writers' (215). Once again, then, the inadequacy of the standard assumption of a distinct caesura between medieval and early modern texts is called into question by the evidence.

As these brief abstracts suggest, the essays in this collection raise a series of questions of equal interest both to medievalists and to early modernists. For the former, they offer reflections on the traditional boundaries of the 'medieval', extend the existing debate on English nationhood and its medieval origins, and bring to light the obscure ways in which the very idea of the medieval was constructed in the early modern period; at the same time, even as they deal with large-scale concerns of this kind, they also sustain a degree of specificity, offering new analyses, for instance, of the minutiae of early modern editions of medieval works. For the latter, they offer new material on the politics of penitence, on the history of editing, on myths of origin and the gendering of national mythmaking, on the creation of historical geographies and cartographies, and on the interrelated appropriations of canonical figures, medieval and early modern, in the construction of a national literary culture. The essays return repeatedly to certain images and issues – to what remains of religious practices and institutions even as those practices and institutions are ostensibly erased, to ongoing debates over historical origin and their engagement with sectarianism, and to the ways in which history always has a certain utility and is thus appropriable to a range of ideological ends – in order to demonstrate in every case the interrelatedness of the understanding we have inherited of what constitutes the 'Medieval' and the 'Early Modern'. Just as early modern Englishmen and women read and re-read medieval texts, so the culture through which they performed those readings was itself at least as much the product of the medieval as it was of the break with the medieval that appears, to us, to define it. This collection thus foregrounds both the ways in which early modern England read the medieval and the ways in which the medieval can always be found in any reading of early modern England.

PART I

Period

CHAPTER I

Diachronic history and the shortcomings of medieval studies

James Simpson

This essay describes and accounts for a vibrant new development in English literary studies; it also offers some more sceptical, correlative reflections on the state and project of medieval studies. My argument derives principally from the experience of writing, over the six years between 1995 and 2001, a literary history for the two centuries from 1350.[1] Writing literary history that traverses the 1530s was an especially exhilarating historical lesson, because writing across the barrier of the Act of Supremacy (1534) was a particularly acute challenge. The challenge, I discovered, derived from the fact that the concepts, and the very tools of historical investigation by which I wrote the book, inevitably became an implicit part of the book's subject. Writing the book therefore inevitably became, on a surprising number of fronts, a way of unwriting and rewriting what I'd taken for granted as part of the way the world was.

The concepts and the tools of historiography, not to speak of a particular notion of the past itself, are, I discovered, the product of revolutionary moments. And for English cultural history the cultural revolution of the 1530s has, among other revolutionary moments, been decisive in forming specific kinds of memory, and specific ways of processing memory. The 1530s in England, that is, initiated not only the theme of 'the Middle Ages', but also, more profoundly, the methods whereby we study these centuries. This is truer of England than of any other European country, since the break in England was not restricted to a given discursive area, such as, say, ecclesiology or education. State-driven as the cultural revolution was in England, it directly affected large tracts of the discursive landscape.[2]

For someone like myself, who was trained in an intellectual culture of synchronicity, and especially in a culture of 'Medieval Studies', the experience of writing across the boundary of 1534 was an awakening. Having been trained as a graduate, that is, from the late 1970s, I entered a field that stressed synchronicity above all, for both institutional and intellectual reasons. Medievalists, who may have felt institutionally beleaguered and vulnerable in individual departments, gathered together for reasons of self-protection. That partial explanation for the founding of centres of medieval studies is, perhaps, more pertinent to the centres founded in the decades of retraction that British and Australian universities have suffered without pause since the 1970s.[3] And intellectually, medievalists recognised that relations with historians of medieval theology, economics, ecclesiology and so on were likely to be more productive than relations with scholars of what was then called the Renaissance in their own departments. An intellectual vision inspired by Foucault was all the more attractive to medievalist literary scholars, in a literary critical environment still trying to shake off the legacy of New Criticism in the USA and Leavisism in the UK, neither of which offered sufficient purchase on most medieval texts.[4]

The institutional result of these pressures were centres of Medieval Studies, such as that in York (founded in 1968).[5] Of course there had been Medieval Centres prior to the late 1960s,[6] but I entered a profession in the early 1980s where I was expected to administer and attend medieval societies (which I dutifully did), and to publish in journals like *Medium Aevum* (which I dutifully, and gratefully, did). Interdisciplinarity was the byword, and synchronicity was the underlying concept that justified the practice. The pedagogy of such a discipline was exacting and vast, involving the mastery of many languages, codicological skills, bibliographical expertise in many fields, a broad historical sweep, and an understanding of analogies between different cultural practices. And that's all before one started reading literary texts. Medievalists practised a new historicism of sorts *avant la lettre* (as they often pointed out, with chagrin, *après la lettre*).

I found some of the work produced from this scholarly matrix fascinating. Where the scholarship dealt with the cultural politics of texts produced, transmitted and received, it was illuminating and refreshing. A good deal of it was, however, in my experience at least, frankly dull. I spent a good deal of time in conferences listening to papers whose relevance to my own field was notional, and based on only loose analogy. These papers were clearly professional pieces, and no doubt would have been interesting had one had the time to have read deeply in that field. Many questions in such conferences were not, however, questions at all, but comments based on the formula 'I don't know the materials you are treating, but in my texts there is something similar . . .' The answer to these comments was invariably, and politely: 'that's very interesting; thank you – I'll follow that up' (that last clause trailing without conviction). I put up with the dullness, and repressed the nagging doubt about why I was there (at what point had I taken the wrong intellectual road?, I often found myself silently asking), because it felt virtuous to be interdisciplinary. The Middle Ages were of a piece; the dull bits would fall into place once the whole picture was established. Until that great day, however, many of these conferences would have found it difficult to reply to the 'so what?' question.

Writing *Reform and Cultural Revolution* persuaded me that the 'Medieval Studies' moment and movement, while enormously productive in its time, might have become a liability and a lost opportunity. It's become a liability because it has cut itself off from the main currents of the institutions (English Departments, say) in which researchers generally continue to have professional homes; from which base they draw salaries; and in which they must fight for replacement (not to speak of new) academic posts. The more medievalists turn to fellow medievalists in other departments, the less credible they become in their own. And, institutional liabilities aside, to my mind medieval studies are becoming a myopic, lost intellectual opportunity, since the subject has lost sight of what made it in the first place. What did make it in the first place was, in England, the sixteenth century, which invested the Middle Ages with a theme and gave us a method for studying that theme.

This essay began, then, as a proposal of sorts, that we redirect our energies away from what in my view has become a shortsighted synchronic medievalism, and that we turn them instead towards a more diachronic historicism. I intended to suggest that medievalists based in English departments in particular reconnect with their early-modernist colleagues, not to speak of reconnecting with scholars of the eighteenth and nineteenth centuries, for example. The study of the seventh to the fifteenth centuries is every bit as much a study of the sixteenth to the nineteenth centuries.[7] The 'medieval' in European society is inseparable from the powerful counters by which it was aggressively formed, Classicism and Protestantism. The stakes of the inexhaustible negotiation between these terms are, at any given moment, potentially very high. I began by proposing that 'Medieval Studies' play for higher stakes.[8]

The preterite tenses in the previous paragraph, about this very essay, serve to underline that what the essay had set out to propose was, well before the essay was redrafted, already happening. Scholars in some fields, particularly book history and certain strands of theatre history, have of course been quietly crossing the lines for a long time. As a movement, though, transgression of the medieval/early modern boundary is of more recent date. Eamon Duffy's *Stripping of the Altars* (1992) perhaps led the way,[9] but influential literary historians have followed suit: *The Cambridge History of Medieval English Literature*, edited by David Wallace (1999);

Seth Lerer's *Courtly Letters in the Age of Henry VIII: Literary Culture and the Arts of Deceit* (1997); Jennifer Summit's *Lost Property* (2000); Sarah Beckwith's *Signifying God* (2001); Deanne Williams's *The French Fetish from Chaucer to Shakespeare* (2004); Helen Cooper's *The English Romance in Time* (2004); David Wallace's *Pre-Modern Places* (2004); and, most recently, Paul Strohm's *Politique* (2005): each points forward to 1547 and often beyond; each finds vibrant resonances between medieval and early modern materials. Influential early modernists are no less interested in what went on before the Reformation: Stephen Greenblatt's *Hamlet in Purgatory* (2001) takes a fascinated look at pre-Reformation accounts of the afterlife, while Brian Cummings's *The Literary Culture of the Reformation* (2002) demands understanding of both sides of the Reformation divide.[10] What the essay began hubristically to propose as a programme, then, turns out in part, more humbly, to be a description of a phenomenon already well under way.

I

What do I mean when I say that the sixteenth century formed not only the theme, but also the methods for studying the later medieval centuries? The text from which I begin is Thomas More's *Supplication of Souls*, written in 1529 in response to Simon Fish's *Supplication for the Beggars* (1528). Fish's short polemical work was addressed to Henry VIII, and was designed to persuade the king to redirect to the living the economy devoted to the dead. The basis of the policy argument is the contention that Purgatory is a fiction, invented by a rapacious Church in order to raise money. More responded with a much longer, more academic though also vernacular work, pleading the case for Purgatory's existence. His rhetorical strategy is to place the argument for Purgatory's existence in the mouths of the dead themselves, crying out to More's readers as if from the very flames of Purgatory. They beg not to be forgotten and abandoned, 'owte of syght owte of mynde' (218.24),[11] as they suffer in purgatorial flame.[12] For much of the treatise, the fiction of this communal voice is invisibly thin, but at moments it rises to great intensity. I cite from the peroration, where the dead remind us of their affection for us, and beg us not to forget them:

Our prayer ys for you so feruent that ye can no where fynde eny such affeccyon vppon erth. And therfore syth we ly so sore in paynys & haue in our great necessyte so gret nede of your help & that ye may so well do yt wherby shall also rebownd vppon your self an inestymable profyte: let neuer eny slouthfull oblyuyon race vs out of your remembraunce . . . Now dere frendys remember how

nature & crystendom byndeth you to remember vs. If eny poynt of your old fauour eny pece of your old loue eny kindnes of kinred eny care of acqauntance eny
fauour of old frendshyp eny spark of charyte eny tender poynt of pyte . . . be left in
your brestys: let neyer the malyce of a few fond felows . . . race out of your hartys the
care of your kynred all force of your old frendys and all remembraunce of all crysten
soulys. (227.29–230.20)

A passage of this kind might move many readers, including those without
any commitment to the Catholic Church. It presents an account of a literally
living past, in which the dead are capable of giving help to, and receiving
help from, the living. The relation between the past and the present is
established through co-operative conversation between living and dead
that can be activated only through acts of generosity. This conversational
opportunity explains and justifies the rhetorical strategy of the text. The
past is not, certainly, a dead fragment requiring decipherment.

More, clearly enough, intended the passage to move its readers. The
text is moving, however, in ways More could not have intended. It intends
to move emotionally, as More underlines the possibility of communica-
tion, between friends and family, across the boundary of death. But it's
also historically moving. Considered in its larger diachronic history, that
is, the passage turns out to bid farewell to a world. We not only witness
the suffering of possibly abandoned friends and kin here; we also observe
a system of communal practice and consciousness bidding farewell to,
or being repelled by, Protestant modernity. Chantries, the institutions by
which prayers were offered for the dead, were abolished, along with a range
of other popular religious and social institutions, in 1545. That Act was
restated and embellished in Edwardian form in 1547: 'Chantries, Hospitalles, Fraternityes and Brotherheddes' are to be suppressed, since they have
come to represent 'superstition and Errors', 'by devising and phantasinge
vayne opynions of Purgatorye and Masses satisfactorye to be done for them
which be departed'.[13] That the conversation between the living and the
dead has come to an abrupt end is vividly exemplified and enacted by the
changes to the Edwardian Prayer Book. In the first edition (1549), the dead
person is addressed by the priest: 'I commend thy soul to God the father
almighty, and thy body to the ground.' In the second, revised edition of
1552, the priest addresses not the dead person, but the bystanders around
the grave: 'We therefore commit his body to the ground.'[14]

This recasting of the dead as an anonymous body in the 1540s is of a
piece with the revolutionary recasting of the past more generally in these
decades. Every revolutionary moment needs to repel the past, or, as in this
case, in some profound sense to *create* the past. The past is created, that is,

by being made very dark, wholly repellent, and sharply different from the brilliant new present. The strategies of what may be called 'past-creation' are everywhere apparent in the 1530s and 1540s. In a variety of practices, what had been a mode of imaginative conversation with the past is now redescribed as plain error (usually, as in the case of chantries, dismissed as phantasy, the work of the purely inventive, groundless imagination).[15] Or else the past is contained by being set out of conversational reach and into the realm of 'remembrance'.

The Second Royal Injunctions of Henry VIII of 1538, for example, order bishops to destroy such images in their dioceses as are used for idolatrous purposes, and to teach their parishioners that such images serve only the purposes of remembrance: by them, the illiterate 'might be otherwise admonished of the lives and conversation of them that the said images do represent; which images, if they abuse for any other intent than for such remembrances, they commit idolatry in the same, for the greater danger of their souls'.[16] In the following year a proclamation declares that 'neither holy bread nor holy water, candles, bows, nor ashes hallowed, or creeping and kissing the cross be the workers or works of our salvation, but only be as outward signs and tokens whereby we remember Christ and his doctrine'.[17] This summarises a series of regulations, in each of which the word 'remembrance', or 'memory' signals a recategorisation: no longer do rituals serve as conduits through which the past flows into the present; instead they provoke memory. Holy water is sprinkled 'to put us in remembrance of our baptism'; giving of holy bread puts 'us in remembrance of unity'; the bread is made of many grains, 'to put us in remembrance of the housel'; the bearing of candles on Candlemas day is done 'in memory of Christ'; ashes on Ash Wednesday are given to put Christians 'in remembrance of penance'; bearing of palms on Palm Sunday 'reneweth the memory of the receiving of Christ'.[18] Key moments from the past are neutralised, or at least contained, by being described as one-off events, worthy of remembrance but without continuing operations in the present.

The treatment of saints provides a good example of both possibilities: some are dismissed from the calendar as not saints at all (e.g. Becket), while others are demoted from the liturgy; authentic saints eventually become sites of memory, but not channels of grace, unable as they are to intercede on behalf of a living suppliant. The Ten Articles of 1536 acknowledge that saints can intercede, but not for specific needs;[19] those same articles, however, abolish many saints' feasts, and the Second Royal Injunctions of 1538 outlawed 'virtually the entire external manifestation of the cult of the saints'.[20] The King's *Primer* of 1545 'jettisons most of the saints normally commemorated',[21] while the 1549 Prayer Book left only the great feasts of Christmas, Easter, Whitsun and a handful of biblical saints' days.[22] By 1547 this diminution of the role of the saints finds explicit theological defence. Whereas the pre-Reformation saints 'could do favours for their friends',[23] the 1547 Edwardian injunction directs that images and relics shall not be set forth for 'superstition or lucre', and that the people shall not be enticed 'to the pilgrimage of any saint or image'. Reproving such practices, the people are to be taught that 'all goodness, health, and grace ought to be both asked and looked for only of God, as of the very author and giver of the same, and of none other'.[24]

Just as some saints are dismissed, and others recategorised as sites of memory, [25] so too with literary texts. Many (i.e. religious texts) are dismissed as the product of mere imaginative error; those deemed worthy of remembrance are refigured as memorials, fragments to be saved against the ravages of time by the ministrations of an incipient philology.[26] The reception of Chaucer in these decades is exemplary of these possibilities.[27] Writers through the fifteenth century (e.g. Hoccleve, Lydgate, Skelton) had entered into kinds of conversation with Chaucer. In the sixteenth century, by contrast, Chaucer became the object of philological grief as the definitively dead and absent author. Textual fragments alone now testify to the existence of the dead author; these fragments now require philological restitution so as to reproduce exactly what the absent author said, nothing more, nothing less. The fifteenth century produced the model whereby Chaucer's poetry 'never shal appallen in my mynde / But alwey fressh ben in my memoyré' (Lydgate, written in 1422),[28] as distinct from the sixteenth century, whereby, in the prints of Chaucer's works, the editor 'deprehended . . . many errours, falsyties and deprauacions, which euidently appered by the contrarietees and alterations found by collacion of the one with the other' (Thynne, published in 1532).[29] The beginnings of English literary history itself as we practise it derive, not coincidentally, from the moment of cultural revolution.

The impulse towards a philological approach to a now lost past is sharp, then, precisely because revolutions create ruptures, and philology needs a rupture in order to legitimate and justify its own project of restoration. The impulse to a philological response to the newly created past in the 1530s was all the sharper given the fact that the historical rupture was not only conceptual, but also physical. The years from the late 1530s to 1553 provided ample material for the philologist and antiquarian, in the form of freshly created ruins of both libraries and buildings, demolished by the asset-stripper's and/or iconoclast's hammer.[30]

Returning to More's *Supplication*, then, we might be tempted to refigure the plea of the dead as a historical plea of sorts: these are the medieval dead, 'our friends and acquaintance', calling to us for a relation of trust and solidarity. In an apparently ineradicable way, Protestant culture, since the late eighteenth century at any rate, has off and on represented the medieval dead very differently, as ghastly Gothic revenants; by contrast, these dead call us to an enlarged sense of communal responsibility. Whereas Protestant propaganda and statute demonised and repressed this world as erroneous, we might be tempted by More to return to the medieval with a renewed understanding of its coherence and integrity.

The invitation offered by More comes into sharper focus by contrasting it with the text against which More writes, Fish's *Supplication of the Beggars*. Despite being locked into each other, these texts are radically different. The voice of More's text is communal; its rhetoric deploys imaginative fiction; the dead address themselves to all Christians; the solution it proposes is one of bottom-up, communal self-help. Fish's text is the opposite of More's on each count: Fish's voice is singular, posing as he does as an intelligent policy maker; he deploys statistics rather than fiction; he addresses himself to the king; and the solution he proposes is one of state-driven economic redistribution of wealth. Take, for example, his statistical arguments about the drain on wealth and war capacity posed by the religious orders. Having affirmed that the religious orders own a third of the realm's property, he goes on to calculate their annual income. He concludes, and further prosecutes his argument thus:

The auncient Romains had neuer ben abil to haue put all the hole worlde vnder theyre obeisaunce if theyre people had byn thus yerely oppressed . . . Ley then these sommes to the forseid therd part of the possessions of the realme that ye may se whether it drawe nighe vnto the half of the whole substaunce of the realme or not, so shall ye finde that it draweth ferre aboue. Nowe let vs then compare the nombre of this vnkind idell sort vnto the nombre of the laye people and we shall se whether it be indifferently shifted or not that they shuld haue half. (414.21–31)[31]

For literary scholars, perhaps the most striking thing about the contrast between More and Fish is the collapse of the realm of the imaginative itself. Revolutionary moments are hostile to the indirections of literature and the inventions of the imagination; they produce instead a culture of the literal sense, ruled by the exiguous and punishing disciplines of the explicit and contractual. In a contrast of the kind between More and Fish, we can see not only how Fish deploys the explicit, rational argument of the revolutionary policy paper, but, more profoundly, how the realm of the imaginative is itself being permanently redefined. For More the community of the living and dead is achieved through exercise of the imagination, by the living imagining their way into the experience of the dead. Fish dissolves that imaginative construction of the world with the solvent of a suspicious hermeneutic. For Fish social relations are determined by social policy, and driven by the state. He isn't concerned with the social function of imagination, precisely because, in his view, imagination merely mystifies the true workings of society. As with all evangelical thinkers in this period, Fish rejects the exercise of the imagination as ungrounded, and banishes it to the domain of the illusory and idolatrous.

If More and Fish offer a stark opposition between a late medieval and an early modern *Weltanschauung*, that opposition might also be perceived as offering a choice of historical alignment for the modern reader. Neither option would be an absurd or irresponsible choice. More's bottom-up concept of society may be more attractive, while Fish's top-down politics and his hermeneutics of suspicion may offer a more efficient version of social practice. He gives priority both to the living over the dead, and to the action of the state over that of an imagined community. The choice is between two sets of practices, one medieval and the other that continues, in some ways, to define our modernity.

Both are coherent positions. Faced with such a choice (and the medieval/early modern divide poses that choice in a myriad of forms), many might decide to become medievalists. One could decide to enter the world of 'medieval studies' as a coherent whole, and, by entering it, to discover the obverse other of modernity, an obverse capable of exposing and rebuking modernity's limitations. In this case one could rebuke, for example, Fish's own mystification of state power as the solution to all social ills. Conversely, one could equally decide to reject the mystifications promoted by the medieval, and (in this case) embrace a world of social policy, which we still inhabit.

A third possibility is to enter the medieval, and yet to subject it to the immensely fertile critique of, and attack on, universalising humanism. That critique will always redescribe accounts of the world such as More offers as ideological. Accounts of the world that pretend to describe a universal nature are revealed, by such a critique, to represent instead the interests of the group that controls representation. In medieval studies such a critique has, with exceptionally illuminating results, broken up any sense of medieval wholeness and insisted instead on cultural plurality and competition.[32] What of vernacular culture? What of women? What of Lollards? What of

urban culture? What of the illiterate?: such a critique will pose questions
such as these in order to undo any universalising claims.

As I say, this approach has been and continues to be immensely productive. It often suffers, however, from the weakness of periodic thinking
itself. It tends, that is, to find the line between medieval and modern already
inscribed within 'the medieval'. Thus studies of Lollardy, for example, tend
in my view to replicate Catholic/Protestant, or, in more coded form, author-
itarian/liberal boundary lines characteristic of the medieval/early modern
divide. The Lollards are taken to be either premature Protestants or (a seri-
ously mistaken view) liberals *avant la lettre*. They are used as the bunker
from which scholars practising as medievalists can finally attack the Catholic
Middle Ages.[33]

II

Such are the choices, I suggest, made by and generating the scholarship of
many scholars, both medievalists and early modernists. One doesn't have to
dig very deep to get to prejudicial layers of this kind in many, dare I say all,
scholars. I don't myself object to the presence of such prejudicial layers –
historical choices are, or inevitably become, ethical *préjugés*.[34] Such a choice
is not, however, so simple, precisely because we are ourselves products of
the very rupture beyond which we are tempted to step, or within whose
boundary we decide to remain. As we witness More's souls, that is, we
cannot help but be aware that they are bidding us farewell. We cannot help
but be aware that these souls are about to evanesce into the phantoms of
error, vaporised by Fish's demystificatory polemic. More himself, after all,
is replying precisely to such 'rationalising' arguments. Indeed, More had
practised such demystification in *Utopia* (1516), thirteen years *before* the
writing of *The Supplication of Souls*. The voice of the modern other, that
is, is *already* present in the very text that we might treat as exemplary of
the medieval 'other'. More offers no escape into a coherent, self-contained
'medieval' world.

Now, someone might reply, that already-inscribed awareness of the 'modern' other might be true of More, but not true of any pre-sixteenth-century
English text. We need simply to draw the distinction between the medieval
and the modern where it is indisputably clear. A reply: when we draw lines
sharply between periods whole unto themselves, *wherever we draw the line*,
we are already falling victim to the logic of the revolutionary moment. It's
the revolutionary moment that needs the sharp breaks in history to define
itself.[35] Wherever we draw the line to create a world whole unto itself,

the wholeness of the world demarcated by that line is *already* informed by inevitable consciousness of what's on the other side. It's that very consciousness that provokes us to draw the line in the first place. Drawing the line might seem to repair the damage of past rupture, by recreating a world whole unto itself. Instead, drawing the line serves to aggravate the damage. The line, that is, is itself a product of revolutionary rupture and of revolutionary ideology. The very ideas of worlds whole unto themselves, or of past civilisations 'in their own terms' are themselves products of revolutionary thought.

Such reflections, if plausible, have powerful implications for the practice of philology. If revolutionary moments create the past as civilisations whole unto themselves, we should pause to observe that this is also, precisely and not coincidentally, what philology does. Historical rupture is the premise of the philological project; the philologist, in attempting to recover the pristine wholeness of segments of the past, posits an intervening period of accretive degradation, which must be cleaned away before the past textual object can be seen 'in its own terms', with, in the remarkably durable terms of an incipient philology, 'nothyng added ne mynusshyd [diminished]'.[36] Philology characteristically treats its objects as definitively entombed and dead. The philologist's characteristic posture is melancholy at the tomb, grieving for loss and absence, even if secretly rejoicing that loss and absence will be supplying payable work for the restorative philologist.[37]

The more one pursues that world 'in its own terms', however, the more, of course, does it lose interest for the present, since the very premise of such historical enquiry is that one should be suspicious of interpretation that serves present interests. If one's premise is that worlds can only be understood in their own terms, then present interest is by definition unlike the terms of the world we reconstruct. Thoroughgoing philology, that is, activates the painful paradox of historicism: the more precisely the scholar historicises the lost object, the less relevant does the object become. In the very act of pursuing its object, philology activates its flight into irrelevance. The more we empathise with More's souls, for example, the more we cannot help but think of them bidding us historical farewell. They might claim to be friends and acquaintance, but if we think of them only historically, they necessarily recede from us into an abandoned, medieval world, even as we reach out to them. There is no going back, no moving into a demarcated world to be understood wholly 'in its own terms', not least because such a conception is itself already the product of a deeply fractured history.

Philology, I am suggesting, is a product of revolutionary consciousness. If this suggestion has weight, then it has particular bearing for 'Medieval

Studies'. The very notion of 'Medieval Studies' implies, that is, a civilisation entire unto itself; and such a notion is itself the product of the moment that created the Middle Ages by rejecting them in the first place. The very concept by which we frame our subject as 'Medieval Studies' concedes its absolute difference;[38] it also, thereby, secretly concedes the historiographical certainties of the revolutionary moment. And the tool by which we study that civilisation, philology, also concedes the same certainty. It concedes the same certainty in the literal sense, the same desire to see worlds 'in their own terms', the same notion of periodisation. The attempt to see historical periods in their own terms, that is, simply replicates the revolutionary philological logic that creates periods whole unto themselves in the first place. The theme and the tools of medieval studies, then, to state the matter baldly, guarantee our alienation from the 'medieval'.

This critique of philology might, of course, be applicable to the study of any other 'period' in European history. For the study of any period *wholly* 'in its own terms' promises, at its logical extreme, nothing but a necessarily ersatz replica, the repetition of a world knowable only to itself. The philologist is ultimately committed to repetition, reproducing exactly what the author wrote, neither more nor less. Such a mode of thinking about any past period must, it could be argued, finally guarantee nothing but the alienation of historicism; it guarantees, that is, that the object of our study eludes us even as we pursue it. In the case of the Middle Ages, however, the paradox it creates is especially acute, since these centuries produced the set of textual practices against which philology initially cut its incisive teeth. It is no accident that exposure of the Donation of Constantine should be one of the founding moments of philology, since that exposure is also a founding moment of the modern world.[39] Scholars of the Renaissance routinely lambast medieval authors for not having a 'sense of the past', by which they mean a sense of the past wholly in 'its own terms'; such a critique ignores the fact that the philological ideal of treating the past wholly 'in its own terms' is the product of a revolutionary moment that needed to create a deeply divided past.

III

Perhaps the scholarly phenomenon (of traversing the medieval/early modern boundary), to which I pointed above, signals the end of this insistently periodised historiography. What effects might reflections of this kind provoke? At its broadest, I observe that many scholars are breaking free of the binary, revolutionary logic that underlies the very notion of periodisation in the first place. A thoroughly periodised historiography is complicit with the revolutionary politics of entirely fresh, idea-driven, clean starts, within whose terms one can approach anterior historical periods on a take-it-or-leave-it basis. To appeal, by contrast, to a Gadamerian version of historiography is to reaffirm the profoundly historical and probably very messy nature of identity, against the economy of revolutionary historiography.

Secondly, reworking the logic of periodisation has particular implications for medieval studies. Strict periodisation, especially between medieval and early modern, always implies a choice to be made. The passion with which we reject one alternative necessarily determines the passion by which we choose another. They are forms of each other, determining, often unconsciously, the forms of the work we do, and committing us to repetitive rehearsal of a five-hundred-year historical agon.[40] Scholars are breaking free of the habit of centuries of historiography that posits the shift from medieval to early modern as an inevitable, natural historical break. They are thinking the rupture less in terms of non-negotiable periodic terms and more as human phenomena produced by specific institutional interests (and using institutional terms such as pre- and post-Reformation rather than medieval and early modern). They are, in short, historicising both the break and, more profoundly, the forms of understanding that flow from it.

Thirdly, in the particular case of literary history, I observe that medievalists are re-engaging early modern writing, in ways that command the attention of early modernists.[41] Such a re-engagement necessarily entails looking across post-Reformation history for the reception of a given topic, in the manner of this very volume. It also entails a discursive, rather than a purely literary history, because the very notion of what literature is, and its range of operations, undergoes radical change across the Act of Supremacy. The historical rupture creates asymmetries and disguised continuities of many kinds between pre- and post-Henrician writing. Only a broad history of discursive practice can delineate the continuities between those two systems.

What implications do such proposals have for interdisciplinarity? That a discursive scholarly practice is necessarily interdisciplinary needs no underlining. But interdisciplinarity is by now so much a part of the fibre of most scholarship in the humanities that it needs no special pleading or promotion. In fact, one might promote a scholarly practice that is rather *less* interdisciplinary, insofar as it might reconnect with the currents of specific departments. The 'Middle Ages' is, obviously, a fabrication common to many European and neo-European traditions. But it is equally specific to each tradition. Rather than assuming and reifying the identity and natural homology of these traditions by studying them in centres of medieval studies, it may be that specific departments are best equipped to understand the vital forces that constructed 'the Middle Ages' in specific traditions. This is no revolutionary call to disband such centres, which would in any case be plainly arrogant and absurd (especially given the undoubted success of many such institutions). I do nonetheless register and welcome a reformist transformation of sorts.[42]

A final conclusion. The proposal that we look beyond revolutionary thinking and philological practice is, of course, too radical a project of self-undoing. There is no easy escape from the paradox of historicism that alienates history from us even as we approach it. We can only start from where and what we are. We are, inevitably and profoundly, revolutionary and therefore philological creatures. Consciousness of what we are, however, is the moment from which to exercise those very skills in the exhilarating act of liberating ourselves from them. Such a process involves the transformation of a rigidly philological historicism into scholarship unashamed of its own historicity. The resultant early modern period will be a little less familiar, seen in the light of the medieval centuries. The resultant 'Middle Ages' will, by contrast, be less alien, much more familiar. The way we engage with the Middle Ages will be much less a matter of finding distant analogies with a past civilisation for the way we do things, and much more a matter of finding friends with whom we want to converse. Of course friends won't agree with us completely (annoyingly, they never do): historical understanding will remain, as it always is for most of us, a complex web of sympathies for practices we find more or less attractive.[43] Repeated traversing of the medieval/early modern divide, will, however, create a new set of sympathies, partially liberated as we could be from the unseen imprisonment imposed by revolutionary historiography.

CHAPTER 2

Friar Bacon and Friar Bungay *and the rhetoric of temporality*

Deanne Williams

The Middle Ages is a retrospective invention, one that has less to do with the particular qualities of the period than with the agenda of those who seek to define it.[1] Recent attempts to dismantle the traditional disciplinary boundaries that separate medieval from Renaissance call attention to the fact that the temporal (or epochal) notion of a 'middle' that falls between the ancients and the moderns is a relatively recent production.[2] As James Simpson argues above, the tendency to define and delimit the medieval says more about the paradoxes and power struggles of the present than it does about the perfections or imperfections of the past. Nevertheless, certain features, assumptions and associations distinguish the Middle Ages long before there was a name for it. Robert Greene's *The Honourable Historie of Frier Bacon* (1594), known to us as *Friar Bacon and Friar Bungay*, offers a near-comprehensive collection of popular images of the Middle Ages. Bringing together an idealised, bucolic world of milkmaids and county fairs, the grand pageantry of the royal court, and the dank, dark lairs of magician/scholars, the play presents a stereotypical, cardboard-cutout vision of the Middle Ages.

Friar Bacon and Friar Bungay portrays the medieval philosopher and scientist, Roger Bacon (1214–*c*. 1292), who lived during the reign of King Henry III (1216–72). The immensely learned Bacon, Doctor Mirabilis, and author of works on everything from gunpowder to magnetism, was familiar to educated Elizabethans. However, Greene engages little with Bacon's intellectual reputation. He follows instead the popular prose narrative, *The Famous Historie of Fryer Bacon* (*c*. 1555), which depicts Bacon as a common-or-garden-variety magician. Called upon to aid lovers in trouble, and trotted out for a competition with the Emperor of Germany's pet magician, Greene's Friar Bacon is a trivial comic figure. At its climax, *Friar Bacon and Friar Bungay* dramatises the apocryphal story of the brazen head: a tale variously attached to the medieval philosophers Gerbert of Aurillac, Albertus Magnus (whose brazen head was broken by Thomas Aquinas), and Robert Grosseteste.[3] Like the story of Faustus selling his soul to the devil, this failed experiment reflects the prevailing Reformation association of the Middle Ages with magic. In order to establish a sense of temporal and epochal break with the Middle Ages, the play characterises the friars, and, by extension, England's Catholic history, as superstitious, foolhardy and credulous. Friar Bacon's proto-Prosperian renunciation of magic at the end of *Friar Bacon and Friar Bungay* engages prevailing notions of the right and proper historical evolution from medieval to modern, from Catholic to Protestant.

But this is not to say that *Friar Bacon and Friar Bungay* presents this as a good thing. To a cynic such as Greene, a text such as *The Famous Historie of Fryer Bacon* would have seemed like a relic from the Dark Ages. Its ardently reformist impulse and clunky anti-clerical satire would have appeared as exceedingly earnest, even misguided, propaganda: as bomb shelter manuals or *Reefer Madness* appear to us today. At the same time that *Friar Bacon and Friar Bungay* charts the trajectory that Keith Thomas calls, famously, 'Religion and the Decline of Magic', it highlights what is lost with rigid distinctions between past and present, or medieval and Renaissance.[4] It resists at an imaginative level the flattening out of the Middle Ages that, Simpson argues, is the result of periodisation at a disciplinary level. As *Friar Bacon and Friar Bungay* reveals, the early modern is the birthplace not only for the idea of the Middle Ages, but also for its deconstruction. With its epigrammatic 'Time is, time was, time is past', Friar Bacon's exploding brass head expresses the enigma of history: impossible to fully control, understand, or contain, yet endlessly demanding formulation and definition.

I

Friar Bacon has seen it all before. Prince Edward sends his friend Lacie to Fressingfield in disguise to woo, on his behalf, the damsel Margaret. Exchanging clothes with Rafe, his father's fool, Edward visits Friar Bacon, hoping he can cast a spell that will make Margaret love him. Thanks to his 'glass prospective', Friar Bacon sees right through Edward's costume. Recognising the prince's true identity, Bacon proceeds to inform him of what is really going on between Lacie and Margaret:

> Edward, King Henries sonne and Prince of Wales,
> Thy foole disguisd cannot conceale thy self:
> . . . Els Frier Bacon had but little skill.

> Thou comest in post from merrie Fressingfield,
> Fast fancied to the keepers bonny lasse,
> To crave some succour of the jolly frier:
> And Lacie, Earle of Lincolne, hast thou left
> To treat fair Margret to allow thy loves;
> But friends are men, and love can baffle lords;
> The earl both woos and courts her for himselfe.
>
> (5.67–77)

Why is this brilliant Franciscan bothering with courtship and country lasses? A student of the best minds of Oxford and Paris, Roger Bacon is one of the most prolific and influential medieval thinkers.[5] Like Boethius and Thomas More, he is also one of the great prison writers. His unorthodox opinions, and, in particular, his views on the importance of studying classical philosophy, prompted Bonaventure to incarcerate him for twelve years. Upon his release, Pope Clement IV, who had heard of his great learning, asked him for a description of his work. Answering the pope's request, Bacon produced his major works, the *Opus Maius*, the *Opus Minus*, and the *Opus Tertium*. Buoyed, perhaps, by Clement's encouragement, Bacon then proceeded to criticise the church in such sharp terms that he was imprisoned once more, following which he wrote his *Compendium Studii Theologiae*, completed shortly before he died, *c.* 1292.

Greene's portrayal of Bacon engages his popular reputation as a magician. *The Famous Historie* constructs Bacon, serious polymath, as the buffoonish friar of medieval stereotype.[6] In its opening woodcut, which was taken up and used in subsequent editions of *Friar Bacon and Friar Bungay* (fig. 1), the sleeping friar represents negligence and lassitude: his study is trivialised by the musician with pipe and tabor, and by the book, abandoned on the desk, with its alchemical symbols casually displayed. As the literary *auto-da-fé* that concludes the treatise constitutes a final example of Bacon's foolishness, it also justifies the giddy destruction of the iconoclasts:[7]

I have found, that my knowledge hath beene a heavie burden, and hath kept downe my goode thoughts: but I will remove the cause, which are these Bookes: which I doe purpose here before you all to burne. They all intreated him to spare the bookes, because in them there were those things that after-ages might receive great benefit by. He would not hearken unto them, but threw them all into the fire, and in that flame burnt the greatest learning in the world.[8]

Bacon here provides the occasion for reformist dogma: the loss of medieval learning is blamed on the errant ways of the past; better simply to burn the books and start over.

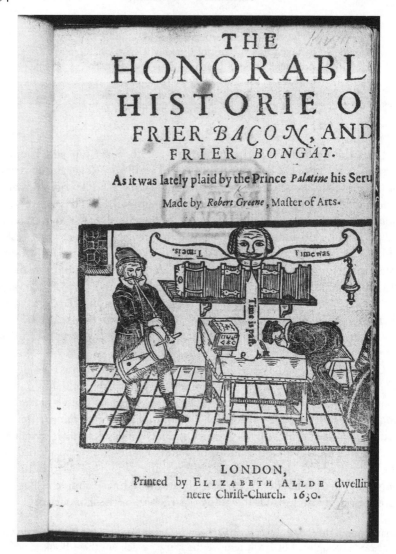

Fig. 1   Robert Greene, *The Honourable Historie of Frier Bacon* (London, 1630), title page, showing woodcut drawn from *The Famous Historie of Fryer Bacon* (London: [*c.* 1555])

Whether they celebrate his work as a theologian and scientist, or ridicule his foolish inventions, Renaissance texts consistently treat Bacon in terms of his temporal affiliation with the Middle Ages. A 1530 edition of Bacon's medical writings, *This boke doth treate all of the best waters Artyfycialles / and the vertues and properties of the same / mocche profitable for the poore sycke, set forth, by syr Roger Becon, freere*, opens with a woodcut of the friar

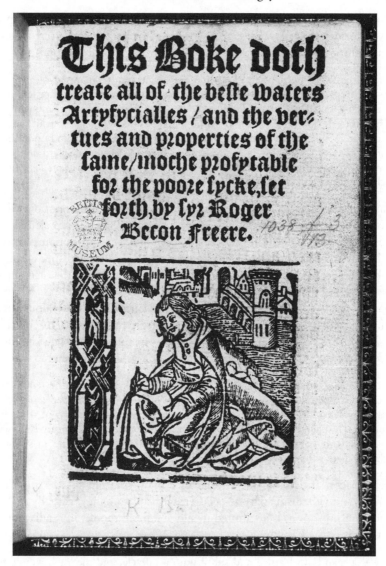

Fig. 2 *This boke doth treate all of the best waters Artyfycialles / and the vertues and properties of the same / mocche profitable for the poore sycke, set forth, by syr Roger Becon, freere* [London, 1530], title page

kneeling, with a river and collegiate buildings in the background (fig. 2): an image of moral probity and religious devotion vastly different from the more famous woodcut. However, Bacon is regarded, not as emblematic of the limitations of the past, but instead as a man ahead of his time. The 1597

Mirror of Alchemy introduces the work of 'the thrice famous and learned Fryer, formerly a fellow of Martin [Merton] Colledge: and afterwards of Brasen-nose Colledge in Oxenford' as a source of wisdom and peace:

> In times past the Philosophers spak: after diuers and sundrie manners throughout their writings, sith that as it were in a riddle and cloudie voyce, they haue left unto us a certaine most excellent and noble science, but altogether obscure, and without all hope utterly denied, and that not without good cause. Wherefore I would aduise thee, that aboue all other bookes, thou shouldest firmly fixe thy mind upon these seuen Chapters, conteining in them the transmutation of mettals, and often call to minde the beginning, middle, and end of the same, wherein thou shalt finde such subtilitie, that thy mind shalbe fully contented therewith.[9]

This preface offers an almost typological structure for interpretation: what was concealed in the past ('in a riddle and cloudie voyce') is revealed in the present. What was not fully apprehended or put to the appropriate purpose in Bacon's day can be better understood under the current dispensation.

By the seventeenth century, the anti-Catholic sentiment that accompanies these discussions of Bacon attached to Bacon's contemporaries rather than to Bacon himself. Attributing his imprisonment to the jealousy and venality of his inferiors, the 1659 edition of Bacon's *Discoverie of the Miracles of Art, of Nature, and Magicke*, translated from a manuscript owned by John Dee, constructs Bacon as an opponent of the Catholic church:

> 'Twas the *Popes* smoak which made the eyes of that Age so sore, as they could not discern any open hearted and clear headed *soul* from an *heretical Phantasme*. The silly *Fryers* envying his too prying head, by their craft had almost got it off his shoulders. It's dangerous to be wiser than the multitude, for that unruly *Beast* will have every over-topping head to be lopped shorter, lest it plot, ruine, or stop the light, or shadow its extravagancies.[10]

Here, Bacon anticipates the Renaissance man: smarter, sharper than his cohort, individualistic. His association with necromancy, actually a Reformation invention, is attributed to silly medieval monks in retaliation of criticisms of the church:

> he was a man both learned and subtil unto a miracle, and did such wonderful things by the help of *Mathematicks*, that by such as were envious and ignorant, he was accused of diabolical *Magick*, before Pope *Clement* the *4th*, and for that cause was detained in prison by him for some time. (A5r)

In each case, Reformation superstition and prejudice are projected onto the medieval past: sixteenth-century fables about the medieval scientist as necromancer give way to anti-clerical stereotypes about the Middle Ages.

Thus, the project of recuperating Bacon's reputation by bringing his work to light and publishing it becomes the occasion to reclaim him from a mistaken and misguided past on behalf of the enlightened (and proto-Enlightenment) present. In the tradition of that other esteemed Bacon, the medieval magician becomes the Reformation scientist:

A Prejudicate eye much lessens the noblenesse of the Subject. *Bacons* name may bring at the first an inconvenience to the Book, but *Bacons* ingenuity will recompence it ere he be solidly read. This as an Apology is the usher to his other Workes, which may happily breath a more free Air hereafter, when once the World sees how clear he was, from loving Negromancy. (A2r–v)

Renaissance treatments of Bacon highlight his distance from the present: as magician or as misunderstood genius. Affiliated in tandem or in tension with a medieval past associated with magic, misunderstanding and superstition, he remains a figure of temporal break.

II

Recognising that to engage Bacon is to engage his association with the Middle Ages, Greene uses Friar Bacon and Friar Bungay to reflect upon the mental and imaginative processes of periodisation itself. Responding to the intellectual gulf that separates Roger Bacon's body of work and the popular tradition that surrounds him, the play shows repeatedly how a stylised rendering of the past may be mistaken for an honest account of events. Greene achieves this by invoking the literary conventions of the past and present, only to undermine any sense of confidence in the idea of the period that they represent.

Recalling happy times in his friendship with Prince Edward, Lacie looks back to the medieval lyric world of the hunt:[11]

> Why lookes my lord like to a troubled skie,
> When heavens bright shine is shadow'd with a fogge?
> Alate we ran the deere, and through the lawndes
> Stript with our nagges the loftie frolicke bucks
> That scudded fore the teasers like the wind:
> Nere was the deere of merry Fresingfield
> So lustily puld down by jolly mates,
> Nor shared the farmers such fat venison,
> So franckly dealt, this hundred yeares before;
> Nor have I seene my lord more frolicke in the chace;
> And now – changed to a melancholie dumpe? (1.1–11)

With images of its 'deere' 'lustily puld down by jolly mates', Fressingfield appears as an ideal place for the prince and his friend to both hunt and chase women. Invoking a lyric tradition associated with merriment and jollity, as well as the occasion for countless allegories of courtship and love, these early lines identify the Middle Ages with the happier times of the past (by contrast to the prince's present 'melancholie dumpe').

However, just as the medieval lyric tradition obfuscates the violence and brutality of the hunt, so, too, are Lacie's welcoming farmers and willing deer, eagerly hunted, so idealised as to be ridiculous. Moreover, the image of untroubled social divisions, with jolly mates happily sharing their flesh with the farmers, looks very different if we interpret the hunt for the 'deere' metaphorically, as an erotic pursuit. The idea of 'dear' country girls being chased and then lustily pulled down by merry hunters, who then 'share' them, suggests the rapaciousness of the aristocratic hunting pastime, while the idea of the bucks being 'stript' implies the farmers' ensuing sexual humiliation. Lacie's speech thus calls attention to how a traditional, inherited, poetic mode can set the terms for misunderstanding. Framing the play through nostalgia, it cautions the audience to adopt a critical perspective on this impulse.

For the Prince is in love. As he relates his own story, he throws the tension between frivolity and violence in Lacie's speech into relief: a girl once regarded as easy prey has become a person, with a name, a character, and a will of her own. Meeting the keeper's daughter has brought Edward's follies into sharp relief: one minute he is 'tossing of ale and milke in countrie cannes' (14), and the next, upon seeing the 'bonny damsel', he is falling 'straight . . . into his passions' (19). One minute he is participating in frivolous fun, and the next he is dreaming of marriage. Greene expresses the paradigm shift that takes place when the prince falls in love with Margaret by lifting Edward out of the medieval lyric and setting him down firmly in the symbolic world of the Renaissance sonnet sequence. The prince recalls:

> She turnd her smock over her lilly armes,
> And divd them into milke to run her cheese;
> But, whiter than the milke, her cristall skin,
> Checked with lines of azur, made her blush
> That art or nature durst bring for compare.
> Ermsbie, if thou hadst seene, as I did note it well,
> How Bewtie plaid the huswife, how this girle,
> Like Lucrece, laid her fingers to the worke,
> Thou wouldst with Tarquine hazard Roome and all
> To win the lovely mayd of Fresingfield.   (78–87)

The sight of the girl immersing her bare arms in milk to make cheese moves Edward erotically. While his allusion to the rape of Lucrece resonates with Lacie's sexually charged recollection of the hunt (even in love, Edward remains a hunter), his recollection as a whole translates a memory into an opportunity for rhetorical display.[12] Edward's account of Margaret's beauty, as contemporary as it is stylised, uses the classical past to turn the living, active milkmaid into a frozen paragon, an emblem of Renaissance beauty.

As the opening speeches of *Friar Bacon and Friar Bungay* evoke a variety of literary modes, they cultivate a consciousness of historical difference. Highlighting the distinction between literary representations and lived reality, they foreground the limitations of any single reading or interpretation of an event. Greene shows medieval characters doing exactly what we might expect of them: Playing with country lasses? Careful: you'll fall in love with one of them. Trouble in love? Consult a magician! 'Why sirra Ned, weel ride to Oxford to Frier Bacon: oh, he is a brave scholler, sirra; they say he is a brave nigromancer, that he can make women of devils, and hee can juggle cats into costermongers' (93–6). However, he consistently thwarts the expectations of plot and character that he sets up. Before we find out that the girl in question is Margaret, her name has been used in Edward's *blazonne* ('her teethe are shelves of pretious Margarites'). The name 'Margaret' itself recalls the medieval French tradition of marguerite poetry, popularised by Chaucer in the *Legend of Good Women*, in which the pearl or daisy symbolises purity and simplicity.[13] Yet even as Margaret is embedded in literary convention, she is *sui generis*. Described making cheese and introduced with a bawdy pun as 'countrie Margaret' (1.119), even describing her own friends as 'countrie sluts' (3.9), Margaret possesses a frank, physical rusticity that pulls her outside of the frame of convention. Her conversation makes her even more impossible to categorise: 'Phoebus is blythe, and frolicke lookes from heaven, / As when he courted lovely Semele, / Swearing the pedlars shall have emptie packs, / If that fair wether may make chapmen buy' (3.13–16). Moving swiftly from the rarefied to the demotic, Margaret makes classical allusions that are quirky and imprecise: Semele was courted by Zeus, not Phoebus/Apollo. Yet these errors also imply individualism: aspiration and reading, as well as independence of mind and self-confidence.

Margaret's off-kilter classical allusions herald a freedom from literary models, enacting a kind of liberation from monolithic formulations of the past. When Edward renounces his claim on Margaret, giving her to Lacie (though she was his already), Margaret expresses her gratitude in the following terms: 'Margret, as milde and humble in her thoughts, / As was Aspatia unto Cirus selfe. / Yeelds thanks' (8.139–41). Aspatia (or Aspasia) was the name given by Cyrus the Younger to the courtesan Milto of Phocaea, one of the least mild and humble figures in history.[14] According to Plutarch, Milto was proudly defiant when Cyrus acquired her as his concubine: at first she refused even to bathe. As he came to value her wisdom, Cyrus named her Aspasia, after the lover of Pericles. A *femme fatale*, known for her learning and rhetorical skills, Aspasia of Miletus is said to have discoursed with Socrates and Plato. A figure of oratory and dialogue, known also for sexual behaviour bordering on the scandalous, she appears in catalogues of famous women, such as Rachel Speght's *Mortalities Memorandum, with a dreame prefixed, imaginarie in manner* (1621): 'Aspatia was in Rheth'ricke so expert, / As that Duke Pericles of her did learne', and inspired Beaumont and Fletcher's *The Maid's Tragedy*.[15] Margaret is not incorrect to associate herself with Aspasia, although 'milde and humble' are not the qualities that come to mind immediately. Like Cyrus's Aspasia, Margaret is beloved by more than one man (after Cyrus died Aspasia was taken by his brother, Artaxerxes II, who dedicated her as a priestess of Artemis to prevent her from being taken by his son, Darius, when he became King of Persia). Like Aspasia of Miletus, Margaret possesses distinctive rhetorical abilities and a knack for outshining her male counterparts. Nevertheless, at the same time that she invokes a paradigm of intelligent womanhood, Margaret, named for her purity, is aligning herself with one of the great courtesans of history. Classical allusion, like medieval lyric, calls into question our assumptions about the past: was Aspasia feisty or meek? Innocent or sexually knowing? And was Roger Bacon a magician or a philosopher? Offering an alternative reading of history, Margaret reveals how the past eludes our grasp, containing possibilities that transcend easy categorisation. As she weaves in and out of classical and medieval literature and transforms them in her own image, Margaret ultimately appears like no one so much as herself.

Although Lacie succeeds in stealing Margaret from Edward, he breaks up with her by means of a brutal letter. Here Margaret is scripted as Patient Griselda, a humanist ideal of feminine submission celebrated by Petrarch and Chaucer's Clerk. Unlike her counterpart in the *Clerk's Tale*, however, Margaret responds, not with resignation and acceptance, but with the active emotionalism of a Senecan tragic hero:

> Fond Ate, doomer of bad boading fates,
> That wrappes proud Fortune in thy snaky locks,
> Didst thou inchaunt my byrth-day with such stars
> As lightned mischeefe from their infancie?
> If heavens had vowed, if stars had made decree,
> To shew on me their forward influence,

> If Lacie had but lovd, heavens, hell, and all,
> Could not have wrongd the patience of my minde.
>
> (10.137–44)

Margaret rails against external conceptions of Fate. Where her medieval counterpart would gesture towards God's will, and accept her fate philosophically, Margaret instead places priority on the personal immediacy of love, which conquers even astrology. Manifesting a thoroughly modern scepticism (she would have been at home with Greene and the other Renaissance 'prodigals', especially Christopher Marlowe), Margaret places inner truth and lived experience above all external forces and structures, which she gives little credence. She acknowledges and even revels in the intensity of her feelings: the very mention of Lacie makes her swoon, 'ah, give me leave to sigh at every thought!' (152). Her decision to retire to a nunnery is motivated not by the occasion to devote 'my loves and libertie to God' (159) but by the opportunity to showcase her broken heart. If she can't take part in a story about personal fulfilment, Margaret may as well shave her head and play another role. Although her disenchantment makes her see the world as 'vanitie; / Wealth, trash; love, hate; pleasure, dispaire' (155–6), Margaret expresses herself wholeheartedly, unselfconsciously and (despite herself) humorously, even as she renounces the world: 'Farewell to friends and father! Welcome Christ!' (14.30).

As the love plot of *Friar Bacon and Friar Bungay* plays with its audience's expectations about the Middle Ages, at times falling into conventional patterns and at other times subverting them, the rivalry of Lacie and Edward fades into the background. Margaret's headstrong and vivacious character emerges out of this jumble of the past, as she enjoys an individual relationship to the traditions and *topoi* that precede her. A female participant in the predominantly male pastime of erotic worship, Margaret's love for Lacie is handled with sympathy.[16] A woman who complains

> I loved once, – Lord Lacie was my love;
> And now I hate my selfe for that I lovd,
> And doated more on him than on my God
> For this I scourge myselfe with sharpe repents
>
> (14.12–15)

deserves love's rich rewards, not self-recrimination. With its lively heroine and multiple editions throughout the sixteenth century, *Friar Bacon and Friar Bungay* enjoyed a popular appeal that reflects the importance of women as theatregoers and as consumers of the printed book.[17] Like any character in a contemporary bodice-ripper, Margaret is a modern girl dressed in period costume. Anticipating debates concerning the early modern (or medieval) invention of the individual, Margaret maintains her individuality as she is held up against a variety of paradigms, from the medieval past as well as from the humanist and theatrical present.[18]

III

At first glance, Greene's handling of Friar Bacon appears anything but independent. He presents only one side of the story: the side that viewed Roger Bacon as a ham-fisted necromancer, and the side that Greene was, himself, unlikely to hold personally. Having studied at Oxford, which preserved a tradition of Bacon's towering intellect, as well as manuscripts of his work in their libraries, Greene must have known better. Nevertheless, he reworks sensational material from the *Famous Historie*, such as the brazen head, the rivalry with Vandermast, and the duel prompted by the glass prospective, to launch an apparent argument against magic, which is presented as faulty, absurd and violent.[19] Yet Greene's handling of the narrative reveals the limitations of a historical trajectory that carves out the Middle Ages as a space for magic and the occult, leaving modernity free to claim reason and science for itself.[20]

Fusing the legend of Bacon constructing the brass head, treated in detail in the *Famous Historie*, with the idea of constructing a brass ring around England (interestingly, the *Famous Historie* does not mention a brass wall, although it does mention a brass *ball*), Greene brings down the ideal of national integrity along with magic: both of which, he implies, are medieval creations. Friar Bacon attaches the idea of a brass wall around England to his other pointless project, that of the brazen head, which explodes instead of spouting philosophy: [21]

> I have contrivd and framed a head of brasse,
> (I made Belcephon hammer out the stuffe)
> And that by art shall read Philosophie:
> And I will strengthen England by my skill,
> That if ten Caesars livd and raignd in Rome,
> With all the legions Europe doth containe,
> They should not touch a grasse of English ground;
> The worke that Ninus reard at Babylon,
> The brazen walles framed by Semiramis,
> Carvd out like to the portal of the sunne,
> Shall not be such as rings the English strond
> From Dover to the market-place of Rie. (2.53–64)

The frequent repetition of these intentions throughout the play does nothing for their stability.[22] Like Margaret, Friar Bacon makes extremely problematic references to the past. In a play that refers to Henry III as a 'brave Plantagenet' (4.13), highlighting his status as a Norman, and conquering, ruler of England, Friar Bacon's desire for an impermeable island appears particularly bizarre. The desire to seal off England from foreign invasion may be noble; however, Friar Bacon's reference to Rome reminds us that it is impossible to reverse the effects of a Roman invasion of Britain that has already taken place in history. Like the wall, the brazen head's 'strange and uncouth' (11.18) words emphasise the impossibility of erasing or preventing a foreign presence in England.[23] By comparing his wall to that of Ninus and Semiramis at Babylon, moreover, Friar Bacon defines his construction project with references to walls that are collapsible and empires that are ultimately destroyed.[24] A classic exemplum for the temporality and contingency of empire, Babylon is the shakiest model imaginable for English nationhood.

Like any good politician, King Henry III speaks as if the wall is already constructed:

> Great men of Europe, monarchs of the West,
> Ringd with the walls of old Oceanus,
> Whose loftie surge is like the battlements
> That compast high built Babell in with towers, –
> Welcome, my lords, welcome brave westerne kings,
> To Englands shore, whose promontorie cleeves
> Shewes Albion is another little world: (4.1–4)

Henry's reference to Babel links the wall once again to Babylon, recalling the biblical story about the division of tongues and its ensuing national and imperial rivalries. For all the play's celebration of England's separateness ('another little world'), Prince Edward's marriage negotiations with Eleanor of Castile, and Henry III's entertainment of the Holy Roman Emperor and his sidekick, Vandermast, illustrate the inescapability of internationalism.[25] Like the brazen head that can speak in tongues, Vandermast has learned to speak in the various tongues of the magic centres he has visited: 'A Germaine borne, past into Padua, / To Florence and to fair Bolonia / To Paris, Rheims, and stately Orleans, / And talking there with men of art, put downe / The chiefest of them all in aphorisms' (4.48–52).[26] While Vandermast's failure as a magician may be read in light of England's imperial rivalry with the Holy Roman Empire in the late sixteenth century, and especially the triumph

of the Spanish Armada in 1588, the play's emphasis upon the instability
of empire produces little confidence in Henry's ambitions for England,
emphasising its vulnerability over its strengths.[27]

Formally renouncing magic, Friar Bacon explains that it is in the best
interests of the nation, drawing upon the longstanding myth of English
descent from Troy:

> I find by deep praescience of mine art,
> Which once I tempred in my secret cell
> That here where Brute did build his Troynovant,
> From forth the royall garden of a king
> Shall flourish out so rich and fair a bud,
> Whose brightnesse shall deface proud Phoebus' flowre,
> And over-shadow Albion with her leaves.   (16.42–8)

Of course, Friar Bacon's dream of a protective wall recalls that other,
famously penetrable, wall of Troy. His belief that magic can serve national-
istic and imperialistic ends ('Thus glories England over all the west' (76)),
is renounced, instead, for a 'mysticall' (63) prophecy of Elizabeth. Although
the Trojan allusion provides the ultimate example of the folly of wall construction, the Tudors, along with many other European royal families,
claimed for themselves a Trojan genealogy.[28] References to 'Troynovant'
and 'Albion' (7, 27, 48, 67) gesture towards Elizabeth's personal mythology,
and the prophecy of how the other flowers shall 'stoope and wonder at
Dianas rose' (62), situates Elizabeth as Virgin (and as huntress) within her
Tudor genealogy. As Greene undoes the dream of national insularity and
integrity, he replaces magic with a myth of Trojan descent. With the image
of the shiny golden rings that wed Prince Edward and Eleanor of Castile,
as well as Lacie and Margaret, losing its power and potential by their visual
association with the bright brass wall encircling England, Greene offers a
canny compliment to a queen for whom marriage and heir-begetting was
no longer a viable option.[29] The play thus concludes, not with an image of
courtship celebrated, but with an image of singularity: 'peace from heaven
shall harbour in these leaves / That gorgeous beautifies this matchless of
flower' (55–6).

With a succession of inappropriate classical allusions and historical references, Greene rhetorically and comically undermines the trajectory from
medieval to modern that the plot of *Friar Bacon and Friar Bungay* paces out.
As references to Babylon and Britain's invasion by Rome suggest the contingency of all empire, weakening Friar Bacon's dream of the wall around
England, they also qualify the notion of replacing a flawed and credulous

past with a far-sighted and far-reaching present. Classical allusions such as Margaret's reference to Aspasia undermine confidence in representations of the past, suggesting that the present never understands or formulates it correctly.

The disruptive effect of classicism on medievalism in *Friar Bacon and Friar Bungay* explains the curiously split personality of Friar Bacon's side-kick Miles. We first encounter Miles reverentially greeting Friar Bacon as *'doctissime et reverendissime doctor'* (2.2). He defends and protects Friar Bacon when Burden expresses doubt at the plausibility of a talking head and a wall of brass. Beaten publicly by Friar Bacon, he drowns his sorrows in drink. In his cups, Miles is a changed man:

> *Salve*, Doctor Burden! This lubberly lurden,
> Ill-shapte and ill faced, disdained and disgraced,
> What he tells unto *vobis mentitur de nobis*.
>   (7.40–2)

Arrested for being a public nuisance, Miles expresses his discomfiture by adopting the verse forms of John Skelton, whose curious combination of scholasticism and alliteration looks back to both the Latin and the native English Middle Ages. Skelton's is the voice of dissent, of crankily pointing out that things are not as they should be, and of using classical learning for political ends. A liminal figure, at once medieval and early modern, Skelton is also associated with resuscitation of the classical past, radically reformulating it in the interests of cultural and political critique.[30]

Recalcitrant to the end, Miles interrupts the grave and grand marriage negotiations between Edward and Eleanor of Castile, chafes at his role as steward at the feast, and, ultimately, produces the climactic moment by failing to awaken Bacon when the head utters its epigrammatic 'Time is . . . time was . . . time is past' (9. 52–71). Bacon laments:

> Villain, if thou had'st cald to Bacon then,
> If thou hadst watcht, and wakte the sleepie frier,
> The Brazen-head had uttered aphorismes,
> And England had been circled round with brasse:
>   (11.98–101)

If it hadn't been for Miles, Bacon believes, he could have kept his magic and built his wall. Having instigated the resulting temporal and epochal break from 'the medieval', Miles is exiled: with a book in his hand, a wide-sleeved gown on his back, and a cap on his head, he is sentenced to 'rome and range about the world' (11.114). A figure of human resistance to the automaton, of internationalism and particularly of Latin learning, Miles, like Skelton, rails against English insularity, and the status quo. As Miles is carried away most happily to hell, *Friar Bacon and Friar Bungay* signals the extent to which Skelton provides a model for Greene's deconstructive purpose by offering an account of hell that closely resembles Greene's idea of heaven:

Faith, 'tis a place I have desired long to see: have you not good tipling-houses there? may not a man have a lustie fier there, a pot of good ale, a paire of cardes, a swinging peece of chalke, and a browne toast that will clap a white wastcoat on a cup of good drinke? (15.31–5)

IV

A collection of discordant classical allusions and a generally uneasy relationship to literary paradigms constitute what we might call Robert Greene's rhetoric of temporality. Together, they prompt a reconsideration of the kinds of pat notion of the past promoted by the brazen head's 'Time is . . . time was . . . time is past', and symbolised by the popular portrayal of Bacon as a magician. Greene's rhetoric of temporality questions this legend and its role in articulating Reformation conceptions about the past that has since come to be referred to as medieval. Ultimately, the play demands renewed respect for the rich and uncontainable history that Elizabethan culture mined for inspiration.

My essay's title takes the phrase 'The Rhetoric of Temporality' from a well-known essay by Paul de Man.[31] In this essay, de Man rejects the Romantic symbol in favor of allegory, a more traditional form of rhetoric that he feels has 'fallen into disrepute'. For de Man, allegory has played Martha to symbol's Mary: the former is tamed, ordered, prosaic, overshadowed by the latter's imagination and spirit. De Man argues that the symbol, associated since the Romantics with a spiritual association between man and nature and a fusion of subject and object, is too universal. Its clunky predecessor, allegory, is not only historical in nature through its association with the Middle Ages and early modern period, but temporal in function. De Man contends that, for all its unabashed constructedness, allegory's emphasis on the distance between the sign and its meaning is more honest. Whereas the symbol obfuscates the truth, which is that the self and the object cannot ever coincide, allegory highlights and is in fact predicated upon what de Man calls 'the temporal predicament'. Dismissing the symbol as a site of nostalgia for a unity that never existed, de Man praises allegory as a site of difference, of historical as well as physical distance from the origin.

Friar Bacon and Friar Bungay deconstructs the ideology of the Middle Ages in much the same way that de Man deconstructs the symbol. Lacie's opening speech gestures toward a pastoral framework that the later Romantic poets associated with the Middle Ages: a time and a place of fusion between nature and humanity.[32] The figure of Friar Bacon is similarly evocative of a firm and fixed conception of the 'medieval', even before such a term had been invented. Yet, as I have shown, *Friar Bacon and Friar Bungay* resists this 'symbolic' or homogeneous vision of the Middle Ages, as the explosion of Friar Bacon's talking head calls into question a linear and compartmentalised vision of history. As the play highlights the distance (and difference) between a historical moment and its imaginary and literary representation, suggesting that history is more fractured and intractable than our representations of it lead us to believe, it demonstrates how easy it is to refashion the past for purposes of the present, and how limited and essentially 'interested' traditional conceptions of period (and of discipline) can be.

In place of a 'symbolic' vision of the Middle Ages, *Friar Bacon and Friar Bungay* engages allegory and its associated tropes and genres that, as De Man argues, highlight the discontinuities between sign and meaning: irony, melancholy and doubling. Friar Bacon's brazen head is ironised when Greene fuses it with an implausible brass wall around Britain, transporting it from the realm of the fabulous to that of the ridiculous. When Lacie laments the prince's 'melancholie dumpe', he shifts from nostalgia, a trope that believes that there once was a true home, to melancholy, the feeling of inescapable exile. For De Man, doubling (or 'dedoublement') is an effect of the alienation produced by allegory: along with allegory and melancholy, doubling frustrates the fusion of sign and meaning by producing multiple signs. In *Friar Bacon and Friar Bungay*, there is even the doubling of doubling. Friar Bacon encounters his German *Doppelgänger* in Vandermast, a figure who recalls Marlowe's Doctor Faustus. If we believe, as is quite likely, that *Friar Bacon and Friar Bungay* followed Marlowe's *Doctor Faustus*, then Vandermast suggests how Greene's play is also doubling Marlowe's. With Vandermast as a double both for Doctor Faustus and for Friar Bacon, the plurality of zany magicians does away with any vestiges of seriousness that may remain.[33] And of course, Friar Bacon has a further double in Friar Bungay, the bungler, who at appears first as an inferior foil to the magisterial Bacon, and then as an anticipation of his limitations.

As it compromises as well as deconstructs nostalgic ideas about the Middle Ages, *Friar Bacon and Friar Bungay* offers a sharp corrective to the readings of the medieval that were taking place in the early modern period. While we may use De Man's felicitous phrase to describe Greene's strategies, 'The Rhetoric of Temporality' also offers some insights into our own constructions of periodicity. His primary move is from the margin to the centre: sidelining symbol, which has enjoyed poetic pride of place since the time of the Romantics, and replacing it with long-maligned and newly recuperated allegory. As a result, De Man enacts a shift in values, with the symbol's limitations expostulated while the virtues of allegory are extolled. To extend this to the wider concerns of this book, the Middle Ages, long considered derivative, secondary and inferior to the Renaissance, are coming to the forefront, as long-overlooked medieval material is increasingly being shown as central to Renaissance texts. De Man's movement from the false certainty of the symbol to the harsher truths of allegory also suits the evolving shift from entrenched beliefs about the Middle Ages as a space of unquestioning faith, untroubled social distinctions, and easy collectivity and communalism to the present agnosticism. Not only do we now see the Middle Ages as a site of conflict; we are conflicted about how we see the Middle Ages. We are unhappy with the traditional distinctions between medieval and Renaissance, yet we nevertheless intuit a Renaissance self-consciousness about the period that was later dubbed the Middle Ages. Even as we try to grasp these elusive differences, we are forced to acknowledge the eternal disconnect between a historical moment and the scholarly terms and literary texts that attempt to represent it.

PART II

Text

CHAPTER 3

Langland, apocalypse and the early modern editor

Larry Scanlon

An unexpected by-product of the triumph of new historicism and its off-shoots has been a persistent boundary dispute between medievalists and early modernists. The dispute concerns the character of modernity in the early modern period and the nature of its difference with the medieval. Over the past decade and a half, beginning with two essays by Lee Patterson and David Aers, a wide variety of medievalists have complained with some regularity that for all of its innovations, new historicist and cultural materialist work on the early modern period retains an outdated, excessively tradition-alist view of medieval culture; that is, as monolithic, static and repressive.[1] To be sure, this dispute has been fairly one-sided. For the most part, early modernist response to these medievalist complaints has been muted, and some medievalists have taken this lack of response as further evidence of the problem they have identified. Speaking on behalf of a misunderstood and illegitimately reified Middle Ages has proven a compelling motive, and it has produced some extremely impressive results, especially when what it defends is medieval culture in its capacious, populist or even progressive mode.

Three major works in particular come to mind: Eamon Duffy's *Stripping of the Altars* (1992), David Wallace's *Chaucerian Polity* (1997) and James Simpson's *Reform and Cultural Revolution* (2002). (I include Duffy's book, though the work of an historian, because of the great impact it has had on Middle English literary studies.) In most respects these works are very different from each other. Nevertheless, they are all alike in striving to recover some aspect of medieval culture that constitutes a lost opportunity. For Duffy, it is the social unity of the liturgy, that great economy 'of ritual observance and symbolic gesture' wherein 'medieval people found the key to the meaning and purpose of their lives'. That unity was destroyed by a Protestant Reformation largely, if not exclusively, imposed from above.[2] For Wallace, it is the possibilities of the late medieval 'associational ideol-ogy' whose contours Chaucer so brilliantly adumbrates in the *Canterbury*

Tales; an autonomous 'process of group formation, where the right to exist *as* a group is simply assumed from within rather than conferred from without'. Chaucerian polity 'represents a singular moment of political confidence that will not be repeated on English territory'.[3] By Shakespeare's time it has been definitively lost, destroyed by the conceptual hierarchies of Renaissance humanism and the absolutism of early modern monarchy. For Simpson, it is the cultural richness of the fifteenth century, a richness of 'unresolved generic juxtaposition', of 'complicated accretion', of 'development and addition' and 'recognition of historical totality'.[4] Simpson provocatively chooses *reform* as the umbrella term to designate this richness, renaming the Reformation and Renaissance a 'cultural revolution'. Stressing 'the values of unity and novelty above all', this revolution achieved a 'simplified and centralized jurisdiction' which 'aggressively displaced [the] culture of jurisdictional heterogeneity' of the later Middle Ages.[5]

Loss is hardly a new theme in Medieval Studies. Indeed, as L. O. Aranye Fradenburg argued not too long ago, memorialising loss may well constitute the field's *raison d'être*.[6] But these works do not figure loss in the traditional manner. Their form of loss is not a fall from some originary unity. On the contrary, the precise character of its pathos lies in its contingency, in the possibility that history might have happened very differently. Moreover, they define what is lost by its congruence with certain values in the present rather than its difference. This is the medieval as decentred, heterogeneous, dispersive, local and popular. In its uncanny anticipation of our own present it puts significant pressure on the progressivist and teleological biases that seem built into historical periodisation as a modern disciplinary structure. As these accounts contest any easy superiority that might be read into the emergence of the early modern, they also perform an even broader and more salutary function, preventing the modern more generally from claiming its freedom from its premodern past too cheaply. Indeed, such contestatory work is one of the postmodern medievalist's most urgent tasks.

However, for that very reason it is worth noting that in some fundamental ways these works remain haunted by the structures of periodisation they contest. For those structures by themselves, with their institutional hegemony and their veneer of scientific precision, constitute a claim for modernity's privilege over its past more sweeping than any specific claim about any specific historical moment that is made within them. Thus, paradoxically, any scholarly project that aspires to speak for the medieval as a period, as against the early modern, or indeed any other moment, as a period, cannot avoid affirming periodisation as a global structure even as it contests the meanings the structure has hitherto assigned to the Middle

Ages. To this perhaps inescapable global paradox we might connect a smaller and more local one. As we all know, new historicism and cultural materialism both began with scholars working in the early modern period or, as it was then exclusively known, the Renaissance. Medievalists were among the first scholars from other periods to adopt this new methodology, although they struggled from the beginning with new historicism's hostility or indifference to the Middle Ages – which is one reason why one rarely finds medievalists who will actually describe themselves as new historicists.[7] Yet if we look at the matter in institutional rather than individual terms, it quickly becomes clear that the methodological innovations that attracted medievalists to new historicism are the same ones which led both to the movement's tendency to oversimplify the Middle Ages and to the characteristic medievalist response to that oversimplification. Perhaps the greatest methodological strength of new historicism is its intensely synchronic bias, its capacity to situate particular texts in a thick description of their own historical moment. New historicism made the immediate historicity of a particular text a matter of great interpretative density. This innovation was extremely attractive to medievalists, particularly in North America, where the reigning paradigm of patristic exegesis threatened to make all of later medieval culture a footnote to Augustine. The cumulative effect of new historicist work in the early modern was to assign the density it discovered in particular texts to the period as a whole, and as medievalists under the influence of new historicism began to uncover a similar density in the later Middle Ages, the reified view of medieval culture which naturally – though perhaps not inevitably – accompanied the synchronic investigations of the early modern new historicists became an increasingly compelling target for critique.

One way through this impasse would be to return to the problem of continuity and to the older historicisms against which new historicism has defined itself. The subject of this essay is Robert Crowley's 1550 edition of *Piers Plowman*, the first print edition of the poem. It appeared in three different versions in 1550, and then was reissued by another printer in 1561. Crowley's edition is also a central feature of what an older generation of historicists, led by Helen C. White, knew as the *Piers Plowman* tradition.[8] As such, the edition eludes all but the most perfunctory explanation on the basis of current synchronic paradigms. It reinforces a still vital tradition, which throughout the sixteenth century offered the figure of Piers Plowman as an enduring model for understanding and examining various zones of social and spiritual experience. In seeking to recover the origin of this tradition and to reconstitute it in the newer medium of print, Crowley's

edition necessarily also asserts a categorical difference between his present
and the past from which the *Piers Plowman* tradition issues. But I will argue
that Crowley mobilises this difference mainly to overcome it. He seeks continuity with his author Langland in a number of ways. First there is the
predictable, mundane historical concerns of the editor of a great poet from
a past now largely obscured. Then, there are the political and philosophical
sympathies Crowley feels unite him with Langland. These sympathies not
only transcend Langland's Catholicism, but also allow Crowley to deploy
Langland's poetic authority against more conservative forms of contemporary Protestantism which Crowley dislikes. Finally there is Langland's
Catholicism itself. Even here, without ever denying the doctrinal differences, Crowley struggles to establish common ground. As we shall see,
these efforts concentrate on Langland's apocalyptic vision and its penitential orientation.

Modern scholarship's response to Crowley's edition has been sporadic,
subordinated to its larger response to Langland. Langland has been read
more or less continuously from his own time to the present, and up until the
beginning of the century just past he had generally been considered a religious and political dissident. The peculiar achievement of modern Langland
scholarship has been to transform him into a quintessentially conservative,
quintessentially medieval poet. One can find the rudiments of this trend at
the end of the nineteenth century, but its real beginning coincided with the
field's response to modern formalism, in the influential readings of C. S.
Lewis and E. Talbot Donaldson.[9] By the 1960s this view had prevailed over
the older one and it has remained dominant ever since.[10] Although some
recent accounts have suggested alternative views, they have yet to achieve
much acceptance.[11] Here is a case of a continuing insistence on medieval
conservatism for which medievalists have no one to blame but themselves.

As the undertaking of a radical Protestant, Crowley's edition might well
seem to present counter-evidence to the prevailing view. Paradoxically, however, the devious logic of periodisation has made it available as a subsidiary
support to the argument for Langland's conservatism. The nearly unani-
mous scholarly view of Crowley's edition is that it constitutes a Protestant
misreading of an essentially medieval text, a view that might be traced at
least as far back as J. M. Manly. Although Manly's 1908 article in the *Cambridge History of English Literature* is better known for its baroque claim that
Piers Plowman was actually five different poems with five different authors,
he combines this claim with a disavowal of then current views of the poem's
dissidence, which he calls a 'misunderstanding' arising from the 'nature of
the interest of the sixteenth century reformers' who took it as 'an inspiration

and a prophecy'.[12] While the claim for multiple authorship has been almost completely discredited, the notion of the sixteenth-century misreading persists. Moreover, this view has even managed to incorporate the strongest piece of contemporary external evidence for Langland's dissidence. Two of the letters produced by the leaders of the 1381 Rising use the figure of Piers as a rallying cry, one of them bidding 'Piers Plowman to go to his work'. These letters have also been long treated as 'misreadings', and two recent and influential discussions of Crowley's edition by medievalists have identified the rebel misreading as the ultimate source for the Protestant one – in spite of the tenuous logic of claiming that a later historical misrecognition had a contemporary source.[13] The most severe verdict on Crowley's edition has come from an early modernist. Although otherwise the best and most sympathetic of Crowley's critics, John N. King has written that 'Crowley kidnapped this orthodox medieval demand for reform of monasticism and society, converting it, through his preface and marginal notes, into a powerful revolutionary attack against monasticism and the Roman Catholic hierarchy.'[14] Subsequent commentators have objected to the severity of this observation, but they have focused on the term 'kidnapped', whereas what I find most salient is the opposition between 'orthodox medieval demand' and 'revolutionary attack'.[15] This opposition might seem another instance of an early modernist reading the Middle Ages as static; and early modernity as dynamic. Yet in this case, King's claim actually defers to the prevailing view among medievalists.

I have called Crowley Langland's 'first modern editor', not only because he is the first to put *Piers Plowman* into print, but because the goals of his edition seem much closer to those of modern editors than to those of Reformation religious polemic. However, in making this claim I am much less interested in the teleology it provisionally invokes than in its potential for increasing the complexity in our understanding of Crowley's motives. For Crowley certainly was a Protestant polemicist, and in general he was much more interested in polemic than either editing or even publishing. But his polemics, though always articulating a fairly radical Protestantism, tended to focus more on politics than on the doctrinal or liturgical, especially at the time he was editing *Piers Plowman*.[16] While his poetry was frequently polemical, its more overriding concern was spiritual discipline, and while his sense of this discipline was also strongly Protestant, what interested Crowley most was its political implications. As these implications were where he sought common ground with Langland, his scrupulous pursuit of doctrinally neutral editorial questions enabled him to protect Langland's historical autonomy and specificity. Robert Crowley was born in 1518 in the

Cotswolds in Gloucestershire. In 1542 he spent a year at Magdalen College, Oxford, leaving as the result of a dispute led by John Foxe against religious conservatives. Foxe would become a life-long ally. Settling in London, by 1548 Crowley was collaborating with the printer John Day, publisher of the sermons of Hugh Latimer and Foxe's *Acts and Monuments*, among other works. The next year Crowley struck out on his own, setting up shop in Ely Rents in Holborn; during the three years from 1549 to 1551, over twenty works appeared with his imprint, though the majority may have actually been printed by Richard Grafton, Printer to the King under Edward VI.[17] Crowley himself was the author of most of these works, and during this same period, he produced five moderately lengthy poems, five polemical pamphlets, the first complete metrical Psalter in English, and three versions of *Piers Plowman*, all of which appeared in 1550. In 1551, he was ordained a deacon and his activities as a printer ceased. There was also a hiatus in his writing. Two years later, with Mary's accession to the throne, he went into exile with other leading radicals, and he did not begin writing again until 1561, after his return.

The apparent rapidity of the successive imprints of the *Piers Plowman* edition is generally taken to indicate that the enterprise was a commercial success. While that may well be true, other circumstances suggest a more complex possibility. The briefness of Crowley's career as a printer, his status as his own chief author, and his abrupt abandonment of the printing business after his ordination would seem to argue his interest in the enterprise was never primarily commercial. Crowley dedicates one of his poems to Lady Elizabeth Fane, whose husband was executed with Edward Seymour in 1552, leading King to identify her as Crowley's patron. Although R. Carter Hailey finds this specific claim dubious, it seems likely that the circle of London radicals within which Crowley moved was heavily patronised by sympathetic aristocrats and well connected to the more radical elements at the court of Edward VI, including Seymour.[18] Hailey, in his own study of Crowley's edition, notes a fascinating codicological anomaly: Crowley produced some copies of his edition in vellum. Although printing on vellum was a regular feature of incunable production on the continent it was quite rare in England. As Hailey explains, Crowley's vellum copies

are the sole extant examples of English printing on vellum between Berthelet's 1544 edition of *Psalmes or prayers taken out of holye scripture* (STC 3001.7, a single copy held by Exeter College Oxford) and the single imperfect copy of *The letany, wyth certayne other deuoute and godlye meditations* in 1562 (anonymously printed; STC 16455 held by the Bodleian.) And the *Piers* copies are one of only five examples of vellum printing from 1544 to the end of the century.[19]

Vellum certainly indicates a more select market, but it also indicates an interest in durability. It seems possible that Crowley's primary motive in producing a print edition of *Piers Plowman* was neither commercial speculation, nor ideological support for current polemic, but canon formation. In putting the poem into print he may have been attempting to secure for Langland the authoritative status Caxton secured for Chaucer nearly seventy-five years earlier. This goal was not ideologically innocent; in Langland Crowley obviously found the medieval *auctor* most amenable to his religious and political beliefs. But in recovering *Piers Plowman* as one of the foundations of these beliefs, he was doing a good deal more than deploying an already established prestigious figure for some immediate ideological advantage.

Crowley based his edition on a now lost manuscript that belonged to the version of Langland's poem modern scholars know as the B-version, which most take to be Langland's second version of the poem and to have been produced during the decade before 1381. Crowley also consulted other manuscripts, including at least one from the C-version, Langland's final version, generally thought to have been completed by 1387. In Crowley's second and third imprints, apparently intended to be indistinguishable, he substantially expanded his supporting apparatus. To the preface of approximately 700 words to the first imprint, Crowley added a passus-by-passus summary of the poem, a little under 3,000 words in length. He also greatly increased the marginal glosses, from 56 in the first imprint to a total of 495 in the third imprint, by my count. To this point no treatment of this edition has produced a detailed reading of Crowley's apparatus. Carter Hailey's excellent 2001 dissertation gives us an exhaustive account of the core of the edition, Crowley's handling of Langland's text. Hailey treats the apparatus more incidentally, though without the tendentiousness I have been criticising in others. These have concentrated on those moments where Crowley is not only at his most polemical, but also at his most anti-Catholic. Across the full extent of his apparatus, such moments are actually comparatively rare. Even when Crowley is most polemical, he is not always anti-Catholic; his remarks are also aimed at the rich, at the nobility and the crown, and at less radical Protestants. This pattern corresponds with much of Crowley's career before he went into exile; like any self-respecting radical he was frequently more interested in attacking insufficiently rigorous members of his own party than in attacking the opposition. Helen C. White rightly describes *An Informacion and Peticion agaynst the Oppressours of the Pore Commons*, a pamphlet Crowley produced in 1548, as 'a pretty sweeping indictment not of the past order but of the present, not of the old regime, but of the new, not just of the church, but of all society, especially lay society'.[20] One could describe many of his other writings from this period in the same way.

There is no doubt this edition expresses Crowley's Protestantism. Nevertheless, it does so in terms that are primarily philosophical, poetic and political. Its sectarianism is occasional and secondary. For what Crowley values in Langland's poem are precisely its philosophical, poetic and political ideals. The continuities which he articulates on these grounds are too subtle, too ambiguous and too complex to be subsumed under notions of appropriation or misrecognition. The most basic and consistent ideological motive his edition and apparatus expresses is the expansion of vernacular literacy. He wants to make *Piers Plowman* available to a much larger audience and he wants to equip that audience with the information necessary to understand the poem in an unmediated fashion. This ideal is certainly Protestant, yet it is not exclusively so. Many late medieval Catholics, Langland included, also advocated vernacular literacy. *Piers Plowman* is an exercise in vernacular theology, one of the most monumental, and certainly by far the most widely disseminated of its own time. As the great social historian K. B. McFarlane memorably remarked, at the end of the fourteenth century, 'the literate laity were taking the clergy's words out of their mouths'.[21] Crowley thus brings to his readers a poem already intent on empowering its readers. This congruence frames the others, and undoubtedly encouraged Crowley to offer the poem in as authentic a form as he could. He locates the centre of Langland's poetic in its negotiations between the imperatives of spiritual discipline and an apocalyptic recognition of the radical contingency of human history. And he moves out from that apocalyptic poetic towards its political and ecclesiological implications in a manner that is also profoundly congruent with Langland's own vision.

We can begin with the preface (see Appendix, 70–71 below, for a complete transcription). Accounts which treat the preface as an instance of anti-Catholic polemic turn on a single sentence. However, when examined in context, this sentence can be shown to support a primarily poetic point. The preface begins in exactly the way most modern readers would expect from the introduction to an edition: by identifying the author and offering some basic biographical details. The first two sentences identify the author as 'Roberte langlande, a Shropshere man borne in Cleybirie, about viii, myles from Malvernes hilies'. The next four explain and justify the conjecture that the poem was written in 1350, 'in the tyme of kynge Edwarde the thyrde', while John Chichester was mayor of London. Then comes the sentence that everyone quotes:

In whose tyme it pleased God to open the eyes of many to se hys truth, giving them boldenes of herte, to open their mouthes and crye oute agynst the workes of darckenes, as dyd John Wicklyfe, who also in those dayes translated the holye Byble into the Englishe tonge, and this writer who in reportynge certayne visions and dreames, that he fayned hym selfe to have dreamed, doth most christianlie enstructe the weake, and sharplye rebuke the obstynate blynde.

There is no doubt that this sentence claims for Crowley's Protestant present a categorical privilege over England's Catholic past, nor that Crowley equates Langland and Wyclif, claiming them both as Protestants *avant la lettre*, or more literally, *voces clamantium*. It may also be, as John King argues, that in associating the two, Crowley responds to the influence of John Bale. In the 1548 edition of his bibliography, *Illustrium maioris Britanniae scriptorum summarium*, Bale mistakenly identifies Wyclif as author of *Piers Plowman* (*Petrus Agricola*), and in the apocalyptic work *The Image of Both Churches*, completed about the same time, Bale, adapting a scheme from Joachim of Fiore, identifies the reigns of Edward III and Richard II with 'the blowing of the fifth trumpet' announcing 'the arrival of Antichrist and the age of "innumerable locustes"'.[22] Nevertheless, all of these polemical possibilities must be returned to their immediate context in this preface. Strictly speaking, the faintly Latinate structure of this sentence, beginning as it does with a relative pronoun, subordinates it to the sentences preceding. Thus, we should read its characterisation of Langland's age as an extension of Crowley's biographical sketch of the poet.

Moreover, even as Crowley endows Langland with prophetic vision, he is careful to assert that Langland's prophecy works through the medium of poetic fiction: the visions and dreams that Langland records are ones 'that he fayned hym selfe to have dreamed'. Crowley returns to this point at the end of the preface, where he discounts the ostensibly prophetic moment concerning an impending famine, which occurs at the end of Passus vi in the B-text. The lines that follow, Crowley explains, 'geveth it the face of the prophecy', but are likely to be the work of another hand. 'For diuerse copies haue it diuerslye', he continues, and then, after quoting the relevant lines from his text, quotes the relevant variant lines from Passus viii in the C version.[23] Crowley uses his editorial knowledge about the variant versions of the poem to make what is for him a crucial point about how to read the poem as a whole. The reader is not to read this text as if it were a prophecy of Merlin, or one of the other medieval prophetic texts sixteenth-century reformers associated with paganism. Nor is the point restricted to that sort of prophecy alone. It applies even to the reformer's own apocalyptic vision:

Nowe for that whiche is written in the .l. leafe concerning the suppression of
Abbayes, the Scripture there alledged, declareth it to be gathered of the iuste
iudgment of God who wyll not suffer abomination to raigne unpunished. Loke
not upon this boke therefore to talke of wonders past or to com but to emend thyne
owne misse, whych thou shalt fynd here most charitably rebuked. The Spirite of
God geve the grace to walke in the way of truthe to Gods glory, and thyne owne
soules healthe.

From Crowley's perspective the dissolution of the monasteries is manifestly the work of Divine Providence and an instance of the True Church
defeating the forces of Antichrist. But the truth this event demonstrates is
fully available to anyone who reads Scripture carefully: God 'wyll not suffer
abomination to raigne unpunished'. Langland's foreseeing of the dissolution of the monasteries illustrates his election by God, the opening of his
eyes to see God's truth, but the revelation takes place not as some miraculous vision or mystical ecstasy. Instead, it comes through the convergence of
Langland's Catholicism with a Protestant virtue. Trusting in the plainness
of Scripture, Langland reads it carefully, as he shows by the Scripture he
'alleges' in making the prophecy.

Crowley makes a similar point three times in the marginal glosses.
In Passus III, when Conscience declares 'I, Conscience, knowe this for
kynde me it taughte / That Reson shal regne and Reaumes governe' (K-D,
284–5),[24] Crowley notes, 'This is no prophecy but a resonable gathering'
(16r). Shortly thereafter, when Conscience goes on to say, 'Kind Love shall
come yet and Conscience togither, / And make of lawe a laborer', (K-D,
299–300), Crowley again notes, 'This is no prophecy but a truth gathered of the Scriptures' (16v). At the end of Passus VI, at the passage he
has already noted in the Preface, he cautions, 'This is no prophecy but a
pronostication' (36r). Thus, for Crowley, a proper reading of Langland's
poem does not look upon it in order 'to talke of wonders past or to com'.
On the contrary, the proper response to an apocalyptic perception is to
emend 'thyne owne misse'. Langland himself transmuted his apocalyptic
vision into fictive dreams in order to instruct the weak, and sharply rebuke
the obstinate blind. Moreover, Crowley finds the ultimate measure of this
apocalyptic poetic in its encyclopaedic scope. In confronting the individual conscience of each of his readers, Langland simultaneously confronts
the social totality as a whole: 'There is no maner of vice, that reygneth
in anye estate of men, whyche thys wryter hath not godly, learnedly, and
wittilye, rebuked.' One might argue this constitutes a tendentious reading
of Langland's poem. If so, however, then the tendentiousness runs along
an unexpected and perhaps even anomalous bias.

Most modern readings of *Piers Plowman* see the B-version taking an irreversibly inward and contemplative turn after the ploughing of the Half-Acre and the Tearing of the Pardon, forsaking concern with social action in a quest for individual perfection. Moreover, this realm of social action, whether forsaken or not, is connected in the poem with the problem of penance. The socially constructive labour of those who put themselves to the plough cannot finally be separated from the works required for penitential satisfaction. The terms of Piers's pardon, and the subsequent quest for Dowel, Dobet and Dobest are enough to make this point, but we might also recall that Piers's entrance into the poem in Passus v follows immediately on the anatomy of the Seven Deadly Sins and the general repentance it engenders. In naming the witty rebuking of vice the poem's central project, Crowley embraces Langland's sensibility at one of the points where Reformation Protestantism found medieval Catholicism most distasteful.

Somewhat closer inspection of this paradox will reveal how misleading generalisations like justification by faith rather than works or the importance of individual conscience can be when wrested out of their original context and used as the basis for a flat distinction between historical periods. As a variety of scholars have noted, Protestant reformers attacked doctrines of works so ferociously precisely because the theology of penance was so important to them.[25] As Martin Luther declared in the opening assertion of the document traditionally held to start the Reformation, 'When our Lord and Master, Jesus Christ, said "Repent", He called for the entire life of believers to be one of penitence.'[26] The goal was not simply to overthrow an illegitimate Roman hierarchy, but to replace its sacrament of penance which a conception of penance that would be more thoroughgoing and rigorous. That such a goal involves an intense emphasis on individual conscience is undeniable; yet it also involves a radical submission to an authority beyond the self that sits very uneasily with more secularist notions of individual conscience which followed the Reformation and are too often read back into it. The displacement of such an authority away from an institutional location which had a direct divine warrant opened up a radical uncertainty as to the exact social form devotional authority should take. No form of Christianity has ever been able to find a purely theological rationale for determining where theology stops and ordinary social life begins; yet such a rationale became an important Reformation imperative because Protestantism's various strands all defined themselves at least in part as the rejection of previously established forms of institutionalisation. The Sacrament of Penance consisted of a complex cluster of rituals and social practices not directly deducible in all their complexity from what reformers understood as the theology of works. Ronald K. Rittgers has recently reminded us that Luther himself declared, 'I will allow no one to take private confession from me and would not give it in exchange for all the wealth of the world.' As Rittgers explains, 'Behind the reformer's well-known disdain for the sacrament of penance was a desire to redeem what he took to be the greatest boon God had provided to the troubled conscience: private confession.'[27] Crowley clearly had similar designs on another aspect of Catholic penitential practice, its production of social discipline, a desire he characteristically expressed in political terms.

Reformist interest in repentance reached a high point at mid-century. It was the topic of influential sermons by such prominent preachers as Richard Wimbledon and John Bradford.[28] Crowley's interest can be seen in two of his own poems, both published around the same time he was producing the Langland edition. *The Voice of the Last Trumpet* (1549) and *One and Thirty Epigrams* (1550) are both indebted to Passus v and Langland's anatomy. While neither poem makes use of the Seven Deadly Sins specifically, both poems present themselves as encyclopaedic taxonomies. Both explore sin in its social causes and effects, and both see Christian virtue articulated in part around social position. The full title to *The Voice of the Last Trumpet* reads, 'The Voice of the laste trumpet, blowen by the seventh Angel (as is mentioned in the eleventh of the Apocalips) callyng al estats of men to the ryght path of theyr vocation, wherin are conteyned .xii. Lessons to twelve several estats of men, which if thei learne and folowe, al shall be wel, and nothing amis'.[29] In a slightly creaky allegory, Crowley presents this last trumpet as the narrative voice of his poem, who addresses each of the estates in the singular: a Beggar, a Servant, a Yeoman, a Lewde Priest, a Scholar, a Learned Man, a Physician, a Lawyer, a Merchant, a Gentleman, a Magistrate and a Woman. This striking juxtaposition of the very last moment of human history and the mundane obligations of the estates of men takes even further the pragmatic application of the Apocalypse Crowley offers in the Preface.

Without in any way relinquishing the commitment to justification by faith, Crowley's poem nevertheless converges with what is often called Langland's semi-Pelagianism, his characteristic conflation of works with the operation of Grace.[30] Like *Piers Plowman*, *The Voice of the Last Trumpet* imagines a polity built on self-sacrifice. Socially subordinate estates, the Beggar, the Servant, the Yeoman and the Woman, are expected to submit to their social position as to the Lord, that is, 'for the conscience thou dost beare / To thy Lorde Gods commaundmente', as the Trumpet urges the

Servant (165–6). Socially superior estates are to strive continually against all the superfluities their superiority entails: the Physician should treat the poor for free, the Lawyer should concern himself only with justice and not his fees, the Merchant should traffic only in necessaries instead of the enclosure and commodification of land, and the Gentleman should pursue knowledge to the exclusion of such pursuits as feasting, hunting and costly clothing, and take delight in defending the poor, instead of raising rents. As the Trumpet explains to the Merchant:

> The ende why all men be create,
> As men of wisdome do agre,
> Is to maintaine the publike state
> In the contrei where thei shal be.
>
> (1025–8)

The good works the Trumpet requires have no sacramental value; they are pure expressions of conscience. Yet the Trumpet also insists on their salvific value, repeatedly promising their reward will come at the Last Judgment. The Trumpet is a transcendent instrument of Christ's Grace; there is no question here of the justification of works in the idolatrous sense in which Protestants attacked it. At the same time, the Trumpet is a poetic fiction, one which enables Crowley to finesse mysteries of Grace which even the most rationalist of Protestantisms proved unable to resolve. Imagining good works from the Trumpet's transcendent perspective, from the apocalyptic edge of human history, where the workings of Grace would be revealed in all their glory, enables Crowley to displace the sacramental value of good works with a moral, and indeed political, imperative that is in some ways even stronger. Langland, by contrast, certainly had no interest in displacing this sacramental value. Yet in founding his political vision on the self-sacrificial labour of Piers the ploughman, he was vigorously proposing to extend this value beyond its strictly sacramental sense. As an allegorical fiction, Langland's extension approaches a displacement. This is the point where his apocalyptic conceptions converge with Crowley's.

This convergence returns us to those other radical readers of Langland, the rebels of 1381. While Anne Middleton and Charlotte Brewer are right to note the similarity between the two, this similarity can be dismissed as a 'misreading' only if we ignore the apocalyptic dimension that connects both readings to Langland's poem.[31] The rebels make Piers an emblem of insurrectionary action, but they also insist on the insurrection's apocalyptic value. Here is John Ball's letter as presented by Thomas Walsingham in the *Historia Anglicana*:

Johon schep som tyme seynte marie prest of ʒork. and now of colchestre. Greteth wel johan nameles and johan þe mullere and johon carter and biddeþ hem þat þei bee war of gyle in borugh and stondeþ [togidere] in godes name. and biddeþ Peres plouʒman. go to his werk. and chastise wel hobbe þe robbere. and takeþ wiþ ʒow johan trewman and alle hijs felawes and no mo. and loke schappe ʒou to on heued and no mo. johan þe mullere haþ ygrounde smal smal smal þe kynges sone of heuene schal pay for al. be war or [ʒ]e be wo knoweþ ʒour frend fro ʒour foo. haueth ynow. & seith hoo. and do wel and bettre and fleth synne. and sekeþ pees and hold ʒou þer inne. and so biddeþ johan trewaman and alle his felawes.[32]

In this enigmatic mixture of coded language and allegory, the implication that the rebellion embodies the spirit of Piers the ploughman either in its decisive taking of action or its fidelity to truth, or both, is balanced against the claim that the rebellion is underwritten by the redemptive power of Christ: 'þe kynges sone of heuene schal pay for al'. This claim may also contain an echo of Langland's poem. In Passus XIX, Christ is said to pay Piers's pardon, a passage that Crowley singles out for glossing, although modern scholars have mainly ignored it.

David Norbrook has argued Crowley would have known the rebel letters and their allusions to Langland.[33] If so, I suspect he would have been less nonplussed by them than some modern Langland scholars have been. There were major rebellions in England in 1548 and 1549 and Crowley wrote at least two pieces on sedition during this period. While he is always careful to condemn sedition – not surprisingly – he always also argues its causes do not ultimately lie with the rebels. In the *The Way to Wealth, wherein is plainly taught a most present remedy for Sedicion*, Crowley begins by counselling the poor to be obedient and to suffer oppression patiently, and by criticising the clergy for a lack of spiritual leadership. Then he turns to the property owners and, addressing them for the balance of the pamphlet, tells them that they are the ultimate cause of sedition, through exorbitant rents and the practice of enclosure.[34] In *An Informacion and Peticion agaynst the oppressours of the pore Commons of this Realme*, a work which does not address sedition *per se* but closely tracks the arguments in *The Way to Wealth*, Crowley argues that 'possessioners', that is, property owners, should consider themselves 'but stywardes and not Lordes over theyr possessions'.[35] And in his most polemical and emphatic treatment of the problem, *Pyers plowmans exhortation unto the lordes knightes and burgoysses of the Parlyamenthouse*, Crowley adopts the *persona* of Piers the ploughman to argue that enclosure has prevented the Reformation from living up to its promise. Because – through enclosure – there is now so much less land to till, the dissolution of the abbeys and removal of livings from the idlers supported by them has been to no purpose. Moreover, Piers pointedly adds, 'a greate part of the sayde abbey lendes be eyther geven, solde or leased unto suche lordes and Gentlemen as had landes before of their owne'.[36] He offers three proposals to alleviate the oppression of the poor, an oppression so great that neither heathen infidels nor ravening beasts would countenance it. He proposes converting arable waste and desolate ground into pasture land, discontinuing enclosure of ploughland for the purposes of pasture, and restraining foreign trade. He concludes by warning that because the realm of England is so firmly in possession of God's truth, God will punish its hypocrisy the more severely if it does not address the suffering of the poor.

The centrality of the dissolution of the abbeys in this, Crowley's own contribution to the continuing *Piers Plowman* tradition, resonates suggestively with his edition. I have already mentioned Crowley's allusion in the Preface. At the actual passage in Passus x to which he refers, Crowley commands, 'Reade thys', and, a bit further down the page, 'The suppression of Abbayes'. On the verso of this leaf he also notes 'The Abbot of Abington', where Langland mentions that figure. Crowley apparently saw this prediction in one other place, Passus v, in Reason's warning to Religion to hold to their rule, 'Lest the kyng and his conseil your comunes apeire / And be Styward of youre stede til ye be stewed bettre' (K-D, 46–7). For here he also notes, 'The suppression of the Abbayes', followed by the exclamation, 'Good counsel' – comments also often cited as evidence of the edition's anti-Catholic agenda. Finally, we might connect to these glosses a more general endorsement of disendowment inspired by Langland's critique of the Donation of Constantine. Adjacent to the line 'Takeþ hire lands, ye lordes, and leteþ hem lyue by dymes' (K-D: xv, 564: 'Take their lands, you lords, and let them live on tithes'), Crowley sardonically observes, 'A medicine for the cleargy' (85v). While anti-Catholic these comments certainly are, the testimony of *Pyers plowmans exhortation* nevertheless suggests a more complex purpose. If the dissolution of the monasteries when it occurred marked a Protestant triumph, recalling it in 1550 in the way that Crowley does serves as a reminder of a Protestant failure.

If we take these glosses away from the handful of other explicitly anti-Catholic marginalia the case for some directly anti-Catholic agenda becomes nearly impossible to maintain. Of the 495 glosses in total in the third imprint, I find only fifteen which are explicitly anti-Catholic. In addition to the four I have just mentioned, five have to do with penitential doctrine – 'The olde satisfaction' Crowley notes at 21v – where, as I have just argued, Crowley's engagement with Langland's belief is at its most complex. That leaves six more. Two point out Langland's anti-papalism: 'Note how he scorneth the auctority of Popes' (39r), and the ironic 'The praise of cardinals' (110v); two point out Langland's anti-fraternalism (54r and 115v); and two take Langland to task for his devotion to hagiography: 'The Legend of seyntes, believe it if ȝe lyste' (81v), and 'He citeth a lye out of the Legend auri' (98r). These last two mark Crowley's acknowledgement and disapproval of Langland's Catholicism. The other four are all supported by the texts to which Crowley adds them. As far as the glosses are concerned, the case for Crowley's Protestant appropriation of Langland's poem seems pretty slight. Moreover, even these fifteen merge without too much effort into Crowley's larger, more purely editorial concern with accessibility. We can class these glosses with the category of glosses we might call interpretative, glosses which make any ideological or philosophical claim at all, beyond neutrally registering some feature of Langland's text. I count 93 of these, still a relatively small number. The largest category of glosses are those giving sources for Langland's citations. There are 237 of these. Crowley makes a systematic attempt to identify all of Langland's scriptural quotations. He also gives the sources for other quotations, but in the main only when Langland has already identified them. The remaining 165 glosses are what one might call narrative or topical summary, the identification of characters, speakers, episodes, or subjects of discussion. Thus in Langland's *Prologue*, Crowley notes 'Common jesters', 'Pilgrimes', 'Hermits', 'Fryers' and 'Pardoners' in the Fair Field of Folk, then later notes the beginning of 'The tale of the ratons'. Slightly longer glosses describe the narrative movement of the allegory; thus, 'The King will know of Mede whom she loveth bett' in Passus III, or 'Pierce profereth Christ to become his servant' in Passus XVII. Or Crowley will mark a theologically important exposition, as in the gloss 'his opinion of fre wyll', in Passus VIII or 'The triniti lyke an hande', in Passus XVII.

In general, then, the predominant character of the glosses corresponds to the goal I named above, to give Crowley's readers the information they need to engage intelligently with Langland's text on their own. Even the interpretative glosses could be seen in that light, in the sense that he wants them to be aware of the sorts of emphases a more learned or experienced reader would bring to the text. These glosses are fairly eclectic in content. Seventeen could be called proverbial: for example, 'Ill gotte goodes muste be il spente', from Passus V or 'Shame is the best remedie for dronkards', from Passus XI. Ten are explicitly political, like 'What harme yll vitillers do and what abuse is in regrattyng', from Passus III, or 'The lawiers kepe the kynge from his right' in Passus IV. The largest grouping, 51, are glosses that might be described as doctrinal or ecclesiological. These range from the very general and non-sectarian, such as 'Christ was pore', from Passus XI, or 'Onli God knoweth the causes of thynges', in Passus XII, to much more pointed observations like 'Curates oughte to have a competent ly[vy]ng certayne', from Passus XX. To the extent it is possible to identify an overarching tendency in this eclec-tic group, I would say it tracks the concerns of Crowley's pamphleteering, especially the conviction that the reformed English church has yet fully to escape its Catholic past. Such comments can be construed as anti-Catholic, but they also apply to more conservative Protestants, who seem more likely to have been their immediate target. One warns 'Wo be to you that turn the tithes to private use' (42v, Passus IX), another 'How covetise of the cleargy wyll destroy the church' (85r, Passus XV), and a third 'A lesson for all that take benifices at wycked men's handes (82r, Passus XV). Yet even these are sufficiently sporadic relative to the marginal glossing taken as an aggregrate, that it would be inaccurate to look to them as the key to Crowley's editorial ambitions.

That leaves the enigmatic figure of Piers himself. The passus-by-passus summary, which Crowley adds to the second imprint, is remarkably diplo-matic. It consists almost entirely of neutral, lucid expositions of the plot. There are very few moments where Crowley allows himself a more ambi-tious exegetical judgement. The most striking occurs in his summary of Passus VIII:

It declareth howe Pierce went to seke Dowell, How he reprouueth the Fryers for saying dowel dwelte wyth them, Howe the Frier proueth by a similitude, that a iuste man sinneth seuen tymes a daye, and sayth hys mynde of frewyl, Howe thought enstructethe him of dowell, dobet, and dobest, And howe wytte (who wyl none excesse) met wyth Pierce, Of whome Pierce desiered to learne what Dowel, Dobet, and Dobest were.

Here is the one point where we might justifiably accuse Crowley of mis-reading. Passus VIII does announce the beginning of the quest for Dowel, Dobet, and Dobest, perhaps the poem's most basic plot division. Following some manuscript rubrication, modern Langlandians see it as the beginning of the Vita, after the opening Visio has concluded with the previous passus. But it is Will, or the Dreamer, who seeks Dowel, Dobet, Dobest, not Piers. On the face of it, this misreading seems simply to illustrate one of the twentieth-century truisms about *Piers Plowman*'s early modern reception, the tendency to confuse Piers and Langland, and the concomitant failures to recognise the poem's fictional status and immense exegetical complexities. Nevertheless, this slip is actually a fairly small one in an otherwise careful summary. Moreover, the confusion in this case is between Piers and Will, not between Piers and Langland, and if the protocols of modern formalism are the invariable standard against which misreadings are to be judged, then we need to acknowledge that Will is no closer to Langland than Piers or any of his other allegorical voices. While it may be true that no modern scholar would explicitly confuse Will with Langland in the way Crowley here confuses Will with Piers, one can find Will and Langland more subtly confused in the modern obsession with Langland's irrecuperable biography – an attempt to make an omelette without eggs if ever there was one – which often depends on Will's (fictional) pronouncements.[37]

We might do better to acknowledge that modern methods of identifying and evaluating textual complexity, despite their power, have their own historical biases – among them of course, the commitment to the autonomy of literary form. The technical inaccuracy in Crowley's summary points to a feature of Langland's text that most modern scholarship has too often ignored, the overriding concern with social action. The standard modern view, which holds that the Vita forsakes this concern, simply reads past whole layers of the very complexity it takes itself as preserving. For this reason, I would offer Crowley's inaccuracy as a momentary overreaching that modern scholars should take not as an appropriation but as a crucial corrective. The displacement of Will by Piers underlines the commitment in Langland's poem to social action, a commitment which many of his otherwise most sensitive and accomplished modern readers have underplayed or missed. The power of Crowley's response can be traced particularly in his treatment of Passus XIX. Passus XIX contains the most sustained discussion of Piers subsequent to the Pardon-tearing episode in Passus VII. It bookends the Dreamer's contemplative quest of Passus VIII–XVIII and, as James Simpson has rightly argued, constitutes a final outward turning.[38] I have already noted Crowley's extraordinary interest in the return of Piers's pardon. What I should now add is that this interest also entails countenancing one of the poem's most Catholic moments.[39]

The passus as a whole extends Piers's significance in a variety of directions, as the ploughman's self-sacrificing labour becomes the figural ground where Christ's promise of redemption merges with the ideal of secular, human justice. Crowley's glosses show him following this allegorical profusion

enthusiastically. The dreamer falls asleep during mass and sees Piers crucified, then turns to Conscience, who explains that while it is Christ who is
crucified he comes in 'Piers armes, / His colours and cote armure'. Crowley
endorses this startling juxtaposition by noting in the margin 'Pierces cote
armour' (104r). Langland's account of the crucifixion and resurrection ends
with the return of Piers's pardon, but not before Langland conflates it with
the power of the keys:

> And when this dede [i.e., the Resurrection] was done do
>   best he taught
> And gave Pierce power, and pardon he graunted
> To all maner of men, mercye and forgiuenes
> Hym might to assoyle men, of all maner of synnes
> In couenaunt that they come, and knowledge to paye
> To Pierces pardon the plowman, *Redde quod debes*,
> Thus hath Pierce power, he his pardon payed
> To bind and unbind, both here and els where
> And assoylen men of all synnes, save of dette onelye . . .
>
>   (106v)

In this passage Langland makes explicit Piers's identification with Peter,
the rock on which Christ builds his church, and through Peter, with the
papal order of succession, the power to bind and loose, and the power
to absolve sins. A clearer claim for the divine origin of the sacrament of
penance and the intercessory authority of the Catholic church is harder to
imagine. There is no way a reader as careful as Crowley did not notice these
claims. Yet his marginal comment passes over them in silence even as it
underlines the equation of Piers with Christ's forgiveness: 'Pierces pardon
is pay that they oweste'.

In my view Crowley tolerates the ecclesiological claims because, as we
have seen elsewhere, Langland is poetically extending Catholic authority
and not simply affirming it, and because as the passus continues he will
use this poetic extension to demonstrate that virtuous social action is an
imperative of individual conscience. Christ retreats to Heaven, and the
Holy Ghost arrives with the gift of grace (duly noted in Crowley's glosses),
makes Piers his 'procuratour' (107v), equips him with a team of four oxen –
the four evangelists – and four seeds to sow, the cardinal virtues of prudence,
temperance, fortitude and justice. Langland will concentrate mainly on justice. On the heels of his provocative suggestion that the pope and cardinals
confine themselves to the papal court, he will declare Piers 'Emperour of
al the world', on the basis of his old plough as well as his new, for Piers

'peyneth him to tyll / As wel for a wastor, and wenches of the stewes / As for him selfe and his servaunts'. Crowley's marginal comment, his last on Piers, is 'Pierce followeth the example of God' (110v). He anticipates this comment in his summary of Passus XIX, with a telling elaboration making its political subtext even more explicit: 'Howe the plowman foloweth the example of god, And what Landlordes and kynges maye take of their tenauntes & subiectes.' It would seem that the poetic figure of Piers negotiates the great diachronic span between a radical Catholic writer and a radical Protestant reader by bringing the example of God to bear on the social privileges of property and political power.

APPENDIX

I. Crowley's Preface to The Vision of Pierce Plowman

The printer to the Reader

[1]Beynge desyerous to know the name of the Autour of thys most worthy worke. (Gentle reader) and the tyme of the writynge of the same: I did not onely gather togyther such aunciente copies as I could come by, but also consult such men as I knew to be more exercised in the studie of antiquities, then I my selfe have ben. [2]And by some of them I have learned that the Autour was name Roberte langlande, a Shropshere man borne in Cleybirie, about viii, myles from Malvernes hilies.

[3]For the tyme when it was written, it chanced me to se an auncient copye, in the later ende whereof was noted, that the same copye was written in the yere of oure Lorde. M.iiii.L and nyne, which was before thys presente yere, an hundred & xli yeres. [4]And in the seconde syde of the lxviii leafe of thys printed copye, i finde mention of a dere yere, that was in the yere of oure Lorde. M.iii.hundred and .L. John Chichester than beyng mayre of London. [5]So that this I may be bold to report, that it was fyrste made and written after yeare of our lord. M.iii.C. L. and before the yere M.iiii.C. and .ix, which meane space was lix yeres. [6]We may iustly coniect therefore that it was first written about two hundred yeres paste in the tyme of kynge Edwarde the thyrde. [7]In whose tyme it pleased God to open the eyes of many to se hys truth, giving them boldenes of herte, to open their mouthes and crye oute agynst the workes of darckenes, as dyd John Wicklyfe, who also in those dayes translated the holye Byble into the Englishe tonge, and this writer who in reportynge certayne visions and dreames, that he fayned hym selfe to have dreamed, doth most christianlie enstructe the weake,

and sharplye rebuke the obstynate blynde. [8]There is no maner of vice, that reygneth in anye estate of men, whyche thys wryter hath not godly, learnedly, and wittilye, rebuked. [9]He wrote altogither in miter; but not after the maner of our rimeres that wryte nowe adaies (for his verses ende not alike) but the nature of hys miter is, to have three wordes at the leaste in every verse which begyn with some one letter. [10]As for ensample, the firste two verses of the boke renne upon .s. as thus

In a somer season when sette was the Sunne

I shope me into shrobbes, as I a shepe were

The next runeth upon H, as thus

In habite as an Hermite unholy of werkes, etc.

[11]This thyng noted the metre shall be very pleasant to reade. [12]The Englishe is according to the tyme it was written in, and the sence somewhat darke, but not so harde, but that it maye be understande of such that wyll not sticke to breake the shell of the nutte for the kernelles sake.

[13]As for that is written in the xxvi, leafe of thy boke concernynge a dearth then to come is spoken by the knoweledge of astronomies may wel be gathered bi that he saith, Saturne sent him to tell, And that whych foloweth and geveth it the face of a prophecy, is lyke to be added by some other man than the fyrst autour. [14]For diuerse copies haue it diuerslye, for where the copie that I folowe hath thus.

And when you se the sunne amisse, & thre mokes heades

And a mayde have the maistrye, and multiply by eyght

Some other have

Three shypes and a shefe, wyth an eight folowynge

Shall brynge bale and battell, on both halte the mone

[15]Nowe for that whiche is written in the .l. leafe concerning the suppression of Abbayes, the Scripture there alledged, declareth it to be gathered of the iuste iudgment of God who wyll not suffer abomination to raigne unpunished. [16]Loke not upon this boke therefore to talke of wonders past or to com but to emend thyne owne misse, whych thou shalt fynd here

most charitably rebuked. [17] The Spirite of God geve

the grace to walke in the way of truthe

to Gods glory, and thyne owne

soules healthe

So be it.

[Transcription of Columbia Univ. 19907 BP 821.15; sentence numbers added.]

II. Categories of marginal glosses in Crowley's Vision of Pierce Plowman *(third imprint) and their relative frequency*

1. Citations		237
2. Narrative or topical summary		165
3. Interpretative		
Proverbial	17	93
Political	10	
Anti-Catholic	15	
Doctrinal/ecclesiological	51	
Total		495

III. Anti-Catholic glosses

12v: The fruites of Popish penaunce
Adj. text: Thanne Mede for hire mysdedes to ȝat man kneled / And shrof hire of hire sherewedness, shameless I trowe; [K-D: III, 43–4]
21r: The suppression of Abbayes / Good counsel
Adj. text: Lest the kyng and his conseil your comunes apeire / And be Styward of youre stede til ye be stewed bettre [K-D: V, 46–7]
21v: The olde satisfacion
Adj. text: Wiþ þat he sholde þe Saterday, seuen yer þerafter, / Drynke but [wiþ] þe doke and dyne but ones. [K-D: V, 73–4]
22r: See howe Envye repenteth
Adj. text: Enuye wiþ heuy herte asked after shrifte [K-D: V, 75]
39r: Note how he scorneth the auctority of Popes
Adj. text: Now hath the pope power pardon to graunte / After peple withouten penance to passen [K-D: VII, 179–80]
50r: Reade thys / The suppression of Abbayes
Adj. text: A ledere of louedayes and a lond buggere . . . /
And there shall come a kyng, and confesse yow Religiouses/ And bete yow, as the bible telleth for brekynge of youre rule [K-D: X, 312; 322–3]
50v: The Abbot of Abington
Adj. text: And thanne shall the Abbot of Abington and al his issue for evere / Have a knok of a kyng [K-D: X, 331–2]
54r: Friers did not seke the bodi but the monie
Adj. text: By my feith frier quod I ye faren lik thise woweris / That welde none widwes but for to welden hir goodes. [K-D: XI, 71–2]
81v: The Legend of seyntes, believe it if ȝe lyste

Adj. text: In *Legenda Sanctorum*, the lif of holy seintes [K-D: xv, 269]

85v: A medicine for the cleargy

Adj. text: Take her lands ye lordes [K-D: xv, 564]

98r: He citeth a lye out of the Legend auri

Adj. text: And there came forth a knight with a kene spere grounde / Hight
Longeus [K-D: xviii, 77–8]

110v: The praise of cardinals

Adj. text: The contree is þe corseder þat Cardinals come Inne / And þer þei
ligge and lenge moost lecherie þere regneþ. [K-D: xix, 417–18]

115v: The fryers are without numbre

Adj. text: Therfore, quod conscience by Crist kynde wit me telleth / It is
wikked to wage yow, ye wexe without noumbre [K-D: xx, 268–9]

116r: Thei that went to the fryers to shrift were like C(S?)antuary men

Adj. text: And fleen to the fryers as fals folk to westmynstere [K-D: xx, 285]

117r: The olde maner of eares shrifte made synners negligent

Adj. text: Thus he gooth and gadereth and gloseth ther he shryveth / Til
Contricion hadde clene foryeten to crye and to wepe [K-D: xx, 368–9]

CHAPTER 4

Public ambition, private desire and the last Tudor Chaucer

David Matthews

The two editions by Thomas Speght of Chaucer's complete works at the end of the Tudor period (1598 and 1602) are by far the most comprehensive and elaborate of the early modern complete Chaucers. Like their Tudor predecessors – the three editions appearing in the name of William Thynne in 1532, 1542 and *c.* 1545–50 and that of John Stow in 1561 – Speght's editions augmented the Chaucer canon (largely, but not entirely, with apocrypha). But in contrast with the earlier, relatively unadorned productions, Speght's presented the poet 'with more grandeur, apparatus, and annotation than he had ever before received', in the form of commentary and explication, illustrations, genealogy, biography and glossary.[1]

Speght's editions, then, seem to represent the apogee of what James Simpson (referring to Chaucer reception in the period 1400–1550) has called the 'philological absence' model of the recovery of Chaucer, in which the poet's text is made the object of scholarly recovery. From Caxton onwards, Simpson argues,

The transmitter of the dead poet is no longer someone who feels in personal contact with him, but rather an expert who rescues and reconstructs the past 'as it was' from the predations of time. For that recovery even to begin demands that the poet is *not* a readily available and personal presence.[2]

In various ways, other commentators have found Speght's editions to be self-consciously historicising the poet and the past in which he lived. Tim William Machan describes Speght's first edition as a monumentalising book which 'recuperates a very humanist Chaucer, one who is presentable in . . . the same format as an Antique poet'.[3] Alice Miskimin regards Chaucer's status at the end of the sixteenth century as 'ambivalent': he is a poetic model, but at the same time 'a remote and primitive ancestor . . .'[4] And Stephanie Trigg writes that Speght's edition aims 'to place [Chaucer] firmly in a medieval context, and to mark out the historical and cultural distance separating manuscript and print, and poet and editor'.[5] In all of these views Chaucer, in 1598, is antique, ancient, classic, canonised and very dead.

Nevertheless, the alternative to philological absence – what Simpson calls the 'remembered presence' model of thinking about Chaucer – was evidently much harder to dislodge than these opinions would suggest. As late as 1613 – as was recalled in the introduction to this volume – Shakespeare and Fletcher were still playing with the notion that Chaucer's ghostly presence might survey their refashioning of the *Knight's Tale*.[6] More famously in the period, Edmund Spenser lays claim to Chaucer's 'owne spirit, which doth in me surviue'.[7] In Thomas Speght's editions, one of the less discussed prefatory items is a poem entitled 'The Reader to Geffrey Chaucer', in which the poet is conjured up to give a blessing to Speght's enterprise. This poem takes the form of a dialogue in which the imagined reader asks, '*Where hast thou dwelt, good Geffrey al this while, / Unknowne to vs, saue only by thy bookes?*' Chaucer replies that he has been in exile until someone brought him forth again, a man '*who hath no labor spar'd, / To helpe what time and writers had defaced*'. The poem concludes in Chaucer's voice:

> *Would God I knew some means amends to make,*
> *That for his toile he might receiue some gains.*
> *But wot ye what? I know his kindnesse such,*
> *That for my good he thinks no pains too much:*
> *And more than that; if he had knowne in time,*
> *He would haue left no fault in prose nor rime.*[8]

Calling up the Chaucerian presence in this way, Speght's edition suggests that *alongside* his advanced philological recovery of the poet, the editor is also laying claim to a form of remembrance of Chaucer. Nearly two hundred years after the poet's death, he seems to be re-inventing, in the manner of Chaucer's fifteenth-century successors, 'some kind of personal relation to the poet', as Seth Lerer puts it.[9] In the suggestion that Chaucer has been 'defaced' by 'time and writers', the poem effectively dismisses, in Chaucer's voice, the work of Speght's predecessors Stow and Thynne. The strange suggestion that until Speght came along to re-edit Chaucer, the poet had been '*Unknowne to vs, saue only by thy bookes*' implies that Thynne and Stow retrieved only the text, while Speght somehow delivers Chaucer himself.

In fact, Speght's 1598 edition offered not much more of Chaucer's text than Stow had given in 1561, in a book with a high degree of page-for-page correspondence with Stow's (though it had been reset). As the fuller edition of 1602 confirmed, however, Speght aimed much higher than his achievement of 1598. Simpson points out the irony, evident in Thynne's edition, of the philological model: setting out to finalise an author and to say all there is to be said, it instead provokes ever more accretion around the author's name. The ultimate result of this is Speght's second edition: a Chaucer edition encrusted with learned additions and apocryphal texts, desperate to assert the primacy of its own philological recovery yet resorting, in order to do so, to the model of remembered presence.[10]

In many ways, different as he wanted to declare himself to be, Speght was simply bringing the Tudor tradition to its logical culmination. He inherited and built upon, for example, the sixteenth-century commonplace that Chaucer was a proto-Protestant. In 1532, Thynne included the Lollard *Plowman's Tale* in his edition, helping to create, as Thomas Heffernan argues, a Protestant-seeming poet 'precisely when an icon of Chaucer as a paragon of clerical reform and a satirist of clerical abuse was most needed'.[11] By 1570, and the second edition of Foxe's *Acts and Monuments*, Chaucer's 'Protestantism was a confirmed fact', as Simpson notes.[12] Speght's own touch was to add the Lollard tract *Jack Upland* to the Chaucer canon in 1602, capping off the process of Chaucer's Protestant conversion.

Speght was even more concerned with a second and related process, in which Chaucer was politically re-envisioned through an emphasis on his links to the Lancastrian dynasty. The starting point for this idea was Chaucer's relation by marriage to the Lancastrian progenitor, John of Gaunt, and the idea of Gaunt's special protection of Chaucer as suggested by the *Book of the Duchess*. As Gaunt was also the protector of John Wyclif, the Lollard Chaucer and the Lancastrian Chaucer conveniently come together here.

In one respect, then, this chapter is concerned with obvious examples, in Speght's editions, of the reading of the medieval in late Tudor England: the process by which Speght reads, in order to rewrite, a medieval author. In another sense, however, Speght is already well advanced on the way to seeing Chaucer as anything but medieval: to regarding him as the first modern poet in the way that, later on, John Dryden will make standard.[13] The Chaucer locked away in the books of Thynne and Stow is medieval; the more transcendent Chaucer whose spirit infuses poets and editors is (in 1598) our contemporary. This tension is only the most fundamental of several which run through Speght's work, and which this chapter explores.

I

The prefatory poem discussed above is not, ostensibly, written by Speght himself, but is signed 'H.B.' These initials, which do not reappear anywhere in the edition, might be no more than a disguise for Speght himself, in mitigation of immodesty. There are no obvious indicators as to the identity behind the initials and they have not, to my knowledge, been attributed. However, the man who signs himself 'F.B'. in Speght's edition is clearly identified as Francis Beaumont, a friend of Speght's since their days together at Cambridge University in the late 1560s. (He was not the dramatist but an older cousin, who would later become the master of Charterhouse school). H.B., I suggest, was Francis's older brother, Henry Beaumont.[14]

Little is known about Henry Beaumont, the eldest son in the Coleorton branch of the Beaumont family who, like his father, represented Leicestershire as an MP. But the one piece of writing he left behind him shows him to have been focused on the age of Chaucer. In a petition presented to King James I, Henry sought to restore his family to the viscountcy it had held in the fifteenth century. Henry claims that his family was 'first highly derived, as appeareth by authentique pedigrees', and goes on to detail '[t]he antiquity and long continuance of them in the state of peers of the realm, as by the records is manifest'. More specifically, Henry links his family to the Lancastrian interest in the fourteenth and fifteenth centuries. He reminds the king that John of Gaunt's first wife Blanche, Duchess of Lancaster and mother of Henry IV, had a Beaumont for a mother; he speaks of the death in battle of one Beaumont who fought for Henry VI, and the capture of another who fought for Henry VIII (a Tudor and hence descendant of the Lancastrian kings).[15]

Henry Beaumont, then, read medieval England in the early seventeenth century in order to produce a very specific meaning. This was that he and his family should regain a nobility inherited from, and authorised by, the medieval past. It cannot be proven that he was the 'H.B.' who appears in Speght's edition of Chaucer. But the circumstantial case is helped by the fact that like Henry Beaumont, Speght's edition goes to great lengths to establish Chaucer's own Lancastrian credentials. Again like Beaumont, Speght reads the medieval past with an eye to what that past might do for him, in 1598.

In Speght's day, the idea of Chaucer's special relationship with John of Gaunt, Duke of Lancaster, was a commonplace. In the earlier Tudor period, it was assumed that Chaucer was of noble birth himself. While

John Stow had exploded this notion with his discovery that the poet's father was a vintner, Speght restored Chaucer's noble connections by printing an elaborate, illustrated genealogy which shows the *later* aristocratic affiliations of Chaucer's family. He also made a discovery of his own, showing that Chaucer had married the daughter of Payne Roet. Speght did not know her first name, but he did know that her sister married John of Gaunt, so that Chaucer 'became brother in law to 'Iohn of Gaunt Duke of Lancaster, as hereafter appeareth' (Biii v). On the basis of such hints, Speght built up the idea of Chaucer as the intimate of nobles and princes: 'Friends he had in the Court, of the best sort: for besides that he alwaies held in with the Princes, in whose daies he lived, hee had of the best of the Nobility both Lords and Ladies, which fauored him greatly' (Bvi v).

The presumed connection of Chaucer with Lancastrian-Yorkist politics is gestured to in both the Stow and Speght Chaucers through the use of an image which explicitly points to the tension between the two houses and its resolution. The *Canterbury Tales* has its own title page in Stow and Speght, in which the words of the title appear in the blank centre of a framing woodcut. The woodcut image depicts a tangled rosebush, growing from the breasts of John of Gaunt, Duke of Lancaster, and Edmund of Langley, Duke of York. The separate branches of the rosebush ascend up either side of the central blank rectangle and in the buds sit monarchs and nobles of the houses of Lancaster and York. At the top of the design the two bushes arrive at Henry VII on the left (heir to the house of Lancaster) and his bride Elizabeth on the right (heir of York); they are clasping hands. Immediately above them is their son Henry VIII, central and at the highest point, holding a sceptre in one hand and a sword in the other.

This image first appeared as the title page to Richard Grafton's 1550 edition of Edward Hall's compendious history, *The Vnion of the Two Noble and Illustre Famelies of Lancastre & Yorke*. The words of Hall's title, appearing in the central rectangle, have an obvious, mutual relationship with the rosebush image. Hall's history illustrates the same outcome as the rosebush, that point at which the division between the families 'was suspended and appalled in the person of their moste noble, puissa[n]t and mighty heire kyng Henry the eight, and by hym clerely buried and perpetually extinct'.[16] The rosebush imagery was evidently a commonplace idea applied to the Tudor monarchs. One pageant celebrating Elizabeth's coronation, Raphael Holinshed records, featured an arch with three stages, the lowest representing the figures of Henry VII and his wife Elizabeth, enclosed by a red rose and a white rose, just as in the image in Hall's chronicle. The second stage represented Henry VIII and the third and highest stage represented Elizabeth herself.

And all emptie places thereof were furnished with sentences concerning unitie, and the whole pageant garnished with red roses and white. And in the fore front of the same pageant, in a faire wreath, was written the name and title of the same, which was; The uniting of the two house of Lancaster and Yorke. This pageant was grounded upon the queenes majesties name.[17]

The appropriateness of the rosebush in these contexts is obvious. The woodcut Grafton used, preserving the image, was then evidently available to Stow's printer, who used it in 1561 for the *Canterbury Tales* title page. The block was by then slightly damaged; it was in even worse shape in 1598 but was still usable in Speght's edition, again to enclose the title of the *Canterbury Tales*. Its appropriateness in this context is far less clear. What did the rosebush, as a frame for the words 'Canterbury Tales', signal to later sixteenth-century readers?

Phyllis Rackin has argued for an almost obsessive interest in late medieval history during the Elizabethan period. 'The story that begins with Richard II and ends with Henry VII', Rackin writes, 'shows the passage from an idealised medieval England through the crime against God and the state that destroyed it and the long process of suffering and penance that led to its redemption in the divinely ordained accession of the Tudor dynasty'.[18] To turn to Chaucer, as Speght did in 1598, is to turn to a figure who was important at the very inception of this period. Speght makes the politic move of making Chaucer appear central in the era of Richard II, aligning him closely with John of Gaunt. As has already been remarked, Speght's Chaucer is usually regarded as a heavily historicised figure. Yet there is a great deal in Speght's edition that wants to drag Chaucer out of that past, or at least, like H.B.'s poem, to reinforce the links between then and now. The reuse of the rosebush woodcut could have been simply an expedient decision by a printer who happened to have the block to hand. But the raising of the issue of York–Lancaster relations half a century after Hall claimed to have settled the question, and the placement of the *Canterbury Tales* at the heart of the thorny politics of the two houses, point to a still living interest in the 1590s in these old tensions. The rosebush imagery suggests that Speght wants to emphasise the effacement of the bloody history of the fifteenth century. Perhaps a little nervously (and he was not, after all, a much-heralded playwright but an unknown schoolteacher) Speght wants to make Chaucer look a logical choice for an Elizabethan editor – a safe topic in an era of tight control on book production. Chaucer is antique, certainly, *antient*, in Speght's own word. But Chaucer's ghost, mocked by Shakespeare and Fletcher, is real and threatening enough. This *retrieved* Chaucer comes with all kind of medieval baggage which is best hidden. The *refashioned* Chaucer, Protestant, politically on the right side, is one who belongs more comfortably in the now.

II

Unlike Thomas More, as already discussed by James Simpson in this volume, or John Bale and John Leland, as described by Cathy Shrank and Jennifer Summit in later chapters, Speght is not a transitional figure, and not an active witness to the destruction of the medieval English past. The Act of Supremacy, the dissolution of the monasteries, the break with Rome – all these were in the past when Speght was born *c.* 1550. Speght's lifetime encompassed a period in which medieval culture began to slip from view. The 'landscape of reform', as Summit calls it, must have been softening in Speght's lifetime, as monastic ruins disappeared beneath weeds and 'the violence that historical change inflicted on [the landscape]' became less evident (160). At the same time, the written records of the medieval past were becoming harder to read and understand, as Speght himself signalled when he added the first glossary to Chaucer's works.

Unlike William Thynne, who held responsible offices under Henry VIII, the king's printer Thomas Berthelette (who produced an edition of John Gower's *Confessio Amantis* in 1532), or the prolific antiquarian John Stow, Thomas Speght was an obscure man. If he had not edited Chaucer no one would know about him. Speght's is the biggest Tudor Chaucer edition but he himself was in a sense the smallest Chaucer editor. Conversely, there was a great deal at stake for him personally in editing Chaucer. Above, I have looked at Speght's Chaucer in the macro-political sense – as Speght's contribution to the Tudor political refashioning of the Middle Ages. I now want to turn to a micro-politics involving Speght's own precarious position as a second- or third-rank scholar at the end of Elizabeth's reign.

On the basis of what Speght says himself and is corroborated elsewhere, it is known that he went to Peterhouse, Cambridge as a sizar, or poor scholar, in the late 1560s, taking his M.A. in 1573. He came from a provincial family, probably in Yorkshire, and received support while studying from Lady Mildred Cecil. How he came to the attention of the famously learned wife of the most powerful man of the day, Lord Burghley, remains the central mystery of Speght's biography.[19] At Peterhouse, he was friendly with the

Francis Beaumont already mentioned. At some unknown point after his Cambridge years, Speght moved to London where he became involved in the literary world and worked as a schoolmaster.[20]

While still at Cambridge, Speght and Beaumont became interested in Chaucer because of the encouragement, in Beaumont's own account, of some 'auncient learned men' at Cambridge, 'whose diligence in reading of his workes them selues, and commending them to others of the younger sorte, did first bring you and mee in loue with him . . .'[21] After Cambridge, Speght kept working on Chaucer in a private capacity (as he implies himself in his edition) from the later 1570s to about the mid-1590s, without intending to publish anything. It must have been known that he was working on Chaucer, however; he was approached to take on the editorship of a new Chaucer edition. Speght accepted and this was the work that appeared in 1598. By 1602, and his second edition, Speght would have been in his fifties; little is heard of him after then. He leased a house near Cripplegate from 1612 at the latest, using part of it as a schoolhouse,[22] and died in 1621. There seems no reason to disagree with Derek Pearsall's assessment of Speght as 'a man on the fringe of the literary and antiquarian and book-collecting circles of London, not in the first rank . . . or even in the second . . .'[23]

The 1598 *Workes of Chaucer* was already in press and partially printed when Speght joined the project. The edition had been entered in the Stationers' Register in 1592 and the way in which it relies on the immediately preceding edition, John Stow's of 1561, suggests that it was probably not intended to be much more than a reprint of that work.[24] But the printer who took out the licence, Abell Jeffes, having 'disorderlie without Aucthoritie and contrarie to the Decrees of the starre chamber. printed a lewde booke . . .', was condemned in December 1595 to have his press 'defaced and made vnserviceable for printinge' – a reminder, if any was needed, of the potential perils involved in publishing.[25]

In Speght's hands the edition, with its wealth of prefatory material and commentary, became something much more elaborate than a commercially driven reprint of Stow. Despite seeming determined to produce the fullest possible Chaucer edition, however, Speght consistently portrays himself as the most reluctant of Chaucer editors. The 1598 edition is full of reservations about the success of the attempt to surpass the Thynne–Stow model. Despite its obvious claims on pre-eminence and newness, Speght's edition is in fact marked by many mitigating *topoi* of modesty and his own dissatisfaction with what he has produced is a constant theme. In the very act of praising the edition, H.B.'s poem laments the lack of time which means that it is not perfect.[26] Elsewhere, in his dedication of the work to Robert Cecil,

Speght writes, 'These collections and corrections vpon Chaucer . . . so might they better haue deserued acceptance at your honors hands, had they ben as fully perfected, as they haue beene painefully gathered. But what is now wanting through lacke of time, may happily hereafter be supplied.'[27]

But there is another tension in Speght's words in 1598 that has nothing to do with the constraints of time. This is a much more fundamental sense of reluctance about the publication, focused on a concern about the public and private faces of scholarship. In 1598, Speght says that he had been engaged on private researches into Chaucer for several years, undertaken at the request of *'certaine Gentlemen my neere friends, who loued* Chaucer', with the aim in view of keeping alive *'the memorie of so rare a man, as also in doing some reparations on his works, which they iudged to be much decaied by iniurie of time, ignorance of writers, and negligence of Printers'*. So Speght's Chaucerian work begins as a private matter but the same gentlemen then prevail on him, along with *'certaine . . . of the best in the Companie of Stationers'*, to go public with his observations by contributing to the Chaucer edition which Jeffes could not now print.[28]

Obviously Speght accepted, yet he laments that as his work on Chaucer to that point *'was done for those priuat friends, so was it neuer in my mind that it should be published'*. He regrets the faults of his own work and the 'importunitie' of these friends, which led him into *'publishing that which was neuer purposed nor perfected for open view . . .'* Speght ends this section with an appeal to *'all friendly Readers, that if they find anie thing amisse they would lend me their skilfull helpe against some other time, & I wil thankefully receiue their labors, assuring them that if God permit, I wil accomplish whatsoeuer may be thought vnperfect'*.

While this appeal might be an extension of the concern over the haste with which the work was put together, Speght's main concern in his address 'To the Readers' is the idea that there is work that should be done in private, for private reasons, and which should not then be publicised. The fact that he *has* publicised his findings is the basis of much of Speght's anxiety. Elsewhere in the prefatory material Francis Beaumont, in his letter entitled 'F.B. to his very louing friend T.S.', makes it clear that there is yet further material that Speght has in fact held back: 'I am sorrie', Beaumont writes, 'that neither the worthinesse of *Chaucers* owne praise, nor the importunate praiers of diuerse your louing friendes can yet mooue you to put into print those good obseruations and collections you haue written of him . . .'[29] Once again, the public and private aspects of scholarship are at issue, as Beaumont goes on to refer to Chaucerian matters he and Speght have discussed in their 'priuate talke', but which, evidently, Speght has seen fit to withhold.

So Speght displays himself as *reluctant* to engage in the 'philological absence' model. Of course the various devices by which he does so – shifting the responsibility for publication on to the importuning private friends and the eager men in the Stationers' Company, attributing his reluctance to lack of time – might be so many modesty *topoi*, the typical, but rhetorical, bashfulness of the poor scholar cringing between the great poet whose work he has edited on one side and the great patron whose attention he hopes to attract on the other.[30] In this case the point of such *topoi* might be to demonstrate the opposite of the ritually expressed inadequacy: the actual *utility* of the work, by showing that it was in demand even before it was produced. Alternatively, what might be operating in these protestations of inadequacy is a version of the stigma of print, more usually deployed by poets taking a deliberately casual attitude towards the printing of their work, but here used by someone who edits a poet. In this respect it might be another indication that Speght sees his labour of Chaucerian recovery as being comparable with poetic labour itself. Presumably there is no doubt in Speght's or anyone else's mind that Chaucer's actual poems ought to be in print; that, after all, is the whole point of the labour, the 'reparations' the private friends judged necessary on the injured work of 'so rare a man'.

Yet the fact that those friends themselves remain so resolutely private while Speght is pushed into the open introduces the notion of nostalgia for a very *private* way of reading and appreciating Chaucer. This is also a very masculine way of reading, suffused as it is with expressions of male homosocial love. Speght, with Beaumont and H.B., projects a vision of Chaucerian study existing in a climate of amity, love and privacy: Beaumont's 'auncient learned men', for example, 'did first bring you and mee in loue with [Chaucer] . . .' Speght's private friends (who may well overlap as a group with the 'auncient learned men') urged that he work on the poet because they too '*loued* Chaucer'. Somewhat paradoxically, this loving reading is not fully compatible with the public sphere and publication, as Stephanie Trigg has argued.[31]

Such expressions of love are no doubt ritual and unremarkable within the norms of sixteenth-century male friendship, but the discourse of love is nevertheless very persistent: Beaumont describes himself as Speght's 'euer louing friend' and refers to 'your vnfained loue towards me'; they both love Chaucer; the Reader, in H.B.'s poem, loves Speght for loving Chaucer enough to bring him into print. Speght's declared reluctance to print is focused in this desire or love for Chaucer. It would be better, he implies, if they all – Speght, Beaumont, the Stationers, the auncient learned men and the private friends – simply went on loving Chaucer in private. Printing – publishing, publicising and therefore dragging a text out of the private realm – inevitably entails a loss of some kind. Meanwhile the private friends, it would appear, have every intention of continuing to love, and discuss, Chaucer privately, even if with copies of Speght's edition in their hands. The fact that their identities remain obscure suggests that this private course of reading is exactly what they pursued.

Such privacy is, of course, the mark of a gentleman. There are similarities between Speght's story of the private friends and the story told by an earlier 'editor' of Chaucer, Caxton himself, in the preface to his second printing of the *Canterbury Tales*. Having sold 'a certayn nombre' of copies of the first printing 'to many and dyuerse gentyl men', Caxton was, he says, approached by one 'gentylman' who 'said that this book was not accordyng in many places vnto that book the Gefferey chaucer had made . . .' The gentleman's father (he told Caxton) possessed a better copy. A negotiation follows; Caxton must guarantee that if the book is 'trewe and correcte' he will print it, regretting the way in which previously, 'by ygnouraunce I erryd in hurtyng and dyffamyng his book in dyuerce places in settyng in somme thynges that he neuer sayd ne made and leuyng out many thynges that he made whyche ben requysite to be sette in it . . .'[32] With this tale Caxton justifies a further edition and makes it indispensable even to those who unfortunately bought the 'certayn nombre' of the now defective first edition that were sold.

While, as Simpson suggests, this story shows Caxton as a philological editor, someone who 'reproduces the text of Chaucer, not Chaucer's presence', there is a degree to which reverence for the Chaucerian text and reverence for Chaucer himself become confused. Caxton makes of Chaucer such a figure of worship that there is a kind of horror involved in the possibility of *dyffamyng* the poet. Speght expresses a similar horror. And, again like Caxton, Speght is licensed by the conviction with which he states that he got it wrong the first time to try a second time to produce Chaucer – a solid commercial ploy, whatever else it might be. Speght's modesty is as convenient, therefore, as Caxton's 'ygnouraunce', perhaps even more so in that it enables him to write off the first edition and promote the second even as the first lands on the booksellers' stalls.

When, however, is a modesty *topos* not a modesty *topos*? Might Speght's modesty be real enough? Could the earnest invitation of corrections from readers and the relatively rapid appearance of the second edition in fact demonstrate Speght's genuineness? For Trigg, Speght's '[g]estures of humility' are decidedly rhetorical, and 'need to be read . . . as ritual expressions of modesty that probably belie a far more confident sense that publishing his research is precisely the gentlemanly thing to do'.[33] Speght's edition, as Trigg suggests, is certainly obsessed with gentlemanliness and gentle men. But the rhetorical sites of his modesty can be read another way: more straightforwardly, as indicating precisely the lack of confidence they appear to betray; consistent with this, I argue, Speght is not at all confident about his own gentlemanliness.

Gentlemanliness is in many ways the crux of Speght's problem as a Chaucer editor. The faceless private friends are the gentlemen in his story. They encourage Speght's work in the first place; it is they who judge that Chaucer's text needs reparation; it is then they, along with '*certaine . . . of the best in the Companie of Stationers*', who change Speght's direction by proposing that he publish. Speght, as we have seen, gives indications of his reservations about publicity. But to him, evidently, the luxurious privacy of his gentleman encouragers is not available. Speght is a schoolmaster, not a fellow of a Cambridge college. Caxton presented the *Canterbury Tales* as entirely for gentlemanly circulation, and his tale about the second printing is one of gentlemanly dealings which conclude when Caxton's interlocutor 'ful gentylly gate of his fader the said book . . .' Speght's *Workes*, by contrast, shows an editor who is obliquely, problematically placed in relation to gentlemanliness. Its editor has, in effect, been pushed out into the public eye in a way he did not seek – or so he says – losing his scholarly privacy. One of the aims of his edition, as I will explore more fully below, is to restore Chaucer to unequivocally gentle status, rectifying any *dyffamyng* of his social status as surely as Caxton looked to the *dyffamyng* of his text. In addition, Chaucer's editor looked to compensate for his own unwanted publicising. Like Henry Beaumont Speght wanted the medieval past to do something for him. There was nothing passive about reading the medieval. But in this respect, the 1598 and 1602 editions of Chaucer were less successful.

III

If we read Speght's reluctance, with Trigg, as a modesty *topos* then what Speght was actually trying to do was to publicise himself and his work while saying that he was not, thrusting himself forward into an inchoate public sphere of discussion that he was helping to constitute by his actions as an editor (which include the pretence that he is *not* trying to constitute such a thing). It was only in such a public sphere that Speght might receive recognition and patronage for his efforts. In H.B.'s poem, as we have seen, there is a coy but nevertheless obvious hint put into the mouth of Chaucer himself that Speght might be rewarded for his labours. But in the poem 'Chaucer' then 'nips the idea in the bud', as Trigg puts it, concluding that it was all done for love. 'Speght's aims are too noble and altruistic to be repaid in monetary terms.'[34]

However, the motif of reward is not confined to H.B.'s poem. In a rather more practical application of his rhetorical powers, Speght dedicated the edition to one of the powerful, and very public, men of the day, Robert Cecil, son of William Cecil, Lord Burghley. In 1598 Cecil had not long before been confirmed as Elizabeth's secretary of state, succeeding his father in that role and confirming his own rise to real influence. Speght was presumably emboldened to make the dedication because of his mysterious link with his one-time benefactor, Lady Mildred Cecil – he reminds Cecil of the connection. By an odd coincidence, Cecil became an even more appropriate choice (in Speght's eyes) in October 1597 when he was appointed Chancellor of the Duchy of Lancaster – a position Speght does not fail to mention in his dedication.[35]

Speght was, in Pierre Bourdieu's term, one of the 'commoners of culture' and it is for that reason that he had to go public while the 'cultural nobility', the members of the shadowy Peterhouse circle, were able to practise the reticence which their accumulated symbolic capital allowed them, but to which Speght could only pretend.[36] Nevertheless, to have been a Cambridge man at this time was more than usually significant given the wide influence under Elizabeth of a clique of Cambridge-educated men: the so-called 'Cambridge connection', of which Robert Cecil, like his father before him, formed part.[37] The Cambridge connection was Speght's link to a cultural, and actual, nobility.

Chaucer, already Protestant and Lancastrian, was about to join the Cambridge connection. On the basis of *The Court of Love* (wrongly attributed to Chaucer by Stow), Speght added to Leland's claim that Chaucer had attended Oxford a fresh claim that he had also been at Cambridge. Chaucer, Speght continued,

became a wittie Logician, a sweete Rhetorician, a pleasant Poet, a graue Philosopher, and a holy Diuine. Moreouer he was a Skilfull Mathematician . . . By his trauaile also in Fraunce and Flaunders, where hee spent much time in his young yeeres, but more in the latter end of the reigne of K. Richard the second, he attained to great perfection in all kind of learning. ('The Life of Geffrey Chaucer', Biii r)

Despite the mention of Richard II here, this Chaucer is hardly the medieval primitive that some have seen in Speght's construction of the poet. In this description (which is based on Leland's conclusions), he is more an idealised version of the Renaissance courtier, perhaps someone like Cecil himself, who had also spent time at Cambridge and had been on diplomatic missions to France before returning to important posts at court. But as Speght goes on, absorbing Stow's detail about Chaucer's humble origins and adding his own inflections to the life of Chaucer, it is the editor whom the poet comes to resemble. Speght highlights Chaucer's successful authorial trajectory, *in spite* of his humble origins. So Chaucer, like Speght, has a humble background but gets to Cambridge University; while thus socially elevated, Speght, like Chaucer, remains modest and self-effacing. Chaucer becomes, in part through literary labour, an associate of a great magnate, the Duke of Lancaster, while Speght engages in literary labours and seeks the intimacy of the duchy's chancellor. So Chaucer is beside the man beside the king, while Speght addresses the man beside the queen. Of all Speght's loving private friends, Chaucer is the nearest.

In these ways Speght's Lancastrianised Chaucer, however carefully constructed to avoid the kind of censure which saw the destruction of Jeffes's press, ultimately participates more in a micro-politics of the self than a macro-politics. Speght, however reluctantly, has left the protective circle of private friends within which it would be possible to go on discussing and improving Chaucer without ever printing a word. We can see the public editorial persona that results as embarked on a trajectory within the public world of letters, seeking patronage via a dedication, hinting at a reward in Chaucer's own voice, seeking in short the kind of trajectory that would simply not be required by a gentleman who could afford to remain within a private circle.

As can be seen in chapters in this volume on earlier Tudor figures, reading the medieval in early modern England is often a matter of selective suppression as, for example, when John Bale takes what he needs from medieval culture for his own literary enterprise while playing down his debt to it. I began here with the example of Henry Beaumont and his petition to James I, a very specific instance of reading medieval history, whereby Beaumont hoped to rewrite his family's present-day fortunes through his reading of its medieval past. Henry Beaumont was perhaps also H.B., who contributed to a rereading of Chaucer by which Thomas Speght reluctantly embraced an attempt to emerge into the public sphere of scholarship and patronage. Henry Beaumont's motivation of medieval history through his petition failed. As far as we know, James I paid it no attention: Beaumont certainly did not get his viscountcy. Francis Beaumont, another prominent participant in the 1598 and 1602 Chaucers, *did* gain from the intervention of James I, when he was awarded the mastership of Charterhouse.[38]

In H.B.'s poem Chaucer's voice speaks of a kind of confinement forced on him by a lack of scholarship. Answering the reader's question as to where he has been Chaucer says, '*In haulks and hernes, God wot, and in exile, / Where none vouchsaft to yeeld me words or lookes*'. Neither *haulks* nor *hernes* was in regular use in the late sixteenth century, as Speght's inclusion of the words in his own glossaries underlines. Their use as self-conscious archaisms tells us that Chaucer is speaking Middle English here, which reminds us (or the Tudor reader) of the work of mediation that needs to go on if '*old words, which were vnknown of many*' are to be made '*So plaine, that now they be known of any*'. These sentiments are not strictly accurate given that Chaucer had been readily available in a series of printings since 1532 and was hardly sequestered in the kind of unwanted privacy – the privacy of oblivion – implied here. Nevertheless, Speght's editions did more than any others to rescue Chaucer from the possibility of oblivion. His extensive use of the philological absence model, through which he piled a mass of commentary on to Chaucer, ensured that. At the same time, the kind of material transformation Speght might have been hoping for – the advancement delicately referred to in H.B.'s poem and which presumably lies behind the dedication to Robert Cecil – did not come about. It is feasible to think that Speght might have had an eye on a position in Cecil's household, perhaps as tutor to Cecil's young son, whose mother had died the year before the appearance of the Chaucer edition. But Speght ended his days a successful schoolmaster, and no more. One of the most extensive readers of the medieval in late Tudor England, he was nevertheless caught up in the moment in which the medieval was passing from view. Within a few years, more and more frequent complaints about Chaucer's language would be written and the remembered presence model of thinking about Chaucer would become, as in *The Two Noble Kinsmen*, a matter for comedy. Speght more than anyone else ensured that Chaucer would be read in the seventeenth century, when medieval literature was most scorned. But he himself, after reading Chaucer, slipped back into private life.

PART III

Nation

CHAPTER 5

The vulgar history of the Order of the Garter

Stephanie Trigg

The Order of the Garter is one of the most familiar, but one of the most enigmatic, traces of ritual practice to survive from the medieval period. Edward III founded his great order of knighthood in 1348 in the wake of his military success at Crécy, but his reasons for choosing the emblem of the garter and its oblique motto – *Honi soit qui mal y pense* – remain uncertain. Could such a venerable institution truly have taken its origins from a careless moment of sexual innuendo amidst the public exposure of a woman's underclothes? Different accounts of the Order offer competing explanations of its insignia, motto and origins, in a pattern of attraction and resistance to the traditional story, in which Edward III gallantly retrieved a lady's dropped garter and silenced the laughter of his courtiers by promising to found a chivalric and military order that would elevate the little item from a despised object of shame and ridicule into a privileged sign of honour.

The stakes in interpreting this foundational moment have always been very high. The Order of the Garter is one of the pre-eminent sites for distributing and regulating the symbolic and mythic capital, as I call it, of the British monarchy; one of the key instruments by which the monarchy constructs and rebuilds its relationship with medieval tradition. This tradition is a key factor in the ongoing mystique, even the charisma, of the royal family. At the same time, the monarchy insists on its capacity to reform, modify or modernise this heritage, whether for reasons of religious, political or more general cultural reform. The history of the Order is one of periodic negotiations between tradition and modernity, between the inheritance of fourteenth-century ritual practice, and the renewal and reform of that practice.[1] Questions of origins are crucial to these debates.

This essay considers some of the narrative and historiographical dynamics around the various accounts of the Order's origins from the late medieval period into the early eighteenth century. These accounts, whether in narrative histories, heraldic treatises, poems or other works, provide an instructive example of the way early modern writers produce and shape their ideas of the Middle Ages. All our reconstructions of the past are partial, of course, and invested with a range of ideological, emotional and psychological charges that are played out in a variety of ways in the institutions and structures of our academic work. The essays in this volume are concerned with some of the early historical moments in the formation of those structures. That is, these readings of medieval culture are not historically discrete: they look forwards as well as backwards, exerting a powerful influence on the cultural trajectories of the medieval into modernity and post-modernity. In the case of the Garter, I will suggest that early modern historiographical method sought to expel or repress the more fantastic aspects of medieval court culture, while still being drawn to the narrative impulses of its romance. The resultant opposition, between the romantic or sexualised story of Edward's garter and the more sober military explanation that came to displace it, has had the effect of dividing scholarly and popular opinion about the Order, in a way that continues to blind us to the nature of Edward's evocative speech-act.

There is little doubt, now, about Edward III's foundation of the Order in 1348;[2] about the institution of St George as the Order's patron saint, and its connection with Windsor Castle. On 23 April 1349, the first formal celebrations of the Feast of St George were held at Windsor, when the Wardrobe accounts record that John of Cologne provided 'six garters and twenty-four robes powdered with garters bearing the motto of the Order, together with matching altar hangings for the Chapel'.[3] The Garter device consistently appears in the form of a buckled blue circle, with the motto spelled out in gold letters. The Garter appears, with the earliest English version of the motto, *Hethyng haue the hathell that any harme thynkes*, in the Middle English poem *Wynnere and Wastoure*, dated between 1352 and 1370.[4] However, there is no medieval English explanation of the Order's origins. The earliest text in English that seems to invoke the narrative of a woman's garter is *Sir Gawain and the Green Knight*, with its suggestive parallel of the garment transferred from a female to a male body, which is then also transformed from a sign of personal shame to one of courtly honour, with the official sanction of heraldic symbolism. Someone, indeed, appended the Garter motto (as '*Hony soit qui mal pense*') to the only surviving manuscript of this poem.[5]

There is no hint, moreover, in the Order's earliest Statutes, dating from the reign of Henry V,[6] that would resolve the question of why Edward should have taken a garter as its emblem. Significantly, the Statutes are principally concerned with practices and systems, and less with origins.

Most discussion of the Order's origins takes place in heraldic or other histories, in poems or prose fictions, while the mystery around the story seems to license narratives that foreground the opposition between reverence for the 'most noble' Order, and fascination with the possible trivial, 'vulgar' or even 'sordid' nature of its origins. My concern in this essay is less to uncover the historical truth of the Order's foundation than with the exercise of scholarly judgement and narrative compulsion in the early modern accounts of that moment.

Joanot Martorell's epic romance of chivalry, *Tirant lo Blanc*, begun in 1460 and published in Valencia in 1490, offers the earliest recorded version of the Order's origins. Martorell claims the text was translated first from English into Portuguese, and then into the Valencian vernacular, or Catalan, excusing himself for any defects since 'the blame lies with the English language, some words of which are impossible to translate'.[7] No record survives of this putative English original; it may function here as an untraceable, but authorising fiction. Martorell's romance was not known to most historians of the Order, so it plays little or no part in the dominant trajectory of the story, but as the earliest and most comprehensive narrative, it commands our attention. David Rosenthal's translation of 1984 makes the task much easier.

Martorell's narrative is a deeply embedded one, framed by the distancing fictions of romance, though it is also situated with some precision around the marriage of an English king to a French princess. Martorell did spend some time in England, so if we seek a historical point of reference, we may suppose the king represents Henry VI, and the princess, Margaret of Anjou: they were married in Tours in 1444, and the king held a three-day tournament to celebrate her coronation at Westminster in 1445.[8] In Martorell's romance, the Breton nobleman Tirant recounts the story of the wedding, and then Diaphebus, another knight, takes over the narration to recite the praise of Tirant, who had been the tournament's champion. He then tells of an order of knighthood the King of England established, 'similar to King Arthur's Knights of the Round Table in olden days'.[9]

The wedding festivities lasted a year and a day (a clear enough signal that this world is governed by the conventions of romance, not history), but the king asked everyone to stay on a little longer, as he wanted to announce his founding of a new order. 'This order's inspiration, as I and all these knights heard it from the king's own lips, came from an incident one day when we were dancing and making merry.' This detailed narrative includes most of the central elements in later versions of the story: a dropped garter; an embarrassed woman; a chivalric king; and, most significantly, the ease with which the king is able to transform a trivial object into a sign of greatness, a sign of shame into a sign of honour.

'Many knights were dancing with ladies, and by chance one damsel named Honeysuckle [Madresilva] drew near the king. As she whirled, her left garter, which was trimmed with silk, fell off. Those nearest His Majesty beheld it on the floor, and do not imagine, my lord, that she was fairer or more genteel than others. She has a rather flirtatious way of dancing and talking, though she sings reasonably well, yet one might have found three hundred comelier and more gracious damsels present. All the same, there is no accounting for men's tastes and whims. One of the knights near the king said: "Honeysuckle, you have lost your leg armor. You must have a bad page who failed to fasten it well."

'She blushed slightly and stooped to pick it up, but another knight rushed over and grabbed it. The king then summoned the knight and said: "Fasten it to my left stocking below the knee."'   ·

The king wore this garter on his leg for four months, until finally one of his favourite servants tells him how concerned everyone is.

'The king replied: "So the queen is disgruntled and my guests are displeased!", and he said in French, "*Puni soit qui mal y pense*. Now I swear before God that I shall found a new knightly order upon this incident: a fraternity that shall be remembered as long as the world endures."

'He had the garter removed and would wear it no longer, though he still pined for it in secret.'[10]

Diaphebus then recounts how the king dedicated a chapel at Windsor to St George, and established an order of twenty-four knights, describing their robes, capes, hoods and garters, and mentioning the rule that they must always wear their garter below the left knee. He recounts the oaths they swear, their ceremonial processions, the rituals for the Installation and Degradation of a knight (which involve dressing a scarecrow in his armour). He also cites the vows sworn by ladies of the Order (that they will never urge their male relatives to return from war; they will do all they can to aid any such relative starving under siege; and that if they are taken prisoner, they will spend up to half their dowry to ransom them). Finally, he comments that the ladies must always wear their garters on their left sleeves.[11]

This account is much fuller than the better-known version recorded by Polydore Vergil in the early sixteenth century. Its historical context bears little relationship to the court of Edward III, while its list of knights in the Order, including the fictional Tirant, matches neither the original company nor the Order under Henry VI. The King's motto is also different, as he invokes punishment, not shame (*Puni*, not *honi*) on any who might think ill of his Order. Most accounts do not foreground the queen's anger or displeasure, as this one does; and it is also alone in making overt the nature of the garter as fetish, as the king pines for it in secret long after he has had it removed from his clothing. Martorell is also unique in naming the lady as Madresilva. In other versions, the lady is not named, or is vastly elevated in status, as Queen Philippa, or the French queen, or more frequently, the Countess of Salisbury, with whom Edward is or is not in love, and whom he did or did not rape.[12]

If there is any kind of kernel of truth in this story, that truth is probably rather a symbolic than a historical truth; that is, the story embodies a first-order truth about the king's power to make symbolic meaning, elevating what is ostensibly humble, even trivial, into what is most worthy; and a secondary truth about that power being beyond the comprehension of many of his courtiers.

This is certainly Susan Crane's view, though she also emphasises the risks the king takes in 'cross-dressing', in transferring the female garment to his own leg.[13] Crane also cites C. Stephen Jaeger who emphasises the king's power to translate signs and symbols from one sphere to another, from what is 'vulgar, obscene and illicit' into what is 'noble, and worthy of veneration'. Jaeger writes of the 'enchantment', the magic circle that surrounds the body of the king and gives additional force to these 'social acts' that reinforce inherent values.[14]

The very richness of the story, and the risks it dramatises for the honour of the court, invites its perpetual re-telling, though the textual tradition of the narrative remains obscure: there is no direct or obvious line of transmission from Martorell's romance to later accounts. His version is unique, too, in being a 'straight' telling of the story, without any anxiety about its veracity as a historical record, or its worthiness as a foundational narrative. Far more common are historical or antiquarian accounts that make apology for the story, dispute its veracity or even discredit its plausibility as an unworthy origin for so great a chivalric order. Whatever their final conclusion, these accounts rehearse the scepticism that characterises much humanist response to medieval or ancient legends, while at the same time gladly succumbing to the narrative pleasures of the story.

For many centuries, the earliest known account was that of Polydore Vergil, who positively relishes the doubt about the story, in his *Historia Anglica*, written around 1512.[15]

But the reason for founding the order is utterly uncertain; popular tradition nowadays declares that Edward at some time picked up from the ground a garter from the stocking of his queen or mistress, which had become unloosed by some chance, and had fallen. As some of the knights began to laugh and jeer on seeing this, he is reputed to have said that in a very little while the same garter would be held by them in the highest honour. And not long after, he is said to have founded this order and given it the title by which he showed those knights who had laughed at him how to judge his actions. Such is popular tradition [*fama vulgi*]. English writers have been modestly superstitious, perhaps fearing to commit lèse-majesté, if they made known such unworthy things; and they have preferred to remain silent about them, whereas matters should really be seen otherwise: something that rises from a petty or sordid origin increases all the more in dignity.[16]

Vergil implies that the tactful silence of the English commentators on the matter is further proof of the story's veracity, or plausibility, but his central point is the metamorphosis of this very humble object into a sign of honour and dignity. In other writings, Vergil had been dismissive of many of the traditional and popular British myths of Trojan settlement and the Arthurian legends.[17] Set against his reputation for scepticism, even irreverence, his apparent support for the popular tradition of the garter narrative sparked equal measures of fascination and resistance: for every writer who accepted the story and revelled in its narrative possibilities, there was another who took a scholarly delight in its vigorous rebuttal.

Perhaps in response to Vergil's story, the *Liber Niger*, or Register of the Order, prepared under Henry VIII, offers an alternative account of its origins. Like many heraldic histories, it constructs a chivalric and military lineage that stretches from the knights of Troy to the warriors of the Old Testament and to Christianity. This tradition passes to Arthur, and then for the first time Richard I at the siege of Acre appears in the context of a Garter history. The siege is proceeding slowly, and to encourage his troops, Richard takes a leather strap, and promises to found an elite order of knights for those who fight most valiantly, promising to reward them with a strap – or garter – of more luxurious form. The *Liber Niger* says Edward III was merely reviving this older order, and emphasises its importance as cementing the affinity and loyalty amongst the Companions.

Not all those who reject Vergil's narrative about the countess accept this retrospective origin for the Order, though its saving emphasis on the Garter's capacity to symbolise loyalty and chivalric brotherhood became an important theme in later commentaries. Vergil's account continued to intrigue, remaining the standard point of reference, either explicitly, in the historiographical discourse of later writers, or implicitly, in the many poetic and fictional accounts of the story.

Elizabethan writers in particular are happy to accept Vergil's account, even if they present variations in the story, or alter his emphases. So

Holinshed reasons, in 1577. He accepts the tale's popular origin ('there goeth a tale amongst the people'), and moves quickly, echoing Vergil's citation of Ovid, to counter any suggestion that this might denigrate the Order:

Though some may thinke, that so noble an order had but a meane beginning, if this tale be true, yet manie honorable degrees of estates have had their beginnings of more base and meane things, than of love, which being orderlie used, is most noble and commendable, sith nobilitie it selfe is covered under love, as the poet Ovid aptlie saith,

Nobilitas sub amore iacet.[18]

Similarly, George Peele's romantic vision poem, *The Honour of the Garter*, from 1593, narrates the story of the queen's garter and concludes 'This beginning had / This honourable order of our time.'[19]

The story's origins in popular tradition (*fama vulgi*) and its associations with romance would count against it, however, amongst those writing from an antiquarian or heraldic context, where there is a discernible transference of 'vulgarity' between the story's mode of transmission, in popular tradition, and the sexualised, or 'sordid', content (Vergil's term) of the story. William Segar can find no alternative account in his *Booke of Honour and Armes* (1590) but gives a brief version of the story: 'thus haue I heard it vulgarlie reported'.[20] Twelve years later, in his *Honor Military and Ciuill*, he expands his discussion, mentioning both the Countess of Salisbury '(of whom the King was then enamored)', and the queen's displeasure. In this more expansive mode, Segar also dutifully reports an alternative explanation: 'Some rather thinke it was made to remunerate those Noble men and Knights, that had best endeuoured and deserued in his most Royall and Martiall affaires of France, Scotland and Spaine, with all which Nations he then had warre and triumphed.'[21] Segar does not choose between these accounts, but as the traditional story expands in its scandalous detail, the more it seems to require the counterweight of scholarly discourse and an alternative account, no matter how unpersuasive.

The most severe account of the matter comes from Peter Heylyn in his *Cosmographie*, first published in 1652. Heylyn dismisses Vergil's account as mere 'popular tradition', in emphatic terms which would be echoed by many later writers:

Of S. George, called commonly the Garter, instituted by King Edward the Third, to increase vertue and valour in the heart of his Nobility; or, as some will, in honour of the Countess of Salisburies Garter, of which Lady, the King formerly had been enamoured. But this I take to be a vain and idle Romance, derogatory both to the Founder, and the order; first published by Polydore Virgil, a stranger to the affairs of England, & by him taken upon no better ground than *fama vulgi*, the tradition of the common people; too trifling a Foundation for so great a building; Common bruit, being so infamous an Historian, that wise men neither report after it, or give credit to any thing they receive from it. But for this fame or common bruit, the vanity and improbabilities thereof have been elsewhere canvassed.[22]

Heylyn offers an influential revisionary reading of the Order as an emphatically masculine and chivalric brotherhood, requiring a serious, fully considered and dignified foundation.

In 1670, Elias Ashmole, writing as the 'Windesor Herald at Armes', summarises Heylyn's view with approval, consolidating the pattern of dismissing the story as 'the vulgar and more general' view, and echoing Heylyn: 'And yet hath it so fallen out, that many learned men, for want of reflection, have incautelously [*sic*] swallowed and run away with this vulgar error; whereupon it hath come by degrees to the vogue it is in now.'[23] Ashmole dutifully reports a number of variants on the story: that the king picked up the queen's garter as he followed her to her room; or that the motto was the queen's own response to the king, when he asked her, what men would say about her losing her garter in such a manner.

In Heylyn and Ashmole we witness a dramatic shift in historiographical method. Both make a virtue of comparing and weighing sources for their accuracy and plausibility, and Ashmole in particular delights in adopting a second-order analytical position:

But both these Relations are remote from truth, and of little credit; nevertheless, they give us opportunity to note here, that it hath thus fared with other Orders of Soveraign Foundation; and an Amorous instead of Honorable Account of their Institution, hath by some been untruly rendred.[24]

Ashmole is emphatic in his dismissal, however, of the 'groundless imagination' that could suppose King Edward might have 'founded this most famous Order . . . to give reputation to, or perpetuate an effeminate occasion'.[25]

By 1724, John Anstis, Garter King of Arms, could confidently describe this and other similar stories as 'absurd' and 'ridiculous', as 'romantick Fancies'.[26] This strategy of associating these stories with a world of fantasy, romance and femininity remains a powerful technique for the Garter's modern historians, for whom this austere view continues to dominate. Accordingly, the Order's recent official historians, Peter Begent and Hubert Chesshyre, quote Anstis with approval, saying it is better such stories be 'left in the dark'.[27] They also comment, 'it is most unlikely that Edward, concerned with his public image, would have adopted an item of a lady's underclothing as a device to be displayed firstly upon a major military expedition and later as a symbol of heroic chivalry'.[28] Hugh Collins, too, in the most recent study of the Garter's early history, is relieved to be able to dismiss this account in terms perfectly reminiscent of Heylyn and Ashmole. 'Although popular in the fifteenth century, this elaborate version of events lacks credibility. It is hardly likely that Edward III, given the serious intent underlying his conception, would have risked trivializing it by selecting such an inappropriate badge.'[29] This is virtually an unbroken trajectory from the early antiquarian, heraldic and historical discourse into the late twentieth century, with a similar pattern of citing the feminised story only to displace it with the voice of masculine common sense and reason.

Nothing short of relief is palpable in such commentators, when they can discover alternative accounts of the Order's foundation, of the motto, and even of the way medieval women held up their stockings. Mercifully, it turns out that the Garter is 'really' a piece of military equipment, 'a small strap, possibly used to attach pieces of armour', or a version of the knight's belt, not a piece of underwear at all, neither men's nor women's.[30] Once the Garter is explained, though, these apologists must still account for the 'shame' *and* the 'evil' invoked in the motto,[31] and so this is said to be a defiant reference to Edward's claim to the French crown, one of the central contentions of the Hundred Years War. The quartering of the French with the English coat of arms on the royal coat of arms dates from this period, while the Garter's colour, blue, signifies the French coat of arms: blue with the gold *fleurs-de-lys*.[32] The imperialist drive to conquer France is seen as the less shameful act, while this alternative derivation, from a tiny and unspecific 'strap', is not seen as shameful at all, especially if it can displace the woman's garter from the centre of the narrative.[33] Curiously, however, Martorell invokes the link between the two forms of the garter; we recall that the courtier who first mocks Madresilva makes this connection between the woman's garter and the piece of armour: 'Honeysuckle, you have lost your leg armor. You must have a bad page who failed to fasten it well.'

In addition to this trajectory from the early modern antiquarians to contemporary historians, however, there is also a counterpoint sequence of alternative narratives that are compelled to dramatise the central scene. These versions have received little or no discussion in the history of the Order, since they are imagined variations on a theme, rather than offering any certainty as verifiable records of fourteenth-century events. I suggest, however, that in their fascination with the motto, and with visualising or dramatising the scene of the woman's garter, they represent a fuller, even a truer response to the king's enigmatic pronouncement. In these more detailed versions, the motto becomes a kind of textual machine for generating both narrative and interpretation, playing a role closer to its original intent. That is, the motto may have been coined and adopted precisely because it is so elliptic, capable of generating such a wide range of interpretations. Those historians who compare the Garter motto with other mottos favoured by Edward – 'It is as it is' or 'Hay, hay, the White Swan, By God's soul I am thy man' – certainly recognise the elliptic nature of courtly play.[34]

Polydore Vergil's *Historia Anglica* was willing to accept that popular tradition might have a purchase on some kind of truth. His anonymous, rather expansive sixteenth-century English translator similarly defends the story of the woman's garter, while also attributing it to 'the ruder sorte'. He continues with a remarkable account of the king's courtiers making sport with the retrieved garter:

that the Kinge on a time tooke upp from the grounde the gartere of the queene or som paramoure which she beefore hadd loste, and that divers of his Lordes standinge bie did pulle it in sonder in ieste or sport for the peaces therof as it has been a [*cancelled*] men are wonte sometime for a jeuill of small importance in somutche that the Kinge sayde unto them. Sirs the time shall shortlie comme when you shall attribute muche honor unto suche a Garteir, whearuppon he didd institute this order and so intituled it. That his Nobles might understond that they hadd caste them selves in their owne Judgement.[35]

This narrative addition conjures up an extraordinary image of courtly play, with the bored knights tossing the garter to and fro, pulling it apart for sport, perhaps to tease the woman who had lost it. This translator is more interested in these lordly games with expensive trifles (the oxymoronic 'jeuill of small importance') than the identity of the woman; and deeply concerned with what their levity reveals about their ungallant attitude. Expounding on the nature of the shame that the king invokes, he emphasises the ethical nature of the king's lesson to his court.

A rather different version is offered by André Favyn, in 1620, a version that is similarly startling in its concrete detail, and its willingness to expose, as it were, the secret source of shame. Where many accounts show the king tying the garter around his own leg – as a trophy, a fetish or a playful symbol of cross-dressing – Favyn has the besotted king attempting to replace the garter, as high as possible, around the countess's leg.[36] The English translation of 1623 (under the name 'Andrew Favin') expands the narrative even further, with a shocking glimpse of white underwear:

Forasmuch as King Edward being wounded with love of faire Alix, the Countesse of Salisbury, one day as hee was devising with her, the left Garter (of Blew Silke) of this Lady, hung loosely down upon her shooe. King Edward, ready at the Ladies Service, and to take up the Garter; by little and little lifted her cloathes so high, that the Courtiers had some sight of her white Smock, & could not refraine from smiling. The Lady reprehended the King for this publick fault before his own people (who carried good lookes, but bad thoughts, and pleased their owne opinion so much, that they made an Idoll of their vaine conceits:) King Edward therefore, to cover his owne honour, stopt all their mouthes with these few French words; Honny Soit Qui Mal y Pense.[37]

This re-telling foregrounds the secret of women's privity that underlines all versions of this story, but which is rarely exposed as dramatically as it is here. Favyn precedes the story with an account of the king's infatuation with the countess, who comes bidden to the festivities, the tournament, and the feasts, dressed as simply as possible (*'le plus simplement atournée qu'elle peust'*).

In contrast to Favyn's novelised account, other writers are concerned with the question of motive. Richard Johnson, for example, attributes the motto to the Queen of France, in his 'Gallant Song of the Garter of England', from 1620. When her garter falls during a feast, the snickering courtiers seem to accuse her of dropping it deliberately to attract the king's attention, so it is she who coins the motto in their reproof:

> But when she heard these ill conceits
> And speeches that they made,
> Hony soyt qui mal y pens,
> the noble Princes said.
> Ill hap to them that evill thinke,
> In English it is thus
> Which words so wise (quoth Englands King)
> shall surely goe with us . . .[38]

Even when commentators dismiss any association with women, the invocation to shame still proves problematic, and capable of generating alternative explanations. In his history of St George, for example, from 1633, Peter Heylyn prefers to think of the motto and the garter symbolising the knights' loyalty to their king, and to each other, citing the Register of the Order:

that as by their order, they were ioyned together as in a fast tye of amitie and concord: so by their Garter, as a bond of love and unitie, they might bee kept in minde to effect each other. *Sic huic ordini cum nominibus, vestes et ornamenta coaptavit, ut omnia hæc ad amicitiam, concordiam, et reliquam virtutem tendere, nemo non intelligat.* Which combination of mindes, and association of affections, lest possibly it might be thought to have some other end in it, then what was just and honourable, *ad adversandum in omni re non male facta malam interpretationem*, as the booke hath it: hee caused that French Motto or Impresse to be wrought in with it, which is still observed: that *viz* of *Honisoit, qui mal y pense*, Shame bee to him that evill thinketh.[39]

In raising the possibility of an unjust, or dishonourable reading of the 'combination of minds, and conjoyning affections', Heylyn seems to countenance a homosexual or homosocial connotation. It is an intriguing instance of the motto's extraordinary capacity to generate interpretation: in defying shame, the motto invokes shame, generating a whole series of shameful possibilities.

This play of heterosexuality and homosociality is seen most dramatically in William Fennor's poem, recited before James I in 1616.[40] Fennor's narrative emphasises the king's chivalry to the countess, then Edward's capacity to turn from courtly dalliance to military endeavour in France, to the greater glory of the Order:

> Saint Patrick's Crosse did to the Garter vayle,
>   Saint Jaques' Order was with anger pale;
> Saint David's leeke began to droupe i'th'tale,
>   Saint Dennys he sate mourning in a dale;
> Saint Andrew lookt with cheereful appetite,
> As though to th'Garter he had future right.

Fennor then tracks a chivalric analogy between the heterosexual transfer of woman's garment to male body, and the presentation of a similar token from king to his knights.

> Say that a man long languishing in love,
>   Whose heart with hope and feare grows cold and warme;
> Admit some pitty should his sweethearte move,
>   To knit a favour on his feeble arme;
> All parts would joyne to make that one joint strong,
> To oppose any that his love should wrong.

> The Garter is the favour of a King,
>   Clasping the leg on which man's best part stands;
> A poesye in't, as in a nuptiall ring,
>   Binding the heart to their liege Lord in bands;
> That whilst the leg hath strength, or the arme power,
> To kill that serpent would their King devoure.

Fennor's analogy is only partly successful, of course, in defending the chivalric masculinity of the Order: the garter, 'clasping' the knight's leg 'as a 'nuptiall ring', seems inevitably to invoke the erotic imagery of marriage and sexuality.

Other writers are less defensive about the Order's origins. John Selden, in his *Titles of Honour*, from 1631, attempts to weigh the evidence, but does not mind admitting defeat in the face of contradictory evidence: 'In this uncertainty of the Occasion, our common stories give us but little light. Nor know I whence wholy to cleere it.'[41] In reporting the story of the countess's garter, Selden compares the Order's motto to the words of Philip upon sight of the Regiment of Lovers slain at the battle of Charonea, as reported in Plutarch's *Pelopida*: 'Ill betide them that thinke any ill of these men.' This is clearly a story of homosexual love and affection, as these were soldiers who fought all the more valiantly to impress the ones they loved in the same division of the army. Selden's final solution to the dilemma is to propose instead that the Order arose at the same time as Edward III's institution of the Round Table at Windsor, suggesting that the story of the garter might have arisen at a later date after some event at the festivities. Significantly, for my purposes, his easy invocation of homosocial love as an analogy for heterosexual desire and courtly play (both defying condemnation) indicates how closely these two are linked, despite the attempts of so many historians to establish an exclusive opposition between them.

For most of the Garter's commentators, then, the problem of origins takes a doubled form. The first problem is the uncertainty and ambiguity of the motto; and the second is the triviality of the Garter as emblem, whatever its original form. If the motto raises the spectre of shame, then sexuality of one form or another is the most persistent scenario to be overcome, but even the other explanations (brotherly companionship; a king's claim to a foreign throne) all seem to invoke more shame. However, the most shameful, the most problematic scenario of all seems to be that Edward could indeed have established such a great Order out of such a small item. Not all the earnest arguments of Vergil and others can write away the oddness of this feature of the Order. And that, after all, is the point. Not being kings, we cannot conceive a sign of such mobility. We are indeed *honi*, shamed, or condemned out of own mouths, as soon as we start to rationalise the king's choice of emblem and motto.

In the face of the Order's success, the only position left to us, as historians and commentators, is to marvel and to wonder, since it makes little difference what we think Edward had in mind. In 1631, Charles Allen throws the whole question open into an issue of careless choice. He gives a brief account of the story about the countess, then summarises the rival account:

Some the beginning from first Richard bring,
(Counting too meanelie of this pedegree)
When he at Acon tyde a leather string
About his Soldiars legges, whose memorie
Might stir their vallour up, yet choose you whether
You'll Edwards silke prefer, or Richards leather.[42]

In offering us a choice of explanations, displaced on to a consumer choice of luxury fabric or utilitarian skin, Allen indicates the insignificance of that choice, and the glamour of the former.

Of all writers, Michael Drayton is the most insouciant about the uncertainty. In the 'Illustrations' to the fifteenth book of his *Poly-Olbion*, published in 1613, which describes the area around Windsor, he comments on the Order:

Whether the cause were upon the word of Garter given in the French wars among the English, or upon the Queens, or Countes of Salisburies Garter fallen from her leg, or upon different & more ancient Original whatsoever, know cleerly (without unlimited affectation of your Countries glorie) that it exceeds in Majestie, honour, and fame, all Chivalrous Orders in the world . . .[43]

Like George Puttenham and Peele, Drayton is writing under the signs of poetry and rhetoric, whereby it seems natural to extol the power of the spoken or written word in the form of the motto to make meaning, and to exercise its capacity to transform the trivial into the magnificent. Any scepticism about the historical origins of the Garter takes second place to these more rhetorical concerns, and the transfer of royal authority from Edward III to James I.

In the move away from antiquarian, chronicle or romance narratives in the seventeenth century, we can identify the emergence of a self-consciously modern scholarly method, taking active pleasure in sifting and sorting various medieval accounts. It is a historiographical method far removed from Polydore Vergil's, replete with marginal annotations, full of respect for historical (that is, written) authority, medieval and classical analogue, and deeply self-conscious about scholarly decorum. At the same time, the narrative impulses of poetry and fiction generate a different kind of pleasure in spinning out more and more complex stories from the merest hint of the shame invoked in Edward's motto.[44] In retrospect, it is easy to see that its very ambiguity, itself a common feature of many mottos, may have been a large part of its appeal for the king. His social power is affirmed once he coins the phrase that leaves us guessing.

The motto thus encapsulates the mixed inheritance of the medieval past for early modernity. Its historians are drawn to the idea of continuity with a national tradition, but they are determined to enact their own critical judgements on that past and its mythologies, attempting to sift truth from rumour, or *fama vulgi*. In doing so they are both producing the medieval period as a historical object worthy of study and dispute, and affirming their own role as modern historians or antiquarians, distinguishing themselves from the poets who are less anxious about the romantic narrative. But there is no reason why they should thereby deny themselves the narrative pleasure of repeating the story about the countess and her garter. Indeed, there is every reason, with Vergil, Heylyn and Ashmole, to articulate a hierarchy of knowledge. There is popular tradition, and there is the academic discussion of popular tradition, just as there is also a hierarchy of sexual and social desire.

In the middle of the sixteenth century, these debates were also played out in the context of an additional dispute about the Garter which deserves brief mention here. William Fennor's poem of 1616 closes with a defence of 'the George', the image of a mounted knight worn on the golden chain of the Order since the reign of Henry VII: 'God keepe our King and them from Rome's black pen', he writes, 'Let all that love the Garter say, Amen!' He was presumably referring to the controversy surrounding the abolition of St George as the Order's patron saint. St George's Day was abolished by Parliament in 1552; and Edward VI had established a commission to reform the Order's Statutes in 1549.[45] Edward himself re-drafted the 'somewhat mangled text' of the statutes to remove all references to St George, and to restore them to their original purity, only to have his reforms thrown out when Mary became queen six months later.[46] In the 1540s, too, the wearing of the George had been taken up as an example in the Reformation debate about images and idols.

In these discussions of the Order's rituals and formalities, the affiliations of the Order with St George play a part analogous to that of the motto and the emblem: all three features signify a medieval past that bespeaks ancient tradition but that also necessitates reform and explanation. The disputes about the meaning of motto and emblem are powerful examples of the potential of medieval tradition itself to confer both shame and honour, both in the regulation and reform of ritual practice, and in the exercise of historical scepticism and explanation.

CHAPTER 6

Myths of origin and the struggle over nationhood in medieval and early modern England

Anke Bernau

In the first half of the twelfth century, between 1130 and 1139, Geoffrey of Monmouth composed what the critic Geraldine Heng has called 'an infamous, celebrated chronicle-history, the . . . *History of the Kings of Britain*'.[1] Controversial even in its own time, it was instantly and hugely popular as well as influential, not least for developing a coherent narrative of the history and glorious origins of Britain.[2] In 1534, three hundred years after Geoffrey's British historiography, Polydore Vergil sparked off the so-called 'battle over Britain' by dismissing Geoffrey's work as 'moste impudent lyeing'. Vergil singled out the long-cherished Trojan heritage myth with which Geoffrey's account begins and which, in turn, was taken up by every subsequent national historiographer of note, into the early seventeenth century.[3] Even before Vergil's attack, in the fourteenth century, the Galfridian account of Brutus was supplemented by the emergence of another, earlier – female – founding figure: Albina. The Albina legend was popular in England as a preface to the Brutus myth until the sixteenth century, after which it was either contemptuously dismissed or ignored.[4] This chapter will examine how gendered foundation myths in English national historiographies of the late medieval and early modern periods were used to negotiate not only national boundaries, but also definitions of progress, civilisation and barbarism as well as the claims to cultural superiority and precedence that underpinned colonial projects.

I

The preoccupation with origin was not new to the fourteenth century. As Susan Reynolds has pointed out, and as Geoffrey's immensely successful Trojan narrative shows, origin myths proliferated from the twelfth century on, increasingly also in the political arena.[5] And whereas Brutus was initially the most well-known of such figures in British history, the naming of land after female founding figures was a familiar motif in medieval historiography. According to John Trevisa's translation of Ranulph Higden's *Polychronicon*, for instance, Asia was named after an eponymous woman, as were Libya, Europa and Corsica. England itself was said by some chroniclers to be named after the Saxon maiden, Inge, or after 'Anglia', 'a quene þat owed þis lond þat heet Angela'.[6] As J. P. Carley and Julia Crick show, the Albina myth, appearing in the first quarter of the fourteenth century, draws on a wide range of well-known literary sources.[7] Jeffrey Jerome Cohen has argued convincingly that it is precisely this combination of familiar motifs from 'biblical, classical, folkloric and ecclesiastical sources' that endowed the new legend with immediate authority, making it appear 'comfortably familiar'.[8] It appeared initially in Anglo-Norman, as an independent work entitled *Des Grantz Geanz* (*c.* 1333), and later 'abbreviated versions of it frequently accompanied copies of the [Anglo-Norman] prose *Brut*'.[9] Its historical and political authority were enhanced when it was translated not only into the other vernaculars of Britain – English and Welsh – but, in a striking and complex reversal of the usual translation process, from the vernacular into Latin.[10] The Latin versions, known as *De origine gigantum*, were used, as Lesley Johnson has shown, either as 'prefaces to the Latin prose *Brut*' or found 'as prefaces to . . . texts of the *Historia regum Britanniae*'.[11]

The Albina narrative starts promisingly enough with a description of Albina and her sisters as beautiful and noble. But the reader is soon introduced to their excessive pride.[12] Shamed by the marriages which have been arranged for them, which they feel compromise their high rank, they plan, at Albina's instigation, to murder their husbands. They are discovered, put out to sea in a rudderless boat, and eventually arrive at an uninhabited island, which Albina claims in her own name, as Albion. Here, they live off the fruitful land, hunting venison and living in caves. Their unruly nature is reconfirmed in Albion. Having shunned lawful union with their husbands, they now pursue their desires and copulate with *incubi*, eventually bearing giant offspring who rule Albion for several hundred years until the arrival of Brutus.[13] This is not a glorious foundation myth *à la* Brutus, but one that posits an inherently flawed and troubled beginning for British history.

In his *Historia*, Geoffrey writes that Brutus has a vision, in which Diana prophesies that he will sail 'past the realms of Gaul' where 'lies an island in the sea, once occupied by giants', which is 'empty and ready for your folk'. They are promised: 'A race of kings will be born there from your stock and the round circle of the whole earth will be subject to them.'[14] The vision manages to promise at once both peaceful settlement and global conquest.

When they finally arrive Diana's prophecy turns out to be inaccurate: the island they reach is not, after all, 'empty'. Geoffrey writes – rather laconically – that 'At this time the island of Britain was called Albion. It was uninhabited except for a few giants . . .'[15]

The remaining giants are killed or driven to the margins of the land before the Trojans inscribe themselves on the landscape, naming it Britannia and erasing all other claims to it; they 'began to cultivate the fields and to build houses, so that in a short time you would have thought that the land had always been inhabited'.[16] Geoffrey's narrative wavers uneasily between the descriptions of Britain as uninhabited *terra incognita* on the one hand, and as populated and already-named Albion on the other. We do not know how the giants got there, why they named it – if it was indeed they who named it – *Albion*. Geoffrey's legend of origins is, arguably, not really a story of origins at all; the prehistory of Britain as Albion is missing.

It is this lack that is addressed by the later Albina myth. Kathleen Davis, citing Homi Bhabha, discusses the 'minus in the origin' – the acts of forgetting that enable a coherent narrative of nation – but what seems to be happening in the Albina story is a deliberate act of remembrance: a *surplus* of origin.[17] And here a tension is evident from the beginning of British national history, between the image on the one hand of Brutus and his men as peaceful settlers and, on the other, of them as forceful colonisers.

The Galfridian narrative was politically potent not just because it posited a glorious origin for Britain in accordance with the demands of the *translatio studii et imperii* topos, but also because it provided a justification of English rights over Scotland and Wales. Edward I and Edward III, in particular, used the Brutus and Arthur myths consistently as evidence of England's ancient right to overlordship over Scotland in the political battle; after all, the chronicles relate how Britain is divided between Brutus' three sons, 'with Locrinus, the eldest, as English overlord'.[18] John Gillingham has traced the introduction of an 'imperialist perception of the Celtic peoples' to the work of William of Malmesbury, who, like Geoffrey, was writing in the twelfth century.[19] He argues that William 'adopted a distinctly different tone' to that taken by earlier chroniclers. For William, 'the Celts, Irish, Scots and Welsh are "barbarians"', and Gillingham concludes that William 'is discarding the familiar concept of barbarian as equivalent to pagan, and formulating a new one – one which allowed for the possibility of Christian barbarians'.

The main characteristics of these Celtic barbarians are familiar and, roughly, threefold. They represent 'fundamentally pastoral economies'; William comments explicitly 'on the absence of towns, commerce and agriculture'.[20] Secondly, they are described as savagely ferocious in warfare, particularly against mothers and pregnant women, as this extract from Richard of Hexham's (*c.* 1140) *Chronicles of the Reigns* illustrates:

By the sword's edge or the spear's point they slaughtered the sick on their beds, women who were pregnant or in labour, babies in their cradles or at their mothers' breasts, and sometimes they killed the mothers too.[21]

Thirdly, their sexual relations are perverse and immoral, as they condone incest, adultery, polygamy and even bestiality. The English (along with the French) are contrasted favourably with this uncivilised behaviour, and these narratives are used explicitly to justify English claims to overlordship over Wales and Scotland.[22] The Scots, in turn, are represented in a manner reminiscent of the description of Albion's originary giants.

Most critics who have worked on the genesis and development of the Albina myth place it in the context of the fraught Anglo-Scottish relations of the thirteenth and fourteenth centuries, in which there was a veritable battle of foundation myths.[23] Carley and Crick cite the example of Alexander III of Scotland's coronation in 1249, where the new king 'heard his royal genealogy recited back to Scota, alleged ancestress of the Scottish race' (55).[24] But the Scota legend was used politically as early as the twelfth century, during William the Lion's reign, when 'two royal genealogies of his time are taken back to Gathelus', Scota's Greek husband.[25] It was used again in 1301, with the intercession of Pope Boniface VIII on Scotland's behalf and again in the 1320 Declaration of Arbroath;[26] then again in 1323, 'when Robert the Bruce demanded [from the English] restoration of the Stone of Scone that Scota had brought from Egypt', and on which all Scottish kings had been crowned.[27]

In the later fourteenth century historiography contributed to the authorisation of this founding myth when John of Fordun, a Scottish priest, 'compiled the first history of the Scottish nation' in 1385.[28] Beginning with the origin of the Scots, he tells of a Greek king living 'in the days of Moses', whose son Gaythelos causes such disruption to his father's kingdom that he is 'driven out by force from his native land' and sails to Egypt where, 'being distinguished by courage and daring, and being of royal birth, he married Scota, the daughter of Pharaoh'.[29] With the downfall of Pharaoh they flee Egypt in the hope of finding 'new lands to settle in, on the uttermost confines of the world, hitherto, as they imagined, unoccupied' (9–10). When they stop in Spain and are plagued by local tribes, Gaythelos sees their suffering as a punishment for not having settled in an empty land:

He perceived that he deserved to suffer the difficulties he had incurred; for . . . he had renounced the design he had originally formed . . . namely to seek out unoccupied lands, without bringing injury upon any one. (12–13)

Eventually his descendants do find Hibernia, which is initially described by John of Fordun as an uninhabited island. However, Fordun becomes as vague on this question of prior habitation as Geoffrey is, adding that '[s]ome, indeed, relate that giants inhabited that island first', while others say that all the inhabitants were slain when Gaythelos' son Hyber claimed the land (14). Fordun concludes that the Scots 'have always had, nearly from the beginning, a distinct kingdom, and a king of their own' (18). The Scots in Ireland multiply and are described as spreading into the 'islands of Albion . . . tenanted by no inhabitants' (24). Scots and Picts intermarry in Albion itself and eventually Fergus, descendant 'of the race of the ancient kings', hears that 'a leaderless tribe of his own nation was wandering through the vast solitudes of Albion, without a ruler' (28) and becomes their first king. All of this is said to have happened long before the arrival of Brutus and Fordun repeatedly emphasises the sovereignty and peace-loving nature of the Scots. He is also careful to explain the division of Albion into the distinct realms of Britannia and Scotia:

This island of Albion, therefore, after the giants, having lost its first name, had, consequently, two names, according to these two divisions, that is, Britannia and Scotia. The first settlers, indeed, in its southern part were Britons, from whom, since that region was first inhabited by them, it got the designation of Britannia. Its northern part, likewise, had Picts and Scots for its first colonizers, and too was afterwards given, in like manner, from the Scots, the name of Scotia. (30–1)

While the Scota myth preceded the Albina myth by several hundred years, both the Scota myth and the Galfridian Brutus myth are derived from the ninth-century *Historia Brittonum* ascribed to Nennius, and there are remarkable similarities between all three myths discussed here.[30]

Perhaps unsurprisingly, given the ubiquity of the trope, all three follow the *translatio studii et imperii* topos, in their migratory stories from east to west, with two of them, the Brutus and Scota myths, positing equally glorious origins for the Britons and Scots. Indeed, the Albina myth reads both like a perfect analogy to and an inversion of the Scota myth: both stories follow the travails of nobles who are turned out of their homeland for causing mischief and threatening authority; but the female founders of Albion are shown to be incorrigibly treacherous, gluttonous and lecherous, while the Scots are portrayed as peaceful and prosperous. Here the Scota myth seems the positive antithesis to the Albina myth: in the former, lawful, patriarchally sanctioned marriage results in noble offspring and political harmony, whereas with Albina, as we have seen, there is pride, rebellion and monstrosity. While in other contemporary, English chronicles this relationship is reversed in that the Scots are the ones depicted as barbaric, this is also done in a manner strongly reminiscent of representations of Albina and the giants. The similarities between the names are suggestive: 'Albina' or 'Albine' and 'Albion' are – in more ways than one – uncomfortably close to 'Albanactus', 'Albany', or 'Alba'.[31]

II

This battle of the chroniclers was renewed (or continued) in the context of sixteenth-century Anglo-Scottish hostilities. Hector Boece, in his 1527 *Chronicles of Scotland*, relates not only the foundation myth of Scota and Gathelus, but also claims that the Scots repeatedly helped the British in their battles against the Romans and the Saxons; assistance which was always repaid with British malevolence and treason. Richard Grafton takes up John Hardyng's *Chronicle*, which includes the Albina myth, and presents it expressly as a weapon to be used against the Scots. The political context for this was already in place, as is seen, for example, in Henry VIII's declaration of 1542 (*A Declaration conteyning the iust causes and consyderacions of this present warre with the Scottis*), which explicitly cites 'Brutus's division of Britain in support of the claim to English sovereignty'.[32]

Grafton states in his dedication that God has sanctioned, '[i]n the right title and querele of England', that the English use their 'stroke as an iron rod / Wherewith to scourge the falsehod of Scotlande'.[33] The Scots, he says, are by nature vicious and false – 'so untowarde / So unstedfast, inconstaunte and unsure' (Dedication ii v). Grafton argues that only their subjection will correct this flawed national character: 'thei will rebel, till by prouision / The kyng of Englande shall haue made them bothe one' (Dedication ii v). Grafton's use of Hardyng builds on the force of precedent and adds its own voice as confirmation of prior knowledge: what Hardyng knew to be true in the fifteenth century – and what was known since at least the twelfth century by English chroniclers – is still true now, concerning both England's right over Scotland and the Scottish native character. The English 'iron rodde of due correccion' (Dedication ii v) will ensure that they are taken in hand; the civilising force of the English must be brought to bear on the Scots, not least for their own good. Left to themselves, they are a quarrelsome and destructive people, like Albina and the giants of Albion: 'Euer sekyng causes of rebellion.' They are, he concludes, a people 'whom

God dooth hate and curse' (Dedication iii r). In this, they are also like
giants.

While the Albina legend was being treated with growing scepticism
in the sixteenth century, the legacy of the giants was kept on, even into
the eighteenth.[34] In the legend one of the sisters' monstrous offspring is
named 'Gogmagog', and as Victor Scherb has shown, 'Gogmagog', passing
from biblical to classical and medieval writings, was a fluid term throughout the Middle Ages and beyond, sometimes referring to 'a single being
(Gogmagog), sometimes separate (Gog and Magog), sometimes ethnic
groups (the races of Gog and Magog), and sometimes lands'.[35] With their
multiple connotations the names 'Gog' and 'Magog' 'functioned as typological metaphors, names that could be appropriated to whatever was alien,
threatening, or actively hostile'. In this role their names 'were at one time or
another attached to the Scythians, Goths, Saracens [and] Jews'.[36] Hardyng's
version, which Grafton is referring to, highlights the giants' essentially perverse, violent and therefore self-destructive nature: 'echone of theim did
other oppresse / That none of theim was left . . . / Of twelue thousande
within a litle date . . .' (chap. vi, fol. ix r). The giants' subhuman ontological
status and their inability to rule themselves lawfully work as justifications
of Brutus's violent colonisation of the land, just as alleged Scottish savagery
and barbarism are used to justify English colonisation. Giants and Scots
share the traits outlined by Gillingham: lack of technology, savagery and
improper sexual behaviour.

The female foundation myth can be read as a precursor explaining and
justifying the Trojan conquest of Albion, as well as conquest and colonisation more generally. The city in particular stands as a symbol of civilisation.
As the fourteenth-century *Anonymous Short English Metrical Chronicle* in
the Auchinleck manuscript states:

> Brut set London ston
> And þis worde he seid riȝt anon
> What kynge þat comes after my day
> Forsothe he segge may
> þat Troy was neuer so faire to se
> So London shall wax after me.[37]

London as new Troy (Trinovantum) is to be read as existing within as well as
continuing an established tradition, symbolising ideal masculine rule, and
therefore associated with law, culture and trade. It is not surprising, then,
that the Scots, like the giants, are not builders of cities: the *Anonymous Short
English Metrical Chronicle* explains all Scottish cities away by claiming that

Hengist built them.[38] If Brutus' rule was already used as proof of English sovereignty over Scotland, then the narrative of his purging of the land of violent, primitive, rebellious and perverse giants who are the offspring of an aristocratic female founding figure who has come from over the sea can be read as further demonstrating the Britons' – and therefore English – cultural superiority, undercutting the Scota myth. The Scottish foundation myth may claim greater antiquity, but original peoples are not, it seems, always desirable. The fact that Albina and her sisters appear to fulfil the demands of *translatio imperii* does not change the fact that they are inherently flawed; arguably they only succeed in translating the *imperii* but not the *studii* from Greece to Albion, therefore making it a garbled or fatally flawed rendition of that trope, which is made visible in their sub-human offspring. The Scots may claim an ancient and noble heritage, but, as the Albina myth shows, this is no guarantee of glory for the descendants.

In the sixteenth century, Albina's story was increasingly derided and dismissed. Edmund Spenser happily refers to the existence of originary giants in his recital of national history in the *Faerie Queene*, but he dismisses the story of Albina as '[t]hat monstrous error'.[39] While the notion of a female founder as well as the fabulous character of the Albina legend undoubtedly caused problems for early modern English historiographers, it was the troubled question of origins *per se* that increasingly exercised them. While Hector Boece was confidently recounting the Scota myth in 1527, Polydore Vergil's attack on the Galfridian version of British history in 1534 sparked a crisis of origins.[40] Precisely at this point, when the veracity of the Albina and Trojan founding myths was being hotly debated, another female British originary figure entered (or, rather, re-entered) national historiography.

The Iceni queen Boudica was rediscovered in the sixteenth century and eventually became a potent and lasting symbol of British national spirit and of British imperialism. Evidence of this can be found in the words of William Cowper (1731–1800), engraved on the statue of Boudica which stands near Westminster Bridge: 'Regions Caesar never knew / Thy posterity shall sway.' Yet in the sixteenth century both Albina and Boudica exemplified what Jodi Mikalachki has called 'the conflicted attitudes towards "their Natives"' in medieval and early modern English historiography.[41] This is not least because the account of Boudica's rebellion was transmitted to sixteenth-century historiographers through classical sources, mainly the writings of Cornelius Tacitus (*c.* 55–120) and Dio Cassius (*c.* 155–235).[42] In England the story of Boudica was made familiar first of all by Polydore Vergil, and it rapidly became a permanent and popular feature in subsequent national histories, such as Raphael Holinshed's *Historie of England*

(1587). Holinshed's account of Boudica, much longer and more detailed than Vergil's, tells the story of how, after the death of Boudica's husband Prasutagus, the Romans take his kingdom, ravish his daughters and, when she challenges their right to do so, flog Boudica publicly.[43] Her ensuing rebellion gets off to a strong start: towns are razed to the ground and thousands of Romans slaughtered. When a host of Britons vastly superior in numbers finds itself opposite the Roman army, victory seems assured. Yet the battlefield chosen by the Roman general Paulinus Suetonius is narrow and the Britons are undisciplined and lacking technology. Their defeat is absolute: Holinshed states that eighty thousand Britons were killed, compared to a mere four hundred Roman casualties. Boudica dies, but the cause of her death remains uncertain.

There are some striking similarities between the Boudica, Albina and Scota myths. Mikalachki reads Holinshed's account as a 'cautionary tale about the dangers of unrestricted female agency and rule'.[44] In this, it echoes the story of Albina. Cohen has suggested that the rudderless boat in which Albina and her sisters are set adrift symbolises 'a state severed from the kind of patriarchal law that Brutus bestows on Britain to ensure that past and future cohere through patrilineage and precedent'.[45] In both cases, originary women and rebellion appear to have an intrinsic and troubling affiliation. Despite his initial sympathy, Holinshed implies that the Britons' acceptance of female rule reveals something disturbingly primitive about their national character. The rebellion is marked by excessive cruelty, which manifests itself most clearly in the Britons' treatment of enemy women, recalling the twelfth-century English descriptions of Scottish attacks:

> They spared neither age nor sex: women of great nobilitie and woorthie fame they tooke and hanged up naked, cutting off their paps, sowed them to their mouthes, that they might seem as if they sucked and fed on them, and thurst them on sharpe stakes. (*The Historie of England*, chapter 12)

On top of this grotesque and savage mimicry of nurturing motherhood, the Britons' gender relations as outlined by Holinshed would have further alienated an early modern English audience: '[the Britons] . . . who also as they haue all other things, so haue they likewise their wiues and children in common, whereby they haue the like audacitie with the men, and no lesse boldnesse in the warres than they' (chapter 11). In this they resemble the Scottish women that Hector Boece praises in his contemporaneous account of the battles between the Scots and the envious heirs of Brutus, pointing out that they were 'even more terrifying than their men, "havand na mercy quhare thay were victorious"'.[46]

Boudica is Amazonian in her martial independence, and Scythia was commonly referred to as the homeland of the Amazons in medieval and early modern sources. Described as noble warriors, the Amazons are nonetheless ultimately tamed by, in turn, Hercules, Achilles and Alexander. Holinshed's account of Boudica and her original Britons recalls once more what Gillingham outlined as the three main characteristics that were believed to demonstrate Celtic barbarism from the twelfth century onwards: a pastoral society, a people viciously cruel and undisciplined in warfare, and 'unnatural' sexual relations and gender behaviour. It also mirrors the defining characteristics of Albina and her sisters, as well as those of their giant offspring. The chroniclers may agree that Boudica has 'iust cause' initially, but the chaos her rebellion causes leads them to argue that she and her followers need to be curbed by the Romans. In this scenario Boudica and the Britons, like the Amazons, represent a feminised savagery that is overcome by the Romans, who act analogously to Hercules, Achilles and Alexander. The Romans come to represent masculine order, as, in the medieval English chronicles, it is represented by Brutus and the English. Like Albina and the Scots, Boudica and her followers are closely associated with the topography of the land: '[T]o us euerie hearbe and root is meat, euerie iuice an oile, all water pleasant wine, and euerie tree an house.'[47] Their razing of London can be read as an attempt to erase Brutus' civilising inscription on the land in order to return to a more 'original' state. In this, they can be read as a threat to the successful continuation of Britain's national history as well as to the survival of Brutus' act of *translatio studii et imperii*. The barbarous heritage, it seems, always threatens to return.[48]

The ongoing tensions and fluctuations between what was perceived as barbarism and what was idealised as civilisation characterised English historiography and the question of English origins throughout the medieval as well as the early modern period. Gillingham sees a knowledge of classical sources as absolutely central to William of Malmesbury's representation of the Celts as barbarians. He argues that this enabled William to '"rediscover" the classical concept of the barbarian, and "discover" that it applied to Celtic peoples in his own day'.[49] In the sixteenth century, English historiographers became concerned with their *own* nation's barbarism as outlined by classical sources. Boudica's proud claim that Britain is like 'an other earth . . . whose name hath beene long kept hid from the wisest of them all' was precisely what was causing early modern historiographers, searching for reliable (increasingly understood to mean 'classical') sources, such a headache.[50] As Vergil pointedly remarks, the story of Brutus and British origins is unreliable without 'cronicles of the Brittons' to refer to, as they

'longe agoe . . . lost all the[ir] bookes . . .'[51] The reason for the obscurity
of English origins, in Vergil's mind, lay not only with the destruction of
native chronicles, but also with the fact that the British 'nation, as it is
placed far from all others . . . was . . . longe unknowne to the Romaines
and the Grecians' (33). Adopting a methodology as well as a history from
a classical tradition that posited the 'original' Britons as colonised barbarians meant that English historians of this period were of necessity adopting
what was arguably not just the viewpoint of the Roman empire, but a more
thoroughly colonising discourse, one in which they necessarily viewed their
own origins and therefore their own heritage as 'other'.[52]

Ultimately, the barbaric other of the medieval English chroniclers and
the barbaric self of the early modern English chroniclers become fused to
serve a teleological progress narrative. Just as the English in the twelfth
century saw themselves as more civilised, more advanced than the Celtic
peoples around them, so the English in the sixteenth saw the Britons as
being at a more 'original' stage of development, one which the English had
long left behind. In this narrative, England is represented as having gone
through the *very necessary* process of colonisation by Rome in its distant
past. This is how Sir Thomas Smith, English secretary of state in the 1540s,
explains it:

[A]s I do understand by histories of thyngs by past . . . this contrey of England,
ones as uncivill as Ireland now is, was by colonies of the Romaynes brought to
understand the lawes and . . . thanncient orders whereof there hath no nacon more
streightly and truly kept the mouldes . . . then we, yea more than thitalians and
Romaynes themselves.[53]

Here the *translatio studii et imperii* trope is used to support the claim
that England has truly become the new Rome – *more* Roman than the
Romans and Italians themselves – and is therefore justified in carrying
the civilising *translatio* into other countries. As Cowper's bellicose words
make clear, Boudica's 'posterity' will 'sway' regions that Caesar himself was
not aware of. At the same time, however, this reading of the trope co-exists
uneasily with its more ambiguous medieval predecessors, suggesting instead
that England has a fundamentally split identity, with barbarous origins
repeatedly popping up to question the success of its own *translatio*.[54]

III

Origin myths were instrumental in medieval and early modern English
colonial ambitions, yet even as they served this function, they also

undermined it. As Fuchs points out in relation to the *translatio studii et imperii* trope, '[w]hat makes the cultural legacy so particularly fascinating is the extent to which it is contested by nations attempting to distinguish themselves from each other even as they claim the same imperial legacy'.[55] The similarities between the Albina and Scota myths meant that they could be read against each other in numerous ambiguous ways, with neither satisfactorily fulfilling its authorising function precisely because of the numerous parallels and overlaps. What John Ganim points out in relation to John of Fordun's nationalist historiography can be applied to both English and Scottish efforts to create authoritative foundation myths: 'Fordun's narrative emerges from an intertextual dialogue with a prior English account, and its frequent modulations and negotiations rest uneasily next to sweeping nationalist claims.'[56] Furthermore, the stubborn presence of originary monsters in early modern English national narratives works against their teleological momentum, for the giants can be read as representing a persisting uncertainty about the legitimacy of a people's claim to the land. Stephen Nichols argues that from the biblical tradition on, '[g]iants embody the forces that resist expansion, conquest, cultivation, and domestication . . . they are an explanation of origins made by cultures that see themselves as invaders or latecomers'.[57] The established nature of the giant's symbolic meanings, as well as the eschatological nature of its biblical contexts, denies the national progress narrative formulated in the sixteenth century. These persistent self-images – either of the barbaric native or of the invading latecomer – ensure that the national identity created is and remains a troubled one.[58] If, as Cohen argues, the figure of the monster in medieval thought, 'living at the margins of the world', has the power to challenge 'traditional methods of organizing knowledge and human experience',[59] then it is perhaps not Albina and her sisters or Boudica and her Britons who represent that 'monstrous error'. Perhaps it is the question of English origins itself.

Exploring national origin through female figures arguably allowed historiographers to articulate – however inadvertently – the ambiguities and fearful uncertainties of writing such histories. While, as Nichols has argued, in medieval thought 'origin is privileged as the moment of essence and purity for both words and their users', this is always disrupted by lingering uncertainties about both 'authentic' written and racial precedents.[60] As the examples of Albina and Boudica show, the writing of, and desire for, English national origins was always haunted by the uncovering of 'disunity' and the unification of 'incompatibilities'.[61] When Boudica summons her people to rebellion, she laments: '[W]e our selues (to saie the trueth) are authors of our owne mischiefe . . .'[62] The bedevilled question of national origins confronted English historiographers and rulers with the benefits and problems of being – and of not being – 'the authors of oure owne mischiefe'.

CHAPTER 7

The colonisation of early Britain on the Jacobean stage

Gordon McMullan

I

Recent essays on *Cymbeline* have chosen to reverse the by now familiar engagement of Shakespeare's last plays with the discourse of colonialism by reading the play alongside *The Tempest* as a colonial text – a text, that is, not of the colonisation of the New World by the English but of Ancient Britain by the Romans. This sets up an inverse thematic link between two plays which, despite their proximity and ostensible similarity as Shakespearean 'late work', are in many obvious ways very different from each other.[1] The representation of colonial relations is complex in both – a complexity which is interrelated, since the example of the Roman colonisation of Britain was cited as a key precedent for English imperialism. As Camden puts it in *Britannia*,

[t]his yoke of the Romanes although it were grievous, yet comfortable it proved and a saving health unto them: for the healthsome light of Iesus Christ shone withal upon the Britans . . . and the brightness of that most glorious Empire, chased away all savage barbarisme from the Britans minds.[2]

The Roman invasion was, for Camden, crucial to the establishment of Britain as a civilised, Christian nation and therefore, despite its rigours and viewed with an appropriate amount of hindsight, an unequivocally good thing. Moreover, its historical value was transferable. Valerie Wayne argues that late sixteenth- and early seventeenth-century English travel literature 'looks back at the colonization of Britain as it advocates moving forward to the colonization of the New World, and the Romans are to the ancient Britons as the English are to the Native Americans'.[3] In this light, *Cymbeline* represents the negotiations of British identity under colonial rule – Innogen is herself Britain, invaded by Roman Giacomo in the darkness of her bedchamber, while Posthumus (like the nation as a whole) discovers his true British identity only by simultaneously absorbing and resisting

Roman civility – and early British history is read in order to make sense of contemporary politics.

Cymbeline has been a troublesome play for Shakespeare critics. Its odd blend of naturalism and stylisation, the curious tone that leaves audiences unsure if they are laughing *with* or *at* the play, the abjection of Innogen, the murder of Cloten by the true princes, the endlessly rehearsed last recognition scene and the awkward capitulation to the Romans at the conclusion have all combined to make critics uncomfortable. Explanations have been sought, and there have been various attempts to ground the play in Jacobean politics – beginning with Emrys Jones's landmark essay noting the play's extension of the Tudor myth by way of repeated references to Milford Haven, the future Henry VII's landing place in Wales, and equating Cymbeline and James as peacemaker kings – but by and large *Cymbeline* continues to be assessed primarily as a 'late play'.[4] Yet reading *Cymbeline* as part of a small group of Shakespearean late plays whose characteristics are assignable to the convergence of a transhistorical mode (late style) and a local obligation (praise of James I) is to ignore the larger issue of the engagement of the Jacobean commercial theatre with the early British past broadly conceived – that is, from the Roman Conquest to the Norman Yoke. *Cymbeline* is in fact neither unique nor bounded purely by the terms of its position late in the Shakespearean canon in its negotiation of early English history; rather it is part of a larger theatrical project to interpret Elizabethan and Jacobean Britain through the reconstruction of a range of different pasts, especially medieval pasts, and it is this larger project that I wish to address.

Since Irving Ribner's account in the 1950s there have been just two surveys of Elizabethan and Jacobean plays with early British settings, Leah Scragg's in her reading of the anonymous *Edmund Ironside* and (though his organisational logic is broader) Benjamin Griffin's in his appendix to *Playing the Past*.[5] In order to develop these accounts and to demonstrate the extent of the engagement of the early modern stage with early Britain in general and with the early medieval in particular, I provide two appendices (see 138–40). The first is a chronology of plays with an early British or Anglo-Saxon setting of some sort (whether historical or mythical); the second is an arrangement of those plays into groupings that indicate their different historical subject-matters. It is immediately apparent that, while plays about early British topics are vastly outnumbered by plays on classical topics or based on classical sources, the subject of early Britain sustained its interest for playwrights right across the reigns of both Elizabeth and James.[6] That interest seems to have come in bursts, to judge at least by the clusters of plays on certain topics, but because of the limitations of the evidence we should be wary of leaping to conclusions. The bunching of plays in the mid to late 1590s addressing the malleable past bounded by the partially historical Hengist and the wholly mythical Uther Pendragon, for instance, rather than marking a politically or historiographically significant moment, may simply be the product of the survival of Henslowe's *Diary*: the bulk of these titles exist only as records of missing Admiral's Men plays of which we would have no evidence were it not for Henslowe, and it may well be that there were plays on these subjects written for other companies of which there is no record. Despite this, however, it seems to me that certain observations can be made about plays with early British settings as an ongoing phenomenon.

One thing these plays manifestly share is their uncertainty about the origins of what James VI and I liked to call Great Britain. Many of them debate the pros and cons of the division of the kingdoms, noting the ongoing threat posed by its neighbours to the aggressive self-determination of the south-east corner of the Atlantic Archipelago. *King Lear*, for us the best-known play to deal with this issue, is in fact only one in a line of plays from *Gorboduc* onwards that deal with the fragmentation of Britain. To the audiences for these plays, the names Albany and Cornwall would have implied not only specific locales but also, synecdochically and proleptically, the associated kingdoms of Scotland and Wales. As Gary Taylor and Michael Warren have argued, Albany, 'the old name for all of Britain north of the Humber, was eventually identified, more loosely, with Scotland'; equally, though Cornwall 'was a separate kingdom until the tenth century, from the fourteenth century the Duke of Cornwall was also always the Prince of Wales, thereby uniting the two western territories under one nobleman' and establishing a conflational shorthand.[7] *Lear* is perhaps an extreme case, but even in a play such as *Nobody and Somebody*, in which they are both uniformly a force for good, the earls of Albany and Cornwall still use the implicit threat of geography and force to manipulate events. All of these plays – even plays such as *Lear* which praise James for healing the division of the kingdoms by occupying the throne of Scotland as well as that of England and Wales – serve to underline the fundamentally divided origins and orientations of 'Great Britain'. J. G. A. Pocock observed in outlining an agenda for the 'New British history' that the term 'British history' 'denotes the historiography of no single nation but of a problematic and uncompleted experiment in the creation and interaction of several nations', and he would find little in early modern dramatic accounts of early Britain to contradict him.[8]

Perhaps the simplest way to see the point reached in the debate over Britain by the time *Cymbeline* was first performed is to look side by side at the frontispieces to two significant Jacobean works of geography (a juxtaposition already familiar to early modern scholars from *Forms of Nationhood*, Richard Helgerson's seminal work on the Elizabethan construction of Englishness): those to John Speed's *Theatre of the Empire of Great Britain* (1611) (fig. 3) and to Michael Drayton's chorographical poem *Poly-Olbion* (1612) (fig. 4).[9] Both appear to support James's project for Great Britain – Speed, as it happens, includes an image of a coin of Cunobelin, or Cymbeline, on his main map of Britain, echoing the peacemaker motif – but both also complicate and undermine that support. Speed presents the reader with five figures from the British past, with one, 'A Britaine', in the commanding position and the other four, 'A Romane', 'A Saxon', 'A Dane' and 'A Norman', arranged below him, suggesting an overarching and ongoing British identity despite the various foreign invasions that took place thereafter. The *Poly-Olbion* frontispiece takes this iconography further, presenting an allegorical personification of Great Britain as a queen who is also a goddess of plenty, complete with sceptre and a cornucopia in place of the orb, a figure whose robe, which is a map of British terrain, associates her directly with the land itself and allows her to replace the tattooed and forbidding-looking Briton at the centre of the Speed frontispiece with an alternative image of peace and fecundity. Around her, as statues on the formal arch within which she sits, are four figures from British history: Brutus, Aeneas' nephew, legendary founder of Britain; Caesar, Roman invader of Britain; Hengist, Saxon invader and king; and William, Norman invader and king. For Helgerson, the location of these figures – and thus the ambitions they represent – 'off at the edge of the frontispiece' indicates that they are being 'pushe[d] . . . to the side': '[m]arginality', he argues, 'is the best they can hope to achieve'.[10] Yet if marginalisation was truly Drayton's aim, it would surely have been easier simply to leave these fragmenting, plurally national figures out of the picture altogether.

What is clear from both illustrations is that Britain was understood to be the product of a series of invasions from overseas – those of Brutus, the Romans, the Saxons, the Danes and the Normans. British history is thus colonial history, an ongoing narrative of the negotiation of national identity in the face of external imposition which does not always view the process of colonisation quite as blithely as proponents of the Virginia venture did the Roman occupation. The theatre responded in a complex way to the advantages and disadvantages of prior occupation, addressing each of the

Fig. 3   John Speed, *Theatre of the Empire of Great Britain* (London, 1611), title page

Fig. 4   Michael Drayton, *Poly-Olbion* (London, 1612), title page

formative invasions. In order to assess that response, I want in the second part of this essay to extend and develop the work of Floyd-Wilson, Wayne and others on *Cymbeline* and the theatrical representation of Roman Britain by taking two of the other occupying nationalities – the Saxons and the Danes – and two of the plays in my list – Thomas Middleton's *Hengist, King of Kent* and Anthony Brewer's rather more obscure *The Love-Sick King*, both dating from fairly late in James's reign – as instances of the Jacobean theatrical engagement with the colonisation of early Britain.

II

I will begin, reversing the order of the history being dramatised, with *The Love-Sick King*. This play, apparently performed in 1617 for James when he passed through Newcastle upon Tyne on progress to Scotland, revisits the subject-matter of the anonymous Elizabethan *Edmund Ironside*, presenting a more complex and fragmented understanding of Englishness than did the earlier play.[11] Where *Ironside* sticks closely to its chronicle sources, *The Love-Sick King* (though showing a clear debt in places to Speed) unashamedly fictionalises, presenting a *dramatis personae* and a plot unrecognisable from the chronicle material.[12] North/south rivalry (embodied in antagonism between the 'true' colliers of the north-east and the cheating charcoal men of Croydon) signifies the absence of a cohering English, never mind British, identity and the southerners show their true colours by inclining towards the Danish (thereby marking the importance of Newcastle within the Jacobean coal industry). A character called Thornton, based on the fifteenth-century Newcastle merchant Roger de Thornton but reshaped by Brewer along the lines of Simon Eyre in Dekker's *Shoemaker's Holiday*, rises from nothing to become the richest Englishman and mayor of Newcastle, flamboyantly fortifying the city out of his own pocket towards the end of the play. The English defeat the Danes, but only just, succeeding in the end for two reasons, firstly because the Danish king Canutus falls for a 'fair English nun', Cartesmunda, who, after resisting virtuously for a while (which of course serves only to provoke him to extravagant lust), becomes his lover and, like a gauche Cleopatra, undermines his military prowess; and secondly because the Scottish king marches south to help the combined force of southerners and Northumbrians to overcome the Danish army – an outcome apparently designed for the command-performance context, implying an early English-Scottish rapport conspicuous by its absence from the chronicles. At the end, King Alured, restored to the throne, fails to execute Canutus because earlier in the play he had fallen in love with the Danish king's sister Elgina, who has since died but who had, when she first met him, declared herself morally if not actually English. Defending the disguised Alured from a Danish officer, she says:

If all the *English* perish, then must I, for I (now know) in *England* here was bred, although descended of the *Danish* blood, King *Hardiknut* my Father, thirty years governed the one half of this famous Kingdom, where I, that time was born an *English* Princess.[13]

Inspired by Elgina's memory, Alured announces that the two nations can be friends as long as the Danes cease to expect tribute and he then abruptly hands the lands between Tweed and Tyne to the Scottish king – an extraordinary move, considering that without the efforts of the Northumbrians Alured would have lost the battle, and only explicable in the context of the royal progress. It also, somewhat ironically, serves to provide instant justification for Thornton's efforts in fortifying Newcastle.

The concluding relationship between the English and the Danes broadly echoes the position the Britons and the Romans reach in *Cymbeline* – Alured's embrace of the Danes is reminiscent of Cymbeline's instruction at the close of the play that 'A Roman and a British ensign wave / Friendly together' as the two armies march through London, though he goes a step further by rejecting the ongoing payment of tribute – to the point that, through Elgina's example, Englishness and Danishness have begun in fact to merge by the close of the play.[14] But the lovely twist here is that underlying this quite careful negotiation of English and Danish identity is a playful – and I think not accidental – choice of source. One of the reasons critics cite for disparaging *The Love-Sick King* (very few have studied the play and even fewer have been impressed) is its lack of historicity – for Madeleine Hope Dodds, the play 'deals very wildly with history and chronology' – especially as regards its entirely fictional characterisation of Canutus himself.[15] There is indeed nothing whatsoever in the chronicles to suggest the plotline in which Cnut falls hopelessly in love with a nun called Cartesmunda to the detriment of his manhood and conquering power (and Cartesmunda's name is of course itself suspiciously playful). It turns out in fact that Brewer did not draw the story from chronicle history at all. He took it from somewhere else entirely – from the story of Mahomet and the fair Irene at the fall of Constantinople, in which the Turkish conqueror, in the midst of sacking the city, comes across a holy maid praying, falls for her, and immediately calls a halt to the violence.[16] This Irene is the 'Hiren' Pistol refers to in one of his outbursts in *2 Henry IV* and would presumably have been known to Brewer from a number of contemporary texts, including a play (now lost) by Peele called *The Turkish Mahomet and Hiren the Fair Greek*, though his demonstrable sources are Richard Knolles's *Generall Historie of the Turke* (1603) and *Hiren: or, The faire Greeke*, a narrative poem by William Barksted dating from 1611, the year of *Cymbeline's* first performance.[17]

The one major change Brewer makes to the story of Mahomet and Irene is to the manner of Cartesmunda's death. Where in the source, Mahomet, chastised for his loss of manhood by a faithful retainer, reclaims his astonishing self-possession and commitment to the cause of conquest by gathering the nobility together and abruptly beheading his lover, in *The Love-Sick King* Canutus – though he announces that 'in strange kind to all your eyes wee'l shew / We can command our self as well as you' (and it is important to remember that 'strange' could mean specifically 'foreign') – lacks the strength of mind to kill Cartesmunda and only does so in the end by accident when his opponent lunges at him and he runs them both through with the same blow. Thereafter, where Mahomet regains his military prowess, Canutus, appalled at what he has done, loses his subsequent battle with the English. Depicting the Dane as a 'stranger', as a 'Turk', Brewer nonetheless pulls back from giving him the exemplary, if atrocious, personal strength of the original. Still, his turn to this particular source inescapably equates the conquering Danes with the conquering Turks and thus sets up two equally difficult possibilities: either Danes, fully alienated, cannot be constituents of Britishness (*pace* the Speed and Drayton frontispieces) or else they are both Turkish *and* British, in which case the British themselves absorb the violent and alien attributes of militaristic Muslims – 'Christians Turn'd Turks' or 'Renegadoes' in the words of two contemporary play-titles.[18]

Not that Jacobean historians cared, by and large, to represent Danishness as a component part of Englishness or Britishness, so perhaps the significance of the double identity set up in *The Love-Sick King* is limited. The Saxons, on the other hand, were seen by some as integral to national identity. For Richard Verstegan, writing in 1605,

Englishmen are descended of German race, & were heertofor generaly called Saxons, and euen vnto this day the Britains which yet retain their ancient habitation in *Cambria* or *Walles* as also in *Cornwall*, & of vs are called welshmen & cornishmen, do not in their own toung call vs Englishmen but Saisons, & our language Saisonaeg, which accordeth to the first and generall name, that our ancestors brought with them out of *Germanie* into *Britaine*.[19]

In this reading, the English *are* Saxons, having driven the British into Wales and Cornwall, converted to Christianity, and become a noble stock.

William Camden, in his *Remains*, echoes this, arguing that once 'this warlike, victorious, stiffe, stowt, and rigorous Nation' had been 'mellowed' by the English air and soil they were 'prepared in fulnes of time for the first spirituall blessing of God'.[20] Mary Floyd-Wilson, noting that Camden's attitude to the Saxons had changed between his *Britannia* and the *Remains*, attributes this to the influence of Verstegan. Together, in Floyd-Wilson's words, they 'fix a line of biological inheritance for the English' which establishes the Saxons as the true precursors of the English.[21]

Thomas Middleton, in his *c.* 1620 play *Hengist, King of Kent*, on the other hand, is having none of this. He depicts the invading Saxons in a way that would have made Verstegan in particular, who saw purely innate qualities in the Saxons where Camden, in his more modulated way, saw potential in their interaction with the English environment over time, very unhappy indeed – though this is hardly surprising, given that Middleton was a militant Protestant and Verstegan a Catholic polemicist, an orientation which underpins his desire to find the roots of Englishness in Continental Europe. The play – which features Ranulph Higden, 'monk of Chester', as Chorus, introducing the action by way of self-consciously archaic dumb shows – begins with Vortiger overthrowing the good but ineffectual Constantius and incurring the wrath of the people. As he casts about for help, an attendant lord appears to announce the convenient arrival of a 'ffleete of valiant saxons newly Landed' and Hengist enters to offer his services. 'We are all my Lord', he says,

> The sons of fortune, she has sent vs forth
> To thriue, by ye redd sweate of o^r owne merritts:
> And since after ye rage of many a tempest
> Our fate has Cast vs vppon Brittaines Boundes
> We offer you ye first ffruites of o^r woundes.[22]

Hengist's men proceed to secure Vortiger's hold on power and we hear a British gentleman comment in awe that 'these saxons bring a fortune wth em / Staines any Romaine success' (2.3.1–2), a neatly modulated assertion which associates the Saxons, whom Vortiger's British faction are treating at face value as highly efficient mercenaries, with the Romans, the first in the historical sequence of invading forces and constituent nations, suggesting that they will prove to be still more effective colonisers than their predecessors and implying, through the resonances of the word 'stains', that their influence will reverse the positive outcomes gleaned in hindsight from Roman colonisation.

Certainly, the play makes it quite clear that the Saxons are pagans and thus thoroughly alien. When Hengist asks for a little land as reward for saving Vortiger, the latter refuses point blank:

> S^r for o^r treasure
> Tis open to yor merits, as our loue,
> But for y'are strangers in religion Cheifly,
> W^{ch} is ye greatest alienation Can bee,
> And breeds most factions in ye bloods of men
> I must not grant yo^u that.   (2.3.33–8)

Faced with this resistance, Hengist proceeds to trick his way into the acquisition of the land he had originally sought as payment and in due course enlarges his holding by a further, murderous deception. In advance of a meeting with the British ruling party at Salisbury, he hands out daggers to his men, to be concealed beneath their clothing. One of them reminds him to give them the code-word that will initiate the coup. 'Thats true', says Hengist, 'the word, I loose my selfe, nemp yor Sexes, / It shall be that' (4.3.35–6). This Old English phrase – from which, in one derivation, the Saxons were thought to have acquired their name and which is the only instance of Old English in the canon of early modern drama – serves to underline the Saxons' foreignness. Hengist, holding Vortiger at knifepoint, makes his demand for power:

HENG: I demand Kent
VORT: Why y'haue ye Earledom on't
HENG: The Kingdome ont I meant, wthout Controll,
    Y^e full possession
VORT: This is strange in you
HENG: It seems y'are not acquainted wth my blood yet
    To Call this strange;
VORT: Never was King of Kent yet
    But who was generall King
HENG: Ile be ye first then,
    Euerything has begining
VORT: No lesse title
HENG: Not if you hope for libertie my Lord.
        (4.3.99–111)

The humour of the lines 'Euerything has begining' and 'It seems y'are not acquainted wth my blood yet / To Call this strange' mocks both Saxon 'Englishness' and the overall idea of national origins as Middleton, like Brewer, demonstrates that one significant constituent component of 'Britishness' – the Saxon – is in fact a form of colonising alien.

I noted early on that a motivating factor in the critical turn to the colonial in recent analyses of *Cymbeline* has been the desire to find a direct, if inverse, connection with another of Shakespeare's late plays, *The Tempest*. *Hengist*, itself late in the Middleton canon, suggests that a quite different form of 'lateness' is in play here – that is, the seventeenth-century sense that history was drawing to a close, that the Reformation and Counter-Reformation signalled the proximity of the endtime at which all disunities, political and ecclesiastical, would be resolved. The last scene of *Hengist* reveals the allegorical significance of the principal characters that has until this last moment been veiled from our sight. This is especially true of the women: Roxena, the daughter of Hengist who becomes Vortiger's queen, is revealed as the Whore of Babylon, female counterpart to the Antichrist, and is finally consumed by fire from heaven. Castiza, Vortiger's first wife, by contrast, disgraced by a vicious take on the familiar bed-trick in which she is kidnapped and raped in darkness by a man she does not realise is in fact her own husband, turns out in the play's last speech to be the proleptic personification of Protestant Truth, celebrated in the speech of the rightful king Aurelius as he praises

> the ffirmness
> Of Truths plantation in this Land for ever,
> Wch always grones vnder som Curse wthout it,
> As I begine my rule with the distruction
> Of this ambitious Pagan, so shall all
> Wth his adulterate faith distaind, and soild,
> Either turne Christians, dye, or liue exild.
>
> (5.2.283–8)

The Saxons have in this final section – which we know from the extant manuscripts but which has been censored out of the published text – become the forces of the Counter-Reformation, as unEnglish as they could possibly be, and Protestant apocalypticism absorbs them into a narrative of the Elect Nation that locates them well beyond the cultural pale. Thus Middleton at the beginning of the Thirty Years War and the opening rounds of the ongoing Spanish Match (which three or four years later he would lampoon superbly in *A Game at Chess*) deliberately turns back to early Britain not only to read Englishness in its origins as the product of colonisation but also to reject those origins as a model for Britain's future by offering an allegory of the threat to England from the Counter-Reformation.[23] *Hengist, King of Kent* thus turns back to a myth of origins, a colonial myth, in order to project an endpoint in the very near future, an endpoint in which there would be neither nations nor conflicts.

III

The contemporary resonances of *Hengist* thus emerge primarily from a sudden and unexpected transformation in our perceptions of the two principal women characters, Castiza and Roxena, and I would argue that this overt gendering of questions of origin is by no means unique in early modern theatre. I want now in the third section of this essay to extend my discussion of Jacobean plays with early British settings by drawing on material addressed by Anke Bernau in her contribution to this collection (see the preceding chapter) in order to consider the dramatic representation of the particular gendered myth of origin she discusses, that is, the story of Albina. I have listed the various plays of which I am aware that engage with Anglo-Saxon or Galfridian history – or, rather, I have listed those plays technically *set* in early times, whether they constitute (as with *Edmund Ironside*) something approaching genuine Anglo-Saxon history or (as with *The Love-Sick King* or with other contemporary plays such as *The Birth of Merlin*) entirely imaginary history either inherited or invented. I am aware, though, that the impact of myths of origin and their connection with early modern colonialism is not apparent only in plays with overt early British settings, and Bernau's material on the Albina myth prompts me to glance at two more Jacobean dramatic texts that lie outside the confines of my list, one briefly, the second at rather more length. The first is a pageant from 1604, *The Triumphs of Reunited Britannia*, in the preface to which, rather clumsily articulating James's pet project for Great Britain, Anthony Munday – to whom Brewer, as it happens, alludes in *The Love-Sick King* – names, so as to exclude, two figures from British mythology because of the rival possibilities they offer to his own preferred derivations for the key words, 'Albion' and 'England':

Concerning the coming hither of Danaus' 50 daughters, and that one of them should be called Albina, and so the land to be named by her: first, not any one of them was so named, neither do I think the story so authentical, but do hold Albion's name for the truest . . . After Brute, I find not any other alternation of our country's name until the reign of King Ecbert, who . . . gave forth an especial edict . . . that it should be named Angles' Land, or Angellandt, for which (in our time) we do pronounce it England. Nor can Hengist the Saxon be the father of this latter name, for Ecbert, because of his ancestors descended from the Angles . . .

called the same after the name of the country from whence he derived his original. So that neither Hengist, nor any qu(een) named Angla, or derivation ab Angulo, is to be allowed before this sound and sure authority.[24]

I have already addressed a theatrical treatment of one of these figures in Hengist and I want now to turn to the way in which the Jacobean stage dealt with his derivational counterpart, Albina.

As Bernau outlines it in her essay, the Albina myth, deriving from an early fourteenth-century Anglo-Norman poem attached to the prose *Brut*, tells the tale of a band of 'beautiful and noble' sisters who are exiled and set adrift on the ocean 'in a rudderless boat' and who

eventually arrive at an uninhabited island, which Albina claims in her own name, as Albion. Here, they live off the fruitful land, hunting venison and living in caves. Their unruly nature is reconfirmed when they give in to their desires once in Albion. Having shunned lawful union with their husbands, they now pursue their desires and copulate with *incubi*, eventually bearing giant offspring who rule Albion for several hundred years until the arrival of Brutus.[25]

The process of conception of the women's children varies from version to version; in one, that of John Hardyng in his *Chronicles*, the women manage to 'impregnate themselves through their own heated and excessively lecherous imagination'.[26] The story thus sees Albion's beginnings as dangerously female, a point of origin which does not augur well for the nation's future until Brutus arrives to reclaim the land for temperate manhood. The Brutus myth was itself viewed fairly sceptically by this time but was nonetheless far preferable to any female myth of origin: as Jodi Mikalachki has argued, early English nationalism involved 'both an exclusion of originary female savagery and a masculine embrace of the civility of empire'.[27] In 1604, Munday acts to type, then, in excising Albina both because of the Jacobean distaste for the absence of gender hierarchies in ancient British culture (the Boudica story being only the best-known instance of British Amazonianism) and because to name the nation after a woman would, as Bernau shows, be unacceptable.[28] At the same time, the self-consciousness of the excision serves the opposite purpose, reminding us of the role of the Albina myth in the construction of English nationalism.

In this context, I want to look closely now not at Munday's pageant but at a King's Men play called *The Sea Voyage*, a Fletcher/Massinger collaboration of 1622 – and thus a play written around the same time as *Hengist* – which displays in its opening moments an overt debt to Shakespeare's late colonial play *The Tempest* – beginning, as it does, with a storm at sea and a shipwreck – but which then moves in a very different direction, eschewing magic and the supernatural to head in a thoroughly material, if imaginative, direction.[29] Because the play is by no means well-known and because plot details are key to the argument I aim to make, I need to offer a brief summary of the action. Driven by a tempest onto a barren island, a group of French venturers led by a pirate, Albert, discover that they are not in fact alone: they encounter two Portuguese men, previously shipwrecked there and hardly recognisable as human beings. The Portuguese, we learn, were displaced from their home by French pirates and separated from their womenfolk by bad weather at sea. They tell the newly arrived French of the lean pickings on the island but also of a wonderfully fecund island nearby across an unpassable gulf. Inspired to learn more, Albert, though injured, braves the channel between the islands and arrives, exhausted, on the far shore, to be greeted by a group of Amazonian women, one of whom, a virgin named Clarinda (a resonant blend of *The Tempest*'s Miranda and Claribel), has never before seen a man and falls for Albert without further ado. Her companions, one of whom has just been describing a lustful dream she had of a 'sweet young man . . . all unbrac'd' who took her 'in his armes and kiss'd [her] twenty times' and who run the island on the model of an originary race of Amazonian natives, start to revive Albert when their matriarch Rosellia, who has vowed lifelong enmity to men, arrives and upbraids them.[30] In the meantime, the Frenchmen on the barren island have stumbled across a pile of gold and begun to fight each other over it, thereby enabling the Portuguese to make off with their ship. Learning of their arrival and faced with the urgent desires of the younger Amazons, Rosellia grudgingly permits interaction with the men, but only (in classical Amazonian fashion) in order to produce girl children, insisting that they return to the men any boys who might be born of their unions. Unsurprisingly, the relations established between the men and the women begins to undermine the purity of the Amazonian society and at the end of the play we discover that the women are in fact the lost wives and daughters of the Portuguese, who return with the French ship, and a reconciliation is effected.

This story emerges, as I have argued elsewhere, from several sources apart from *The Tempest* – from the *Odyssey* (Albert's arrival, soaked and exhausted, at Clarinda's feet on the beach is a parody of the Nausicaa sequence), from Book 5 of *The Faerie Queene* (which provides an account of Amazons as well as a barren/fertile island pairing), from Joseph Hall's *Mundus Alter et Idem* (which offers a further account of Amazons) and from John Nicoll's narrative of colonial shipwreck, *An Houre Glass of Indian News*.[31] Fletcher and Massinger's principal source, however, is William Warner's 1597 'novel' *Syrinx*, whose frame-narrative of disharmony, shipwreck and eventual reconciliation provides the basic storyline. The play, however, reworks Warner's narrative in ways that do not derive from the other sources so far named and which suggest that it is, at least in part, a reinterpretation of the Albina story.[32] In the sections entitled 'Arbaces' with which he begins and ends his narrative, Warner describes the tempest that drives an Assyrian ship under the command of a captain called Sorares onto a barren island and the surprise experienced by the sailors when two apparently monstrous figures, barely 'men in shape', address them.[33] These turn out to be Medes, forced to take refuge on the island years before by the previous generation of Assyrians and all that remain of a larger group destroyed by internecine conflict over a trove of gold. The newly arrived Assyrians, repeating the error of their predecessors, begin to fight over the gold, and the Medes escape with their ship. From here on, the narrative offers a sequence of moral tales, loosely focused on debates over the faith of women, which make up the bulk of the text. In the concluding section, Sorares' sons, who have been searching for him throughout the narrative, land on a 'verye pleasaunt and delectable Iland' and are captured by the forces of a cruel tyranness named Dircilla, who is described as 'armed much to the *Amazonian* fashion . . . more warlike then *Penthesilea*, or rather more terrible then *Bellona* her selfe' (s2r, s2v), but who eventually turns out to be the long-lost wife of one of the Medes, who have by now returned to rescue the Assyrians. Warner's framing story thus provides the plot and a good deal of the detail for Fletcher and Massinger's play: the Assyrians become the French, the Medes the Portuguese, and the outcome, by way of capture by a tyrannical woman stranded long before who turns out to be the wife of one of the protagonists, is identical.

Warner's narrative embraces certain elements of the Albina myth, then, but Fletcher and Massinger turn more directly to that myth – itself dependent upon Amazonian tales – in reshaping certain aspects of the story for the stage. In *Syrinx*, Dircilla is alone when abandoned on the island and she becomes ruler over the island's aboriginal inhabitants, who are not Amazons but a relatively kind-hearted society composed of both men and women; without the Amazons, there are no images of hunting or of archery and there is no equivalent of the erotic dream that excites one of the frustrated, manless women. These are details that derive from a fuller version of the Albina myth than is available in Warner, most probably the account in the medieval *Chronicle* of John Hardyng, as reprinted by Richard Grafton in 1543. Hardyng recounts in detail the story of the daughters of 'Danao / The kyng of Egipte' – the eldest of whom is Albina – who, condemned for murdering their husbands, are

putte in the sea
In shippe to passe echeone fro there countree
As fortune woude, to make there auenture
Whiche by processe, with streames to and fro
And tempestes greate, and sore disauenture
Of sickenes greate and mikell other woo
And moste of all, thei knewe not wether to goo
Till at the laste thei came vnto this isle
That then was waste, as chronicles dooe compile.[34]

Hardyng notes that 'Dame Albyne', the eldest sister, 'gave this Isle a pro-
pre name / Of Albion, out of hir name as chief / And called it so, from
thens forwarde the same' (fol. viii r). He describes how Albina's instructions
enabled the women to survive:

She ordained theim bowes to their relief
Arowes & boltes and bowstrynges made in brief
To slea the dere, the Bull and also the Bore
The Beer and byrdes, that were therin before. . .
Eche daye they made wyttie cheuesaunce
To helpe theim selfe at their necessitee
For hungre, that they should not perished bee.
(fol. viii r–v)

He then notes that once the women had satisfied their hungers and were
'of nature reuigured corporally', they '[h]ad great desyre to playe theim
womanly / . . . And bryng forth frute, the land to rule and led' (fol.
viii v). And he claims (as Bernau notes) that, in the absence of men, the
women managed through the sheer strength of their imaginations and the
intervention of incubi to become pregnant:

So wer they tempted with inwarde meditacio[n]
And vayne glory within theyr hertes implyed
To haue conforte of mennes consolacion
And knewe nothyng, howe of them to prouyde
But inwardly theim they glorified
So hote that spyrites in mannes forme
Laye by theim their desyres to performe.[35]
(fol. viii v)

Hardyng thus provides Fletcher and Massinger with details missing from
Syrinx and allows them to develop the story they drew from Warner into
effective drama.

Interestingly, one place the playwrights would *not* have found a helpful
version of the Albina myth is in the book for which Warner is best known,

his chronicle-history *Albions England* (first published in 1586 and reprinted as recently as 1612), in which he discusses the derivation of 'Albion' (he could hardly do otherwise, considering his chosen title) without mentioning Albina and without offering an actual original for the name:

> . . . [*Brute*], landing here, suppressed so the state
> Of all the fiend-breed *Albinests*, huge Gyants fearce and strong,
> Or race of *Albion Neptuns* Sonne (els some deriue them wrong)
> That of this Isle (un-Scotted yet) he Empire had ere long.[36]

Warner thus slightly awkwardly elides Albina, only returning to the story later when it could safely be displaced into a fictional and geographically alienated narrative. Holinshed, too (a familiar source for Fletcher, who had worked closely from the *Chronicles* when writing *Henry VIII* with Shakespeare shortly after the latter had written *Cymbeline* and *The Tempest*), though he recounts a foundation narrative involving a group of women adrift at sea arriving on an island, is, like Warner and like Munday later, mainly intent on rejecting Albina as the root for the name 'Albion'. He tells the story of the daughters of the Assyrian Danaus, who plot to murder their husbands, describing how they,

left to the mercy of the seas, by hap were brought to the coasts of this Ile then called Albion, wher they tooke land, and in seeking to provide themselves of victuals by pursute of wilde beasts, met with no other inhabitants, than the rude and savage giants mentioned before, whome our historiens for their beastlie kind of life doo call divells. With these monsters did these ladies (finding none other to satisfie the motions of their sensuall lust) ioine in the act of venerie, and ingendred a race of people in proportion nothing differing from their fathers that begat them.[37]

He acknowledges that, in telling this tale, he makes 'no mention of Albina, which should be the eldest of the sisters, of whome this land should also take the name of Albion', but explains the omission as follows:

though we admit that to be true which is rehearsed . . . of the arrival here of those ladies; yet certeine it is that none of them bare the name of Albina, from whome this land might be called Albion . . . So that, whether the historie of their landing here should be true or not, it is all one for the matter concerning the name of this Ile, which undoubtedlie was called Albion, either of Albion the giant . . . or by some other occasion. (A3 v)

Holinshed, then, in the tradition recounted by Bernau, denies Albina her derivational role and minimises the details of the story. Neither he nor Warner provides a workable version of the myth for use by the playwrights, who go against the grain in turning instead to Hardyng's mid-fifteenth-century chronicle. Interweaving that account with its derivative in Warner's

Syrinx and with certain features drawn from Shakespeare's *Tempest*, Fletcher and Massinger write a play which quietly explores a suppressed foundation myth for Britain, transferring it to an early modern colonial context and blending it with Homeric material and with reworked accounts of Amazons that draw resonances both from the classics and from early British culture. To list only plays with *overt* early British settings, it seems, is by no means to delineate the full extent of the early modern theatrical engagement with the question of British origins. Foundation myths also haunt and inform plays with settings that are ostensibly more recent and geographically distant.

A year prior to collaborating on *The Sea Voyage*, Fletcher had already dramatised colonial enterprise in his romantic tragicomedy *The Island Princess*, an account of the alternately violent and erotic encounters between the inhabitants of the Moluccas, the Indonesian 'Spice Islands' of early modern mercantile desire, and Portuguese venturers, turning, as Shankar Raman has argued, to Portuguese colonial material in order to celebrate the belatedly projected dominance of England in Spice Island trade.[38] In writing *The Sea Voyage* with Massinger, Fletcher seems to have turned backward and inward to early British myth in order to make narrative sense of the process of colonisation – dramatising a fertile island with an originary Amazonian history and implicitly acknowledging the reversibility of colonial roles over time best expressed in Theodor De Bry's celebrated observation that 'the Inhabitants of the great Bretannie have bin in times past as sauvage as those of Virginia'.[39] It may well be that *The Sea Voyage*'s barren and fertile islands (mis)represent Ireland and England respectively, arguably obliging us to look back at *The Island Princess* (which also has a basic good/bad island structure in the rivalry between Tidore and Ternata which initiates the action) and recognise in the proud, royal and embattled title character, Quisara, an oblique representation of a quite different island princess rather closer to home, whose negotiations for and evasions of a potentially colonising marriage had intrigued and disturbed her subjects for a substantial part of her reign and whose successor is celebrated in Fletcher and Shakespeare's *Henry VIII* by way of a prophecy spoken at the moment of Elizabeth's christening, as a maker of 'new nations'.[40] However you approach these Jacobean colonial plays, you find that their Portuguese or French (or, for that matter, Amazonian or Indonesian) characters modulate readily enough into English men and women just as the Trojans, Romans, Saxons, Danes and Normans in plays with Anglo-Saxon and early British settings enter into, and multiply constitute, Britishness. Through a careful deployment of source and implication, then, British origins are read

covertly in the early modern theatre as colonial history and contemporary
colonial tensions are rehearsed through myths of foundation.

APPENDIX I: PLAYS WITH EARLY BRITISH SETTINGS, 1560–1625

Date	Playwright	Title	Production context	Publication
1562	Norton and Sackville	*Gorboduc*	Inner Temple	1565
1588	Thomas Hughes et al.	*The Misfortunes of Arthur*	Gray's Inn	1587?
1590	Wilson, Robert (?)	*Fair Em*	Strange's	1593
	Anon.	*King Leir*	unknown	1605
1591	Peele? Greene?	*Locrine*	unknown	1595
1592	Anon.	*A Knack to Know a Knave*	Strange's	1594
1594	Anon.	*King Lud*	Sussex's	lost
	Anon.	*William the Conqueror* (? *Fair Em*?)	Sussex's	lost
	Anon.	*Guthlac* (*Cutlack*)	Admiral's	lost
1595	Anon.	*Edmund Ironside*	unknown	ms
1596	Anon.	*Vortigern* (*Valteger*)	Admiral's	lost
1597	Anon.	*Hardicnut* (revival of earlier play)	Pembroke's/ Admiral's	lost
	Anon.	*Hengist* (revival of earlier play)	Admiral's (same as *Vortigern*?)	lost
	Anon.	*Uther Pendragon*	Admiral's	lost
1598	Chettle, Dekker, Drayton and Wilson	*Earl Godwin & his Three Sons*	Admiral's	lost
	Dekker and Drayton	*Conan, Prince of Cornwall*	Admiral's	lost
	Chettle and Dekker	*The Second Part of Earl Godwin*	Admirals's	lost
	Richard Hathaway	*Arthur, King of England*	Admiral's	lost
	Richard Chettle (?)	*The Conquest of Brute*	Admiral's	lost
	William Rankins	*Mulmutius Dunwallow*	Admiral's	lost
1599	Thomas Dekker	*Old Fortunatus*	Admiral's	1600
	Anon.	*Brute Greenshield*	unknown	lost
1600	William Haughton	*Grim, the Collier of Croydon*	unknown	1662
	William Haughton	*Ferrex and Porrex*	unknown	lost
1602?	Anon.	*Nobody and Somebody*	Queen's	1606
	Charles Massey	*Malcolm, King of Scots*	Nottingham's	lost
1604	Anthony Munday	*The Triumphs of Reunited Britannia*	civic pageant	1605

Date	Playwright	Title	Production context	Publication
1605	William Shakespeare	*King Lear*	King's	1608
1606	Francis Beaumont	*Madon, King of Britain*	unknown	lost (SR 1660)
	William Shakespeare	*Macbeth*	King's	1623
1608	William Rowley	*A Shoemaker a Gentleman*	Queen Anne's	1638
1610/11	William Shakespeare	*Cymbeline*	King's	1623
	John Fletcher	*Bonduca*	King's	1647
1612	R. A. (Robert Armin?)	*The Valiant Welshman*	Prince's	1615
1615	Anon. (T. W.)	*Thorney Abbey*	unknown	1662
1617	Anthony Brewer	*The Love-Sick King*	unknown (Newcastle?)	1655
1619	Thomas Carleton	*Fatum Vortigerni*	Douai	ms
	William Drury	*Aluredus, sive Alfredus*	Douai	1620
1620	Thomas Middleton	*Hengist, King of Kent*	unknown	ms & 1661
	Thomas Carleton	*Emma Angliae Regina*	Douai	lost
1622	William Rowley	*The Birth of Merlin*	Prince's (Curtain)	1662
1623	Thomas Dekker	*The Welsh Ambassador*	Red Bull	ms

APPENDIX 2: PLAYS GROUPED BY HISTORICAL SETTING

Constantine (1591; lost)	Roman Britain
A Shoemaker a Gentleman (1608)	
Cymbeline (1610–11)	
Bonduca (1610/11)	
The Valiant Welshman (1612)	
Gorboduc (1562)	Brutus/Arthur/legendary
The Misfortunes of Arthur (1588)	
King Leir (1590)	
Locrine (1591)	
King Lud (1593–4)	
Guthlac (1594; lost)	
Uther Pendragon (1597; lost)	
Conan, Prince of Cornwall (1598; lost)	
Arthur, King of England (1598; lost)	
The Conquest of Brute (1598; lost)	
Brute Greenshield (1599; lost)	
Ferrex and Porrex (1600; lost)	
The Triumphs of Reunited Britannia (1604)	
Nobody & Somebody (1602?)	

King Lear (1605)
Mador, King of Britain (1606; lost)
The Birth of Merlin (1622)

Vortigern (*Valteger*) (1596; lost)   Hengest/Vortigern (*c.* 450)
Hengist (1597; lost)
Fatum Vortigerni (1619)
Hengist, King of Kent (1620)
The Birth of Merlin (1622)

Old Fortunatus (1599)   Athelstan/Edmund (*c.* 930)
The Welsh Ambassador (1623)

A Knack to Know a Knave (1592)   Edgar/Dunstan (*c.* 960)
Grim, the Collier of Croydon (1600)

Edmund Ironside (1595)   Cnut/Edmund/Ethelred
                                                 (1016)

Hardicanute (1597; lost)
The Love-sick King (1617)
Emma Angliae Regina (1620; lost)

Fair Em (1590)   Norman Conquest
[*William the Conqueror* (1594; lost)]
Earl Godwin & his Three Sons (1598; lost)
The Second Part of Earl Godwin (1598; lost)

Malcolm, King of Scots (1602; lost)   early Scottish
Macbeth (1606)

PART IV

Geography

CHAPTER 8

Tamburlaine, *sacred space, and the heritage of medieval cartography*

Bernhard Klein

Historians of European cartography have grouped medieval maps into three main types: world maps, regional or local maps, and portolan charts (navigational maps of coastlines).[1] Among this triad, the *mappaemundi* (or world maps) have long attracted particular historical interest in the speculative geographic framing of their moral and didactic narratives. Such maps are symbolic in the sense that they provide a myth of origin, a visual history of God's presence in the world, and a theory of salvation; a symbolism dictated by the duty of 'truthful' representation that weighs as heavily on these images as the commitment to mathematical 'accuracy' troubles their early modern successors. Mapping styles show continuity within change: cartographers across history have visually encoded in their maps a human and social address to the world, in accordance with prevailing descriptive conventions, and they have used maps to present in pictorial form a meaningful fusion of spatial and emotive data. By making visible God's master plan for a beleaguered humanity, the *mappamundi* – a common pictorial form in Europe from about the eighth century onwards[2] – made a particularly powerful and 'effective' statement about the emotional investment in human geography. This essay considers the extent to which this 'effect' of medieval maps is owed to their 'affect' – to their emotional impact on notions of self and identity, and to the sense of home and belonging they evoke.[3]

How did early modern mapmakers, in revising the image of the world, negotiate the heritage of medieval cartography? On one level, the answer is simple: it did not bother them. The rediscovery of Ptolemy's classical exposition of geography and map projection gave them a new, seemingly superior paradigm in which they could work, a universal frame for the world picture based on geometric principles that held infinite possibilities for internal variation. One of the most flamboyant spectacles of cartographic hubris in early modern English drama, occurring in the first of Christopher Marlowe's two *Tamburlaine* plays (*c.* 1587/88), makes this point with particular force.

In a memorable scene (discussed in more detail below) Marlowe has his title character Tamburlaine, a cartographer of sorts, eloquently 'confute those blind geographers' that came before him, and dismiss out of hand all maps based on a principle of projection he calls the 'triple regions'[4] – a phrase that applies equally to the traditions of classical and medieval cartography, both of which divided the world into its three continents Asia, Europe and Africa.

But on another level, the discursive violence practised on the medieval world image by both Tamburlaine and early modern cartographers hides deeper anxieties. For one, the makers and readers of early modern maps were acutely conscious of the 'folly' and worldliness of these maps, and of the extent to which their sheer expansiveness transgressed the moral boundaries expressed in such classical injunctions as *Nosce te ipsum*.[5] Another, related source of anxiety, which this essay will be mainly concerned with, is obliquely alluded to in the scene from Marlowe's play. Tamburlaine makes his iconoclastic speech in order to legitimise the sacking of Damascus, including the brutal murder of all its citizens. This bloody act of real violence has its origins, I want to argue, not only in the 'natural' cruelty of a Scythian savage whose transgression of geographic boundaries has unleashed ferocious, barbaric forces on the world around him, but also in his rage over the lingering properties of medieval maps that prove resistant to his aggressive attempt at cartographic erasure.

The affective power of the *mappamundi* which enrages Tamburlaine has two main sources: the intimate relationship it entertains with the human body, and the comfort and community its sacred spaces promise to that body. These residues of an ancient geographic epistemology made the *mappamundi* speak to the map-gazing body in ways that the most widely celebrated successors of medieval world maps – the global images produced under the rubric of a 'New Geography' by early modern cosmographers such as Abraham Ortelius and Gerard Mercator – explicitly refused to do. The disembodied, desacralised and entirely secular spaces of the New Geography were (and still are, of course) a huge and long-lasting success story, but they did not immediately displace the deep-rooted understanding that geography had to serve a moral purpose. As I shall argue below, Tamburlaine's rage is just one indication that the spiritual authority inscribed in the old maps could not simply be suppressed or ignored in the sixteenth century. Here, as in many other examples noted in this volume, the compelling but (in this case) literally 'superficial' impression of radical change obscures the more subtle historical continuities between the medieval and the early modern. For the purposes of this essay, Marlowe's Tamburlaine will exemplify just these contradictions, for as an observer of changes in the early modern landscape he is – like the chorographer John Leland and the antiquarian John Speed, discussed in this volume by Jennifer Summit – a reader of medieval and a maker of modern maps, and his aggression and geographic *furor* suggest a related (if very differently articulated) desire to break through the perceived limitations of a moralised medieval geography.

I VERSIONS OF SACRED SPACE

To get a measure of just what was at stake in Tamburlaine's assaults on medieval geography, we need to briefly consider the meanings of sacred space. The phrase is no retrospective imposition, for the sacred begins with its spatialisation. The word *sanctum*, 'holy ground', refers to what is set apart, 'consecrated', for religious purposes; the word thus denotes a specific place that is delimited, enclosed, spiritually encompassed, hence sacralised and rendered inviolable. The word *profane* technically describes what lies before and outside the *fanum*, the sacred zone. The opposition between sacred and profane, which Durkheim elevated into the defining characteristic of religious thought,[6] thus has to be imagined, in the first instance, as a clash of differently conceived spatial entities. Historically, the principal impulse to declare (or dedicate) space as sacred appears to have been the experience of order arising out of primeval chaos. When rough land assumed shape and structure, when visible order was carved out of the surrounding wilderness, the resulting territorial pattern was human insofar as it was accommodating to man, and divine insofar as it suggested the imprint of God's will to order on the wild and inhospitable surface of the earth.

The emphasis on human habitation is central in this context, for sacred space is in a very immediate sense keyed to the human body. Sacred sites emerge at the intersection of man and landscape, of body and world. They are places that can be visited, literally walked into. To sacralise space is thus to map the earth on a human scale, to index the divine within the intimate reach of the body. This conceptual centrality of the body is mirrored by the directional centrality of sacred sites. Sacred space is nearly always centripetal in its gravitational pull, pointing inwards to some imagined core or privileged interiority. (By contrast, *representations* of sacred space – whether visual or textual – are centrifugal in character, urging the viewer or reader to rise and start the pilgrimage.) The *omphalos* stone at Delphi, the 'navel of the earth', or the city of Jerusalem – 'set', according to Ezekiel 5:5, 'in the midst of the nations and countries that are round about her' – are just two related expressions of the typically centred structures of the sacred, also characteristic of such exalted toponyms as *China*, the 'Middle Kingdom'; *Samoa*, the 'centre of the world'; the *Mediterranean*, the 'middle of the earth'; or of such body-bound geographic fantasies as the *umbilicus urbis Romae*, the civic 'umbilical cord' of the Roman Forum.

Specifically localised sacred sites were always *hauts lieux* distinguished from their profane surroundings by acting as sources of revelation. They were governed by a logic of exchange that fashioned them as sites and rites of passage, places that offered access to a higher cosmic order, implying a proximity, even presence, of the Divine. The form of this access has been variously imagined as a tree, a ladder, a pole: variations of the *axis mundi*. The heightened intensity and concentrated energy of these places also made them, literally, into *landmarks*, fixed nodal points in a matrix of (moral and spatial) *orientation*. In Christianity, sacred places have also been perceived – historically in roughly that order – as sites of memory, wonder and mercy: they resonate with the memory of some great historical deed, with the wonder that a place so infused with spiritual energy can still perform, and with the mercy locally available for the pilgrim willing to undergo the hardship of travel.

There is another, more global sense of a sacred spatiality, prominent in medieval times and principally geographic in essence. The world, as the work of the gods, is itself a sacred place; and the divine effort is visible in the particular territorial layout of the earth, in the internal relationship of its constituent geographic parts: this is the sacred idea of the *oikumene* in its original meaning of the 'house-world' with different rooms (i.e. continents). It is an idea that is recorded in graphic simplicity on the ancient TO-maps associated since the sixth century AD with Isidore of Seville – on which the T inside the O divides the world into its three constituent parts, 'houses' or continents – and in far greater visual complexity on the late medieval *mappaemundi*. As this framework offered – in its various adaptations – an explanation of man's place in the world, it also protected the sacred core of the haven or home: the bodily comfort zone. It is this divinely sanctioned geography that a character in the second *Tamburlaine* play – significantly, a non-Christian – evokes as he appeals to the justice of the Christian deity:

> . . . he that sits on high and never sleeps,
> Nor in one place is circumscriptible,
> But everywhere fills every continent
> With strange infusion of his sacred vigour . . .
>   (2 *Tamburlaine*; 2.2.49–52)

The 'strange infusion' is the numinous quality that defines all sacred space as inhabited by the divine spirit, as suffused by a transcendental presence. As a concept, 'numinous' here is owed to Rudolf Otto, whose pioneering description of the sacred singled out precisely this quality as its defining characteristic.[7] In Marlowe's play it is a Muslim who addresses these words directly and deliberately to the Christian God, appealing to his divine justice and asking him to punish one of his own followers as a traitor (Sigismund, the King of Hungary). Though this shaming of Christians by non-Christians is a fairly conventional trope (which Marlowe culled straight from one of his sources),[8] it draws attention to what Alan Sinfield has called 'the disorderly concatenation of classical, Christian, and Islamic religious terminology'[9] so prominent in the play. It might also serve simply as a reminder that the notion of sacred space is not unique to the Judaeo-Christian traditions. Most religions, most cultures, have organised their self-image around spaces and sites defined in some form as set apart from the rest, removed from the everyday flow of time and the world.[10]

II   THE SCOURGE OF GOD

The evocation in these lines just quoted, of the world as a structured whole, an 'everywhere' inclusive of 'every continent', in conjunction with a ubiquitous (and hence placeless) God who cannot be 'circumscripted in one place', is characteristic of the global ambitions of the play's central character. The biographical tradition on which Marlowe drew – widely available in several Elizabethan retellings – shows 'Timur the Lame', the original Tamburlaine, 'as a meteoric figure, embodying sheer will, "symbolising the naked fanaticism of expanding power, the lust and horror of destruction"'.[11] The purveyors of the legend that Marlowe consulted – especially Whetstone and Perondinus[12] – all seem daunted by this figure, never knowing 'whether to praise him for his military prowess . . . be grateful to him for defeating a contemporary other (the Turk), reverence him as the living sign of God's displeasure, or shudder at his appalling ferocity'.[13] The awe that Tamburlaine evokes in his followers and opponents bears a close similarity to the nature of the sacred as described by Otto: a *mysterium* that is dreadful or terrible, *tremendum*, as well as uniquely attractive, *fascinans*, and an experience of overpowering *majestas*: imperious majesty, allure, fascination. For his fellow stage characters as well as for his readers, the response to Tamburlaine is divided; he commands our admiration even while exciting terror and revulsion.[14]

These responses are, in the first instance, provoked by Tamburlaine's extreme violence and his shocking contempt of everyone and everything that stands in his way, but also, importantly, by his geographical excess and violations of the sacred. The 'scourge of God' (as Tamburlaine is referred to repeatedly by himself and others, quoting Isaiah 10:26) imagines himself rhetorically outside all temporal and spatial constraints, the founder of a new world order, who indulges in wild fantasies of conquest. Conquest appears in many forms in the play – military, rhetorical, sexual, but especially spatial. Most prominently, it expresses itself as a form of cartographic conquest. Tamburlaine himself is a maker of maps, an 'arbiter of meridians',[15] the creator of global cartographies. His maps are chiefly rhetorical, as in the scene briefly referred to above, when he wants to topple the 'blind geographers / That make a triple region in the world' (1 Tamburlaine, 4.4.81–2), suggesting with this ex-orbitant (and hence blasphemous) conceit that he will map regions outside the world's natural orbit, spaces that neither man nor God have ever even heard of. They are also physical, especially when he appears in front of a world map at the end of the second play, to survey what technically amounts to the failure of his outrageous ambitions, when he almost despairs – shortly before his final demise – at the sight of all the spaces he must now leave unconquered (2 Tamburlaine, 5.3.151).

Tamburlaine prides himself on the modernity of his maps, and his dismissal of the 'blind' medieval geographers is clearly conceived as a deliberate attack on the symbolism of the mappamundi and the notional centrality of its sacred space: by first destroying Damascus, a sacred centre he does not respect, and by then reducing it to a geometric fantasy, a purely virtual 'point / that shall begin the perpendicular' (1 Tamburlaine, 4.4.87–8), he openly defies all ruling deities by anchoring the map of the world in a centre entirely of his own choosing. Yet in spite of the swagger and audacity of his rhetoric, it is precisely this verbal assault on medieval maps that shows him still in the grip of just the geographic symbolism he tries so hard to displace. His reference to a 'point' or centre implies that he is not at all in command of the decentred, flattened out spaces of the sixteenth-century planisphere but trapped within a cartographic paradigm that still relied on notional centres or 'points' – which the TO-maps and mappaemundi assumed must exist in the world, but not the New Geography.[16] His mention of the 'triple regions' is a similarly ambiguous moment: the self-conscious foregrounding of the ancient model against which his new map is defined only betrays the lack of confidence in the qualities of its innovations.

Most notably, the retrograde element in his cartographic thinking is revealed in his exchange with Zenocrate, the abducted Asian princess suffering from Stockholm syndrome, who learns to love her captor. It is Zenocrate who prompts Tamburlaine's rant against 'blind' geographers in the first place when she pleads with him to spare Damascus. In making this request, Zenocrate evokes the city as the town of her father – as a family home, in other words: an accumulation of intimate bodies. She does not see it as Tamburlaine sees it, as a mere point in the map. Importantly, though, it is through the violent erasure, the brutal killing, of all the city's bodies – rather than through the destruction of its buildings – that Tamburlaine frees the map for his 'perpendicular', or vertical line, the new imperial meridian. Thus, even though he ignores Zenocrate's plea to save the father-city and refuses to acknowledge Damascus as a social rather than a virtual reality, he responds in his actions to her implicit understanding of physical space as a world made up of bodies. On all three counts, then – in the anchoring of the map in a visual centre; in the continued emphasis on a tripartite world; and in the equation of space with the bodies that inhabit it – he shows himself still under the spell of the geographical paradigm he openly rejects.

III   MAP, WORLD, BODY

The links between the geographical musings in the *Tamburlaine* plays and Mercator's New Geography are thus more critically inflected than the title character, who loudly advertises these links, wants us to think. We know, of course, that in writing *Tamburlaine* Marlowe was working from a copy of Abraham Ortelius' 1570 world atlas *Theatrum Orbis Terrarum*, and that whole speeches are based on the toponyms he found there in individual maps.[17] But if Tamburlaine was devised as a particularly aggressive implied reader of the early modern atlas – and by further implication, as a commentator on the medieval geography that these atlases consciously attempted to supplant – he also reminded his audience of the risks and difficulties involved in the attempt to overcome the authority of the ancient world with its limits, boundaries, and moral strictures on movement and freedom of access. The intensity of his rage certainly suggests that these limits are by no means as effortlessly transgressed, or removed from the map, as he repeatedly claims they are.

Just how radical a break with the medieval past the New Geography promoted in works such as Ortelius' 1570 *Theatrum* becomes especially apparent in its reconfiguration of the relationship between body and map.

Fig. 5   The Hereford *mappamundi* (*c.* 1290)

What appears obvious in Tamburlaine's spatial mastery is his utter disregard for any possible divine inscription in the spaces he simply annexes, annihilates, or otherwise refashions as his fancy takes him. Such an interference with world geography would have been a literally unthinkable response to the medieval *mappaemundi*, on which spaces are epistemologically fixed, locked in 'houses' or parts of the body of Christ. The value of the sacred frame of such images – the body of Christ – far supersedes the relevance of any particular place within the map, as is evident from the carelessness that led the cartographer of the Hereford *mappamundi* (fig. 5) to reverse the toponyms Africa and Europe, attributing them to the wrong continents. Another famous example of such maps, the thirteenth-century Ebstorf *mappamundi* (which was destroyed in World War II), made the point even more strongly by adding small drawings of Christ's head, hands and feet at the four cardinal directions of the image.

Medieval world maps of this kind are less wayfinding tools than visualised narratives of the sacred, pictorial encyclopaedias of geographical and biblical knowledge, which speak directly and immediately to the map viewer or potential pilgrim.[18] Indeed, the frame of the *mappamundi* defines the relation between the world on display and the human body gazing at it in a way that emphasises the primordial character of this link. The body is not only used as a defining structural principle of the world picture, it is also in a very immediate sense the whole point of the image to give this body shelter. The *imago mundi* constructed by such maps, John Gillies writes, 'glows with affect'.[19] The world on display is a sacred place that energises the body, enwraps it by manifestations of the divine. It also invites all human bodies to share a common home, binds them together into social groups, and is thus centrally engaged in the work of community-building and preservation.[20] This is even more apparent when we consider where such images were to be found: they were hung in churches, in public places where many bodies congregated for communal worship, thus defining both their own self and their community through a literal performance of sacred space.

Early modern versions of the world map were no longer found in churches but most commonly in private homes (fig. 6). Here a new definition of the nexus between body and map emerges. The invisible body in front of the map is recast as the omniscient, all-seeing observer, but in the image itself the body no longer plays a constitutive part. Space produces meaning in relation to the external world entirely within its own representational orbit and without any reference to the body. Human corporeality is literally relegated or emptied from the new world picture.[21] The visual result is a decentred image that encodes placelessness, the loss of home and orientation, the surrender of cartographic affect. On the *mappamundi* the body was not only the model or frame for the space of the globe, it was also its natural extension and first addressee, to whom it offered comfort and a sense of home. It is this comfort of the body and all its associated features – identity, self-knowledge, belonging – which disappears from the global image in early modern times, and which comes most under threat in Tamburlaine's world-shattering rampage.

Seen in direct relation to their cartographic source, the two plays offer a disturbing comment on the implications of the new map of the world. As they progressively widen their geographical scope, Tamburlaine's fury only increases, generating images of a disembodied and desacralised landscape

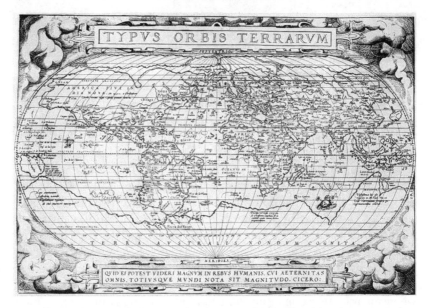

Fig. 6   Abraham Ortelius, 'Typus Orbis Terrarum' (1570)

that has lost all regard for authority or tradition. This space is as inhuman as the Scythian shepherd himself who 'was never sprung of human race' (*1 Tamburlaine*, 2.6.11). It is a world where only kings and princes reach up high enough to be visible to the human eye, a world which no longer caters for the body that once enjoyed its comforting hospitality. Significantly, when Tamburlaine imagines himself as a god on equal terms with the reigning deity, he strips himself of his body, carrying his crusade to celestial heights, 'dissevered from this flesh' (*2 Tamburlaine*, 4.3.132).

Theatre and atlas suggestively converge at such junctures, both in hubris and in visionary force. The power of cartography to propel viewers, Tamburlaine-like, into imaginary space on bodiless, ethereal flights was noted by many contemporaries, who could see nothing unusual in the close conceptual affinity between map and stage.[22] The analogy is persuasive but not without its limits: while the stage is defined through the physical *presence* of bodies, the new map trades on their *absence*. Indeed, Marlowe's plays are hardly as seamlessly mapped on to Ortelius' atlas as Tamburlaine's confidence in his own, god-like omnipotence suggests. In the long dramatic action, the flesh is never transcended or 'dissevered', except finally in death. In image and hyperbole, the cartographic fantasies are indulged to the full, but for the human actors on a narrow stage, they remain dream visions of the *Theatrum Orbis Terrarum*, elusive 'idols of the theatre'. Of course, theatre audiences across time have gladly accepted the illusion, but even within the imaginative logic of the dramatic fantasy, Tamburlaine illustrates nothing more powerfully than the wide gap between his high-flying, atlas-fuelled, flesh-transcending rhetoric and the dead weight of his own body. Rather than championing the cause of the modern map, the whole play might be seen to expose its incomparable folly, showing up the human loss incurred in Tamburlaine's arrogant rejection of the body-centred *mappamundi*. These ironies are most fully explored in the final scene of the play, but before turning to that concluding moment I want to briefly evoke one further context and suggest that a similarly divided response to the New Geography, one that qualifies the belief in its supreme value with an unease about its moral implications, characterises instances in which the new-fangled map was made to serve a timeless religious purpose.

IV   RELIGION AND CARTOGRAPHY

The desacralising impulse the play inherits from the new world map might suggest a growing divide between modern cartography and contemporary religious thinking, but this does not appear to have been broadly the case. One relevant observation in this context is the increasing use of maps or map images in bibles printed in the sixteenth century, especially by Protestant printers.[23] The emphasis on individual conscience in the reformed faith meant that geographical illustrations were accepted as useful guides to a better understanding of the biblical narrative. However, most of these maps or map images – and many of these are not plans, but perspectives, picture maps, or 'views', which imply a ground-level observer subject to the limitations of human eyesight, not the cartographic omniscience encoded in the geometric map – were inserted into bibles in tight explanatory contexts, where the surrounding sacred narrative dominated and contained the geographical image. These were not the spatial explosives that blew up old pieties on every page of the *Tamburlaine* plays. Despite their hesitant acceptance, scale-maps remained suspect to theology, introducing alien ideas, and affording views on the globe naturally reserved for the divine gaze.

Heinrich Bünting's *Itinerarium totius sacrae scripturae*, 'All the Travels of the Holy Scripture', might serve as an example here. First published in German in 1581, the book was quickly translated into English and other

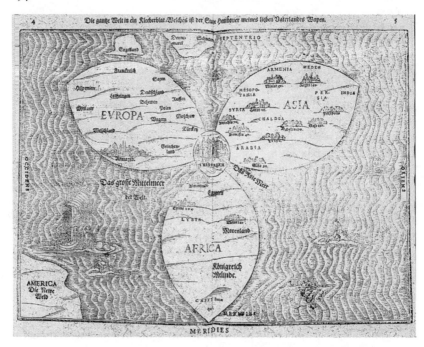

Fig. 7   Heinrich Bünting: the world in form of a shamrock (1581)

European languages, remaining in print for several decades. It is a curious amalgam of modern travelogue and biblical exegesis, translating (as
the title-page of the English edition announces) the 'Trauels of the Holy
Patriarchs, Prophets, Iudges, Kings', and indeed of 'our Sauior Christ, and
his Apostles, as they are related in the Old and New Testaments',[24] into
the modern cartographic idiom of longitude and latitude, direction, angle,
perspective, distance. To serve this purpose, the travel sections are accompanied by treatises on the 'Weights, Monies, and Measures mentioned in
the Scriptures',[25] already converted into local standards, and thus adapted
to the different national contexts and potential markets where the book
circulated in its many translations.

Typically, a straightforward historical and geographical description of
a particular place is followed up by Bünting with an exposition of its
spiritual or allegorical meaning. From the early editions onwards, the book
contained maps, including a rather eccentric depiction of the world in the
form of a shamrock (fig. 7). Bünting explained that it was in honour of his
native city, Hannover, which carries a shamrock in its coat of arms, that
he used this particular conceit, but the whole idea is owed of course to the

ancient partition of the world into the 'triple regions' that we have seen Tamburlaine railing against – the same kind of narrow, trinitarian world encoded in the medieval TO-maps.

This map might serve as evidence that the ancient idea, so central to medieval cartography, of the world as a house with separate rooms, and its sacred centre at Jerusalem (the hearth, so to speak), together with all the associated symbolic resonances of orientation, fixity of centre, belonging and rootedness of identity, still carried enough persuasive power to challenge the wild visual innovations of the New Geography. Significantly in this context, in the preface to the original German edition Bünting refers to himself and his readers as God's 'housemates'.[26] In a move typical of sixteenth-century cosmographical works, which often paraded ancient and modern images of the world side by side, Bünting added a second world map – 'the actual and truthful shape of the earth and the sea'[27] – based on geometric representation and, like the shamrock map, making a hesitant gesture towards the New World by including it as a featureless blob of land in the bottom left-hand corner of the image. But this map is added almost as an afterthought, and in its graphic simplicity follows the symbolic shamrock map, rather than invoking the New Geography. 'Home' and 'belonging' remained properties of the ancient discourse of 'triple regions'.

Not all early modern mapmakers that turned to religious themes articulated their continued faith in medieval cartography quite so openly. Jodocus Hondius' *Christian Knight Map of the World*, printed in 1596 (fig. 8), combines in visually complex terms the modern world map and the deeply moralised Christian narrative inherited from medieval times. The geographical information depicted here is as up to date as on any world map of the time. But the scene along the bottom of the image tells a much older story. Here we can see the Christian Knight, 'armed with the Sword of the Spirit, the Shield of Faith, and the Helmet of Salvation',[28] ready to take on (from right to left) Death, the Devil, Flesh, Sin and the World itself. That an allegorical 'Mundus' should be included here surely requires an explanation, for this pits a negative, anthropomorphised image of the world – in its guise as 'Lady World', or worldly temptation – against a geometric and entirely affirmative representation of the very same thing: the world. One explanation that has been put forward emphasises the split character of the New Geography as a whole, which was divided against itself, and which continued to be haunted, even while it celebrated the modern in maps and atlases, by the ancient moralising discourse of *contemptus mundi*.[29]

Are there shades of a conqueror-figure like Tamburlaine in the Christian Knight? Though his armour and the drawn sword, if taken literally

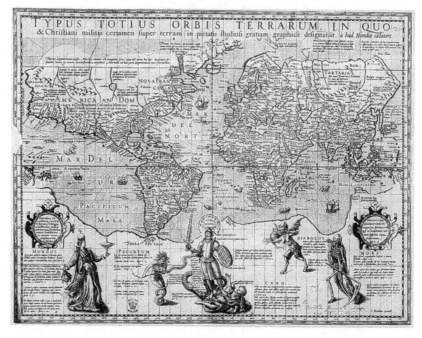

Fig. 8 Jodocus Hondius, 'The Christian Knight Map of the World' (1596)

rather than allegorically, might superficially suggest this, a direct equation is surely untenable. Far more relevant is the juxtaposition on this map of two different world views that have to coexist within the same representational frame: one moralistic, body-bound, almost tribal, the other heady, intellectual, geometric. If the former suggests the *mappamundi*, the latter is the province of the New Geography. The two are hardly reconciled in this image: they are made to clash. And it is not as if the conventions of medieval allegory are evoked only to be dismissed, for it is his moral armour alone that the Christian Knight can rely on for his protection. This makes the scenario all the more precarious, given that the real challenge to religious man seems to be not so much the traditional seductiveness of Lady World and all the sinful temptations she represents but the unprecedented seductiveness of the sheer intoxicating expanse of the globe – making the knight's head (as is perhaps visually suggested by the curious halo) almost spin in response. The Christian Knight must make sense of a world that is overwhelming in its vastness, dangerously attractive in its visual pull, and purged of its sacred coordinates. That might be where the Tamburlaine effect is indeed present on this map: in the cartographic vortex that threatens to suck the Christian Knight into a geographical dynamism that will dislodge him, eject him, from his spiritual home.

V   THE DISLODGED BODY

Such moments of dislodging or ejection – whether from home, field, church or any type of sacred place – have wider contemporary resonances, of course. As Jennifer Summit shows in the next chapter in this volume, the English Reformation was driven by a distinct desacralising impulse in its assault on monasteries, churches and other holy sites. Dislodgings of a different kind took place all over the English countryside, where the new economy commodified rural space, pushed it away from a feudal system of mutual obligations towards the open market, and thus severed the ancient links between people and land. I have suggested in this essay that as an aggressive and violent defender of a newly globalised and 'virtual' space, Tamburlaine is heavily implicated in these dislodgings and ejections. But in spite of ten acts of seemingly unstoppable carnage and spatial disembodiment, not even he can *fully* annihilate the human corporeality encoded in the medieval map, or obliterate from its visual surface all traces of man's spiritual home – in the same way that neither Bünting nor Hondius could or would simply eliminate old world meanings and morals from their maps.

On the stage, the continued centrality of the body to all spatial imaginings is affirmed – even as that body is finally ejected – when the dying Tamburlaine collides with a world map at the end of the play. The corporeality of the medieval map could not be more subtly redeemed than by ending Tamburlaine's violent dream of an empire of maps with this huge clash in scale between a global fantasy and a local body. The confrontation suggests that the modern world map – Tamburlaine's global theatre of conquest – can be seen to hide or obscure (perhaps protect) rather than to fully erase the presence of bodies within the spaces it depicts. The body may have left no *visible* traces on the post-Ortelian world map, having been removed to a viewing position beyond the frame, only to be formally reintroduced – originally on Dutch pictorial maps appearing in the 1590s – in the form of marginal portraits that further consolidate the split between people and land.[30] Yet the body is still notionally there, leading some kind of subterranean, subliminal existence; for instance, in the individual, particularised toponyms spread over its surface, mini-narratives of human experience and history, that even as they are rewritten or 'silenced'[31] live on in the historical memory and spatial practice of the people. Maps are still, and have always been, used by both locals and strangers, opening up spaces of experience and experiment beyond the map which even the most resolutely imperious cartography can never fully occlude.[32] Marlowe, by making these spaces elude his hero in the end, may have been more aware of this than most.

Critical readings of maps that explain their 'power'[33] in terms of the visual transformation of lived spaces into sterile, depopulated and uniform images have, of course, become familiar in recent times. By hiding the human investment in place, the argument runs, the modern world map allows itself to be appropriated for all kinds of purposes, political and otherwise, precisely because the universalising – or globalising – appeal embedded in its visual rhetoric effaces the attention to detail and particularity. In a way, the argument can be turned against both cartographic traditions I have touched on in this essay, the *mappamundi* and the New Geography. Both are universalising in the sense of forcing discursive homogeneity onto the world, and both turn a blind eye to the particularity of place and its human or social dimension.

But only the latter consciously writes the body off the map as a superfluous adjunct of its desacralised space, turning the vast empty planes of the new world image into a fantasy of mental possession. The lesson that lingers on from medieval maps – that this fantasy will always be frustrated on the material level – is perhaps the real reason for Tamburlaine's mourning at the end of the play: maybe his final tears are not so much shed over the immense spaces he must now leave 'unconquered' (2 *Tamburlaine*, 5.3.151, 159), but over the realisation that the world map he has created and before which he now expires ultimately dislodges everyone, including the 'scourge of God'. Even world conquerors have only particular bodies. In the play, the reminder that all bodies, including Tamburlaine's, will fade away not in virtual space but in a particular place with a particular history, puts a final human perspective on the early modern globalising discourse of the New Geography.

CHAPTER 9

Leland's Itinerary *and the remains of the medieval past*

Jennifer Summit

John Leland's *Itinerary*, a work once obscure to all but antiquarian readers, has experienced a resurgence of attention in recent years, thanks to rising scholarly interest in Renaissance geography.[1] By many accounts, Leland's was the inaugural work of Renaissance geography in England, spurred on by a set of exceptional historical circumstances: in the early years of the English Reformation Leland was personally employed by Henry VIII to survey the holdings of the newly dissolved monastic libraries, which gave him the opportunity 'to se throughlye all those partes of thys your opulent and ample realme', as he wrote to his royal patron. Touring the English countryside, Leland carefully noted each topographical feature and landmark with the intention of creating a magnificent map, in which he promised Henry, 'yowr grace shaul have ready knowledge at the firste sighte of many right delectable, fruteful, and necessary pleasures, by the contemplation therof, as often as occasion shaul move yow to the sight of it'.[2] To that map Leland proposed to append 'an history, to the which I entende to ascribe this title, De Antiquitate Britannica, or els Civilis Historia' to be separated into books by 'shires . . . whereof eche one severally shaul conteyne the beginninges, encreaces, and memorable actes of the chief tounes and castelles of the province allotted to hit' (xlii). The letter describes a massive geographical and historical enterprise that is well suited to the nation-building aims of Henry's Reformation. But before he could complete his mission, Leland went mad, leaving behind a multivolume set of fragmentary and sometimes illegible manuscript notes that would be collected by early modern antiquarians and eventually preserved in the Bodleian, where they remained unpublished until the Bodleian librarian Thomas Hearne's nine-volume edition of 1710–12.[3] Despite their obscurity, Leland's manuscript notes became a treasure trove for later Elizabethan and Jacobean geographical writers, whose published works – which include the maps Leland envisioned but never saw completed – have been seen as the fulfilment of Leland's patriotic project. Camden's *Britannia*, writes

F. J. Levy, 'is the book that Leland might have written', not only in its attempt to conceive the nation as a geographical entity, but also in its effort to give that nation a history – one that is, like Leland's, divided by county.[4] Indeed, Camden appears to claim Leland's mantle for himself, invoking the title of Leland's proposed 'De Antiquitate Britannica' by proclaiming in the famous maxim opening the *Britannia*, 'I would restore antiquity to Britaine, and Britain to his antiquity.'[5] Camden's statement has long been taken to signal his intention to recover a specifically classical past – a goal that has been similarly projected backwards, through Camden, to Leland. Read through Camden and his contemporaries, Leland's work becomes a proto-Renaissance project whose ultimate incompletion owes as much to its author's incapacity as it does to that of its age, in which limited historical knowledge and geographical scholarship made the ambitious work impossible to realise until the antiquarian movement of the later sixteenth and seventeenth centuries.[6] But this essay rethinks the relationship between Leland and his Elizabethan and Jacobean followers by reversing the direction of influence. Rather than establishing Leland's proto-Renaissance credentials, I find that Camden's and other early modern geographers' uses of Leland reveal the persistence of the religious and political concerns that formed Leland's immediate context in the 1530s and 1540s. This point redefines the historical investments of early modern geography by making them the product less of Renaissance than of Reformation – less, that is, of a newly awakened, classicised self-consciousness than of an ongoing, politically driven struggle to redefine and contain the nation's own medieval past.

The geographical project identified with the Renaissance has been called 'the discovery of England', and has been seen as complementing, or turning inward, the exploratory projects that early modern England promoted overseas.[7] But tracing this project to Leland's *Itinerary* reveals the limitations of the term 'discovery' as a description of the project's origins and aims. Scholars of early modern colonialism have shown how rhetorics of 'discovery' disguise acts of conquest by ignoring their inhabitants, effectively depopulating lands and turning them into empty and pristine canvases that invite repopulation.[8] Similarly, the notion of the 'discovery of England' empties the English landscape of its immediate history by replacing it with an illustrious, ancient past waiting to be 'discovered'. But, as Leland's work shows, in the wake of the Reformation it was impossible to experience the English landscape without also confronting physical evidence of the medieval past and the violence that historical change inflicted on it. While Protestant propaganda cast the Reformation as an organic development within England, the English landscape suggested otherwise, in the ruined monasteries and shrines newly littering the countryside.[9] As these ruins indicated, England was not 'discovered' but forcibly remade, its formerly sacred spaces actively converted, like its inhabitants, to support new structures of belief and government.

In Leland's *Itinerary*, geography advances the political and cultural aims of the Reformation. As James Simpson and David Lawton have recently pointed out, Leland was part of the same project of reform that wrought the very destruction that he observes and records; yet if Leland's employment by Henry made him literally 'an agent of destruction', Leland's *Itinerary* is not simply an extension of brutal, Cromwellian, iconoclasm.[10] In Leland's own attempts to theorise it, his work represents an effort less of destruction than of translation, a word that recurs throughout the *Itinerary* to describe what Leland observes to be a world in flux. As such, it offers a pivotal instance for reflecting on the nature of the cultural movement that separated, and thus created, the 'Renaissance' and the 'Medieval'. If the Reformation represents a watershed of sorts between these two periods, the *Itinerary* forces us to re-examine and revise the terms by which we understand the nature of its periodising work, particularly the assumption that it was a historical moment of total, cataclysmic destruction on the one hand or of 'continuity' on the other.[11] As a work of translation, Leland's *Itinerary* commits itself to the historical task of making the old world legible and meaningful to a new one. Leland's project was to rewrite the violence of the Reformation and to re-incorporate the ruins it left into a topography of the newly Protestant nation, a project that involved rethinking, and actively remaking, the relationship between landscape and history, place and time.

I

At this stage, let me offer one preliminary argument: the English landscape was not 'discovered' by the Renaissance but rather became a vital subject of post-Reformation antiquarian knowledge, starting with Leland, *because* it was so vital to medieval religious practice and thus urgently required re-writing. Medieval narratives of sanctity and salvation both structure and are structured through experiences of landscape.[12] The 'Life of St Kenelm', from the *South English Legendary*, for example, opens with a description of England which, as Lesley Johnson and Jocelyn Wogan-Browne point out, seeks to '[locate] English history within Christendom, and [makes] West Midland regional and topographical detail part of English history

and part of the sacred geography presided over by Rome'.[13] An experi-
ence of this sanctified geography is recorded in a fifteenth-century text by
Leland's nearest pre-Reformation counterpart, William Worcester, whose
'Itinerarium' records a series of journeys undertaken in 1478–80.[14] Like
Leland, Worcester left a voluminous record of his travels and observations
that was also preserved by Elizabethan antiquarians (in Worcester's case, by
Leland's friend Robert Talbot, and then by Matthew Parker's library at Corpus Christi College, Cambridge).[15] Employed as an estates manager for Sir
John Fastolf, Worcester turns his surveying skills to the English landscape,
revealing a curiosity about distances and placenames that anticipates and
perhaps sets the pattern for Leland. But Worcester, unlike Leland, structures this landscape by reference to pre-Reformation religious practice; his
travels through Cornwall follow a well-travelled pilgrimage route, and his
experience of topography is framed by the *loca sancta* of saints' shrines and
the abbeys and friaries that still dominate the landscape. As John Howe has
recently shown, the Roman Church established through the sites of saints'
martyrdom and burial "'sacred center[s]" where heaven and earth meet'.[16]
Even while Worcester betrays a Leland-like interest in genealogies of local
historical figures, or topographical details such as distances between cities
and the courses of waterways, he also describes a landscape that is infused
with a history of miracles:

> St. Elevetha, virgin and martyr, one of the 24 daughters of the petty king of
> Brecknock in Wales, 24 miles from Hereford; she lies in the church of Virgin nuns
> of the town of Usk and was martyred on a hill one mile from Brecon where a
> spring of water welled forth, and the stone on which she was beheaded remains
> there, and as often as someone in honour of God and the holy saint shall say Lord's
> prayer or drink of the water of the spring, he shall find each time a woman's hair
> of the saint upon the stone; a great miracle. (154, 155)

When the Reformation abolished pilgrimage and appropriated religious
buildings for secular uses, it effectively desacralised the English landscape,
which needed a new geography to replace the one that Worcester records.[17]
Leland – who may well have known Worcester's manuscript through its
early sixteenth-century owner, Talbot – produces the first geographical
description of this desacralised landscape. If the Dissolution desacralised
the country through force and decree, by defacing, mocking and destroying
the topographical landmarks of medieval pilgrimage and worship, Leland's
Itinerary pursues related goals through a different method, using the tax-
onomic and quantitative procedures of antiquarian study to produce a
landscape without miracles.

Leland's divergence from Worcester is evident in the opening of the *Itinerary*, which records a journey 'Begunne about 1538. 30. H.8'. Of Eltesley, a site in Cambridgeshire, Leland notes:

From Cambridge to Eltesle village al by champeyne counterey 8. miles. At Eltesle was sumtyme a nunnery wher Pandonia the Scottish virgine was buried, and there is a well of her name yn the south side of the quire. I hard that when this nunnery was destryid a new was made in Hunchingbroke by Huntendune. (1: 1)

Like Worcester's landscape, Leland's is defined by a saint – Pandonia, a name that Leland coins as a classicised version of Pandwyna, the obscure tenth-century saint whose remains were translated into Eltesley church in 1344.[18] Leland's Pandonia is no longer a sacred presence but a fragment of local history; no longer a saint but a 'Scottish virgine', the source not of miraculous waters but of placenames, those of the well and the former nunnery destroyed in the Reformation. The medieval past is not erased but rather absorbed into a desanctified landscape; in Leland's world, saints are history.

Throughout the *Itinerary*, Leland's description of the landscape serves as an extended meditation on historical change. While Leland's letter to Henry VIII suggests that his notes will form the basis of a map – providing 'such a description . . . of your reaulme yn writing, that it shaul be no mastery after for the graver or painter to make a like by a perfecte exemple' (xli) – it is unclear how a map could be made from the descriptions he leaves. The *Itinerary* offers no objective or consistent coordinates of distance and scale that could guide a mapmaker; where a map presents a bird's-eye view, Leland's *Itinerary* records the experience of a landscape from the ground. The perspective it provides of the English countryside is endlessly mobile; its fluidity suits the itinerary form, which, as Michel de Certeau points out, represents space from a perspective of movement, as opposed to the map, which freezes it into a single moment.[19] Leland's *Itinerary* lends itself to analysis along lines that Richard Helgerson suggests in his assertion that 'chorography defines itself by opposition to chronicle. It is the genre devoted to place, and chronicle is the genre devoted to time.'[20] Yet as Leland shows, places are always in time, and time is always sedimented in place. Leland describes a remarkably fluid landscape, always in a state of passing, like the traveller who records it, from one point in time to another.

Given the fluidity of Leland's geographical perspective, it is appropriate that he follows a landscape dominated by rivers; indeed, Leland has been called 'the invisible source . . . of British river literature' because of his sustained attention to rivers not only in the *Itinerary* but also in his Latin poems, the *Genethliacon* and the *Cygnea Cantio*.[21] But Leland is not the first to structure his geographical description around rivers; in so doing, he follows Worcester, who habitually notes rivers and their sources as the ongoing touchpoints of his travels. Such is the case in one page from his 1478 travels, where again, as in the case of St Elevetha above, the resting-place of a saint is linked to the source of a river:

St. Morwinna the virgin lies in the church [Morwenstowe] which stands 2 miles from Welcombe where the springs of two rivers rise, viz. The river Tamar that divides Cornwall and Devon and ends in Saltash haven, 3 miles from Plymouth, flowing within 3 miles of Launceston and to the ferry called Calstock Hatch 3 miles from Tavistock, to Cargreen and thence to the port of Saltash where it falls into the sea harbour, and in all it flows for some 40 miles.

The other river is called Torridge and flows through Hatherleigh [near] Torrington, Bideford, and falls into the sea at the port or haven of Appledore, and thus it flows circuitously northwards for some 40 miles by estimation. (27–8)

Worcester repeatedly identifies rivers by their sources:

One Salisbury stream rises at Frome Selwood and is called the Bourne [Wylye] flowing thorugh Warminster and Heytesbury and falles on the west side of – [*sic*].

A second stream begins about Theale town near Reading and flows by Collinbourne and – and by Amesbury Abbey and by Old Sarum.

Another stream rises near Andover and flowing through Stockbridge and Romsey falls into the sea at [Sout]Hampton, but does not pass through Salisbury.

Another stream rises in the direction of the town and Abbey of Wilton . . . (146–7)

In contrast, Leland identifies rivers by the bridges that traverse them. Thus he charts his travels in the same region that Worcester describes in the first passage above by listing the bridges he comes across:

The river of Turege risith in a morisch ground a 3. miles by north est from Herteland almost by the principale hedde of Tamar: and first rennith south south est by a few miles
The first notable bridge on Turege is Kissingtun bridg.
Thens half a mile to Pulford bridg.
Thens a 2. miles to Woddeford bridg.
Thens a 2. miles to Depeford bridge of 3. arches.
Thens to the south bridge of Torigton. Or ever Turege cummith ful to Torington he turnith from the south to north west.
Thens to the west bridge of Torinton.
Thens to Bedeford bridge about a 4. miles.
And a 2. miles lower is the confluence of Turege and Taw, and so strait into Severn by the haven mouth. (173)

And again in Cornwall:

The river of Tamar risith a 3. miles by north est from Hertelande, and thens cummith to Tamertun, a village on the est ripe yn Devonshire, and ther is a bridg over Tamar of stone: and from this bridg to Padestow xx. Miles.
Yalme bridge of stone 2. miles lower.
New Bridg 2. miles lower.
Greistoun bridge a 2. miles or more lower (etc.) (174)

Leland's preoccupation with bridges has been noticed by John Scattergood, who finds it indicative of Leland's ongoing representation of how 'the natural yields to the human', since bridges establish that 'rivers are not unnegotiable forces of nature, but channels to be negotiated'.[22] But the literary history of rivers, as in Leland's Latin poetry, is rich with representations of the fluid passage of time.[23] Leland's interest in bridges underscores his own function as a metaphorical bridge, as he continually seeks to represent perspectives defined by in-between-ness; if as a traveller he is in a constant state of transition from one place to another, he is also similarly transitioning between a Catholic past and a Protestant future.

This passage between Catholic past and Protestant future is visible in the land itself, which is likewise described as in a state of in-between-ness. In the North Riding of Yorkshire, Leland notes that he 'passed over a broke cumming from Shirifwottes Castelle quarters. The place where I passed over it is communely caullid the Spitel, corruptly for hospitale' (1: 56). Hospitals were among the religious institutions suppressed officially in 1545 and then 1547, when 'Chantries, Hospitalles, Fraternityes and Brotherheedes' were put down as breeding-grounds of 'superstition and errors'.[24] But in Leland's account, the former 'Hospital' in the North Riding does not have to be forcibly suppressed; rather, it assumes a new identity as a popular placename. Thus the land absorbs the medieval past in a way that both memorialises and neutralises its former identity. As Victor Watts points out, many existing English placenames owe their current form to Leland and his antiquarian successors, who shaped English nomenclature in order to 'satisfy the need . . . to establish affective relationships with places by locating them in feelings about history, social context, or status'.[25] The 'Spitel' represents a similar place of transition: just as it enables Leland's own passage 'over a broke' (as 'the place where I passed over'), the 'Spitel' itself undergoes an almost organic transformation through a process of linguistic corruption, declining from its former religious identity into a site of common memory.

The most dramatic and consistent sign of transition on the landscape appears in the former abbeys and houses of religion that continue to exert a topographical presence. Leland's notes on Exeter, for example, reveal the architectural afterlife of the medieval past. He notes: 'There was a priorie of St. Nicolas, a celle to Battaille-Abbey, in the north side of Town', and: 'There was an house of Blake Freres in the north side of the cemiterie of the cathedrale chirch . . . The Lord Russelle hath made hym a fair place of this house' (1: 228). These observations both invoke and sublimate the stormy history of the Reformation in Exeter: the priory of St Nicholas, which Leland observes in the past tense, was dissolved only five years before Leland's visit in a more contentious event than Leland's characteristically laconic description betrays: in 1537, when workmen began to tear down the rood loft in its chapel, they were accosted by a small group of protesting women, who left one of the workmen with a broken rib.[26] Two years later, in 1539, the Dominican house that Leland describes was dissolved and deeded to John Russell, first Earl of Bedford, just as the hospital of St John, which Leland also mentions ('Joannes de Grandisono Bisshop of Excester made an hospitale of S. John, and endowid it with landes. This hospitale is hard by the est gate' (1: 228)) would be deeded to a local nobleman, Sir Thomas Carew, after its surrender in 1540.[27] These secular appropriations of formerly religious property reflect Henry VIII's calculated effort to remake English geography by transferring monastic landholdings to sympathetic aristocratic owners – an especially key strategy in remote areas like Exeter, which still maintained strong Catholic factions long after the Reformation. Indeed, not long after Leland's visit, in 1549, the city was the focus of the so-called Prayer Book Rebellion, which was quelled with the help of a small mercenary army run by the same John Russell who built his house out of Exeter's former Dominican house.[28]

Leland avoids any direct mention of the political or religious controversies of the Reformation, despite their immediacy and his indirect involvement in them as an agent of Henry VIII. Instead, he retells the Reformation as a story about land and buildings, as property is seamlessly transferred from one set of owners to another.[29] Thus, of an impressive house he encounters in Hampshire, Leland writes: 'Mr. Wriothesley hath builded a right stately House embatelid, and having a goodly Gate . . . yn the very same Place where the late Monasterie of *Premonstratenses* stoode caullyd Tichfield' (1: 281). Like Lord Russell's house in Exeter, Thomas Wriothesley's house at Titchfield appropriates religious property on behalf of the state and its secular agents; it does so, moreover, in a way that made the new building's symbolic power strikingly apparent to outside viewers. As

Fig. 9   Nave conversion, Tichfield Abbey

is still visible today, the same 'goodly Gate' that Leland admires was built in the very nave of the former monastery's chapel, demonstrating, in the starkest of terms, the Reformation's desacralisation of space (fig. 9).[30] The sacred architecture of the past, reduced to raw substance, became building material for the secular uses of the present – this was the view of the king's commissioners who drew up the deeds for the property and assessed the costs of its conversion, noting, 'As for plucking down of the church [it] is but a small matter.'[31]

Leland's *Itinerary*, I have argued, creates a new geography for a post-Reformation England. But it does so not by erasing the medieval past, still less by destroying it or participating in its destruction. Instead, it presents a record of translation, Leland's term of choice to describe the passage of religious people and property after the Reformation; for example, in his notes from Fotheringay, Northamptonshire, Leland remarks: 'The chirch and place where the college is now was sumtyme a nunnery. The nuns of this house were translatid to De la Pray [by Nor]thampton' (1: 4). The act of translation describes not only the physical transportation of individuals, such as the nuns discharged from their convent, but the transformation of properties like Russell's or Wriothesley's from religious to secular uses. Thus in Hertfordshire Leland describes the site of a former convent, noting that 'Humfrey Boucher, base sonne of the late Lorde Berners, did much

coste in translating of the priorie into a maner place: but he left it nothing endid' (1: 104). And similarly, shortly after this account, he notices a
wood 'wher of late tyme was a priorie of nunnes. Master Page the knight
hath it now in exchaunge for landes of his in Sutherey about the quarters of Hampton-Courte. Master Page hath translated the house, and now
much lyith there' (1: 104). Page and Boucher epitomise the Tudor 'new
men' whose fortunes rose as a result of Henry's massive transfer of land
following the Dissolution. That transfer unsettled the medieval landscape
by transforming base-born men into landed ones, while transforming former religious houses into new seats of local, secular power; the fluidity of
Leland's geographical perspective reflects and participates in this historical
shift. Leland's *Itinerary* represents an effort to come to terms with historical
change by charting its material effects within the landscape. The effect is
a historiography without political agency; just as the meanings of words
like 'Hospital' decay over time, buildings like convents or even chapels are
similarly transformed through a process that appears harmonious with the
natural changeability of places. By reading the landscape through this lens,
we could say that Leland naturalises the Reformation by writing it into the
land. But, as Leland's records of his travels also show, such transformations,
however organic, are never complete; the past never disappears without a
trace. As he notes in Worcestershire:

There was a place of nunnes at the very northe side of the cemiteri of St. Oswald.
It was caulyd Whitestan, now suppressyd, the churche clene rasyd downe, and a
ferme place made of the resydewe of the buildings. (11: 91)

Even what is 'clene rasyd downe' leaves a 'resydewe', which retains traces
of its past even after its transformation. Leland's *Itinerary* is a record of the
residual; it maps a new landscape of Protestant England not by extirpating
the traces of the past but by incorporating them into a topography of
change. The medieval past survives in vestigial form, becoming the ground –
and sometimes quite literally, the material framework – on which the new
nation is forged.

II

After Leland, chorographical accounts of the English landscape increasingly
circulated with maps, which promoted new conventions for representing
space visually. With their tendency to freeze space in a single moment,
maps made it more difficult to represent the kind of sedimented history

that Leland portrays in his *Itinerary*, and the former monasteries offered
a particular challenge for portraying the vestiges of the medieval past in
the post-Reformation landscape.[32] In 1595 the Protestant propagandist and
mapmaker John Norden included a key to his map of Hampshire that indicated 'places decaid' and 'places sometime monastical', betraying a Leland-
like interest in representing the layers of material history under the visible
present.[33] Norden's attempt to represent the former monastic sites visually
was followed by Camden, who adopted many of Norden's maps as the
models for those in his *Britannia*, and whose map of Hampshire similarly
includes a key indicating 'Monasticall places' (1: 258–9). Such a symbol
marks the site of 'Titch=house' in 'Titchfeld', whose history is filled in
by the narrative chorographical account that constitutes the main feature
of Camden's *Britannia*: '*Tichfield*, sometime a little monasterie founded
by *Petre de Rupibus* Bishop of Winchester where the marriage was solem-
nized between King *Henrie* the sixth, and *Margaret of Aniou*; and now the
principall seat of the Lord *Writheosleies* Earles of South-hamton' (1: 267–8).

Camden's chorographical descriptions follow Leland's *Itinerary* in reading the pre-Reformation past through its post-Reformation incarnations,
as when he describes 'Osney', 'a most stately Abbay, as the ruines doe yet
shew' (1: 379). Or when he notes of a town in Northumberland that he
calls Haledon, after 'Heaven-field' (now Havenfelt, near Hexham) where
St Oswald was killed – a name that classicises but commemorates its former
status as a *locus sanctus* – 'all the glory that it hath, is in that ancient Abbay,
a part whereof is converted into a faire dwelling house, belonging to Sir
Iohn *Foster Knight*' (11: 807–8). Following Leland, Camden transforms the
medieval past into the raw material for a Protestant nation.

But unlike Leland, Camden does not shy away from describing the
Reformation explicitly as an act of violence. In his British history that
opens the *Britannia* Camden compares it to a 'sudden floud' that brought
the medieval past to ruin:

About the xxxvj. yeere of the reigne of the said Henrie the Eight, a sudden floud (as it
were) breaking thorow the banks with a maine streame, fell upon the Ecclesiasticall
State of England; which whiles the world stood amazed, and England groned therat,
bare downe and utterly overthrew the greatest part of the Clergie, together with
their most goodly and beautifull houses . . . And in the yeere next following,
under a faire pretence & show of rooting out superstition, all the rest, together
with Colleges, Chanteries and Hospitals were left to the dispose and pleasure of
the King . . . After which for the most part, shortly after were every where pulled
downe, their revenues sold and made away, and those goods and riches which

the Christian pietie of English nation had consecrated unto God, since they first professed Christianity were in a moment as it were dispersed, and (to the displeasure of no man be it spoken) profaned. (1: 163)

In Camden's account, the Reformation is entirely about property, which is 'profaned' through its seizure and redistribution by the Crown. Also following Leland, Camden structures *Britannia*'s account of the landscape around rivers.[34] But Camden develops the river's allegorical significance when he describes the Reformation as a 'sudden floud' that '[breaks] thorow the banks with a maine streame' and lays the 'goodly and beautifull houses' of the medieval church to waste. Invoking the two contemporary meanings of 'main streame', the 'principal current of a river' and 'prevailing trend of opinion', Camden transforms the river into a destructive force of both nature and human history that overthrows the former stability of the land.[35]

Camden was forced by critics to defend his representations of the monasteries and to fend off charges of papist sympathies that such representations raised.[36] Thus in the opening to his 1610 English edition of the *Britannia* he notes:

There are certaine, as I heare who take it impatiently that I have mentioned some of the most famous Monasteries and their founders. I am sory to heare it, and with their good favour will say thus much, They may take it as impatiently, and peradventure would have us forget that our ancestoures were, and we are of the Christian profession when as there are not extant any other more conspicuous, and certaine Monuments, of their piety, and zealous devotion toward God. Neither were there any other seed-gardens from whence Christian Religion, and good learning were propagated over this isle, howbeit in corrupt ages some weeds grow out over-ranckly. ('To the Reader', n.p.)

Camden's testy response to his critics reflects the divided expectations of early seventeenth-century readers and consumers of geography. If the middle-class taste for maps arose from a patriotic impulse to see the nation represented as a visual entity, chorographical texts like Camden's undercut that patriotism by recalling the conditions under which that nation came into being, showing that it was the product not of nature but of conquest.

III

As Michel de Certeau has asserted, after the fifteenth and sixteenth centuries, 'the map . . . slowly disengaged itself from the itineraries that were the condition of its possibility', a historical development that has been noted and explored by Helgerson and others working in the field of early modern geography.[37] John Speed's *Theatre of the Empire of Great Britaine* (1611) shows how the growing division between maps and chorographies played out in the representation of the medieval past. Published a year after the English translation of Camden's *Britannia*, Speed's work acknowledges both Camden and Leland as sources.[38] Like Camden, Speed has been seen to 'fulfil the design of Leland in a single work' by joining maps and chorographical narratives.[39] But in Speed's work the historical projects of the chorography and the geographical work of the map are at odds, a point signalled in a prefatory verse by John Davies. Davies praises Speed's book as 'Times Library, Places Geographie', drawing a distinction between the textual basis of history and the visual basis of geography. Where for Leland the two are complementary, Davies locates a tension between them in Speed's work:

> Here Time and Place, like friendly foes doe warre
> Which should shew more desir'd Particulars;
> But Place giues place, sith Time is greater farre;
> Yet Place, well rang'd, gets glory by these warres.[40]

In Speed's *Theatre*, time and place – text and map – tell different stories about the nation each takes as its subject, with history clearly relegated to the narrative, chorographical medium and evacuated from the map. While Speed used many of John Norden's maps as the basis for his own, he rejected Norden's system of indicating 'places sometime monasticall' in the key. Instead, in the maps themselves Speed leaves the sites of former monastic buildings either blank or designated only by the names of the stately homes that replace them; and in the margins of the maps, instead of the keys that might identify the monastic sites, Speed reproduces the arms of local aristocratic families. Thus, in contrast to Leland, Speed's map of Exeter identifies 'Bedford House', the name that Lord Russell gave to his stately home, but not the Dominican monastery it replaced (fig. 10). Similarly, Speed identifies Thomas Wriothesley's house at Tichfield, but leaves no indication of the house of Premonstratensians on which it was situated (fig. 11). Even when monastic ruins were not rebuilt as secular houses, Speed leaves them blank. Thus, when Speed represents Whitby, site of one of the most celebrated monastic houses in the Middle Ages, he identifies the town of Whitby while leaving blank the site of the former abbey across the inlet, whose ruins still dominate the skyline. By removing all signs of the former monastic buildings and replacing them with aristocratic homes and coats of arms, Speed's maps produce a Protestant English landscape in an idealised present, while subjecting the signs of the medieval,

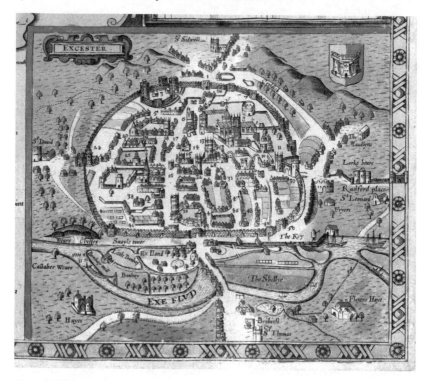

Fig. 10 John Speed, *Theatre of the Empire of Great Britain* (London, 1611), map of Exeter

Catholic past to what J. B. Harley calls the 'toponymic silence' that
early modern mapmakers imposed on unruly populations or historical
memories.[41]

But what is invisible is not necessarily absent.[42] While they are removed
from Speed's maps, the monasteries reappear in the narrative descriptions
that are interleaved with the maps in Speed's book, which record the region's
topographical features, principal landmarks, and chief architectural sites,
including its former monastic buildings. Despite their absence from his
maps, monasteries were a special interest for Speed. He wrote specially to
Robert Cotton requesting him to 'send a Note of all Monasteryes in the
Realm', which apparently formed the basis of a table Speed publishes at the
end of the *Theatre* as 'A Catalogue of the Religious Houses with the Realme
of England and Wales, with many their Orders, Founders, and Values, most
of them being suppressed by King Henry the eight. Together with such
other sacred places, as either then were by him left standing, or since have

Fig. 11 John Speed, *Theatre of the Empire of Great Britain* (London, 1611), map of Tichfield, showing the house

been erected.'[43] The chorographical narratives that Speed appends to the maps, along with excavating the monasteries, offer explanations for their transformation and ruination; thus in the description of Hampshire, Speed notes:

Chiefe Religious houses within this countie erected and againe suppressed were these, *Christs-church, Beaulieu, Whorwell, Rumsey, Redbridge, Winchester, Hyde, South-Hampton,* and *Tichfield.* The honour of this shire is dignified with the high titles of Marques, and then Earles of *Winchester* and *South-Hamton,* whose armes of families are as thou seest. (13)

Speed's chorographical text invokes the monastic past and then re-enacts its suppression, by rooting the description of Tichfield among the religious houses 'erected and againe suppressed', while representing the present 'honour of this shire' through the arms of the Earl of Southampton, identified in a cartouche on the map ('as thou seest') as Thomas Wriothesley. The present that Speed pictures is a land of stately homes, not of monasteries; accordingly, it is to Wriothesley, not to the Premonstratensians, that the county owes its identity.

Speed's historical narratives account for the disappearance of the monasteries by presenting the Reformation as a seasonal or meteorological event from which human agency has been totally removed. These descriptions echo Leland in picturing the Reformation as part of the cycle of time, rather than of political agency or force. But where for Leland the past continues to exert a desacralised presence in the landscape, Speed's descriptions explain the monasteries' absence from the landscape represented in his maps by suggesting that they were swallowed up by time, which he metaphorically describes as a deluge. Thus, describing the disappearance of the religious houses in Herefordshire, Speed writes that 'some faults [in them] were apparent, whereby they were laid open to the generall deluge of Time, whose stream bore down the walles of all those foundations, carrying away the shrines of the dead, and defacing the Libraries of their ancient records' (17–18).[44] Similarly, in his description of the former monastic houses in Buckinghamshire, Speed imagines the Reformation as a storm at sea: 'These all in the stormes and rage of the time, suffred such shipwracke, that from those seas their merchaundize light . . . [Made them] wreaks indeed' (43). In his metaphor-laden history, Speed adapts Camden's image of the Reformation as a 'sudden floud', while also developing and extending the focus on waterways that was a feature of English chorographical writing since Worcester and that, I have argued, takes on the allegorical significance of historical time working through the landscape.

But where Worcester links English waterways to their sources, often the miraculous sites of saints' martyrdoms and burials, and Leland defines them by the bridges that traverse them, metaphorically linking past and present, Speed's 'deluge of Time' sweeps the medieval past underwater, washing the landscape clean of its presence and producing the timeless Protestant topography that he represents in his de-medievalised maps. If Camden's 'sudden floud' produces ruins that he will excavate in his chorographical descriptions, Speed's 'deluge of Time' produces blankness.

By washing away England's monasteries, Speed also helps to define England's identity as a Protestant island, separated from the Catholic continent as from its own Catholic past by bodies of water that represent geographical as well as historical chasms. These are not to be traversed, like Leland's rivers. Rather, they circumscribe England as an island, enforcing what Roland Greene calls the 'Island logic' of the Renaissance that erects geographical borders in place of the 'holistic worldview' that for Catholic geographical writers, like the writer of the 'Life of St Kenelm', united England with Rome.[45]

IV

I have argued that domestic geography in the sixteenth century developed from Leland's Reformation attempt to assimilate the material remains of England's Catholic past into a newly Protestant landscape. Thus, rather than a 'discovery of England', it represented and helped produce England's desanctification, as former religious sites became the property of a new generation of Henrician landowners and their families. Like the so-called 'discovery' of the Americas, this geographical project attempted to neutralise the unruly reminders of the land's previous identity. While some have seen John Leland's Reformation project of domestic mapping as a turning inward of a project of colonial exploration and settlement, I would argue instead that it formed a template to project outward in the colonial enterprises, providing a model of how the unruly past could be incorporated and its incorporation naturalised in the description of the landscape. This point could explain why, when early modern explorers encountered native Americans, they saw Catholics: thus, for example, when Thomas Harriot describes the Algonquians, he finds their rituals redolent of Catholicism and their ornaments reminiscent of pre-Reformation idols.[46] Or why Speed's own maps of Ireland pictured the landscape as pristine and empty space, thus enabling the 'conquest and colonization of Ireland', in Christopher Ivic's words, through the 'displacement and erasure of the native Irish'.[47]

Such acts of conquest take their pattern, I argue, from the displacement of the medieval past in geographical representations of England. In other words, before England could domesticate its colonies, it first needed to domesticate itself, starting with its own recent past. Speed's maps went on to circulate independent of their original context within his *Theatre*, further popularising an image of the English landscape purified of its medieval past. But that past continued to interpose itself in narrative chorographies, which, while reading English history layered in the land, reveal the conditions behind the national vision that maps like Speed's freeze in time.[48] From Leland to Speed, such texts show that the past never disappeared but continued to exert an influence as palpable as the ruins it left behind.

PART V

Reformation

CHAPTER 10

John Bale and reconfiguring the 'medieval' in Reformation England

Cathy Shrank

Born at the end of the fifteenth century and dying in the first decade of the reign of Elizabeth I, John Bale (1495–1563) is a transitional figure. His lifetime spans our institutionalised chronological boundaries between 'medieval' and 'Renaissance' (or 'early modern'), boundaries which – as James Simpson has shown – Bale did so much to help construct by consistently setting out to distinguish what he portrayed as his enlightened era from the preceding aeons of 'horrible darkenesse'.[1] This drive towards periodisation is a recurrent concern of Bale, manifested across the full range of his many and varied works. His rhetoric of chronological difference is characteristic of the period's religious polemic in that it is emphatically binary and more often than not phrased as an opposition between light and darkness, as in *A brefe Chronycle concerynynge . . . syr Iohan Oldecastell*, where Bale categorises the early fifteenth century as a time when 'whyght [was] iudged blacke and light darkenesse / so yll was mennes syght in those dayes'.[2]

The incessant imagery of light and dark has, of course, spiritual resonances. The title-page of Bale's 1530s drama *A tragedye or enterlude manyfestyng the chefe promyses of God vnto man* cites the first chapter of John to prove the point: 'In the worde . . . was lyfe from the begynnyng and that lyfe was the light of men. Thys light yet shyneth in the darkenesse, but the darkenesse comprehendeth it not' (A1r).[3] Darkness, then, is not simply the lack of scholarship and literary panache bemoaned by Bale's contemporary John Leland, but is the darkness of religious error which, for Bale, is synonymous with papistry (as it was for many others of his religious persuasion). Leland laments John Gower's failure to attain Ovidian eloquence inhabiting, as he did, 'a semi-barbarous age' (*semibarbaro saeculo*),[4] an era that can be distinguished from 'this, our most flourishing age' (*hac nostra tam florenti aetate*).[5] Bale, in contrast, habitually makes religious, rather than literary, distinctions, as in his *Epistle exhortatorye of an Englyshe Christyane*. Here Bale announces a new age of spiritual clearsightedness, declaring 'no doubt of yt / but the mercie of our eternall father hath opened vnto vs in these latter dayes what ther forked fatherhede / the oyled auctorite / and ther shauen holynesse is'.[6] England's break with Rome, that is, marks an end to what is described in the *Yet a Course at the Romyshe foxe* as 'the most pestilent tyme of papystrye'.[7]

Yet Bale's attitude to the past is far from simple. As Simpson has argued in his work on Bale and Leland, 'both reveal . . . a division of consciousness with regard to the past: as the new age is announced triumphally, so too does triumphalism undo itself'.[8] Bale's 'new age' is consequently shown to be as hedged with the shadows of barbarity and ignorance as the preceding centuries, as the papists continually threaten to rise up and blot out the new-found light, leading the people of England into 'a palpable kind of darkenesse by their masses, and other sorcerouse witchcraftes', a darkness so menacing that it is analogous to the ninth Plague of Egypt, that of 'darkness which may be felt'.[9] The murk of the past is at the same time shown to be punctuated by the pinprick lights of proto-reformers, such as John Wyclif, remembered in Bale's *Catalogus* – an extensive bibliography of British writers – in Christ-like terms as 'the morning star in the midst of cloud' (*stella matutina in medio nebulae*).[10] Bale's 'triumphalist' vision of his present is further undone by his recurrent attempts to align himself, and other reformers, with previous victims of persecution. Early Christian history, for example, provides precedent for Bale's publication of Anne Askew's examinations, issued with extensive commentary by Bale in 1546 and 1547. As Bale writes in the preface of *The first examinacyon*: 'In most terrible persecucyons of the prymatyue churche, were the examynacyons & answers, tormentes and deathes of the constaunt martyrs written, and sent abroade to all the whole worlde ouer, as testyfyeth Eusebius Cesariensis in hys ecclesyastycal hystorye. Their coppyes habounde eueryewhere.'[11]

Bale's version of history is that of an ongoing, epic struggle between the forces of light and darkness. This essentially repetitive view makes history cyclical, rather than something that can be divided into distinct periods, challenging – or at least complicating – Bale's efforts at periodisation. History is given a pattern, with particular use made of prefiguration: the martyr Askew is equated with Blandina, the first-century French martyr;[12] in the autobiographical *Vocacyon* Bale places continued emphasis on parallels between his own sufferings and those of St Paul, whose status as a notable convert from spiritual error to enlightenment proves especially resonant for Bale, the former Carmelite friar who had turned from the teachings of the Roman church in the early 1530s.[13]

The past, then, is presented both as different from, and worse than, the present and (contrariwise) as justifying the actions of Bale and his fellow reformers. This essay examines Bale as a Janus figure, looking back as much as forward. On the one hand, he endeavours to differentiate his age from 'that most blynde and ignoraunt tyme';[14] on the other, despite his loud avocation of the 'new learnyng', he is rooted in and dependent on medieval sources, traditions and genres – such as chronicle, morality play and miracle play – which he infuses with Reformation thought and the new antiquarianism, which valued and interpreted original artefacts.[15] As such, Bale illustrates continuities between the 'medieval' and 'early modern', and the use made of the 'medieval' by early modern writers who strove to fashion a national literary tradition, national history and national religion.[16] The essay focuses above all on Bale's enthusiasm for texts and the written word, a passion which is both symptomatic of his attempts to differentiate his own era from the past, and central to the ways in which he used his medieval material. Bale was a prolific writer, under his own name and pseudonyms: as we shall see, publication was for Bale a national and spiritual duty, and his generic range encompasses prayers, religious polemic, didactic dialogues, drama, catalogues of writers, biography and autobiography.[17] Books were more than polemical tools, however: as Philip Schwyzer has argued, it is the knowledge contained within them that holds aesthetic power for Bale, and which awakens an insistent language of 'bewtie' from the habitually derisive and abrasive reformer.[18]

The significance of books in the author's world-view is reflected in memorials to Bale, which recurrently link him to bibliographical study. Barnabe Googe's sonnet 'To doctor Bale', written close to Bale's death in 1563, addresses 'good aged Bale' 'that with thy hoary heares / Doste yet persyste, / to turne thy paynefull Booke' and 'leavst not yet / On Papers pale to looke',[19] whilst the woodcut portraits of Bale which appear in his works – in certain copies of the *Summarium* and in the printed edition of *A Comedy concernynge thre lawes, of nature, Moses, & Christ* – both portray him book in hand. The pose in the *Summarium* portrait even resembles that of Wyclif, champion of the holy book, in the same volume (the only other writer depicted visually in the work): both men appear in profile, facing left, in academic dress, against a classical background; Wyclif's left hand rests upon a book, Bale's upon a stone lintel (Bale holds a book in his right hand, while Wyclif's is raised, as if gesturing to emphasise a point whilst preaching to an off-stage congregation).[20]

The word for Bale is – naturally, for one of such religious convictions – first and foremost God's word, as can be seen from the sentiments which

Bale puts into the mouth of his eldest son in *A dialogue or communycacyon to be had at a table betwene two chyldren*. Here John Junior cites John's gospel at his younger brother Paul (a choice of names which highlights the significance for Bale of prefiguration, and of St Paul and John the Evangelist). The elder boy reminds his brother that 'In the beginning was the worde, & the word was with God, & God was that word' before proceeding to explain that, contrary to the teachings of the 'popyshe churche', God, not St Matthew, was the first writer of God's word: 'God wrote it fyrst in the naturall hart of man, & so yt remained here styll tyll Moyses and the prophetes ded leaue it in outward wrytinge to the peoples farder erudicyon' (A3v). The imparting of belief is thus made scribal: the text is initially inscribed in men's hearts, and later transcribed by the prophets into actual books. That key message is then reiterated, as John Junior continues: 'Godde is their secrete instructour & preacher, which taught it first withoute voice & wrote it without penne in the hidden hart of man' (A4r). Further evidence of Bale's imagining God's word as written text can be found in the woodcuts which appear in both parts of the examinations of Askew and *The Vocacyon*. These devices adapt the traditional Catholic icon of the Virgin Mary crushing the serpent of heresy under her foot. In Bale's texts a female figure – not identified as the Virgin, but variously interpreted as either 'Truth' or a martyr – holding a book, the Bible (inscribed in *The Vocacyon* with the words '*Verbum Dei*'), treads down the snake of papistry, identifiable in the examinations of Askew by its triple papal crown.[21]

As well as a written word, God's word is a living text, as can be seen from the characteristic terminology of Bale's defence of the Duke of Northumberland in 1552, in which Bale declares that 'I have always known the same a most mighty, zealous, and ardent supporter, maintainer, and defender of God's *lively word*'.[22] The emphasis placed on God's word as 'the lyvynge wurde' infuses Bale's texts.[23] As befits a good reformer, Scripture becomes a guide by which to live and write. The title-pages of Bale's works are habitually heavy with text: lengthy, explanatory titles; the occasional potted summary (as on the title-page of *The epistle exhortatorye*); and, invariably, biblical quotation. The use of biblical quotation is commonplace on title-pages of the period, but what is particularly interesting about Bale's choice of quotations is that they are not confined to advice on spiritual matters. The title-page of *The laboryouse Iourney*, for example, cites the apocryphal Machabees on the act of composition: 'ii. Macha. ii / He that begynneth to wryte a storye, for the fyrste, muste wyth hys vnderstandynge gather the matter togyther, set hys wordes in ordre, and dylygently seke out on euery parte' (A1r).

The consciousness of the word as God's word can be seen to shape Bale's construction of himself as author. Bale habitually depicts himself as a compiler or collector of texts, and not as their first original. Hence we have *The tragedy or enterlude manyfestyng the chefe promyses of God vnto Man . . . Compyled by Johan Bale, anno domini 1538*, or *A brefe comedy or enterlude concernynge the temptacyon of our lorde and sauer Jesus Christe by Sathan in the Desart. Compiled by Johan Bale, anno 1538*.[24] Bale is not unique in his use of the term *compile* to mean composition: Caxton, for example, writes of the intention to 'compyle an epistle' in his translation of Raoul Lefèvre's *The Hystorie of Iason* (*c.* 1477).[25] However, Bale is notable for the consistency with which he writes of compiling, collecting or gathering his works. This stress on composition extends beyond works based on biblical sources, where compilation is an obvious sign of authenticity (in comparison with what is characterised in reformist polemic as papist neglect or even falsification of Scripture).[26] Bale's promotion of his role as that of compiler, or collector, is also found in his more 'biographical' works, such as the *Chronycle concerynynge . . . Oldecastell*, 'collected togyther by Johan Bale / out of the bokes and writynges of those Popyshe Prelates which were present then both at his condempnacyon and iudgement' (2r). As Diarmaid MacCulloch comments, Bale's recovery and dissemination of Lollard history, 'built on the pioneering work of Bible translator William Tyndale', has 'the added refinement that he used sources captured from the enemy, books written by the official medieval Church, in order to illuminate the past in a new way'.[27] Bale's method of composition is thus inflected both by his antiquarianism and by his religious beliefs, as the study of old documents is used to bring forth historical 'truths' allegedly suppressed whilst those texts were 'kepte . . . vndre duste' in monastic libraries.[28]

When it comes to the promulgation of Bale's views, of his vein of religious polemic, and of his version of national history, his age is seen to have a distinct advantage over preceding eras. Like his friend John Foxe, whom he met in the late 1540s at the household of Mary Fitzroy, Duchess of Richmond,[29] Bale applauds the power of the printing press, using possibilities provided by the technology – and the illusion of the ready and easy access that print publication supposedly supplies – as further means of distinguishing his age from that of his predecessors, when the 'lyuely memoryalles of our nacyon' had been sequestered in the monasteries.[30] The monasteries are here transformed by Bale into sites, not only of lechery and religious error, but also of disloyalty to the nation, for 'a more sygne of ignobylyte can not be sene than to hyde such noble monuments' (c2r). The dissolution of the religious houses consequently offers an opportunity – admittedly at risk of being squandered – to recover and celebrate a national culture, as Bale exhorts his compatriots to 'brynge you into the lyghte, that they kept longe in the darkenes':

As ye fynde a notable Antyquyte, such as are the histories of Gildas & Nennius amonge the Brytaynes, Stephanides & Asserius among the Englyshe Saxons, let them anon be imprented, & so brynge them into a nombre of coppyes, both to theire and your owne perpetuall fame. For a more notable point of nobylyte can ye not shewe, than in suche sort to bewtyfie your contrey, & so to restore vs to suche a truthe in histories, as we haue long wanted. (B2v–3r)

This is not a rejection of the past, but an assimilation of it, as the shards and fragments of the monastic libraries are used to shore up a new version of national history and a new national religion.[31] To this end, 'the noble art of prentynge' becomes a gift of God 'geuen' 'in thys age' to 'send' the noble monuments of Bale's nation 'a brode amonge men'.[32] These sentiments demonstrate first, Bale's conviction of the novelty, and hence superiority, of at least some aspects of his own time, and secondly, God's conscription into the religious struggles on the side of the reformers. Publication – and print publication above all – thus takes on the weight of a national and spiritual duty.

Bale's emphasis on the primacy of the word has obvious repercussions in his role as playwright, particularly when coupled with an aversion to idolatry typical of reformers such as Bale, since drama is a genre that is dependent on the visual.[33] The onus on avoiding idolatry is obviously under greatest pressure in Bale's 'bible' plays, of which three survive: *A tragedye or enterlude manyfestyng the chefe promyses of God vnto Man*; *A brefe comedy or enterlude of Johan Baptystes preachynge in the wyldernesse, openynge the craftye assaultes of the hypocrytes*; and *A brefe comedy or enterlude concernynge the temptacyon of our lorde and sauer Iesus Christ, by Sathan in the desart*. As scholars such as Thora Blatt and E. S. Miller have argued, these can be seen as part of a cycle of plays, drawing on the medieval mystery tradition, which in the words of Peter Happé was 'still being actively promoted in many English towns and cities'.[34] Despite his enthusiastic embracing of the 'newe learnynge', that is, Bale is the product of a 'medieval' upbringing, and it is therefore unsurprising that he should turn to didactic genres familiar from his boyhood – such as mystery and morality plays – to instruct his audience in the 'true' religion.[35] Indeed, techniques and motifs from medieval drama permeate his prose works, as well as his plays. As Rainer Pineas has shown, Bale uses the Vice as a means of identifying and vilifying Catholicism, utilising a tradition that categorises the Vice as 'craftye' and intent to 'dyssemble'.[36] However, it is not just figures from Bale's plays, such as the Pharisee and Sadducee in *Johan Baptystes Preachynge*, or Satan in *The Temptacyon*, who display Vice-like characteristics. The papist figures who haunt Bale's biographical and polemical works are similarly distinguished as a 'dyuersely dysgysed host of anointed hypocrites' eager to ensnare and delude the unprepared.[37] Medieval dramatic conventions, in other words, bleed into and inform Bale's non-dramatic works, providing a familiar and culturally resonant shorthand by which to excoriate the Roman church.

However much Bale is indebted to medieval drama in his prose works, his adaptation of it on-stage, in his bible plays, is (unsurprisingly) distinctly anti-dramatic. *Gods Promyses* is probably the most striking example. Its structure is repetitive, reflecting Bale's cyclical view of history. Seven prophets – Adam, Noah, Abraham, Moses, David, Isaiah and John the Baptist – appear before God. In every case, the prophet hears the Heavenly Father's complaints against humankind (namely, that humans disregard God); the prophet pleads on humankind's behalf; God announces his prescribed punishment and makes a promise which gives humankind, and the prophet, hope for the future; the prophet praises God; and the act ends with an antiphon sung in English (illustrating Bale's commitment to vernacular worship). We never see enacted the behaviour of which God laments, or the fulfilment of his promises. Instead, the play relies simply on dialogue, informing us what has happened, and what will happen. All opportunity for dramatic representation is consequently removed: despite the presence of Noah, for example, we never witness the building of the ark, depicted in plays such as Towneley 3; likewise, despite Abraham's role, we are not shown the infamous and undoubtedly dramatic near-sacrifice of his son Isaac (the subject of Chester 4 and the Brome play).

Bale chooses to tell, not show. Discourse, not representation, is the way to enlightenment, as in the *Dialogue* staged between his two sons. This deliberate emphasis on word over spectacle is also conveyed in one of the few records we have of Bale's plays in performance, which appears in Bale's *Vocacyon*. There, Bale's three extant bible plays are used alongside his preaching as part of a counter-attack against the outbreak of papist ceremonies – 'processions / musters and disgysinges' – that erupted in Kilkenny on the death of Edward VI (24r). As Bale relates, in order to inoculate his flock against the spectacle of 'prebendaryes and prestes abought wearing the cope / croser / and myter in procession',

I toke Christes testament in my hande / & went to the market crosse / the people in great nombre folowinge. There toke I the .xiii. chap. of S. Paule to the Roma. declaringe to them bravely / what the autoritie was of the worldly powers & magistrates, what reverence & obedience were due to the same . . . The yonge men in the forenone played a Tragedye of Gods promises in the olde lawe at the market crosse / with organe plainges and songes very aptely. In the afternone agayne they played a Commedie of sanct Johan Baptistes preachinges / of Christes baptisynge and of his temptacion in the wildernesse. (24r–v)[38]

His plays, in short, are explicitly aligned against spectacle.

As Blatt argues, Bale rejects the liturgical basis for the mystery plays and returns to scripture for his biblical dramas. According to Blatt, 'this faithful adherence to the source shows how far his plays are removed from the miracle plays, to which his dramas may be considered a corrective'.[39] Or, as James Simpson puts it: '"Drama" becomes . . . the occasion for scriptural summary.'[40] In this, Bale would seem to be following his namesake, John the Baptist in *Johan Baptystes Preachynge*, who announces his inability to veer from, or embellish on, God's word:

> My preachynge was it,   from it can I not go,
> For grounded it is   on Gods mighty worde trulye,
> Uttered long afore   by the prophet Esaye.
>   (lines 59–61)

Yet for all his self-representation as a compiler and collector and his apparent adherence to Scriptures, Bale does elaborate on his biblical material. This is not elaboration of the type we see in the mystery plays, with the introduction of details such as Noah's nagging wife in Towneley 3, or the sheep-rustlers Mak and his wife in the Towneley Nativity play (Towneley 13). In keeping with his preference for word over spectacle, Bale's embellishments do not provide local colour or comic digressions: instead, they introduce the idea of disputation and, in particular, argument that is based on precedent – additions that once again exemplify Bale's interest in the power of words, and in historical patterning. Hence we have, for example, the manner in which a number of the prophets in *Gods Promyses* almost seem to bargain with God by pointing out previous examples of his mercy. As Noah argues, 'Of all goodnesse, lorde, remember thy great mercye / To Adam and Eve' (lines 230–1). In turn Abraham has recourse to the example of both Adam and Noah ('. . . mercyfull lorde, thy gracyousnesse remember / To Adam and Noah both in thy worde and promes', lines 322–3); and David to Moses ('Remembre yet, lorde, thy worthye servaunt Moses', line 563). The encounter between Christ and Satan in *The Temptacyon* is similarly transformed into a disputation, in which Christ recurrently looks back to past figures, such as Adam, Helias and Daniel (lines 133, 139), to vindicate his own path of (in)action and in which the two protagonists cite chapter and verse in a way that is much expanded from the scriptural source (Matthew 4:1–11).

A polemical writer in a time when the future of the English church and English souls were under contention, Bale predictably elaborates on his biblical material to make a series of political and doctrinal points, as when at the end of *Gods Promyses* Baleus Prolocutor argues for justification through faith alone, and attacks those familiar targets of Reformation polemic: the papist belief in 'fre wyll' (line 976) and salvation by good 'workes' (line 973). Contemporary religious controversy also haunts *The Temptacyon*, requiring Bale to differentiate Christ's abstinence in the wilderness from the papist practice of fasting. As Christ explains to his audience in forceful and partisan terms, 'Thynke not me to fast bycause I wolde yow to fast, / For than ye thynke wronge and have vayne judgement' (lines 43–4). Bale's biblical plays thus take on immediate contemporary relevance within the context of Reformation England. With their concerns for their 'lyvynges' (line 210) and 'outwarde pretence . . . of holynesse' (line 225), the Pharisee and Sadducee of *Johan Baptystes Preachynge* represent the Roman clergy (whom Bale condemns in the *Chroncyle . . . of Oldcastle* as 'styfnecked Pharysees', 11v) as much as they do their biblical sects. John the Baptist, meanwhile, is reprimanded by these papist prototypes for his 'newe lernynge' (line 316), a stance for which sixteenth-century papists are mocked in the *Laboryouse Iourney*, when Bale comments on how 'we had never good worlde (saye they) sens thys new learnynge come in' (A4r).

Bale's use of his biblical plays for Reformation point-scoring – and his emphasis on obedience to magistrates and rulers in the market place at Kilkenny (cited above, 185) – are a reminder of crucial differences between the composition of the mystery plays and Bale's own biblical dramas. The mystery plays, from what we can tell, were organic compositions, evolving over many years, and the product of more than one hand (even the existence of a single 'Wakefield Master' is now being questioned by scholars such as Happé).[41] These plays also had a local and often civic dynamic, performed and funded by members of various city guilds. In Bale's plays, these local dynamics have been replaced by a national dimension. The effacing of the local is perhaps inevitable in the works of a man who had been rendered socially and geographically mobile by the monastic training which wrested him from his birthplace, and by his university education, which further alienated him from his roots. This trajectory was, however, compounded by the technological and religious changes of his time: namely, the printing press and the English Reformation. *The Temptacyon*, *Gods Promyses* and *Johan Baptystes Preachynge* were – like the *Thre Lawes* – printed *c.* 1547–8 for the benefit of a book-reading public who, unlike the audience at mystery plays, were not associated with any one locale, whilst the original plays were themselves responses to political and religious upheavals on a national scale.[42] Many of Bale's dramas were originally written under the patronage of John Vere, the reformist Earl of Oxford.[43] These were then revised and supplemented under the auspices of Henry VIII's chief minister, Thomas Cromwell, whose patronage Bale received between 1537 and Cromwell's death in 1540. Bale appears to have come under the statesman's influence and protection after he interceded to secure Bale's release from prison in Greenwich, where he was being held on the order of John Stokesley, Bishop of London, after complaints in 1536 about Bale's unorthodox preaching. According to Bale's *Catalogus*, Cromwell's intervention was 'on account of his comedies'.[44] Subsequent to his liberation, Bale used the plays which had caught the Lord Secretary's eye to promote the new religion to which they both subscribed, organising a company of actors ('fellows'), active *c.* 1538 and 1539 – possibly known as 'the Lord Cromwell's Players' – who staged plays for Cromwell and were paid for their performances directly out of his purse.[45]

Cromwell's awareness of the power of propaganda to buttress the religious changes he promoted is well documented by G. R. Elton.[46] If not quite the works of the 'official' playwright which Jesse Harris claims Bale to be, his plays nevertheless seem to have won favour with influential men of reformist tendencies at the Henrician court, such as Cromwell and Thomas Cranmer, Archbishop of Canterbury. Contemporary testimonials of Bale's dramas recurrently highlight their topicality and political function. Bale's own description of the performance of his plays in Kilkenny in 1553 (noted above) reveals the appropriation of public, civic space – the market place – to endorse obedience to the royal authority of governors and magistrates, as Bale endeavours to cling to the structures of the Edwardian regime which had upheld and promoted the reformed religion. The connection between loyalty and religious affiliation was certainly apparent to at least one audience member at a performance of *King Johan* at Cranmer's house in 1539: afterwards, one John Alforde stated that 'it would be a pity "that the Bisshop of Rome should reigne any lenger, for if he should, the said Bisshop wold do with our King as he did with King John"'.[47] Perhaps most striking of all is the tantalising record of a play performed before king, court and archbishop at Canterbury in 1538 on St Stephen's Day (7 September), the night before the destruction of Thomas Becket's shrine in the city's cathedral, and for which 'Balle and his Fellows' were 'given . . . by my lorde commaundement for playing before my lorde – xl^s'.[48] As MacCulloch argues, 'it is hardly stretching coincidence too far to suggest that the work performed was Bale's *On the Treasons of Becket*', one of the lost plays named in *Anglorum Heliades* as 'The Betrayal by Thomas Becket'.[49] If – for once – Bale's play is pertinent to the locale in which it was performed, the purpose and effect of that setting is not to celebrate the local, but to justify and approve royal policy, the furtherance of royal supremacy in matters of religion and the destruction of local, 'papist' cults.

This emphasis on religion as a national religion permeates Bale's works. For all its depiction of its eponymous protagonist as a 'blessed martyr of Christ', the *Chronycle concernynge . . . Oldecastell* begins not with examples of others who died for their religion, but of those who 'moche commended and thought worthy of eternall memorye / . . . haue eyther dyed for theyr naturall contreye or daungered theyr lyues for a commonwelthe', a glorious roll-call which includes pagan and even mythical heroes such as Theseus, Ulysses, Scipio Africanus and Quintus Curtius (2r), a classical motif reflected in the depiction of Oldcastle in classical armour on the title-page. Subscription to the reformed faith is aligned with national loyalty. *King Johan*, for instance, is a play which fuses allegiance to nation and monarch with repudiation of the Roman church,[50] whilst the dedicatory epistle to Edward VI in *The laboryouse Iourney* explicitly blames the recent uprisings in Devon and Cornwall on 'papist' clergy leading people into error (A5r).[51]

Bale's works, that is, fully endorse the processes of Reformation as they occurred within England. The 'true' religion is not only reformed; it is also authorised by the state, a stance most consistently demonstrated in the *Vocacyon*, in which Bale continually insists on the primacy of the crown in religious affairs. He consequently offends the Irish clergy by being installed as Bishop of Ossory in a ceremony 'after that boke of consecratinge bishoppes / which was last set fourth in Englande by acte of parlement' (18v), and through his continued promotion of 'that only boke of commen prayer / whych the kynge & hys counsel had that yeare put fourth by acte of parlement' (21v). A corrupt justice of the peace, meanwhile, is castigated as 'not only a vyolatour of Christes institucion / but also a contempnor of his princes earnest commaundement / and a provoker of the people by his ungraciouse example to do the like' (23r). An enemy of the prince is an enemy of God and of civil harmony to boot; or, as it is put in the printed marginalia of *Yet a Course at the Romyshe foxe*: those that support papist ceremonies 'do but dally and mocke with the kynge' (A5r).

The relationship between crown and author-scholar is highlighted in the illustrations that accompany Bale's works. The title-page of the expanded 1551 edition of *The actes . . . of the Englyshe Votaryes* depicts a writer in academic dress presenting a book to a king, whose diligence in letters is suggested by his position, standing at his writing desk, whilst – in a design familiar from medieval woodcuts – the *Summarium* shows Bale kneeling before the throne, as he presents the volume to the beardless boy-king, Edward VI.[52] Both illustrations draw attention to the scholar's role as royal servant; the *Summarium* even positions that service within the context of an assertion of royal authority in religious matters: Edward is seated on a throne which is modelled on that of Solomon, with its sphinx support, the Reformation iconography of which has been explored by Margaret Aston.[53] Displayed prominently in the lower left-hand corner of the picture is the royal coat of arms of England under the closed imperial crown, which – since 1533 and the Act in Restraint of Appeals – had symbolised the autonomy of the realm and its monarch from foreign powers, including and especially the pope.[54]

With their stress on obedience in both civil and religious affairs Bale's works are, in other words, very much products of the English Reformation, of which one defining characteristic was the evolution of a national, centrally controlled church. However, there is another, further way in which his texts epitomise English Reformation writing, and that is in their manifestation of a tension between access to texts – particularly religious texts – and control of their subsequent interpretation.[55] Bale's promotion of print as a means of making the 'truth' readily, cheaply and widely available is thus circumscribed by his concern to ensure the 'right' reception of his works. To this end, he makes much use of the format of his printed books to assemble, and then mould, an audience of like-minded readers, whose experience of reading is shaped by the author. From the outset, Bale's readers are coerced by the labels he habitually attaches to them: 'the Christen' (i.e. reformed) and 'diligent' readers of *The first examinacyon of Anne Askewe* (♣2r); the 'true English men' to whom he directs his *Excellent and A right learned meditacion* in 1554 (A1r); the 'good readers' of *The Actes of the Englyshe Votaryes* who are instructed to 'lerne herin . . . to iudge false myracles' (A1r); or the reader of the *Chronycle concernynge . . . Oldecastell* who, having 'iudgement in the sprete / shall easelye perseyue by this treatyse / what beastlye blockeheades these bloudye bellyegoddes were in theyr vnsauerye interrogacyons' (3r). The epithets and intended outcomes stated presuppose and demand particular readings.

The heavy use within Bale's works of paratext – such as glosses, indices and tables of contents – is similarly directive. This paratext is ostensibly present as an aid to reading. Bale even laments in *Yet a course at the Romyshe foxe* about 'how shamefullye are the bibles handled, which . . . hath neyther annotacyons nor table[s]' (7r), and Bale's *Image of Both Churches* depicts the absence of paratext as a papist plot, orchestrated by 'the disciples of

antichrist with their bifurked ordinaries' who 'violently pluck from the true
Christian church . . . the eternal word of the Lord': 'Already have they taken
in England from the bibles the annotations, tables, and prefaces, to perform
this their damnable enterprise.'[56] In contrast to this diabolic project, Bale's
own texts boast extensive indices and tables. *Yet a course at the Romyshe foxe*
even advertises on its title-page the 'alphabettycall dyrectorye or Table also
in the ende therof, to the spedye fyndynge out of the pryncypall matters
therin contayned' (A1r). These indices and tables not only allow readers
ready access to the texts, however: they also exercise authorial control over
the text, steering readers to certain highlighted passages which lambast
the papacy or insist on the scriptural basis for Bale's own views. Like the
English authorities who sanctioned and even promoted a vernacular Bible,
Bale is similarly concerned to regulate and contain the interpretations of
his readers. He is consequently an intrusive presence, breaking into his own
texts through paratext just as he habitually intervenes in, and interprets,
the texts of others: be they the examinations of Askew, initially recorded in
her own hand and words, or the scholarly meditations of Leland's *A Newe
yeares gyfte*, published with Bale's extensive interjections as *The laboryouse
Iourney of Johan Leylande*. Bale's on-stage persona in his extant plays –
'Baleus Prolocutor', 'Bale, the spokesman, one who speaks for others' – is
thus symptomatic of the author's recurrent attempt to retain interpretative
responsibility for the actions or ideas he recounts.[57]

In conclusion, there are elements in Bale's works which distinguish his
writing from that of a previous, pre-Reformation era, not least his emphasis
on a national church, governed through acts of parliament, and his own
attempts to control interpretation of his works in a controversial age. We
should be careful, however, of being seduced by Bale's own rhetoric of
difference, which – as we saw at the start of this essay – is less assured
than Bale himself would posit. For all his apparent rejection of the past,
Bale assimilates its relics in his works: through printing the documents surrounding Oldcastle's examinations, for example, or through the adaptation
of medieval devices and genres (the portrayal of Satan, for instance, is based
not so much on Scripture as on the medieval dramatic tradition). The parallels Bale draws with earlier martyrs also serve as a reminder that, throughout
his version of Christian history, there are those who suffer persecution for
adherence to God's word and the rejection of false ceremonies: there is no
sudden break from the past, that is; rather, the past has a tendency towards
repetition.

Similarly, despite Bale's emphasis on printing as a tool of enlightenment, we should remember (as he does) that publication occurred before

and without printing. Askew publishes – 'sent abroade' – her examinations 'by her owne hande writynge'; the examinations of Oldcastle in the
early fifteenth century, 'wrytten by [the Archbishop of Canterbury's] owne
notaryes and clarkes', are 'dyrected vnto Rycharde Clyfford than Byshhope
of London with a generall commaundement to haue it than *publysshed* by
him & by the other Bysshopes *the whole realm ouer*'.[58] And, despite Bale's
focus on the nation, we should be wary of sealing off Bale's England from
the Continent that still provided an important audience. Bale tapped into
a network of Continental printers, whose presses he used for works too
dangerous for London-based workshops.[59] Indeed, one of the key messages
of the *Epistle exhortatorye* is that good Christians 'manifest [the] mischeues
[of the Roman church] to the vniuersall worlde / euerye manne accordinge
to his talent geuen of God / some with his penne / and some with tonge'
(3r). To this end, the use of Latin, as well as English, is acknowledged as
necessary for spreading news of English martyrs. As Bale writes in *The first
examinacyon of Anne Askewe*:

> nothynge at all shall it terryfye vs, nor yet in any point lett vs of our purpose, that
> our bokes are now in Englande condemned and brent . . . But it wyll from hens
> forth occasion vs, to set fourth in the Latyne also, that afore we wrote onlye in
> the Englysh, and so make their spirytuall wyckednesse and treason knowne moche
> farther of. (5v)

Bale's recognition of the international language of Latin is an additional
reminder of continuities between the 'medieval' and 'early modern'. Despite
the investment in English as a language of literature and scholarship during
the sixteenth century – witnessed, for example, by the publication of arts
of rhetoric in the vernacular – as Françoise Waquet has shown, throughout
that century, the level of Latin learning rose across England, as it did on
the Continent.[60] The early moderns did not reject the language that had
dominated medieval scholarship and diplomacy: like other aspects of their
medieval inheritance, they used it for different purposes.

CHAPTER II

Medieval penance, Reformation repentance and Measure for Measure

Sarah Beckwith

> Those actions are properly called human actions that proceed from a
> deliberate will. And if other actions are found in man, they can be
> called actions of a man, but not properly human actions, since they
> are not proper to man as man. (Thomas Aquinas)

'I think if you handled her privately, she would sooner confess; perchance
publicly she'll be ashamed', says Lucio to Escalus in the last act of *Measure for
Measure* (5.1.274–5).[1] Escalus has asked leave of Angelo to question Isabella
and anticipates his questioning as an exemplary display of the workings
of justice: 'You'll see how I'll handle her' (5.1.270). Lucio's comment is a
semi-apologetic gloss on his salacious aside that Escalus will handle Isabella
no better than Angelo 'by her own report' (5.1.271). Lucio leans on such
language as he dwells on the obscene connotations of 'handle' as managing
and man-handling. Escalus' private handling, like Angelo's, he suggests, is
erotic, but it is also juridical, designed to elicit evidence for a court of law.
It might include other forms of handling – the racking and tousing with
which he threatens Friar Lodowick a few lines later. But Lucio's comments
also exploit an older usage of 'handling', the penitential contexts in which
sins are handled by a confessor. *Handlyng Synne* is the title of a much-read
medieval confessional manual translated from the French.[2] In the confessional manuals and other medieval penitential literature sins are groped
and handled, discerned and brought to light by the priest or friar as diagnostician, healer and absolver on behalf of the church. Lucio's words refer
to a practice (auricular confession) that had been abolished as a mandated,
component part of the practice of penance or repentance as it was known in
post-Reformation England. So, in the context of the play, it would be quite
possible for 'handling sin' to be reduced to either the eroticising ridicule
so common in anti-fraternal satire, or to the purely juridical contexts to
which it is so often confined in Elizabethan and Jacobean England. I shall
be arguing in this essay that *Measure for Measure* is part of an extraordinarily

penetrating exploration of the transformation in penitential practice that is an enduring, compelling and much overlooked facet of Shakespeare's inheritance of medieval culture. An analysis of the play in these terms, I believe, will help us see the *radical* nature of Shakespeare's medievalism, a medievalism that is almost invariably seen by modern readers as nostalgic, conservative or both. I hope too that we might begin to perceive the sheer complexity, the unforeseen consequences and unintended effects of a reformation that is far too often reduced to doctrines and dogmas that, once identified, subsume complex explorations to pre-emptive apologetic positions.

Sin is currently far more likely to be conceived along the lines of bad behaviour proscribed by an authority conceived as wholly external to an autonomous subject in protection of his freedoms, or more metaphysically, as a merely unaccountable evil. Such a conception makes it hard to see the densely linked social and psychic explorations made possible by the medieval and the reformed understanding of sin, one intimately bound up with actions, relations and behaviour. And it obscures the continuities of Renaissance theatre, in particular of Shakespeare's theatre, with medieval theatre's penitential preoccupations and with the rethinking in theory and practice of penance in the Reformation.

Sin was a deeply theological category bound up not merely with social relations but also with the very structure and reflexivity of self. It was the category through which, as a human creature, one encountered and learnt about oneself. It involved epistemological questions not simply for the priest who, as a curer of souls, was doctor and diagnostician, but also for the self and the self's relation to its past and present actions. As a fully theological category it involved too a relation to a natural created order. Scholars have recently considered the abolition of purgatory and consequently the ways in which links between the living and the dead were severed, and they have examined the changes in the rites and theatre of death, and there has been much recent emphasis on the sacrament of the altar from medieval mass to communion table in the *Book of Common Prayer*.[3] But there has been very little attention paid to the sacrament of penance, even though, in reality, there can be no understanding of the eucharist without penance because the body of Christ was inseparable from a reconciled community in both the medieval and the Reformation practice of penance and repentance.[4] Moreover penance and repentance are forms of cognition and practice that are themselves technologies of memory; they involve the shaping and practice of remembering the past.

An investigation of the transformation of penance to repentance in Shakespeare's theatre has the benefit of addressing two problems currently dogging the rethinking of Shakespeare's relation to religious culture. One problem, deriving from the anthropological concerns of such critics as Stephen Greenblatt and Louis Montrose, has to do with their understanding of Elizabethan and Jacobean theatre as taking over the ecclesiastical functions of the medieval church, whilst simultaneously evacuating those rituals.[5] Such a treatment tends to render too functional the concerns of medieval ritual as it renders the theatre complicit with a deeply polemical account of that ritual (as magic, myth, con-trick). Such views have nevertheless, and for good reason, seemed more plausible and attractive than the accounts of Shakespeare's Christian theatre that reduce the massively *theatrical* explorations of that theatre to a set of doctrinally stated propositions that follow creeds and catechisms extractable from them with such alarming ease it remains a question why they ever had to be posited in theatrical terms at all.[6]

Measure for Measure, of all Shakespeare's plays, deals most overtly with the problem of the reform of sin, and it deals with it in such a way as to make clear the potentially deforming and even paradoxical effects of attempts to reform sin which loom as large as the fruits of sin itself. In dealing with such questions we are in the jurisdictional territory of the much-disputed ecclesiastical courts, institutions which in the eyes of their detractors were remnants of the popish past and obstacles to the discipline that alone was the sign of the true church. The ecclesiastical courts historically dealt with heresy, simony and sacrilege, the refusal to pay church tithes, and with that thorn in the side of Duke Vincentio – *defamatio*. Indeed in the presentments of the churchwardens as a result of episcopal visitation, *publica fama* supplied the substance of ecclesiastical cases brought by the reports of neighbours as, through the practice of compurgation, it could also release the defendant from the charges brought against him. After the Reformation, failures to conform to the liturgies and practices of *The Book of Common Prayer* came under the jurisdiction of the spiritual courts and provided further reasons for non-conformists to detest them.[7] They also addressed questions of usury, probate of wills, advowson and patronage, contracts where oaths had been sworn, bastardy and matrimony – the last three also the complex terrain of the play's investigation of legitimacy and consent in marriage. Indeed the canonistic doctrine of consent in marriage produced some astoundingly perplexing questions. For in establishing that a binding sacramental marriage was instituted by the single exchange of consent between two parties, without any other formalities, canonists had developed a form of marriage that was incapable of proof. If the two witnesses required to establish the fact of the marriage themselves disagreed about whether a secret marriage had taken place, such proof was impossible to establish and as one historian charmingly described the situation: 'many couples all over the Christian world may have been uncertain whether they were actually married or not'.[8]

The faculty of canon law was itself ended by Henry VIII's royal injunction in 1535.[9] The reform of ecclesiastical law promised in the *Reformatio Legum Ecclesiasticarum*, a comprehensive revision of the canon law for the English polity, never occurred and in the event civil lawyers took over canon law by another act of parliament in 1545, which allowed them to exercise ecclesiastical jurisdiction.[10] Thus canon law was administered often by lay officials, cut off from the living body of the law in Rome and without a university faculty trained in the continuing study of such law. The crown in parliament was the ultimate arbiter of ecclesiastical discipline and loyalty to the church and the state were indistinguishable as a result of the Erastian path taken in the English Reformation.

Apart from the probate business of the court, church court business was divided between so-called 'instance' cases which involved the hearing of cases brought by one party against another, and the significantly more controversial *ex officio* cases in which sins were judged and corrected by a judge in virtue of his office. In *ex officio* cases the laity were refused the right of compurgation and were unable to confront their own accusers.

That the church courts were maintained after the abolition of the sacrament of penance was one of the contradictions of a Reformation that was radically Calvinist in theory yet that maintained continuity with the Roman Catholic institution of the spiritual courts even in the absence of legitimating ties with Rome. The wholesale abolition of compulsory auricular confession created further contradictions. It was abolished because the notion of priestly absolution deriving from the power of the keys seemed an obscene usurpation of divine authority. But church reformers also argued that penance had once been open and public and had been suborned in the repugnant secrecy of the 'ear-confession'. Furthermore the secrecy of the confessional suggested to reforming sensibilities a corrupt and easily sexualised relation. Yet the abolition of auricular confession paradoxically had the effect of separating the internal from the external forum of confession. Canon law had since the end of the twelfth century distinguished between the internal forum of confession (the 'court of conscience') and the external forum of the ecclesiastical courts.[11] The first was governed by the power of orders (*potestas ordinis*) and was largely the domain of the priest in the confessional imposing penances in the cure of souls. The second forum was properly speaking in the jurisdiction of the bishop and his officers, rather than the priest, and was understood as a jurisdiction (*potestas jurisdictionis*) with the power to punish in the ultimate medicinal aim of curing the soul. Precisely because, after the abolition of compulsory auricular confession, there was no regular, mandated recourse to the priestly admonitions and penances that might result from such private confessions, penance became more punitive, public and juridical in ways that could have been neither intended nor anticipated. Precisely the sorts of minor offences that might once have been dealt with in the internal forum of confession to a priest were now brought before the courts.[12]

Medieval confessional handbooks, for instance, give ample testimony to the degree to which the boundaries of the private and the public were carefully adjudicated at the discretion of the confessing priest. For example, in *Speculum Sacerdotale*, a fifteenth-century collection of sermons, the priest is advised to deal tactfully with a woman who has committed adultery and does not dare fast in penance in case her husband becomes suspicious of her. The penance recommended in *Speculum Sacerdotale* enjoins common days of fasting only and so tactfully allows her to keep her secrets and protects her from the prospect of her husband's rough justice.[13] The abolition of auricular confession entailed that only public penances, not private ones (such as fasting and the recitation of prayers or psalms), were allowed. Confession was of course allowed, even encouraged in the *Book of Common Prayer* – in the general confession in the liturgies of morning and evening prayer, in the litany, and in the general confession for the service of Holy Communion. It was also a possible implication of the injunctions to the parish priest to ensure that parishioners were in charity before communing, injunctions that might have entailed significant pastoral mediation including, perhaps, confession, but that also often resulted in the exclusion altogether from the communion.[14] But such confessions were no longer enjoined on all and shared by all. From a practice that was mandatory at Easter and woven into the penitential season of the liturgical year, confession was essentially relegated to the last dying speech of the criminal penitent in the context of punishment and execution.[15] Without question the abolition of mandatory auricular confession reduced the complexity and indeed the permeability of the boundary between public and private adjudicated by the parish priest. In hardening that boundary, the abolition assured that penance would also be automatically shameful and humiliating because the resort to public exposure was unmitigated and unmediated by any prior stages of private penance. 'Nothing', says

Patrick Collinson, 'can have made a greater negative impact than the lapse of the universal obligation to confess to a priest, as the condition both of receiving the sacrament and of remaining an acceptable part of what was still a compulsory Christian society.'[16] From its original and pastoral purpose in the cure of souls, penance became more exclusively the means of the punishment and exposure of souls and bodies and again, paradoxically and as an unintended effect, ecclesiastical authority was further externalised.

In *Measure for Measure*, the Duke as friar is the instigator and conduit of a technique whereby all that has been uttered to him in the privacy of the confessional is produced in a public judgment. In Simon McBurney's savage staging of *Measure for Measure* in the 2004 production at the National Theatre, the conversion of the knowledge gained through the confidence and trust of the confessional into humiliating exposure and profound exploitation of the confessee is given painfully extended play. Mariana and Isabella, having been induced to 'confess' to the assembled community at the gates of the city, are brutally cast aside. The feeling is given voice in Isabella's devastated 'And is this all?' (5.1.117). After the Duke's refusal of her suit for the life of Angelo with its hope that he may be moulded out of his faults, and after his hasty proposal to Isabella, who has just been confronted with the brother she is assured is dead, a bare few seconds after she has pleaded for the life of his murderer, McBurney has the two women gazing at each other in bewildered, utterly uncertain shock and in the nascent realisation that they themselves have been 'played'. In McBurney's dark and brilliant reading, the Duke, played by David Troughton, has manipulated and engineered all the proceedings to win Isabella for himself. To the astonishment and horror of all on stage, the lights go up on the backstage in which there lies a bedroom framed by bars like the prison that has dominated the set as he speaks the play's last words: 'So bring us to our palace, where we'll show / What's yet behind that's meet you all should know' (5.1.535–6). McBurney's staging responds to the play's subordination of all interior movements of the soul to the brutal logic of exposure in the Duke's theatre. It is only in the interests of the public shaming and exposure of Angelo that Isabella is encouraged to make a false confession (a confession that is really an accusation). Furthermore, although Isabella's point that thoughts are merely subjects and cannot be judged under the law seems reasonable (though not of course legally correct in view of the laws of treason), and that therefore Angelo cannot be held accountable for an act intended but not committed, such a view evacuates the vital, even constitutive, terrain of the canon law. For it was the burden of the canon law developed in the twelfth and thirteenth centuries that the intent of the sinner could convert a seemingly neutral act into a heinous sin and thus the thoughts, will, intentions and reasons for an act rather than the act itself were what might determine the degree of guilt involved.

This revolutionary and consequential seismic shift in the very terrain of the law is of course the very subject of the Sermon on the Mount from which this play takes its title (the only Shakespeare play containing a biblical allusion).[17] This is also why the distinction between whether an act might be adjudicated juridically or in the confessional was always difficult in medieval penitential theory and practice. It is this entire realm that is simultaneously exploited (as a technique of surveillance) and then utterly and conspicuously evacuated and subordinated to the Duke's logic of exposure. It is fascinating in this respect that Aquinas actually mentions what has come to be known as the bed-trick as part of his dialectical and capacious investigation of intention in the *Summa Theologiae*. Could a man be held responsible for adultery if he slept with another woman thinking her to be his wife? The footnote of the Blackfriars editor finds the example 'naïve', but its presence there is indication of the longevity of its role in the history of narrative, a role precisely guaranteed by the question of what constitutes a human act. This version of the conundrum is of course reversed in the case of Angelo: can a man be held responsible for rape when he has not so much violated his chosen object but rather slept with the woman to whom he is betrothed, who, moreover, wants to marry him?[18] And moreover, is it even possible that such a marriage can be regarded as consummated as the Duke's pseudo-providential plot wants it, when as far as Angelo is concerned he slept with Isabella, not Mariana and so there was neither volition nor consent on his part?

Shakespeare's Duke as friar is not, as Debora Shuger would have it, a 'gesture towards the sacerdotal nature of royal authority, and thus what it means to bear the sword of heaven'.[19] Far from it. His character is, rather, part of a discourse on dominion which anciently pairs the notion of sexual and political consent, and which therefore sees sexual ethics as an intrinsic part of the exploration of tyranny where tyranny is understood as the ruler who acts for his own personal pleasure above the common good.[20] It is also a thoroughgoing critique of the inseparability of church and state invested in the person of the monarch as supreme governor of the church, and the 'primacy of the crown in religious affairs', as Cathy Shrank puts it in her chapter in this volume (189). This critique incidentally is shared by Catholics and non-conformists alike, though for different reasons. Finally it is an economical and hilarious *theatrical* joke on the king's two bodies.[21]

Shuger's understanding of the Duke as friar as a defence of the sacerdotal authority of kingship depends on our admiration for the Duke's role
as a disguised confessor.[22] But this is to misread the complexity of Shakespeare's subtle inversion of an entire theatrical tradition, and the extent
to which the confessions of the play traduce the speech act of confession
altogether. In the Duke's own confession (here understood transitively), it
is striking that what he wishes to avoid, in his surrogation of Angelo, is
the imputation of tyranny: 'Sith 'twas my fault to give the people scope, /
'Twould be my tyranny to strike and gall them / For what I bid them do'
(1.3.35–7). During the course of the play he will solicit the confessions of
others (Juliet, Claudio, Barnardine and, by implication and puzzling past
reference, Mariana). His tactic here systematically converts the discourse
of self-knowledge and transformation into the acquiring of information.
In the staging by McBurney and Complicite, one of the most moving
scenes in the play is that point when the Duke has told us that he will
not tell Isabella that her brother has after all been saved by the 'accident'
provided by Ragozine's head: 'But I will keep her ignorant of her good, /
To make her heavenly comforts of despair / When it is least expected'
(4.3.108–10).

Isabella's response is devastating in McBurney's gripping staging. In her
grief she moves forward to gain comfort from the consoling friar whose
gratuitous cruelty is the very cause of her grief. Forgoing her customary
control and restraint, she rushes forward and, almost prostrate, clutches
hold of the friar, beating her fists on his back. They are thus framed in a sort
of pietà where the friar is definitively imaged as mother church. But he does
not embrace her. In fact, aware of her physical proximity he keeps his arms
and body separate from her, stretching them out into thin air. After a long
moment he deliberatively encloses her in an embrace that unites calculation
with withholding in a deeply disturbing combination. There is not one
ounce of natural warmth in this movement and no grain of compassion;
the sheer viciousness of his retention of this piece of information is drawn
out to expose its inherent sadism. It richly informs Isabella's sense of shock
and betrayal at the end of this version of the play, and her sense of despair
and entrapment.

Utterly hidden himself and so incapable of being known by others,
he can, or so he thinks, discover them in the truth of the confessional.
The confessional for him is then a form of effective espionage, an entirely
effective means of surveillance. As confessor, he has no compunction in
casually breaking the seal of the confessional, a secrecy enjoined again in the
canons of 1604, even in the utterly reduced and confined new circumstances

of post-Reformation confession. 'I have confess'd her', he says to Lord Angelo of Mariana, and 'I know her virtue' (5.1.524). (He lies to Claudio that he has confessed Angelo and 'knows' that he is only testing Isabella, his sister (3.1.165–6).) To him the confessional is the mechanism by which 'all difficulties are but easy when they are known' (4.2.204–5).

In the long genealogy of anti-fraternalism which is turned to new uses in Protestant theatre, friars are conventionally associated with pretence, disguise and deceit. The most notable examples can be found in the work of John Bale, particularly his longest and most sustained piece of agitprop drama, *King Johan*, but the conceit is by no means confined to Protestant theatrical texts alone; it is the central accusation against Catholicism itself.[23] For the late Middle Ages, friars cathected many of the problems associated with voluntary poverty and spoke to the contradictions and convictions of a religion that had at its heart a notion of sanctified poverty.[24] Yet friars were also traditionally confessors, often to kings, and worked outside the parishional system, directly under papal authority. In John Bale's theatre, the friar is the quintessential conspirator and suborner of England by Rome, and quintessentially the figure of disguise. Indeed in Bale's theatre, fraternal identity is only possible precisely as disguise because it is *essentially* duplicitous, essentially histrionic.

Shakespeare's own friars, prior to *Measure for Measure*, are emphatically not in this tradition. On the contrary, the friar is the figure who benignly circumvents the problems paternal authority brings to the legitimate desires of the young. The friars in Shakespeare generally help the young to marry, or engage in providential fictions. Above all, they are trusters of time. Their fictions have the effect of halting the rash, destructive and violent impetuosity of false judgements – such as Claudio's viciously public denunciation of Hero in *Much Ado About Nothing* or the revengeful animosity of the parents in *Romeo and Juliet*. In these plays friars are represented not as a royal priesthood, but as a church unsubordinated to the state, capable of acting quite independently of the state's jurisdiction. In transforming his prior treatment of the friar to the Duke as friar in *Measure for Measure*, Shakespeare *reverses* the import of Protestant theatre's deployment of this figure. For here, the combined anti-fraternalism and anti-theatricalism of the tradition works against the theatricality of the crown/dukedom/monarchy, rather than the theatricality of the church, and what results is precisely an inversion of anti-Catholic theatre using its own techniques. The wolf in sheep's clothing is not friar but Duke. For here confession has become utterly theatricalised and fake. The contrition and confession of subjects are deployed in an epiphany of ducal/monarchical power enacting a fantasy of itself as 'grace divine' and pardon becomes a one-way donation which substitutes for forgiveness and reconciliation.

Moreover, the hole-and-corner secrecy of this Duke-friar's confessions are provocatively juxtaposed with the emphatically public staging of the last act. The Duke declares that he is 'bound / To enter publicly' (4.3.95–6) and he sends a message to Angelo which soberly puns on 'procession' as both trial of justice and public entry:

> Him I'll desire
> To meet me at the consecrated fount
> A league below the city; and from thence,
> By cold gradation and well-balanc'd form,
> We shall proceed with Angelo.
>   (4.3.96–100)

The pun is preceded and underlined by another one on the notion of gradation as both step and status.

Indeed the whole of the last long act of *Measure for Measure* takes place at the gates of the city and thus draws on some of the conventions of the royal entry. In medieval cities with their parcelised sovereignty and mixed jurisdictions, the protocols of entry to the formal frontiers of the city were elaborate and minute in their observations of deference and preference. Sometimes for example, the mace, or other symbols of authority vested in the most senior office of the city, would be relinquished to the visiting sovereign, kissed and returned. In this economically eloquent gesture, authority is ceded and then granted again. It is a renewal of trust, authority and delegation; it marks out borders and territories in a ritual that laid bare the structures of governance, displayed and re-affirmed mutually by the giver and the recipient. These forms of ceremony were invented in the Middle Ages alongside the processional drama of Corpus Christi. Royal entries borrow from the advent liturgy as they stage the coming of the king as the coming of Christ.[25] In such kingly appropriations of Christology a fully developed sacramental understanding of kingship is modelled. Vincentio might be understood to be staging an entry then, an entry that stops at the gates of the city to reveal the structures of governance there. We think we are about to witness the ceremonial and public transfer of authority; what we see is a scripted performance that stages the epiphanic presence of the Duke-like 'grace divine'. Yet in the double genealogies of Christ and king, the Christological motifs of advent are re-modelled through the inventive theatricalisation of the king's two bodies. The theatrical joke of *Measure for Measure*'s last act is precisely that an actor can only play in one body at a time. That body can stand for the friar's body. It can stand for the Duke's body. It cannot stand for both at once when both need to be present. Vincentio has spent most of the play in his disguise as a friar; his theatrical problem at the end of the play is that these two bodies (Vincentio and the fake friar) must both be produced at once which, of course, they cannot be. The fiction works when one of the bodies is necessarily absent and so can be referred to without presencing. But as soon as the mechanisms of plot require both at once (as does the Duke's own plot) that fiction will collapse. The Duke has to disappear for the friar to re-appear ('I for a while will leave you' [5.1.256]). Even in the dizzying substitutions of *Measure for Measure*, where beginning with Angelo for Vincentio, one body is so often standing in for another – Mariana's for Isabella's, Barnardine's for Claudio's, Ragozine's for Bernardine's, a maidenhead for a brother's head – the friar's stand-in for the Duke can only operate for as long as they never have to appear together.

The legal fiction of the king's two bodies gives the king one body that dies and one that is immortal and incorruptible, thus allowing for the permanent legal existence of kingship in the absence of a mortal incumbent, or during the passing of one mortal incumbent to another. Here the king's two bodies are not so much a glorious fiction of inviolable monarchy, and a literal embodiment of the king as prince and head of the English church, ruler of temporal and spiritual jurisdiction, as an instance of and an insistence upon the real limits of embodiment – that even as actors we can be only one body at a time.

In his speech to parliament in 1603, James VI and I brings into conjunction precisely the connections of the king's two bodies so richly explored in *Measure for Measure*. Using the language of the marriage service, anticipating at once the union of Scotland with England and the union of crown and people, James says, 'What God hath conjoined then, let no man separate. I am the Husband, and all the whole Isle is my lawful wife; I am the Head, and it is my Body; I am the Shepherd, and it is my flocke.'[26] The pastoral image of the shepherd, the conjugal image of husband and wife, and the image of the body politic are benignly united, but it is the underside of this subsumption of church by king that is explored in the play.

In *Measure for Measure*, Shakespeare imagined a society which had lost the institutions, understandings and capacities for confession and for whom therefore remorse was becoming, in Rowan Williams's phrase, a lost icon.[27] In converting confession into accusation and surveillance it is precisely vulnerability to others that the Duke denies. For it is the thrust of the Duke's own confession to the friar who aids and abets his disguise that he wishes to be invulnerable to the perception of others. In surrogating Angelo he wishes to escape from his own past actions and their consequences. This is the import of the 'confession' he makes to the friar in a conversation that he is even here attempting utterly to script and control: 'Now, pious sir, / You will demand of me, why I do this' (1.3.16–17). What the play explores, then, is the sort of state and the sort of theatre that occurs where interiority is hollowed out – in short, a theatre of exposure and humiliation. That it can effect such an extraordinary and penetrating exploration derives not from its obliteration or forgetting of medieval pasts and practices, but, on the contrary, by virtue of a fidelity to the astonishing legacy of those practices in the cure of souls.

The therapeutic model of confession that subsumes contemporary Anglo-American culture is likely to understand confession as a story about the self in which introspection will lead to greater self-mastery. In this fantasy there is a denial of the shared nature of language, in the way in which our words and actions are part of the history of others, bound up in our relations with others. Thus it is that confession is never exclusively about the self but always about an acknowledgement of the self in relation to others. It is just such painful imbrications that are part of the extraordinary understanding of sin and self excavated in *Measure for Measure*.

CHAPTER 12

Medieval poetics and Protestant Magdalenes

Patricia Badir

[A ghost story] instructs its hearers to create an image whose own properties are second nature to the imagination: it instructs its hearers to depict in the mind something thin, dry, filmy, two-dimensional, and without solidity. Hence the imaginers' conviction: we at once recognize, perhaps with amazement, that we are picturing, if not with vivacity, then with exquisite correctness, precisely the thing described.

Elaine Scarry[1]

In the following description of the crucifixion, Aemilia Lanyer's speaker provides for her reader – at this moment the Countess of Cumberland – a 'briefe description of [Christ's] beautie':

> This is that Bridegroome that appeares so faire,
> So sweet, so lovely in his Spouses sight,
> That unto Snowe we may his face compare,
> His cheekes like skarlet, and his eyes so bright
> As purest Doves that in the rivers are,
> Washed with milke, to give the more delight;
>   His head is likened to the finest gold,
>   His curled lockes so beauteous to behold . . .[2]

The passage, from *Salve Deus Rex Judeorum* (1611), is palpably corporeal. And yet the speaker withdraws before the text becomes at all incarnational. Then, in a subsequent stanza, visceral description is all but abandoned as the speaker requests permission to lay aside 'this taske of Beauty' for she fears she may 'wade so deepe' and in so doing deceive herself before she has completed the image ('before I can attaine the land'). Perfection seems to lie in the partial obscurity of the reader's experience. While the addition of more visual material may make the scene appear more real and even more magnificent, the speaker claims it would also diminish the reader's role in the aesthetic experience. While it is important that the Countess see Christ as 'a God in glory, / And as a man in miserable case' it is also crucial that she 'reade his true and perfect storie', for in words '[h]is bleeding body [she]

205

may embrace' (108). It is Cumberland's insightful readership that prepares her to be touched by divinity:

> Sometime h'appeares to thee in Shepheards weed,
> And so presents himselfe before thine eyes,
> A good old man; that goes his flocke to feed;
> Thy colour changes, and thy heart doth rise;
> Thou call'st, he comes, thou find'st tis he indeed,
> Thy Soule conceaves that he is truely wise:
>   Nay more, desires that he may be the Booke,
>   Whereon thine eyes continually may looke.
>
> (109)

The Countess is exemplary because her reading allows her to figure forth that which has no corporeal presence at all and yet is nonetheless very real. Rather than fully describe Christ, Lanyer shows Cumberland's sensual reading: hearing Christ's words as they echo in her ears, seeing Christ's person as it appears just beyond the full perception of her eyes, feeling his touch as it presses down upon every pore of her skin. Lanyer sees Cumberland finding Christ's 'perfect picture' deeply engraved, or printed, in 'that holy shrine' of her heart. His presence before her is spectral, figurative even, remarkable for the impression that it leaves behind.

Cumberland's posture is familiar. She is a reading Magdalene, a relatively common figure in the devotional poetry of the seventeenth century whose affective quality often associates her with what has been dubbed 'tears literature' – an important subset of penitential writing including the famous treatments by Southwell, Constable, Marvell and Crashaw.[3] Because Mary's grief can be exhausting in its lugubrious detail, many have found the poetic illustrations of the penitent to be aestheticised.[4] This is certainly the case, but I want to suggest that the moment cannot be simply dismissed as such, for the maudlin aesthetic or, more precisely, the poetics that are informed by that aesthetic are precisely at issue here. Like their medieval counterparts, early modern Magdalenes were exalted for their expert negotiation of vision, memory and language. In particular, Protestant poets like Lanyer borrowed from late medieval treatments of the sepulchre scene that focus upon the vicissitudes of the saint's memory – that is, her prior experience of corporeal touch brought to the foreground of consciousness through the strange vision of the resurrected Christ particularly as described in the Gospel of John.[5] Importantly, in many of the medieval treatments of the scene, Christ's presence is not corporeal. The only tangible body is that of the Magdalene, whose sight – withdrawn and intimate, for it resides in the depths of her soul – is privileged as a record of the resurrection while her person becomes the pliable material upon which Christ's ghostly and no-longer-human presence is impressed. This important precedent allows Protestant writers, including Lanyer and Nicholas Breton, to figure the palpable presence of an invisible god in an iconoclastic world. These poets make Christ's presence known, not by describing the resurrected man himself, but rather, by describing the eerie effect the sight of his untouchable, phantasmal form had upon its first witness. The medieval Magdalene's privileged vision, and the effect it has upon her, becomes, in the Protestant tradition, the basis of a devotional poetics dedicated to Magdalene-like women, including the Countess of Cumberland, whose readerly forms likewise register the effect of the ghostly return of their Saviour.

I

The medieval Magdalene is recalled by Lanyer because the saint was perceived to have special knowledge of the Passion and, moreover, because she was recognised for her ability to bring the vision of Christ's suffering to mind in the absence of his physical body. When Julian of Norwich alludes to Mary Magdalene, for example, she longs for her forerunner's immediate and intimate access to the suffering body of Christ; she wants to see, as Mary did, the 'bodily sight' of his suffering so that she might have more 'knowledge of the bodily peynes of our saviour'. Only with this kind of memory ('shewing') can she 'have the more trew minde in the passion of Christe'.[6] Mary's sensual experience of Christ or, more precisely, her vivid recollection of that experience, is the key to more perfect knowledge and thus to more perfect love. But Julian's dilemma, akin to Lanyer's, is how to do so without the benefit of the Magdalene's privileged physical intimacy.

The potency of Mary Magdalene's access to Christ, as acknowledged by Julian, has an even more ancient history as a part of the Easter liturgy in the form of the *Quem quaeritis* trope. In this text, four members of the clergy enact the discovery of the empty sepulchre by the three Marys and the exchange between the women and the angel who announces the resurrection. The importance of this brief scene, still widely understood as the first manifestation of liturgical drama, lies in the emphasis it places upon sight – that is the ability to see absence – as evidence for the resurrection and, consequently, Christ's continuing presence in the world. For Michal Kobialka, the answer to the question '[w]hom do you seek' (which is 'He is not here; he has risen, as was foretold. Go and announce that he is risen from the sepulchre') becomes an imperative not only to preach the resurrection, but also a reflection of 'the desire to give visibility to the body, which had disappeared' and to give 'representational form to a complex theological thought'. The fact that the Magdalene is one of the Marys participating in the exchange locates her at a moment in which discursive and mutable definitions of the nature and substance of Christian representation were formulated and revised.[7]

Sarah Beckwith, who has also considered the centrality of the Magdalene to medieval Eucharistic theory, reads the dramatisation of John 20 in the York play as subversive because it wrests the tropes of sacrament from the arms of the church and re-establishes them in a communal and lay setting. That is, one possible way for medieval Christians to come to terms with their relationship to Christ was through the dramatic exploration of Christ's relation to Mary Magdalene. For Beckwith, the York 'Magdalene in the Garden' sequence dramatises the question central to sacramentality itself by asking '[h]ow do we encounter the glorified God who has withdrawn himself from our sight?' Along with the other Passion plays, this one provides 'the regained sight that shows that we too can see that Christ is the sign of God'. In particular, the Magdalene sequence explores the implications of Christ's absence and 'the transition between Christ as a living contemporary to a Christ who henceforth exists in memory – in the sacrament and in the church founded on and by those who witnessed his resurrection'. That the discussion of absence and presence, as posited by the Magdalene's encounter with the empty sepulchre, is enacted in theatrical ways is important. The moment is sacramental because it gives a scriptural idea tangible substance by introducing living form.[8] Theatre does, to a certain extent, solve Julian's problem by enacting Mary's experience for an audience hungry for evidence of Christ's living presence. However, as Beckwith is quick to point out, the Reformation makes it impossible to further exalt the Magdalene's role in the business of making Christ materialise.[9]

And yet in her reading of the frontispiece to the 1611 edition of Richard Hooker's *The Lawes of Ecclesiastical Polity* (fig. 12), Debora Shuger has observed that the presence of the Magdalene in an image that serves as preface to a (if not *the*) canonical text of English Protestantism shows how the figure had become 'the decorous symbol for the Protestant *individual* subject, the *suppositum* existing apart from the mystical conjunctions of both church and state, with room (and book) of her own'.[10] Shuger's point is that Mary's 'erotic fragrance' – a vestigial remnant of medieval 'ocular eroticism' – presupposes the importance of Mary's physical knowledge

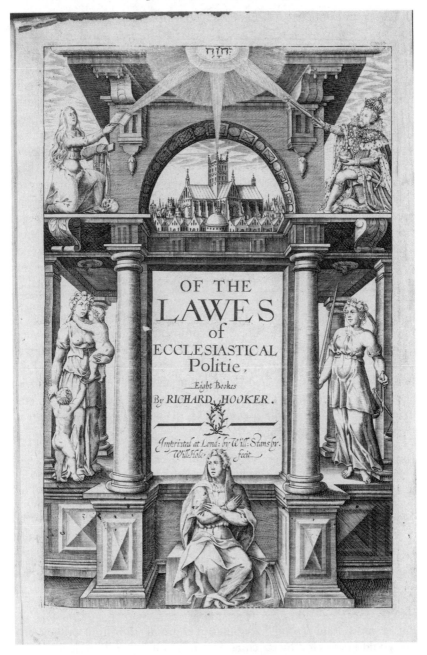

Fig. 12   Richard Hooker, *Of the Lawes of Ecclesiastical Politie* (London, 1611), title page

of Christ and undercuts absolute adherence to the non-corporeal, purely spiritual devotion that tends to be associated with post-medieval religion. 'The Magdalene narratives', concludes Shuger, 'concern the *body* of Christ, that is, the real presence. The emphasis on Christ's body is Eucharistic as well as erotic – or, rather both at once.'[11] Their early modern Anglo-Catholic treatments of the Magdalene, the sermons and poems of Robert South-well, the poems of Henry Constable and the poems of Richard Crashaw, do turn to the Magdalene to lament the loss of Christ's physical body in the terms Shuger suggests.[12] However, nostalgia for a more corporeal piety is not integral to the poetics of the seventeenth-century Protestant writers who use the Magdalene specifically to honour their aristocratic dedicatees as devout readers of the Gospels. Much of the Magdalene writing of the seventeenth century is, in fact, neither sacramental nor Eucharistic. Instead, poets like Lanyer and Breton make use of the Magdalene's clairvoyance, located at the crux of memory and vision, to articulate divine presence in purely figurative terms. In so doing they render portraits of Protestant devotion: images of reading women whose posture is an uncanny semblance of the Gospels' blessed sinner.

Post-medieval, Protestant fascination with a figure so sacramental in nature is partly explained by Erasmus's commentary on John 20. The Mag-dalene's singularity here is, once again, her unfaltering commitment to Christ's person. She lingers at the sepulchre because she longs to tend the body of him 'whome she had loued being aliue'. When she sees Christ again, and falls to the ground to touch his feet, she does so in 'remem-braunce of thyr olde familiaritie'. And yet, the wrenching prohibition, *noli me tangere*, is glossed as follows:

Jesus knowying that as yet she thought no great excellent thyng of hym, although she loued him sincerely and ardently, did prohibite her to touche his bodye for Marie saw well that he was aliue agayne, but she thought that he was reuiued for none other cause, but as he dyd before, to liue familiarlye with his frendes, beyng now a man aliue where as before he was deade, & ignoraunte she was that he now caryed about with hym an immortall bodye whiche was to be handeled with muche greater reuerence, whiche bodye the Lord did neuer exhibite or present to the wicked, nor suffered it to be handled of euery man, to thentent he might little by little, altogether withdrawe them from the loue of that bodye. Touche me not (sayeth he) it is the same bodye whiche hong upon the crosse, *but it is nowe beautified and adourned with the glory of immortalitie.*[13]

For Erasmus, John describes a significant epistemic shift from a time when one could know God by touching him to a time when knowledge could come only to the blessed and only to those who had altogether withdrawn from physical attachment. More notably, the presence that Mary sees, and that Erasmus describes, is 'nowe beautified and adourned with the glory of immortalitie'. This is not a tangible presence; it is rather a phantasmal presence figurable only by means of the effect it has upon its beholder.

While Shuger finds medieval affect in Protestant interiority, Erasmus's Magdalene opens a window on medieval spiritual insight – a facet of the Magdalene's pre-Reformation biography that is as significant as her association with matters of the flesh. Erasmus, like many before him, is suggesting that Mary is special because she demonstrates a form of 'spiritual seeing', or what Herbert Kessler identifies as an intermediate level of perception between the corporeal and the intellectual that relies upon the 'eyes of the mind' (the term is Augustinian) to 'think of bodies previously known but now absent'.[14]

Theresa Coletti reminds us just how harsh and jarring the *noli me tangere* prohibition seemed to Margery Kempe, who saw the biblical figure as 'pursuing an utterly tactile religious epistemology, forever at odds with the deeper spiritual implications of the *noli me tangere*'.[15] And corroborating Beckwith's observations cited above, Coletti further suggests that the Magdalene drama (the Digby play, the York Winedrawers' play, the Townley *Resurrection* and the N-Town *hortulanus* scene in particular), challenges Christ's reproof of Mary's touch by recognizing her attachment to Christ's body. But, for Coletti, the medieval story does not end here: the body/spirit dichotomy is more productively engaged elsewhere. In the *Wisdom* play, for instance, the character of Anima is bound to Mary when she is purged of seven devils and Coletti determines that, 'far from being empty of a meaning of her own, the Anima/Magdalene figure signifies the most basic connections between body and soul, humanity and God'. More specifically, the *Wisdom* play constitutes the character as a 'permeable body' in order to remake her as the 'clene sowll [that] ys Godys restynge place'. The idea of the Magdalene as a 'real' container for some kind of essential, non-corporeal presence is also found in the N-Town play where Mary Magdalene is metaphorically figured as a 'chawmere' or chamber for her Lord's 'swete sowle'.[16] It is this medieval tradition – one that posits a meditative Magdalene whose body is the site upon which an image, or idea, of Christ appears to materialise – that I want to pursue because it begins to articulate a ghostly poetics of presence that would appeal to writers coming at the issue of spiritual affect from a very different religious perspective.

In the pseudo-Chaucerian *The Complaynt of Mary Magdaleyne* (1526), Mary's lingering memories of ablution and crucifixion lead her to describe the body she has recently known so completely. And yet, while her intimacy with Christ's person may be the source of her mourning, the power of her image lies, precisely, in its measure of *her* experience of bodily absence.

> Whiche rufull sight whan I gan beholde
> Out of my wytte I almost distraught,
> Tare my heer, my handes wrange & folde
> And of that sight my hert dranke such a draght
> That many a fall sownyng there I caught;
> I brused my body, fallying on the grounde
> Whereof I fele many a greuous wounde.[17]

When Christ appears only to deny the anchoring capabilities of touch, the Magdalene finds herself, at least initially, even further at sea. Susan Stewart suggests that Christ's interdiction 'outstrips the possibilities of comprehension and reference' and produces 'effects of sublimity, magnitude and ungraspability'.[18] What the reader sees is thus not Christ's renewed presence but rather the effects of that untouchable presence upon its privileged witness. It is of great consequence, then, to acknowledge that the Magdalene's vision of the intangible Christ is rationalised and explained with reference to the printed page. She says: 'Thy blessed visage', is the place '[w]herin is printed my parfyte solace' (F3r). In anticipation of the Magdalene of Hooker's frontispiece, Mary's meeting with a ghost is explained as a kind of reading.

The image of the reading Magdalene has a long history traceable back to Gregory.[19] The lecherous eyes of the sinner become, through Christ's mercy, contrite, tearful eyes and tearful eyes, in turn, become contemplative or reading eyes invoking what Beckwith has described as the long-standing association between tears and words, weeping and reading.[20] There are also many visual examples of this posture: Correggio's penitent reads in a grotto; Tintoretto's nude Magdalene holds a book in her hand; Titian depicts the saint with eyes looking upward and away from a book that rests upon a skull and Rogier van der Weyden paints her more modestly with downcast eyes looking upon a book. Another English Magdalene – this time a late medieval sculpture on an outside wall of the Church of Mary Magdalene in Launceston, Cornwall (fig. 13) – illustrates the same moment.[21] These visual images, like the Hooker frontispiece, draw upon medieval iconography in which Christ, the Word, is figured as a book, and the Magdalene, in a rather bizarre moment of reflexivity, is the exemplary reader of her own story.[22] In many of these images the subject's eyes look down or look away from the pages open before her – these eyes have been interpreted as 'come-hither' bedroom eyes and, as such, reminders of the penitent's sinful past.

Fig. 13 Sculpture of Magdalene, Church of Mary Magdalene, Launceston, Cornwall

But Mary's diversion registers, rather, the effect of reading. The beauty of the image resides in the interplay between the sign of absent presence – the book – and the passionate experience of that presence as registered by the reader's senses.

The reading trope undergoes one further extension in *The Complaynt*, as the Magdalene herself is transformed into an imprint or impression of the original word. Mary promises:

> The wounde, hert, and blode of my darlyng
> Shal neuer slyde from my memoriall;
> The bytter paynes also of tourmentyng
> Within my soule be *grauin* principall
> The spere, alas that was so sharpe withall
> So thyrled my hert as to my felyng,
> That the body and soule were at departyng.[23]

If Mary finds solace in the pages of Christ's face, then other readers, in turn, find comfort in the image of Christ they see impressed upon the pliant pages of her soul. She becomes, quite literally, a printed repository of Christian memory. 'Chirled my soule by inwarde resemblaunce / Whiche neuer shall out of my remembraunce', she pledges, for her heart is 'impressed ful sore' of 'His royall forme, his shap, his semelynesse, / His port, his chere, his godenes evermore, / His noble person, with al gentylnesse'.[24] This depiction of Mary recalls Matthew's pronouncement on the significance of the saint's attention to Christ: 'Wheresoever this Gospel shall be preached in the whole world, there shall also this, that this woman hath done, be told for a memorial of her' (26:13 [Geneva]). For Matthew, at least, the image of the Magdalene is always attendant upon the reading of Christ.

Mary Magdalene's figure, understood as an engraved memorial to Christ's living presence, is at the root of her vocation as it is authorised in John: 'go to my brethren, and say unto them [. . .] (John 20:17)'. The N-Town Mary interprets the command as a call to preach:

> There kan no tounge my joye expres
> Now I haue seyn my lorde on lyve.
> To my bretheryn I wyl me dresse
> And telle to hem anon ryght belyve;
> With opyn speche I xal me shryve
> And telle to hem with wurdys pleyn,
> Howp at Cryst from deth to lyve,
> To endless blys is resyn ageyn.[25]

The importance of Mary's teaching to the mendicant culture of the Middle Ages has been well established by Katherine Jansen, whose magnificent book saves the Magdalene from the pitfalls of her reputation and establishes her as the *sine qua non* of the *vita apostolica*.[26] But the N-Town passage also describes, in as precise terms as possible, the public vocation of devotional writers charged from the middle of the sixteenth century onward with the exclusive responsibility of representing Christ in verbal or textual terms: '[a]nd telle to hem with wurdys pleyn, / How þat Cryst from deth to lyve, / . . . is resyn ageyn'. Another example of medieval precedent for a maudlin poetics is found in the York play. 'In thyne hart thou write / Myne armoure riche and goode' says Jesus to a bewildered Mary after he forbids her touch.[27] If Christ's impression as left on Mary's person becomes the real subject of meditation, she, like the devotional poet, is earnestly compelled to copy and circulate that impression upon every occasion and in every possible instance. Mary's intimate encounter with Christ acquires its force only when it enters the realm of words and thus representation. The power of the sepulchre story, in the late medieval tradition, does not, therefore, reside entirely in an incarnational poetics – Christ is not made to appear to the reader – instead the task of beauty each poet undertakes is the reproduction and circulation of the image of a woman marked by a ghost no one else can see.

Thus far, my project has been to illustrate that pre-Reformation treatments of Mary Magdalene are not exclusively eroticised manifestations of the corporeal piety of the late Middle Ages. Now I want to turn more concertedly to the early modern to show that the medieval Magdalene's importance to matters of form and narration, briefly alluded to in Lanyer's *Salve Deus*, is also identifiable in other works by seventeenth-century Protestant writers. There are a number of examples that I could turn to at this juncture but none more fascinating than the works of Nicholas Breton that play with the bewildering and enthralling possibilities of the Magdalene's poetic vision.[28]

The prefaces to many of Breton's writings express concern for the fate of the feminine soul. His explicitly female readers are often asked to turn their 'good mindes' to the memory of 'some women in his especiall fauour' including Mary Magdalene.[29] Breton's appeal to the female reader is, at least in part, a reiteration of the opinion that women were, like the Magdalene, particularly prone to visionary lapses of the imagination induced by an excess of passionate feeling. But the urge to associate Breton's construction of female readership with anti-feminist suspicion needs to be qualified by the fact that most of Breton's Magdalene work was dedicated to Mary Sidney, Countess of Pembroke – a woman whose formidable mind was certainly beyond reproach.[30] In 'The Blessed Weeper' (1601), Breton draws attention to his dedicatee's election in terms of the imaginative talents of her remarkable intellect. He explicitly addresses Sidney's contemplative gifts in the hope that his poetry will 'lay before [her] eyes a diuine humour of a rauisht soule' – a vision Breton hopes will be pleasing to the Countess's 'good fauour'. The matter of Magdalene is offered to a woman whose eyes and mind are already turned toward the matter of God:

Matter of most worth to most worthy mindes, is most worthily presented. What matter, in worth may compare with diuine meditation? What minde more worthy honour, then the heauenly enclined? and whose minde more truly worthy of that blessed Title, then your Ladiships.[31]

By thinking upon Mary, Sidney thinks upon Christ. By presenting his dedicatee *à la Madeleine*, Breton sheds light on the Countess's own role in the creation of a literature of spiritual insight. As is true of the medieval representations of the reading Magdalene, what Breton's readers see is not an image of the Passion but an image of the passions of a devout and creative soul.

The Blessed Weeper appears to Breton's speaker as the first witness of the Resurrection. As is conventional, Mary Magdalene's grief is intensified by the fact that Christ's body has apparently been removed from the tomb. Referring to Jesus as '[t]he heavenly substance of my life and loue', Mary asks '[w]hy should I liue and look vpon the light? / Now that I have lost the ioy of such a sight?' Because Mary's soul was attached to the physical body of Christ, the disappearance of that body means that her soul is jettisoned into the world leaving her body bereft of sense:[32]

> But what speake I of either sinne or grace?
> My sinnes too greeuous, and my gace [*sic*] is gone;
> My life is dead, the earth is all too base,
> For my loues Lord, to deigne to looke vpon,
> Where liues not one good creature, no not one,
> And what should I but weepe to liue to see,
> I cannot see where my sweete Lord may be.[33]

Not only has Mary become blind, but in Christ's absence, seeing becomes a base and even loathsome experience.

In spite of her distraction, however, or more likely as a consequence of it, Mary's tears ultimately provide a kind of optic lens for a spiritual insight that refocuses the senses to see differently. Mary says: 'Let me see thee, and I desire no more.' She would be as satisfied with the ethereal vision of Christ as with the phenomenal, corporeal presence of his body:

> Oh sight more pretious then tongue can expresse,
> Wherein the eye doth comfort so the heart,
> The heart, the soule, and all in their distresse,
> Doe find an ease, and end of euerie smart.
> When eie and heart, and soule and euerie part
>   Concluded in ioy, that comfort did beginne;
>   Better to weepe in grace, then laugh in sinne.[34]

Breton's Mary does eventually see 'the substance of her bliss' and experiences the return of her senses. More importantly, the *noli me tangere* moment is glossed as reflecting Mary's understanding that she needs 'but a looke of that sweet heavenly holy eye of Thine'. Breton's penitent is ecstatic, for her lover's 'substance' resides within her heart and soul. Breton references this moment with a familiar appeal to the act of reading – the complete passage is:

> I wil not presse one foote beyond the line
> Of thy loue's leaue, vouschafe me but a looke
> Of that sweete heauenly holy eye of thine,
> Of my deere Loue the euer-liuing Booke.[35]

Wherever one finds the Gospels then, one also finds Mary Magdalene and, I would argue by implication, Mary Sidney – the Scriptures' two most inspired readers. This idea is consistent with the observation that Breton's departure from the Eucharistic tradition entails the effectual abandoning of the missing body and the acceptance that the replacement is a kind of literary contract or figurative exchange in which one form of seeing will be replaced with another.[36] In concert with his pedagogic vocation, directed as it is to an ideal Protestant woman who is both reader and writer (the speaker wishes 'that all women might such weepers be'), the overtly corporeal demonstration of devotion associated with female piety and with late medieval Catholicism becomes bound up in a poetics that understands reading as liberating, rather than harnessing and restraining the authorial potential of the female imagination.[37]

One imagines Breton's noble patron and the Magdalene becoming one as both read the Gospels: both look away to imagine that place where the reading gaze meets the likeness/presence of another – of Christ that is. Breton recreates this scene over and over again in his work dedicated to Sidney. In 'The Countesse of Penbrookes Loue', the Countess is represented as lamenting her sins in the fashion of the Magdalene ('looke on thy Mary with her bitter teares, / That washt thy feet and wipte them with her heares'). In *The Passions of the Spirit*, Sidney is found sitting with the Magdalene 'at the grave / As full of grefe as ever love maye live'.[38] The sensuality of a representation premised so vividly on sight means that the Pembroke/Magdalene figure is not just the subject of Christ's scrutiny – she is also looked at, even admired, by Breton as by any reader who happens upon the scene of her devotional reading. Such an observation could, I suppose, be used to bolster theory on the politics of voyeurism or even as evidence of a romantic relationship between Pembroke and Breton. However, I would suggest that Breton puts the speaker/writer, subject/patron problem at some remove by situating his Magdalene behind a shroud of language that partly obscures her person. I am referring specifically to a poetic practice that aestheticises and disarms erotic potential by accentuating Mary Magdalene's expert negotiation of vision, memory and language so as to complement Mary Sidney's like aptitudes.[39] In other words, it is more productive to consider the oddness of the optics as a matter of poetics, particularly a poetics of portraiture, that transcends both the politics of the male gaze and the specifics of biography. The speaker of 'The Blessed Weeper' recognises the cognitive conditions under which he writes and this recognition allows him to draw attention to the narrative that his speaker recounts, collapsing, in the process, the distinction between the way she looks and what she says.

And yet, the speaker has difficulty keeping both portrait and speech in mind:

> As to her words my vision witness beares,
> And my remembrance may for truth approoue;
> The whole discourse, her passions seem'd to moue;
>   In hearts deepe griefe, & soules high ioy conceiued,
>   Was as I write, were not my thoughts deceiued.[40]

His sight should prove her words true and yet the speaker distrusts his own authorial ability to sustain the presence of the shadowy figure his words have summoned. The sepulchre scene seems to be used by Breton and Lanyer to describe a kind of vertigo experienced by the poetic persona in the face of a devout patron, who, by virtue of her status, utters an interdiction, 'touch me not' that denies the speaker's complete access to his subject. As with the Magdalene, the poet's instability is instigated by the loss of the stabilising capabilities of touch – because the subject of poetry is in some sense ungraspable, the speaker's vision is rendered subject to doubt.[41] The sensual passion and depth of the Magdalene's encounter with Christ is repeated in an analogous encounter between shadowlike muses and a tormented speaker/poet touched and bewildered by the hauntingly beautiful intensity of inaccessible presence.

At the end of Breton's poem, the Magdalene suddenly disappears, leaving the speaker alone to contemplate what he may or may not have witnessed:

> And with that word, she vanisht so away,
> As if that no such woman there had beene,
> But yet me thought, her weeping seem'd to say
> The Spirit was of Marie Magdalene,
> Whose bodie now, although not to be seene,
>   Yet by her speech, it seemed it was she,
>   That wisht all women might such Weepers be.[42]

The tenuous claim this speaker has to any kind of certainty comes with the words spoken to him by the maudlin spectre, making her apparition a poignant example of what W. J. T. Mitchell articulates as 'the necessarily verbal character of imagining the invisible'.[43] Breton uses the opening and closing stanzas of his poem to remind us that presence can be made known as much by means of words that linger as by visions that vanish.[44] Perhaps, then, it does not matter that the speaker cannot trust either the clarity of his vision or the accuracy of his memory. The possibility of deception or misperception that troubles the somnambulist speaker (he was 'halfe in a slumber and more halfe a-sleepe') may be an acknowledgement that one of the lessons the Magdalene teaches is that figurative language can only succeed when it haunts the mind, challenging it to question the substance of the forms it makes manifest.[45] It is not coincidental then that Lanyer also describes the inspiration for her account of the Passion as 'delivered unto me in sleepe many yeares before I had any intent to write in this maner'.[46] Like the ghost story which, according to Scarry, 'instructs its hearers to depict in the mind something thin, dry, filmy, two-dimensional, and without solidity' producing the effect that 'we at once recognise, perhaps with amazement, that we are picturing, if not with vivacity, then with exquisite correctness, precisely the thing described', Breton's and Lanyer's speakers constitute presence darkly. Breton shows us the features of two Marys, one saint and one saintly patron, both phantasmal reader-writers remarkable for the vivid impressions Christ's ghostly presence has made upon them. Lanyer's speaker-poet is herself a Magdalene who comes face to face with, and then withdraws from, the memories that haunt her in order to acknowledge a pliant space within the heart of her reader – a space where Christ's form can be felt most intimately.[47]

I argue elsewhere that the convention of representing aristocratic ladies *à la Madeleine* would eventually become decadent as the erotic features of the penitent reader would prove, in a different political context, impossible to contain.[48] In dedicating their poems to Cumberland and Pembroke, however, Lanyer and Breton move a medieval memory of Mary Magdalene into conformist court culture where she serves to render these aristocratic patrons not only as Magdalene figures but also as the very image of English Christian subjectivity – figuring Magdalenes. Both Breton and Lanyer seek to attribute to their patrons something of the sensory experience of Mary Magdalene by dwelling not just on the scene that impresses both Pembroke and Cumberland but also upon the women's ability to impress the poetic imagination. The Magdalene is thus not always the vestigial remnant of a more erotic, Eucharistic piety, nor is she an aestheticised emblem of a newly formed female devotion premised upon silent reading and meditation. Like Pembroke and Cumberland she is, as she has always been, a gifted seer whose impressions haunt the devotional writing of the age.

Afterword

David Wallace

This is a timely volume, or a volume just ahead of its time. New initiatives in medieval and Renaissance studies are appearing on a monthly basis: special issues of journals, conferences, curricular reforms, book proposals, study centres. So far, most of the running has been made by medievalists reading forwards rather than by Renaissance scholars reading back. The editors have an explanation: medievalists are more eager to do this, 'for institutional reasons' (6). This might be taken to mean that the Renaissance will always be assured of its place in English curricula, given the long-established dominance of Shakespeare, whereas fourteenth-century English might go the way of Anglo-Saxon. Twenty years ago, in my first job, I was told by a prominent Renaissance scholar that Shakespeare would always be the 'strutting stage' of every English Department: an assertion supported by his tendency to regard departmental politics as akin to those of a self-fashioning world of Renaissance courtiers. Now he might not be so confident, surveying the parcelised sovereignty of contemporary curricular space: Postcolonial Studies, Gender and Queer Studies, Cinema Studies and Creative Writing all demand their market share. Even American Studies (traditionally a conservative or at least monolingual field) is reinventing itself, to embrace 'literatures of the Americas'; some English professors are even learning Spanish. The Shakespeareocentric Renaissance was also bolstered by filmic adaptations: as someone said, there will never be a *Chaucer in Love*. Now, however, it might be argued that Jane Austen outperforms Shakespeare as film author of choice; and that, what with *Spamalot* and a rash of Crusader epics (to say nothing of US Foreign Policy), the Middle Ages is making a strong stage and celluloid comeback. For whatever reasons, be it curricular constriction or recognition of common interests, medieval and Renaissance scholars increasingly keep company with one another. This volume is one of the first to recognize this new state of affairs: one that sees us moving from occasional dialogue to incipient cohabitation.

The space around which scholars of medieval and Renaissance English gather seems a fathomless pit, formed by acts of institutional destruction – chiefly the spoliation of monasteries – that have ruined or fragmented medieval systems of learning, devotion and written record. Increasingly, attention has been paid to the furious decades of the Reformation: these function, for medievalists, as something akin to the Middle Passage in African-American historiography. 'It will be clear to readers', the editors write, 'that the term "Reformation" is central to the concerns of this volume in a way that "Renaissance" is not' (7). Medievalists contemplating the Reformation in England feel mixed emotions: resignation to the patient task of textual reconstruction (the business of editing with which medievalists, especially in England, are famously associated); and a kind of road rage directed at Renaissance Studies. Such animus derives from recognition that the English Renaissance first creates English medieval studies (by fragmenting its textual culture and physical remains) and then ignores it: for the key motif of Renaissance is to proclaim the new and abjure the superannuation and darkness of the old; to move on and not look back. It is thus fitting to scrutinise those key decades that see Tyndale debating More and More responding to Fish; that see Anne Askew crushed between Catholic and Protestant factions (each willing to see her die, as heretic or martyr); that nurture John Bale, the sometime Carmelite friar. The emergence of Bale in this volume, particularly in the fine chapters of Cathy Shrank and Jennifer Summit, suggests that he more than anyone is the natural creature of darker English Reformation spaces. As an author, he is not especially talented: indeed, it can be argued that his finest moments are parasitic, sucked from poor creatures such as Askew and John Leland. But he is a passionate, indeed incendiary, writer; he bears authentic witness to the temperature of the times. Thomas More writes and imagines better: his *Supplication of Souls* (1529) offers a most poignant account of those suffering unremembered in Purgatory. James Simpson argues persuasively that our interpellation by such appeals speaks not only to our sense of 'possibly abandoned friends'; it also evokes 'a system of communal practice and consciousness bidding farewell to, or being repelled by, Protestant modernity' (21). Here and elsewhere, our imaginative and indeed emotional experience of a literary text is coloured by knowledge of greater historical forces; and by a sense, at least as professional medievalists, that these supplicating souls of a vanishing Catholic culture cry out to *us* as their last hope of textual memorialisation.

Some risks accrue, however, from accentuating the Reformation as the organising centre of English medieval/Renaissance thinking. One ironic effect is that the very passion that imbues Reformation writers – the sense that there is everything to play for, in a short span of years – also affects those who write about it (even from a great historical distance); and one notices that, then as now, such writers are almost all men. The vigour and urgency of Brian Cummings's 'Reformed Literature and Literature Reformed,' the final chapter of *The Cambridge History of Medieval English Literature* (1999), threatens to swallow up all that has gone before. James Simpson's *Reform and Cultural Revolution* (2002), part of the new Oxford English Literary History, gives Reformation polemic and violence newly foundational status; his second chapter opens with Lord Protector Somerset's destruction of murals based on verses of Lydgate at old St Paul's. Cummings and Simpson can hardly be blamed for being powerful and compelling writers. One danger of their very persuasiveness, however, is that attention may become *over*-fixated on the Reformation decades; their sheer intensity may come to condition or predetermine readings of all that follows. Larry Scanlon might well have anticipated greater anti-Catholic sentiment in setting out to read the glosses of Robert Crowley's edition of *Piers Plowman* (1550): but 'of the 495 glosses in total in the third imprint', Scanlon reports, 'I find only fifteen which are explicitly anti-Catholic' (65). Protestant Crowley, Scanlon finds, seems more concerned to seek common ground with Catholic Langland than to proclaim difference of religion; this leads Scanlon to meditate upon 'the problem of continuity' (53). Over-emphasis upon the Reformation – as *the* decisive, epoch-making break in English cultural tradition – may ironically conserve the ideal of a Middle Ages possessing originary wholeness (rather than the 'decentred, heterogeneous, dispersive, local and popular' character that allows it, in Scanlon's view, to dialogue so powerfully and directly with postmodern culture (52)). And, as with the post-modern, there are *other* historiographical fractures, other phases of violence and 'cultural revolution' (to recall Simpson's key phrase), which come between us and medieval/Renaissance textuality. It is often difficult to know, for example, whether medieval manuscripts disappeared from cathedral libraries at the Reformation or during the Cromwellian civil war. And with the Restoration, Catholic culture began to flourish again: friars frequented London palaces, nuns returned to York, and a Catholic king produced a Catholic male heir. Much of *this* Catholic English history is later subdued, of course, by the 'Glorious Revolution' of 1688. The 1707 Act of Union employed anti-Catholic discourses to unite regions disaggregated by differences of cultural tradition and local loyalty; the Gordon Riots of 1780 killed over seven hundred Catholics or suspected Catholics in London. In this same eighteenth century, however, many Catholics and

Protestants found common intellectual ground: one of the commonplace assumptions of our own time is that Christianity and Judaism pass through Enlightenment, whereas Islam did not. Finally, difference of religion came to matter less than difference of skin colour: blackness signified enslave-ability, and whiteness freedom. These are historiographical fractures every bit as great as the discourses of sixteenth-century religious Reformation; they too come between us and our retrieval of premodern texts.

The English Middle Ages, before ending in ruined shrines and charred madonnas, itself keenly sensed and imagined historical fracture. Malory's Arthurian saga, which ends in terminal destruction, was itself written dur-ing a civil war that Malory himself would not survive. Chaucer's only Arthurian adventure, *The Wife of Bath's Tale*, begins by looking back from a disenchanted time: one that sees friars – a relatively recent addition to English landscapes – pry panoptically into every corner of the realm (3.857–81). Like their Renaissance counterparts, medieval Englishmen think back selectively: Chaucer's Man of Law knows all the *doomes* or judicial deci-sions made *since* the 1066 Conquest (1.323–4). English guilds, obliged to submit self-descriptions to the Chancery at Westminster early in 1389, show lamentable forgetting of Anglo-Saxon saints; Johns and Margarets abound in all walks of life. Medievalists whose expertise begins in 1300, or on 16 July 1377, have been as unwilling to read backwards through time as those Renaissance scholars they accuse of period-bound fixity. It is thus encouraging to see a scholar of the Renaissance, Gordon McMullan, draw-ing representations of Anglo-Saxon history into *longue durée* discussion. McMullan, in introducing us to Thomas Middleton's *Hengist, King of Kent* (*c.* 1620), alerts us to 'the only instance of Old English in the canon of early modern drama' and, in the very same play, to the extraordinary prospect of Ranulf Higden, 'Monk of Chester', as Chorus (129, 128). It is amusing to imagine the quintessentially medieval author of the *Polychronicon* tread-ing the boards in Jacobean England, although it is worth recalling that Trevisa's translation of his work (1387) was treated to printed editions by Caxton (1482) and Wynkyn de Worde (1495). McMullan's chapter meshes beautifully with that of medievalist Anke Bernau. Here again, across the Reformation divide, models of continuity seem more persuasive than any search for fundamental alteration of historiographical design – except that the continuity in question, before and after 1547, is creative adaptation of sedimented pasts to current political need. Most striking here is the recur-rent conceit that unruly females – 'originary women', in Bernau's phrase (114) – need both to display native courage and (by way of authorising imperial designs at future dates) to be subjected to masculine conquest.

Albina and Scota prefigure Boudica; Boudica, whose statue stands close
to Westminster Bridge, comes to symbolise (again, especially for the eighteenth century) the kind of native pluck which, transformed through subjection to an *imperium*, whether Roman or, later, British, develops into
world-conquering power.

The adroitness with which many authors in this volume, in addition to
McMullan and Bernau, narrate backwards through time has considerable
potential. This would not be achieved simply by reversing the terms of
the title, namely seeking 'the early modern' in the 'medieval': that might
rekindle medievalist 'it happened here first' grievances while strengthening
conventional teleological schemata. But a topic such as personification allegory, pursued back into the Middle Ages from seventeenth-century starting
points, might prove instructive. We might begin with Bunyan's Christian,
Evangelist, and Mr. Worldly Wiseman and pass by way of Miltonic Sin
and Death to pause halfway with, as ever, John Bale. Bale is not, as Cathy
Shrank demonstrates, a gifted dramatist: even when he has Noah on stage
he would rather ply us with doctrine than entertain us with arkbuilding.
The morality drama which precedes Bale, and from which he borrows, has
its moments: but it cannot achieve the subtleties of personification allegory
one finds in Chaucer and especially Langland. Wrath is actually a character
sine nomine in Chaucer's *Summoner's Tale*: for at any moment in the tale,
someone embodies wrath, or is embodied by it. Similar things happen in
Piers Plowman, both with Wrath (momentarily embodied by the biting
and scratching nuns of c vi) and through personified aspects of the human
mind (such as Imaginatyf). A convenient end to this Merlinesque temporal
movement might be the first part of the *Roman de la Rose*: a text of acute
psychological subtlety that employs personification to explore the shifting
movements of a young girl's mind, welcoming (Bel Acueil) or resisting
(Daunger) strategies of masculine seduction. Compared to the *Rose*, those
seventeenth-century texts possess the subtlety of sandwich boards ('I am
Mr. Worldly Wiseman'); a teleology that leads us *back* to superior interior analysis of a female mind in love thus might challenge assumptions
conventionally associated with the *rise* of the novel. Reverse chronological
narration (and this can be said more briefly) would certainly lead us from
insularism, that of English Protestantism, to Catholic internationalism. It
is amusing to observe, with Shrank, Bale perforce employing continental
printers and the Latin tongue to wage war in England against the would-be
universalism of Rome and its Latin Bible. But such glimpses of 'abroad' are
relatively rare in this volume, which (in depicting 'the medieval in the early
modern') is notably Anglocentric. Stephanie Trigg's advertence to *Tirant*

lo Blanc, a Catalan romance inspired by *Guy of Warwick*, offers glimpses of the expanded internationalism of medieval centuries: a culture in which King Henry VI of England entertained a claim for *batalla a ultrança* issued by an insulted Aragonese nobleman (Joanot Martorell, the future *Tirant* author). Moving back further still, impelled by the spectre of Clare Lees (10), we might contemplate the contents of Cuthbert's sarcophagus at Durham: silks and ivories imported along trade routes of the extraordinarily internationalist kind recreated by Michael McCormick's magisterial *Origins of the Medieval Economy: Communications and Commerce AD 300–900* (2002).

One of the joys of a collaborative volume such as this, perhaps one of its rationales, is its insight into texts and dramas such as *Tamburlaine* and *Measure for Measure*. In reading across periods, rather than circulating within them, fresh insights emerge. A case in point here is Sarah Beckwith's account of the *accidental* making of Protestant English consciousness (or at least of one of its most characteristic modes, still with us today: public denunciation of the sinful). Many scholars, after Foucault, trace reflexively modern selfhood back to the confessional (although we should speak of confessional practices, since those closed boxes are postmedieval). This seems a hard sell to me, since most medieval people – excepting professional religious, the class that writes the manuals – confess infrequently (once a year minimum, after 1215): a peasant has a more organic relationship with the rear end of his ploughing horse than with his father confessor. Nonetheless, medieval people did maintain some form of private relationship, more or less intimate, with their parish priest. Within the bounds of such privacy, as Beckwith suggests, priestly discretion might be exercised. Thus according to the *Speculum Sacerdotale*, it might be better *not* to assign fasting as penance to a woman confessing to adultery, since her spouse might grow suspicious and she might face 'the prospect of her husband's rough justice'. But with the abolition of compulsory auricular confession, Beckwith argues, 'penance became more punitive, public and juridical in ways that could have been neither intended nor anticipated' (197): for anomalously, church courts lived on in England even after the sacrament of penance had been abolished. It is but a short step from here to the seeming outrages of *Measure for Measure*, where the Duke as friar divulges all that has been revealed to him in confessional privacy in a self-constituted court of public judgement. Such simultaneities of 'medieval' and 'Renaissance' imagining occur in the accounts of mapping provided by Jennifer Summit and Bernhard Klein, and in the very body (as Klein tells it) of Marlowe's Tamburlaine. Bale works in the Reformation divide; Tamburlaine, perhaps a bit like Leland, is *of* that divide: the agon of world views warring within one body precipitates rage in Tamburlaine (and in Leland, madness). Medieval *mappaemundi* promise the comfort and community of public, sacred space (they hang in churches): something quite different from 'the disembodied, desacralised, and entirely secular spaces of the New Geography' (whose maps hang in private homes) (144). Tamburlaine the Great, ungodly Scythian savage, would exceed all geographical limits to conquer the world. 'Timur the lame' would thus be a TO-map God in a new world of abstract cartography: impossible, medieval clerics might argue – except that the mixing of new and old geographies lives on, Klein argues, in Protestant bibles that are not quite ready to relinquish faith in old-style mapping.

Earlier in this 'Afterword' I made a passing comparison between the Reformation and the Middle Passage as historiographical points of rupture. This might seem wholly irresponsible, given the after-effects, and intrinsic suffering, of each: except that it might entice medievalist philologists – 'whose characteristic posture is melancholy at the tomb, grieving for loss and absence' (27) – to consider more contemporary work, poetic and scholarly, achieved in the face of social and cultural disintegration. As premodernists converge on the Reformation, so African-Americanists have turned to the ocean implicit in their hyphenated identity: to the *Black Atlantic*, in Paul Gilroy's famous formulation. Marilyn Nelson, in plotting a 'pilgrimage to Africa' in her 2005 *Cachoeira Tales* (11), finds Chaucerian couplets and a 'fellowship' structure to be the perfect medium. Africa proves too expensive, so she takes her Fellowship with her to visit a son working in Salvador da Bahia, Brazil. This might seem a problematic or random *telos*: except that black diaspora ('we all over the globe') questions the logic of western pilgrimaging that would turn only to 'that piece of desert they fighting about over there' (22). When Marilyn Nelson paddles 'in the waves' she thinks 'of Matthew Arnold. Then, of slaves' (43). The comma after 'then' here is devastating, analogous but different to the separating hyphen of African-American. As a good *mulier academica*, Nelson thinks first of Arnold on Dover beach, hearing the 'melancholy, long, withdrawing roar' as 'the Sea of Faith goes out': a response that is primarily academic, I would guess, since Nelson is both a Professor of English (at the University of Connecticut) and a woman of faith (52). 'Then, of slaves' sees her contemplate the ocean as both sustaining element and 'bone highway' (in an earlier phrase) (36): the double consciousness of all Caribbean writing and African-American thought. Hunger for contact with authentic, carried-over culture begets ironies, some of them comic: the 'grocery store Muzak' played by local Bahia musicians proves grossly inferior to that of '"our" musicians, drunk with beverage / and fellowship' (41). Again on the sea shore, Nelson observes young people practising *capoeira* kicks, a martial art compared to *tai chi* in its graceful complexity: 'self-defence disguised as dance / That is another slave inheritance' (35). Such rueful and wilful wishing to see true fragments of a ruined culture reminds us, once again, of medievalist desire: structuration of desire is comparable here, even if the personal stakes are not. This concluding turn to Marilyn Nelson means to perspectivise, and not to belittle, medieval/Renaissance work: it is Nelson, after all, who chooses to employ Chaucerian rhyme and structure for her own pilgrimage poem. But *The Cachoeira Tales*, in joining the medieval to the postmodern, might further encourage us to connect our work to greater and longer mappings of human experience.

Notes

INTRODUCTION: READING THE MEDIEVAL IN EARLY MODERN ENGLAND

1. John Fletcher and William Shakespeare, *The Two Noble Kinsmen*, ed. Lois Potter, Arden Shakespeare (Walton-on-Thames: Thomas Nelson, 1997), Prologue, lines 15–21.

2. Ann Thompson, *Shakespeare's Chaucer: A Study in Literary Origins* (Liverpool: Liverpool University Press, 1978), 30.

3. The terms 'Renaissance' and 'early modern', though treated often enough as interchangeable, are of course nothing of the sort. The current general use of 'early modern' by literary scholars and historians represents a concerted attempt to negotiate both the ethos embodied in 'Renaissance' – a positive view of the period as a revolutionary rebirth of classical cultures which privileges northern Italy – and a broad time-span from the fifteenth to the eighteenth century, that is, between the 'medieval' and the Industrial Revolution. Although our materials take us only into the seventeenth century and although our premise of course questions the *terminus a quo* of the 'early modern', it seems to us to be preferable to 'Renaissance' as a working term, though in citing a range of critics we inevitably deploy both. On the recent construction of 'early modernity' see Moshe Sluhovsky, 'Discernment of Difference, the Introspective Subject, and the Birth of Modernity', *JMEMS* 36 (2006): 169–99.

4. Wallace K. Ferguson, *The Renaissance in Historical Thought: Five Centuries of Interpretation* (Boston: Houghton Mifflin, 1948), 73.

5. Jacques Le Goff, 'For an Extended Middle Ages', in *The Medieval Imagination*, trans. Arthur Goldhammer (Chicago: University of Chicago Press, 1988), 18–23 (19). See also his most recent work, *The Birth of Europe* (Oxford: Blackwell, 2005).

6. Jacob Burckhardt, *Die Kultur der Renaissance in Italien* (1860); translated into English by S. G. C. Middlemore as *The Civilisation of the Renaissance in Italy* (1878).

7. Lee Patterson, 'On the Margin: Postmodernism, Ironic History, and Medieval Studies', *Speculum* 65 (1990): 87–108; David Aers, 'A Whisper in the Ear of Early Modernists; or, Reflections on Literary Critics Writing the "History of the Subject"', in David Aers (ed.), *Culture and History 1350–1600* (New York: Harvester Wheatsheaf, 1992), 177–202.

8. David Wallace (ed.), *The Cambridge History of Medieval English Literature* (Cambridge: Cambridge University Press, 1999); David Wallace, *Premodern Places: Calais to Surinam, Chaucer to Aphra Behn* (Oxford: Blackwell, 2004); James Simpson, *Reform and Cultural Revolution*, The Oxford English Literary History, vol. II (1350–1547) (Oxford: Oxford University Press, 2002).

9. Eamon Duffy, *The Stripping of the Altars: Traditional Religion in England, 1400–1580* (New Haven: Yale University Press, 1992); Berndt Hamm, *The Reformation of Faith in the Context of Late Medieval Theology and Piety: Essays by Berndt Hamm*, ed. Robert J. Bast (Leiden: Brill, 2004), 271. A more cautionary note is sounded by Sluhovsky, who in 'Discernment of Difference' sees the early modern period as having been 'demodernized' in recent criticism; 'early modernity' has been 'absorbed into the growing alterity of the Middle Ages and thence distanced from modernity' so that 'rather than connecting modernity with the Middle Ages, [early modernity] has become an extension of the later Middle Ages' (173, 174). For other critiques see Lorraine Daston, who believes the term '"[e]arly modern" is as screamingly anachronistic and teleological a label as the "Middle Ages" . . .' ('The Nature of Nature in Early Modern Europe', *Configurations* 6 (1998): 149–72 (149)) and Randolph Starn, 'The Early Modern Muddle', *Journal of Early Modern History* 6.3 (2002): 296–307.

10. Greg Walker, *Plays of Persuasion: Drama and Politics at the Court of Henry VIII* (Cambridge: Cambridge University Press, 1991); Paul Whitfield White, *Theatre and Reformation: Protestantism, Patronage, and Playing in Tudor England* (Cambridge: Cambridge University Press, 1993); Scott McMillin and Sally-Beth MacLean, *The Queen's Men and their Plays* (Cambridge: Cambridge University Press, 1998).

11. John Cox and David Scott Kastan (eds.), *A New History of Early English Drama* (New York: Columbia University Press, 1997).

12. SunHee Kim Gertz, *Chaucer to Shakespeare, 1337–1580* (Basingstoke: Palgrave, 2001); Derek Pearsall, *Chaucer to Spenser: An Anthology of Writing in English, 1375–1575* (Oxford: Blackwell, 1999); Pearsall and Duncan Wu, *Poetry from Chaucer to Spenser* (Oxford: Blackwell, 2002).

13. Helen Cooper, *The English Romance in Time: Transforming Motifs from Geoffrey of Monmouth to the Death of Shakespeare* (Oxford: Oxford University Press, 2002); Benjamin Griffin, *Playing the Past: Approaches to English Historical Drama, 1385–1600* (Woodbridge: D. S. Brewer, 2001); Cathy Shrank, *Writing the Nation: Literature, Humanism and English Identities, 1530–1580* (Oxford: Oxford University Press, 2004); Jennifer Summit, *Lost Property: The Woman Writer and English Literary History, c. 1380–1589* (Chicago: University of Chicago Press, 2000); Deanne Williams, *The French Fetish from Chaucer to Shakespeare* (Cambridge: Cambridge University Press, 2004).

14. Andrew Hadfield, *Literature, Politics and National Identity: Reformation to Renaissance* (Cambridge: Cambridge University Press, 1994); Philip Schwyzer, *Literature, Nationalism, and Memory in Early Modern England and Wales* (Cambridge: Cambridge University Press, 2004). Other significant contributions to the study of early nationhood include Richard Helgerson, *Forms*

of Nationhood: The Elizabethan Writing of England (Chicago: University of Chicago Press, 1992); Claire McEachern, *The Poetics of English Nationhood, 1590–1612* (Cambridge: Cambridge University Press, 1996); and David Baker and Willy Maley (eds.), *British Identities and English Renaissance Literature* (Cambridge: Cambridge University Press, 2002).

15. Seth Lerer, *Chaucer and His Readers: Imagining the Author in Late Medieval England* (Princeton: Princeton University Press, 1993); Theresa Krier (ed.), *Refiguring Chaucer in the Renaissance* (Gainesville: University of Florida Press, 1998).

1 DIACHRONIC HISTORY AND THE SHORTCOMINGS OF MEDIEVAL STUDIES

Versions of this essay were read at Harvard University, King's College London, and the University of Melbourne; I thank participants in these events, no less than the editors of this volume and its anonymous readers, for critical comment.

1. Simpson, *Reform and Cultural Revolution*. For a series of penetrating responses to this book, see the volume of *Journal of Medieval and Early Modern Studies* devoted to consideration of *Reform and Cultural Revolution*, *JMEMS* 35 (2005).

2. Of course many strokes followed from the cultural revolution of 1534. See, for example, Patrick Collinson, *The Birthpangs of Protestant England: Religious and Cultural Change in the Sixteenth and Seventeenth Centuries* (London: Macmillan, 1988), and Michael Walzer, *The Revolution of the Saints: A Study in the Origins of Radical Politics* (London: Weidenfeld and Nicolson, 1966).

3. I speak of Britain and Australia simply because I have experienced this retraction at first hand in these countries.

4. Though New Criticism, it should be said, had very much more purchase than Leavisism, whose few medievalist exponents accented Leavisite nostalgia for an English tradition of high art in living touch with its popular roots. Compare, say, the evergreen study of Charles Muscatine, *Chaucer and the French Tradition: A Study in Style and Meaning* (Berkeley and Los Angeles: University of California Press, 1957), with the always already sere John Speirs, *Medieval English Poetry: The Non-Chaucerian Tradition* (London: Faber and Faber, 1957). For the development of Chaucer Studies and of Medieval Studies more generally, see the indispensable essays of Lee Patterson, 'Historical Criticism and the Development of Chaucer Studies', and 'Historical Criticism and the Claims of Humanism', both in his *Negotiating the Past: The Historical Understanding of Medieval Literature* (Madison: University of Wisconsin Press, 1987), 3–39 and 41–74 respectively.

5. I have been helped by many British colleagues in my investigations into the foundation dates of centres of medieval studies. Wendy Scase reports on two periods of foundation:

The first era was the mid sixties, when the earliest centres were founded on the North American model. Examples are the centres at Leeds, Reading, and York. But the foundation of many centres is much more recent, clustering in a period from the mid 1990s. Nottingham's Centre for the Viking Age dates to 1995, Kent's Canterbury Centre for Medieval and Tudor Studies . . . was founded in 1996, Glasgow's Medieval and Renaissance Centre in 1997, and Hull's Centre for Medieval Studies in the same year. I imagine the most recent foundation must be the Hilton Shepherd Postgraduate Centre for Medieval Studies at Birmingham (2002).

Extract from Wendy Scase, 'Decentring Medieval Studies', a paper presented to the symposium '"Undisciplined"?! Where are Medieval Studies Going?', 29 November–1 December 2002, The Canterbury Centre for Medieval and Tudor Studies, University of Kent. To this one should add that the University of Bristol's Centre for Medieval Studies was founded in 1993–94 and the Centre for Medieval Studies at Cardiff University in 1996. I thank Ad Putter and John Hines for help with these dates.

6. The Pontifical Institute of Mediaeval Studies in Toronto, for example, was founded in 1929.

7. Thanks to superb recent work, we are in a much better position to understand aspects of this claim as it applies to historiography. See David Matthews, *The Making of Middle English, 1765–1910* (Minneapolis: University of Minnesota Press, 1999), now accompanied by an anthology of texts, *The Invention of Middle English: An Anthology of Primary Sources* (Turnhout: Brepols, 2000). See also the excellent earlier study, Arthur Johnston, *Enchanted Ground: The Study of Medieval Romance in the Eighteenth Century* (London: Athlone Press, 1964).

8. The argument of this essay runs parallel to that of Patterson in his penetrating article, 'On the Margin: Postmodernism, Ironic History, and Medieval Studies', but develops the following point in particular: 'Perhaps then it is time to reconsider the wisdom of relying upon centers and programs of medieval studies as the institutions centrally responsible for graduate education. The traditional justification for these kinds of institutions is that they are necessary to provide an opportunity for interdisciplinary work . . . Above all, interdisciplinary work is thought to be peculiarly appropriate for the medievalist: just as medieval culture is a unified whole, so runs the argument, the training of the medievalist should be equally coherent. Yet just here is the problem, for of course the very claim of a unified Middle Ages is itself part of the post-renaissance mythology of difference' (105).

9. See the editors' introduction to this volume for further confirmation of the scholarly movement now under way.

10. Renewed activity in the early Tudor field is also providing crucial bridges. See, for example, Greg Walker, *Persuasive Fictions: Faction, Faith and Political Culture in the Reign of Henry VIII* (Aldershot: Scolar, 1995); Ramie Targoff, *Common Prayer: The Language of Public Devotion in Early Modern England* (Chicago and London: University of Chicago Press, 2001); Shrank, *Writing the Nation in Reformation England*; and Tom Betteridge, *Literature and*

Politics in the English Reformation (Manchester: Manchester University Press, 2004).

11. All citations from the *Supplication of Souls* are drawn from the following edition: Thomas More, *Letter to Bugenhagen*; *Supplication of Souls, Letter against Frith*, ed. Frank Manley, Germain Marc'hadour, Richard Marius and Clarence H. Miller, The Yale Edition of the Complete Works of St. Thomas More, VII (New Haven: Yale University Press, 1990). All references will be made in the body of the text, by page and line number.

12. For a penetrating discussion of these texts, and the implications of the repression of Purgatory for the representation of ghosts, see Stephen Greenblatt, *Hamlet in Purgatory* (Princeton: Princeton University Press, 2001).

13. *Statutes of the Realm*, ed. T. E. Tomlins et al., 11 vols. (London: Dawsons, 1810–28; repr. 1963), 1 Edward VI, ch. 14, art. 1 (IV.1: 24). (The Edwardian statute restated and embellished a Henrician statute of 1545: 37 Henry VIII, ch. 4.)

14. I am indebted to Greenblatt, *Hamlet in Purgatory*, 244–5, for this point. For the impersonality of the vernacular Book of Common Prayer, see Targoff, *Common Prayer*; see also Duffy, *Stripping of the Altars*, 475.

15. For the attack on the inventive and thereby erroneous capacities of the imagination by Protestant polemicists in these decades and beyond, see James Simpson, 'The Rule of Medieval Imagination', in Jeremy Dimmick, James Simpson, and Nicolette Zeeman (eds.), *Images, Idolatry, and Iconoclasm in Late Medieval England* (Oxford: Oxford University Press, 2002), 4–24.

16. For a conspectus of Henrician and Edwardian legislation against images, see Margaret Aston, *England's Iconoclasts*, vol. 1: *Laws Against Images* (Oxford: Clarendon Press, 1988), 223–300.

17. In P. L. Hughes and J. F. Larkin (eds.), *Tudor Royal Proclamations*, 3 vols., vol. 1: *The Early Tudors (1485–1553)* (New Haven: Yale University Press, 1964), no. 188, p. 279.

18. Hughes and Larkin (eds.), *Tudor Royal Proclamations*, vol. 1: no. 188, pp. 278–9. For a penetrating discussion of the cultural function of 'remembrance' in the English Reformation, see Summit, *Lost Property*, 143–7.

19. For the treatment of the saints in Henrician and Edwardian legislation, see Duffy, *Stripping of the Altars*, 379–477.

20. *Ibid.*, 407.

21. *Ibid.*, 446.

22. *Ibid.*, 465.

23. Brad S. Gregory, *Salvation at Stake: Christian Martyrdom in Early Modern Europe* (Cambridge, Mass.: Harvard University Press, 1999), 34.

24. See Hughes and Larkin (eds.), *Tudor Royal Proclamations*, vol. 1: no. 287, p. 394.

25. It should be noted that the relocation of spiritual energies and events to the realm of 'memory' is precisely the opposite of what is meant by 'memoire' in Pierre Nora (ed.), *Les Lieux de Mémoire*, 3 vols. (Paris: Gallimard, 1984–92). Nora's principal distinction is between critical, academic 'history' (whose very existence implies a total rupture with the past), and 'memoire' as the experiential preservation of the past (e.g. 1: 23–37).

26. For the beginnings of English literary history in the 1530s, see Simpson, *Reform and Cultural Revolution*, chapter 1.
27. See Lerer, *Chaucer and his Readers*, chapter 5, and James Simpson, 'Chaucer's Presence and Absence, 1400–1550', in Jill Mann and Piero Boitani (eds.), *A Chaucer Companion*, 2nd edn (Cambridge: Cambridge University Press, 2003), 251–69. This paragraph summarises some of the argument in the essay just cited.
28. Robert R. Edwards (ed.), *John Lydgate, The Siege of Thebes* (Kalamazoo, Mich.: TEAMS, 2001), lines 44–5.
29. Thynne's preface is available in Derek Brewer (ed.), *Chaucer: The Critical Heritage*, 2 vols. (1978; London: Routledge and Kegan Paul, 1995), 1: 87–90. I have punctuated the text. The work is ostensibly written by Sir Brian Tuke, but the voice of the actual text shifts between that of Tuke and of Thynne. I attribute the whole text to Thynne as a matter of convenience.
30. For which see Simpson, *Reform and Cultural Revolution*, chapter 1.
31. Fish's *Supplicacyon for the Beggers* is edited in Manley (ed.), *More, Letter to Bugenhagen; Supplication of Souls, Letter against Frith*, 412–22. Citations are from this edition, and made in the body of the text by page and line number.
32. David Aers deserves great credit as the first to bring such perspectives most forcefully to bear in Middle English Studies. See, for example, his attack on the 'quiet hierarchies' version of the Middle Ages espoused by D. W. Robertson, in his 'Introduction', *Community Gender and Individual Identity: English Writing 1360–1430* (London: Routledge, 1988), 1–19.
33. If David Aers deserves the credit of introducing such thinking, he also sometimes exemplifies this tendency. Thus, for example, Aers asserts that 'Lollards strongly opposed religious forms that necessarily set people apart from their fellow Christians involved in the daily practices on which the preservation of their communities depended'; he refers to the Lollard 'will to integrate Christianity in the daily life and daily groupings of the working community'. See David Aers and Lynn Staley, *The Powers of the Holy: Religion, Politics and Gender in Late Medieval English Culture* (University Park: Pennsylvania State University Press, 1996), 57. The Lollard *Lantern of Light*, for example, asserts the existence of three churches (the true Church, the material Church, and the Devil's Church), and is evidently certain about who belongs to which. Texts of this kind will give pause to ready acceptance of Aers's communitarian account of Lollard theory. The long history of determination to extract Chaucer from 'The Middle Ages', and to make him an honorary representative of modernity, would suggest that the attempt to create lines of division between medieval and modern *within* the medieval period is of long standing. See, for example, Simpson, *Reform and Cultural Revolution*, chapter 2, and Linda Georgianna, 'The Protestant Chaucer', in C. David and Elizabeth Robertson (eds.), *Chaucer's Religious Tales* (Cambridge: Brewer, 1990), 55–69.
34. The positive reference to *préjugés* is evidently indebted to Hans-Georg Gadamer, whose defence of the inevitability and desirability of 'prejudice'

in historical exegesis is made in his *Truth and Method*, 2nd edn, trans. Garrett Barden and John Cumming (first published in German 1968; 1st edn first published in German 1960; London: Sheed and Ward, 1975), Part 2.2, pp. 235–341. Gadamer is clearly the guiding spirit of this essay.

35. For an excellent and diachronic account of historiographies that 'make history whole', versus those that attempt to create absolutely clean historiographical breaks, see Anthony Kemp, *The Estrangement of the Past: A Study in the Origins of Modern Historical Consciousness* (New York and Oxford: Oxford University Press, 1991).

36. Cited from Caxton's Prologue to his 1484 reprinting of *The Canterbury Tales*, printed in Norman Blake (ed.), *Caxton's Own Prose* (London: Deutsch, 1973), 61–3 (62).

37. For examples drawn from the history of the reception of Chaucer, see Lerer, *Chaucer and his Readers*, chapter 5. The Renaissance cult of authorial tombs is chronicled by J. B. Trapp, 'Ovid's Tomb: The Growth of a Legend from Eusebius to Lawrence Sterne, Chateaubriand and George Richmond', *Journal of the Warburg and Courtauld Institutes* 36 (1973): 35–76.

38. At one of the discussion sessions after I had read an earlier version of this essay as a paper, one auditor reported that a long-retired (and now deceased) Cambridge professor held this view: if an idea about the Middle Ages had obvious contemporary relevance, it was *ipso facto* wrong.

39. The tension between the past as wholly relevant and wholly foreign is embedded within philological humanism from its fifteenth-century beginnings; as Anthony Grafton says, some humanists wished to 'make the ancient world live again, assuming its undimmed relevance and unproblematic accessibility', while others sought to 'put the ancient texts back into their own time, admitting . . . that success may reveal the irrelevance of ancient experience and precept to modern problems'. See his *Defenders of the Text: The Traditions of Scholarship in an Age of Science, 1450–1800* (Cambridge, Mass.: Harvard University Press, 1991), 26–7. For the consequences of pre-fifteenth-century philological practice for our own reception of such texts, see Tim William Machan, *Textual Criticism and Middle English Texts* (Charlottesville: University Press of Virginia, 1994). For the replicative tendency of synchronic history, see Louise O. Fradenburg, '"Voice memorial": Loss and Reparation in Chaucer's Poetry', *Exemplaria* 2 (1990): 169–202.

40. For the best survey of that agon, see Ferguson, *The Renaissance in Historical Thought*.

41. A bracing first salvo in this re-engagement of medieval and early modern studies was given by David Aers, 'A Whisper in the Ear of Early Modernists'.

42. J. A. Burrow has recently made a similar critique of Medieval Studies; see his essay 'Should We Leave Medieval Literature to the Medievalists?', *EiC* 53 (2003): 278–83.

43. My position, if impelled by the same motive, arrives at slightly different conclusions from that of Nicholas Watson in his championing of 'affective historiography'. Like him, I propose a hermeneutics of empathy, and like him, I

think we should be able to acknowledge that we can learn, directly, from the past. I nevertheless allow that many texts will fascinate us without at the same time being assimilable within an 'affective historiography'. I propose a model of texts as friends rather than lovers. See Nicholas Watson, 'Desire for the Past', *SAC* 21 (1999): 59–97. I have replied more fully to this article in 'Confessing Literature', *ELN* 44 (2006): 121–26.

2 *FRIAR BACON AND FRIAR BUNGAY* AND THE RHETORIC OF TEMPORALITY

I would like to thank the Social Sciences and Humanities Research Council of Canada, and Clare Hall, Cambridge for generously supporting my research.

1. See, *inter alia*, Simpson, *Reform and Cultural Revolution*; Aers, 'A Whisper in the Ear of Early Modernists'; Patterson, *Negotiating the Past*.
2. On the temporal or epochal notion of a 'middle' see G. S. Gordon, 'Medium Aevum and the Middle Age', Society for Pure English Tract no. 19 (Oxford: Clarendon Press, 1925), 1–25 and Brian Stock, 'The Middle Ages as Subject and Object', *New Literary History* 5 (1974): 527–47. For discussion see Ruth Morse, 'Shakespeare's Ages', forthcoming in *Shakespeare Survey*.
3. See the discussion of Roger Bacon in A. W. Ward and A. R. Waller (eds.), *The Cambridge History of English and American Literature* (New York: Putnam, 1911).
4. See Keith Thomas, *Religion and the Decline of Magic: Studies in Popular Beliefs in Sixteenth and Seventeenth Century England* (Oxford: Oxford University Press, 1970). Thomas demonstrates the persistence of occultism well into the seventeenth century.
5. See J. Hackett, 'Roger Bacon: His Life, Career and Works', in J. Hackett (ed.), *Roger Bacon and the Sciences: Commemorative Essays* (Leiden: Brill, 1997), 9–23; on the legend see E. Westacott, *Roger Bacon in Life and Legend* (New York: Rockliff, 1953). See also René Pruvost, *Robert Greene et Ses Romans* (Paris: Les Belles Lettres, 1938) and John Clark Jordan, *Robert Greene* (1915; New York: Octagon Books, 1965).
6. See A. G. Molland, 'Roger Bacon as Magician', *Traditio* 30 (1974): 445–60. Bryan Reynolds and Henry S. Turner explain Bacon's divergent reputation as a function of his celebrity as a professional writer and the increasingly public face of academic culture. See their forthcoming articles, 'From *Homo Academicus* to *Poet Publicus*: Celebrity and Transversal Knowledge in Robert Greene's *Friar Bacon and Friar Bungay* (*c.* 1589)', in Edward Gieskes and Kirk Melnikoff (eds.), *Writing Robert Greene: New Essays on England's First Professional Writer* (Aldershot: Ashgate, forthcoming), and 'Performative Transversations: Collaborations Through and Beyond Greene's *Friar Bacon and Friar Bungay*', in Bryan Reynolds, *Transversal Enterprises in the Drama of Shakespeare and his Contemporaries: Fugitive Explorations* (London: Palgrave, 2006). I would like to thank them for giving me access to their work before publication.

7. The text concludes, 'Thus was the Life and Death of this famous Fryer, who lived most part of his life a Magician, and dyed a true penitent Sinner, and an Anchorite.'

8. *The Famous Historie of Fryer Bacon* (London, [*c.* 1555]), F4v.

9. Roger Bacon, *The Mirror of Alchemy* (London, 1597), A2r.

10. T. M., *Frier Bacon His Discovery of the Miracles of Art, Nature, and Magick* (London, 1659), A3 r–v.

11. There are no recent scholarly editions of the play: one is sorely needed. Existing editions include Daniel Seltzer's (1963; London: Edward Arnold, 1964) and J. A. Lavin's (London: Ernst Benn, 1969). It also appears in *English Renaissance Drama: A Norton Anthology* (New York: Norton, 2002). I have used the edition in *The Chief Elizabethan Dramatists*, ed. William A. Nielson (New York: Houghton Mifflin, 1911).

12. See Stephanie Jed, *Chaste Thinking: The Rape of Lucretia and the Birth of Humanism* (Bloomington: Indiana University Press, 1988).

13. See James I. Wimsatt, *The Marguerite Poetry of Guillaume de Machaut* (Chapel Hill: University of North Carolina Press, 1970) and John Livingston Lowes, 'The Prologue to the *Legend of Good Women* as Related to the French Marguerite Poems and to the *Filostrato*', *PMLA* 19 (1904): 593–683.

14. On Aspasia see Plutarch, *Pericles*, ed. and trans. Bernadotte Perrin, Loeb Classical Library (Cambridge, Mass.: Harvard University Press, 1916); Plutarch, *Artaxerxes*, ed. and trans. Bernadotte Perrin, Loeb Classical Library (Cambridge, Mass.: Harvard University Press, 1926) and, for discussion of the tradition of Aspasia see Madeleine M. Henry, *Of History: Aspasia of Miletus and Her Biographical Tradition* (Oxford: Oxford University Press, 1995).

15. Rachel Speght, *Mortalities Memorandum, with a dreame prefixed, imaginarie in manner* (London: Edward Griffin, 1621).

16. Like Doctor Faustus's 'all is dross that is not Helena', (5.1.103). *Friar Bacon and Friar Bungay* references *Doctor Faustus* in its handling love as much as magic: 'Shall I be Hellen in my forward fates, / As I am Hellen in my matchless hue, / And set rich Suffolke with my face afire?' (10.93–5).

17. See Jean Howard, *The Stage and Social Struggle in Early Modern England* (London: Routledge, 1994); David Scott Kastan, *Shakespeare and the Book* (Cambridge: Cambridge University Press, 2001). Editions of *Friar Bacon and Friar Bungay* were printed in 1630 and 1655.

18. See the discussion of this debate in the Introduction, 3–5.

19. Bacon even imagines it as adding to the trials of Christ: 'And from those wounds those bloudie Jews did pierce, / Which by thy magick oft did bleed afresh, / From thence for thee the dew of mercy drops, / To wash the wrath of hie Jehovah's ire, / And make thee as a new borne babe from sinne' (13.102–6). It seems that this speech might have anticipated Shakespeare's 'The quality of mercy is not strained / It droppeth as a gentle rain from heaven' in *The Merchant of Venice* (4.1.184–85)

20. On the limitations of this historical framework from a postcolonial perspective, see the introduction to Carolyn Dinshaw's *Getting Medieval: Sexualities and Communities, Pre- and Postmodern* (Durham: Duke University Press, 1999).

21. Marlowe's Doctor Faustus plans to 'Search all corners of the new-found world, / For pleasant fruits and princely delicates . . . wall all Germany with brass / And make swift Rhine circle fair Wittenberg' (1.1.85–92).

22. Examples include: 'I tell thee, Bacon, Oxford makes report, / Nay, England, and the court of Henry saies, / Th'art making of a brazen head by art, / Which shall unfold strange doubts and aphorisms, / And read a lecture in philosophie; / And, by the helpe of divels and ghastly fiends, / Thou meanest, ere many yeares or daies be past, / To compasse England with a wall of brasse' (2.22–9); 'Thus, rulers of our academic state, / You have seene the frier frame his art by proofe; / And as the colledge called Brazennose / Is under him, and he the Maister there, / So surely shall this head of brasse be framed, / And yeelde forth strange and uncouth aphorismes; / And Hell and Heccate shall faile the frier, / But I will circle England round with brasse' (2.162–9); and '. . . the brazen head / That, by the inchaunting forces of the devil, / Shall tell out strange and uncouth Aphorismes, / And girt faire England with a wall of brasse' (1.18–20).

23. 'Strange' is a word typically applied to foreignness in early modern England.

24. *A Midsummer Night's Dream*, composed the year after *Friar Bacon and Friar Bungay* was printed, also engages with the idea of the permeability of the Babylonian walls. Ninus and Semiramis built the famous Hanging Gardens of Babylon; it was actually Nebuchadnezzar who built the walls. On Babylon and the idea of empire in Middle English literature see Deanne Williams, 'Gower's Monsters' in Ananya Jahanara Kabir and Deanne Williams (eds.), *Postcolonial Approaches to the European Middle Ages: Translating Cultures* (Cambridge: Cambridge University Press, 2005), 127–50.

25. As Greene was writing *Friar Bacon and Friar Bungay*, Elizabeth's longstanding enmity with the Holy Roman Empire had prompted an alliance with the Ottomans.

26. Orleans is a place associated with magic in Chaucer's *Franklin's Tale* (see *Canterbury Tales*, v.1118) and in Shakespeare's *Cymbeline* (1.4.35).

27. We may compare this to the additions in the B-text of *Doctor Faustus* concerning the Holy Roman Empire. See, for discussion, Leah Marcus, 'Textual Instability and Ideological Difference: The Case of *Doctor Faustus*', *Renaissance Drama* 20 (1989): 1–29.

28. See Heather James, *Shakespeare's Troy: Drama, Politics, and the Translation of Empire* (Cambridge: Cambridge University Press, 1997).

29. See, for further discussion, my 'Dido Queen of England', *ELH* 71 (2006): 31–59.

30. On Skelton, see my *The French Fetish from Chaucer to Shakespeare*, 121–80.

31. Paul de Man, 'The Rhetoric of Temporality', in Charles S. Singleton (ed.), *Interpretation: Theory and Practice* (Baltimore: Johns Hopkins University Press, 1969), 173–209.

32. In reaction against the mechanisation of modernity, the Romantics dwelled on imaginary pasts: a nostalgia that was occasionally classical (as in Keats's 'Ode on a Grecian Urn') but just as often medieval, especially among the German Romantics.

33. Just as *The Historie of the Damnable Life and Deserved Death of Doctor John Faustus*, an English translation of what is known as the German Faust-book, provides the material for Marlowe's *Doctor Faustus*, so *The Famous Historie* constitutes a prose outline for *Friar Bacon and Friar Bungay*. Like Faustus, Bacon conjures figures to entertain royalty, invokes the devil, and gets into all kinds of trouble. See *The Historie of the Damnable Life and Deserved Death of Doctor John Faustus* (London, P. F. Gent, 1592) and *The Famous Historie of Fryer Bacon* (London, London: G. Purslowe for F. Grove, 1627). On the dating of these texts and their relationship to the plays, see John Henry Jones (ed.), *The English Faust Book* (Cambridge: Cambridge University Press, 1994).

3 LANGLAND, APOCALYPSE AND THE EARLY MODERN EDITOR

1. Patterson, 'On the Margin'; Aers, 'A Whisper in the Ear of Early Modernists'.
2. Duffy, *Stripping of the Altars*, 11.
3. David Wallace, *Chaucerian Polity: Absolutist Lineages and Associational Form in England and Italy* (Stanford: Stanford University Press, 1997), 2.
4. Simpson, *Reform and Cultural Revolution*, 2.
5. *Ibid.*, 1.
6. Louise Fradenburg, '"So That We May Speak of Them": Enjoying the Middle Ages', *New Literary History* 28 (1997): 205–30 (217–19).
7. The term *new historicism* was coined by Stephen Greenblatt in the introduction to a special double issue of *Genre*, 'The Forms of Power and the Power of Forms in the Renaissance', *Genre* 15.1 and 2 (1982). From the very beginning its status was largely heuristic (Greenblatt describing it 'as no single critical practice', 5).
8. Helen C. White, *Social Criticism in Popular Religious Literature of the Sixteenth Century* (New York: Macmillan, 1944), 1–40.
9. Ironically, what now has become a historicist commonplace began as a formalist-inspired attempt to focus attention on the specificities of Langland's poetic achievement, and to insulate that achievement from the exigencies of history. Thus, Lewis in *The Allegory of Love: A Study in Medieval Tradition* (London: Oxford University Press, 1936) equates Langland's poetic genius with a political quietism: 'Scholars more interested in social history than in poetry have sometimes made this poem appear much less ordinary than it really is as regards its kind, and much less extraordinary as regards the genius of its poet . . . As a politician, Langland has nothing to propose except that all estates should do their duty' (158–9). Donaldson, in *Piers Plowman: The C-Text and Its Poet* (New Haven: Yale University Press, 1949), calls Langland 'a moderate and a traditionalist, if not a reactionary' (108). For further discussion of this point see Larry Scanlon, 'King, Commons, and Kind Wit: Langland's National Vision and the Rising of 1381', in Kathy Lavezzo (ed.), *Imagining a Medieval English Nation* (Minneapolis and London: University of Minnesota Press, 2004), 191–233 (198–9).

10. For a recent, authoritative statement of the standard view see Kathryn Kerby-Fulton, '*Piers Plowman*', in David Wallace (ed.), *The Cambridge History of Medieval English Literature* (Cambridge: Cambridge University Press, 1999), 520–6. Other influential discussions of Langland's politics which view him as a conservative include Ralph Hanna, 'On the Versions of *Piers Plowman*', in *Pursuing History: Middle English Manuscripts and the Their Texts* (Stanford: Stanford University Press, 1996), 203–43; Steven Justice, *Writing and Rebellion: England in 1381* (Berkeley, Los Angeles and London: University of California Press, 1994), 102–39; David Aers, *Community, Gender, and Individual Identity: English Writing 1360–1430* (London and New York: Routledge, 1988), 20–72; Derek Pearsall, 'Poverty and Poor People in *Piers Plowman*', in Edward Donald Kennedy, Ronald Waldron and Joseph S. Wittig (eds.), *Medieval English Studies Presented to George Kane* (Cambridge: D. S. Brewer, 1988), 167–85; Anna Baldwin, *The Theme of Government in 'Piers Plowman'* (Cambridge: D. S. Brewer, 1981); Janet Coleman, *'Piers Plowman' and the 'Moderni'* (Rome: Edizioni di Storia e Letteratura, 1981); Morton Bloomfield, *'Piers Plowman' as Fourteenth-Century Apocalypse* (New Brunswick: Rutgers University Press, 1961); D. W. Robertson, Jr., and Bernard F. Huppé, *'Piers Plowman' and the Scriptural Tradition* (Princeton: Princeton University Press, 1951). Robertson and Donaldson were to become the emblematic leaders on either side of the Exegetical/Formalist debate that constituted the central debate in Middle English Studies in the United States from the late 1950s into the late 1970s. Nevertheless, on the matter of Langland's politics both sides agreed: he was a conservative. Moreover, this conviction became such a fundamental structuring force in the field that it expressed an even broader influence indirectly, as an accepted part of the intellectual landscape against which critical projects were shaped. It lurks in two of the most widely accepted and frequently reiterated assertions about the structure of the poem. The first is that Langland intended the revisions of the C-version as a repudiation of the 1381 Rising, revealing the 'latent social conservatism' that was there all along (Kerby-Fulton, '*Piers Plowman*', 522). The second is that in both the B- and C-versions the poem's most fundamental division occurs after the Pardon scene, where the *Visio* ends and the *Vita* begins (B VIII, C X). At this point the poem is held to turn inward: it renounces all interest in social action in favour of an entirely individual quest for spiritual perfection.

One can find the shaping authority of these readings at work in a variety of influential accounts of the poem which either bracket the question of its politics, or are not entirely satisfied with the standard account. Thus, the essay by Aers I cite above is simply one part of an extremely variegated body of work that has always stressed the political significance of the poem but has also insisted on the conservative rudiments of a medieval political ideology that Langland could not get beyond even when he struggled against it. Mary Carruthers's *Search for St. Truth* (Evanston: Northwestern University Press, 1973) is without doubt one of the best books on the poem in the last fifty years, and remains the best sustained formalist reading of it. In this reader-response-influenced account, the experience of reading Langland's poem impels one to search for 'a redeemed rhetoric, which will make divine truth meaningful in comprehensible human language' (197). The complexities and ambiguities of Langland's language enact the ethical and intellectual difficulties that attend such a search. Carruthers has very little to say about Langland's politics, yet her argument takes the Pardon scene as a crucial turning point, marking a definitive inward turn: 'Piers's society fails so abjectly to be effective in any way at all' that he is forced out of a reliance on the Old Law and a literal conception of justice into the transcendent spirituality of the New Law. The book thus depends on the assumption of a conservative or quietist Langland even as it brackets the question of politics.

A similar observation can be made about the work of Anne Middleton, who after an early essay classifying Langland as a public poet ('The Idea of Public Poetry in the Reign of Richard II', *Speculum* 53 (1978): 94–114) has produced a series of dazzling, tightly argued essays (including 'Narration and the Invention of Experience: Episodic Form in *Piers Plowman*', in Larry Benson and Siegfried Wenzel (eds.), *The Wisdom of Poetry: Essays in Early English Literature in Honor of Morton W. Bloomfield* (Kalamazoo: Medieval Institute Publications, 1982), 91–122; and 'William Langland's "Kynde Name": Authorial Signature and Social Identity in Late Fourteenth-Century England', in Lee Patterson (ed.), *Literary Practice and Social Change in Britain, 1380–1530* (Berkeley, Los Angeles and Oxford: University of California Press, 1990), 15–82) arguing that Langland was attempting to carve out an autonomous space for the literary. In the most recent of these, 'Acts of Vagrancy: The C Version "Autobiography" and the Statute of 1388', in Steven Justice and Kathryn Kerby-Fulton (eds.), *Written Work: Langland, Labor, and Authorship* (Philadelphia: University of Pennsylvania Press, 1997), 208–317, Middleton suggests that Langland constructs the autobiographical interpolation he adds to C v as an ironic response to the 1388 Statute of Labourers. Aggressively proclaiming himself a vagrant of the sort the statute was meant to prosecute, Langland also 'appears to be making a deft, if wittily indirect, plea for renewed or altered patronage' (211). Middleton's argument is itself deft and indirect; one of its many virtues is its implicit demonstration that arguments for the autonomy of the literary have their own political and historical integrity. Nevertheless, while her argument does not necessarily depend on treating Langland as quietist or conservative, that assumption still lurks in at least one respect. In arguing that Langland embraces the identity of the vagrant in order to carve out an exception for the idleness of the poet, Middleton never considers the possibility that he might also have been identifying with the subversive labourers who constituted the statute's actual target. To cite two other examples more briefly: in '*Piers Plowman* and the Peasants' Revolt: A Problem Revisited' (*Yearbook of Langland Studies* 8 (1994): 85–106), Anne Hudson suggests 'we should hesitate' before accepting the traditional view that John Ball and his fellow rebels misread Langland's politics (98), yet goes on to reiterate Langland's negative reaction to the Rising as the primary motive driving his revisions, arguing that it explains not only C, but B as well. James Simpson's *'Piers Plowman': An Introduction to the B-Text* (London and New York: Longman, 1990) is the first major account of the poem to dispute the finality of the inward turning in the latter two-thirds of the poem, arguing that the poem turns outward again at its conclusion. However, for Simpson this outward turning is exclusively ecclesiological, directed at the Church alone, a point he amplifies considerably in *Reform and Cultural Revolution* (322–82).

11. These include John M. Bowers, *'Piers Plowman* and the Police: Notes toward a History of the Wycliffite Langland', *Yearbook of Langland Studies* 6 (1992): 1–50; Susan Crane, 'The Writing Lesson of 1381', in Barbara Hanawalt (ed.), *Chaucer's England: Literature in Historical Context* (Minneapolis: University of Minnesota Press, 1992), 201–21; Lawrence M. Clopper, *'Songs of Rechelesseness': Langland and the Franciscans* (Ann Arbor: University of Michigan Press, 1997), esp. 145–75; Scanlon, 'King, Commons, Kind Wit'; and Anne M. Scott, *'Piers Plowman' and the Poor* (Dublin: Four Courts Press, 2004) esp. 68–119.

12. J. M. Manly, '"Piers the Plowman" and its Sequence', in A. W. Ward and A. R. Waller (eds.), *The Cambridge History of English Literature*, vol. II: *The End of the Middle Ages* (Cambridge: Cambridge University Press; and New York: G. P. Putnam's Sons, 1908), 1.

13. Anne Middleton, 'Introduction: The Critical Heritage', in John A. Alford (ed.), *A Companion to 'Piers Plowman'* (Berkeley, Los Angeles and London: University of California Press, 1988), 5; Charlotte Brewer, *Editing 'Piers Plowman': The Evolution of the Text* (Cambridge: Cambridge University Press, 1996), 7.

14. John N. King, *English Reformation Literature: The Tudor Origins of the Protestant Tradition* (Princeton: Princeton University Press, 1982), 322.

15. Brewer, *Editing 'Piers Plowman'*, 18; see also Simpson, *Reform and Cultural Revolution*, 332, n. 21.

16. One can see his interest in the doctrinal and the liturgical both in his very earliest writings, of 1548, *The Confutation of the Mishapen Aunswer to the Balade, called the Abuse of the blessed Sacrament* (Day and Seres, STC 6082) and *The Confutation of the .XIII. Articles, whereunto Nicolas Shaxton subscribed* (Daye and Seres, STC 6083), and in many of the works he produced after his return from exile, such as *A Briefe Discourse against . . . Apparell* (1578, STC 6080) and *A Deliberat Answere Made to a Rash Offer, which a popish catholique, made to a learned protestant . . .* (Charlewood for Woodcock, 1588, STC 6084).

17. Robert Carter Hailey, 'Giving Light to the Reader: Robert Crowley's Editions of Piers Plowman (1550)' (Ph.D. dissertation, University of Virginia, 2001), 15–19.

18. For another view, see Jennifer Loach, *Edward VI* (New Haven and London: Yale University Press, 1999), 61–2.

19. Hailey, 'Giving Light to the Reader', 243.

20. White, *Social Criticism*, 115.

21. K. B. McFarlane, *Lancastrian Kings and Lollard Knights* (Oxford: Oxford University Press, 1972), 317; cited in Vincent Gillespie, 'Vernacular Books of Religion', in Jeremy Griffiths and Derek Pearsall (eds.), *Book Production and*

Publishing in Britain, 1375–1475 (Cambridge: Cambridge University Press, 1989), 317.

22. King, *Reformation Literature*, 61–2; 66–71; 324–5.

23. Brewer, *Editing 'Piers Plowman'*, 14.

24. George Kane and E. Talbot Donaldson (eds.), *Piers Plowman, B Version* (London: Athlone Press, 1975); hereafter abbreviated as K-D.

25. Katharine Jackson Lualdi and Anne T. Thayer (eds.), *Penitence in the Age of Reformations* (Aldershot, Burlington, Vt., Singapore, Sydney: Ashgate, 2000); Richard Strier, 'Herbert and Tears', *ELH* 46 (1979): 221–47; Thomas N. Tentler, *Sin and Confession on the Eve of the Reformation* (Princeton: Princeton University Press, 1977), 349–62.

26. Martin Luther, *Ninety-Five Theses*, in *Martin Luther: Selections from His Writings*, ed. John Dillenberger (Garden City: Anchor Books, 1961), 490 (Thesis 1).

27. Ronald K. Rittgers, 'Private Confession and Religious Authority in Reformation Nürnberg', in *Penitence in the Age of Reformations*, 51. The citation comes from *D. Martin Luthers Werke, Kritische Gesamtausgabe* (Weimar, 1883–), vol. X, pt. 3, p. 62.

28. Ian Green, *Print and Protestantism in Early Modern England* (Oxford and New York: Oxford University Press, 2000), 325.

29. Robert Crowley, *The Last Trumpet*, in *The Select Works of Robert Crowley*, ed. J. M. Cowper (London: Early English Text Society, 1872; rpt. Millwood, NY: Kraus Reprints, 1987), 53. All subsequent citations are from this edition. Line numbers will be given in the text.

30. For the classic exposition of this view, see Robert Adams, 'Piers's Pardon and Langland's Semi-Pelagianism', *Traditio* 39 (1983): 367–418.

31. See 55 and n. 13 above.

32. Transcription from Justice, *Writing and Rebellion*, 14–15.

33. David Norbrook, *Poetry and Politics in the English Renaissance* (London and Boston: Routledge & Kegan Paul, 1984), 54.

34. Crowley, *Select Works*, 134–42; 143–50.

35. *Ibid.*, 157.

36. *Pyers plowmans exhortation, vnto the lordes, knightes and burgoysses of the Parlyamenthouse* (Imprinted at London by Anthony Scoloker dwelling in the Sauoy tentes. without Templebarre, 1550); Early English Books Online facsimile of copy from Bodleian Library, 11. This work was first attributed to Crowley by Barbara Johnson; the attribution has been accepted by King, *Reformation Literature*, 474. Cf. Norbrook, *Poetry and Politics*, 50n.

37. The best of these include Middleton, 'William Langland's "Kynde Name"', and the essays in *Written Work*. James Simpson, 'The Power of Impropriety: Authorial Naming in *Piers Plowman*', in *Langland's 'Piers Plowman'*, 145–65, is a long overdue corrective.

38. James Simpson, *'Piers Plowman': An Introduction to the B-Text* (London and New York: Longman 1990), 203; cf. Scanlon, 'King, Commons, and Kind Wit', 203.

39. Norbrook argues that Crowley 'regarded the more obviously Catholic elements in the poem, such as praise of the Virgin Mary and references to transubstantiation, as later interpolations' (*Poetry and Politics*, 42). He cites no evidence for this claim, and I certainly haven't been able to find any.

4 PUBLIC AMBITION, PRIVATE DESIRE AND THE LAST TUDOR CHAUCER

1. See Thomas Speght, *The Workes of our Antient and lerned English Poet, Geffrey Chavcer, newly Printed* (London, 1598). The book was produced in three impressions in early 1598, by the booksellers George Bishop, Bonham Norton and Thomas Wight. They vary slightly; I quote from the Bishop impression (STC, 2nd edn, 5077). On Speght, Thynne and Stow, see Derek Pearsall, 'Thomas Speght', James Blodgett, 'William Thynne' and Anne Hudson, 'John Stow', in Paul G. Ruggiers (ed.), *Editing Chaucer: The Great Tradition* (Norman: Pilgrim Books, 1984), 71–92, 35–52, 53–70. See also Robert Costomiris, 'Some New Light on the Early Career of William Thynne, Chief Clerk of the Kitchen of Henry VIII and Editor of Chaucer', *The Library*, 7th ser., 4 (2003): 3–15.
2. Simpson, 'Chaucer's Presence and Absence', 254.
3. Machan, *Textual Criticism and Middle English Texts*, 90.
4. Alice Miskimin, *The Renaissance Chaucer* (New Haven: Yale University Press, 1975), 251.
5. Stephanie Trigg, *Congenial Souls: Reading Chaucer from Medieval to Postmodern* (Minneapolis and London: University of Minnesota Press, 2002), 130; see also Miskimin, *Renaissance Chaucer*, 251, 259.
6. See above, 1–2.
7. *Faerie Queene* IV.2.34. On appropriations of Chaucer in the early modern period, see Krier (ed.), *Refiguring Chaucer in the Renaissance*. On the uses of ideas about the poet's body, see Thomas A. Prendergast, *Chaucer's Dead Body: From Corpse to Corpus* (New York and London: Routledge, 2003).
8. Speght, *Workes of Chavcer*, n.p.; italics in original.
9. Simpson, 'Chaucer's Presence and Absence', 257; Lerer, *Chaucer and His Readers*, 18–19.
10. Thomas J. Heffernan estimates that 40 per cent of the texts attributed to Chaucer in the 1602 edition are spurious. 'Aspects of the Chaucerian Apocrypha: Animadversions on William Thynne's edition of the *Plowman's Tale*', in Ruth Morse and Barry Windeatt (eds.), *Chaucer Traditions: Studies in Honour of Derek Brewer* (Cambridge and New York: Cambridge University Press, 1990), 155–67 (161).
11. *Ibid.*, 160.
12. Simpson, *Reform and Cultural Revolution*, 41.
13. See further on this James Simpson's essay, 26 above, n. 33.
14. Among others who signed themselves with these initials in the relevant period, or those who actually bore the initials, no candidate looks remotely likely to have been an occasional versifier who might have contributed to a Chaucer

edition. It is of course possible that the letters are a deeper encryption than simple initials. Although Henry Beaumont displayed no overt signs of an interest in Chaucer, he was at Peterhouse, Cambridge around 1560, where there certainly was an interest in Chaucer (see 80–1, above for discussion). There was until recently no obvious connection between Speght and Henry, other than the former's friendship with the latter's brother. But Speght's will, recently unearthed by Professor Alan Nelson, shows that there was certainly a connection, as Henry owed Speght £1,200 at his death. I am grateful to Professor Nelson and Henry Summerson at the *ODNB* for bringing this to my attention.

15. The petition is printed in Revd William Betham, *The Baronetage of England*, vol. II (London: Printed by W. S. Betham for E. Lloyd, 1802), 218–19n.

16. Edward Hall, *The vnion of the two noble and illustre famelies of Lancastre [and] Yorke* . . . (London: Rychard Grafton, 1550). STC, 2nd edn, 12723. The quotation is taken from [Henry Ellis] (ed.), *Hall's Chronicle* (London, 1809), 1.

17. *Holinshed's Chronicles of England, Scotland and Ireland*, 6 vols. (London: J. Johnson, 1806–08), IV (1808): 161. I owe the reference to Emrys Jones, *The Origins of Shakespeare* (Oxford: Clarendon Press, 1977); see 122.

18. Phyllis Rackin, *Stages of History: Shakespeare's English Chronicles* (Ithaca and New York: Cornell University Press, 1990), 59.

19. Speght tells us himself of Mildred Cecil's support in the dedication prefaced to the 1598 *Workes of Chaucer*. Her support of a poor scholar is not in itself surprising: at least one other instance is known. See Alan Haynes, *Robert Cecil, Earl of Salisbury, 1563–1612: Servant of Two Sovereigns* (London: Peter Owen, 1989), 13.

20. See further my entry on Speght in *ODNB* online edn, October 2005, which supersedes the print version of this biography.

21. 'F.[rancis] B.[eaumont] to his very louing friend T. S.' Speght, *Workes of Chaucer* (1598), n.p.

22. D. E. Wickham, 'An Early Editor of Chaucer Reidentified?' *Notes & Queries* 240 (1995): 428.

23. Pearsall, 'Thomas Speght', in Ruggiers (ed.), *Editing Chaucer*, 72.

24. Edward Arber (ed.), *A Transcript of the Registers of the Company of Stationers of London, 1554–1640*, 5 vols. (London, 1875–94), II (1875): 293, 395, 316. On Speght's relation to Stow see Derek Pearsall, 'John Stow and Thomas Speght as Editors of Chaucer: A Question of Class', in Ian Gadd and Alexandra Gillespie (eds.), *John Stow (1525–1605) and the Making of the English Past* (London: British Library, 2004), 119–25.

25. Arber (ed.), *Transcript of the Registers*, II: 621. W. W. Greg (*Some Aspects and Problems of London Publishing between 1550 and 1650* (Oxford: Clarendon Press, 1956)) finds the 'lewde booke' to be 'obscure but pious and innocent' (20).

26. See the closing couplet quoted above. As this couplet breaks the otherwise regular scheme of a poem of three quatrains, it was perhaps an apology tacked on when the editor realised that he was not going to do all that he would have liked. In the fuller edition of 1602, the couplet is dropped.

27. Speght, *Workes of Chaucer* (1598), 'To the Right Honorable Sir Robert Cecil . . .', n.p.

28. Speght, 'To the Readers', *Workes of Chaucer* (1598), n.p. According to Pearsall the Stationers to whom Speght refers would have included George Bishop, a long-time Master of the Company, and the wealthy Bonham Norton (Pearsall, 'Thomas Speght', 73). These men were responsible for two of the three impressions of Speght's 1598 edition. Caroline Spurgeon suggests that one of the 'auncient learned men' was John Whitgift, Archbishop of Canterbury, who had previously been at Peterhouse at the relevant time; see Caroline F. E. Spurgeon, *Five Hundred Years of Chaucer Criticism and Allusion, 1357–1900*, 3 vols. (Cambridge: Cambridge University Press, 1925), 1: 146.

29. Speght, *Workes of Chaucer* (1598), n.p.

30. On the ritual nature of such disclaimers in Renaissance prefaces (in relation to literary rather than scholarly works), see Wendy Wall, *The Imprint of Gender: Authorship and Publication in the English Renaissance* (Ithaca and London: Cornell University Press, 1993), 173–5.

31. Trigg, *Congenial Souls*, 130–1.

32. William Caxton, *Prohemye* to *Canterbury Tales*, 2nd edn (1484), in Brewer, *Chaucer: The Critical Heritage*, 1: 76–7.

33. Trigg, *Congenial Souls*, 131.

34. *Ibid.*, 133.

35. Dedications of books to Robert Cecil are commonplace. After his elevation as secretary of state in 1596 until his death in 1612, roughly half a dozen a year were addressed to him, many by figures claiming, like Speght, some connection to him, but at least one by a writer who acknowledges that he and Cecil had never met. Cecil held the Lancaster position only a short time and Speght's is the only dedication to mention it.

36. Pierre Bourdieu, *Distinction: A Social Critique of the Judgement of Taste*, trans. Richard Nice (Cambridge, Mass.: Harvard University Press, 1984), 23, 24.

37. Winthrop S. Hudson, *The Cambridge Connection and the Elizabethan Settlement of 1559* (Durham: Duke University Press, 1980).

38. 'The appointment of Mr. Beaumont was made "by the King." This seems to be the only instance in which the election was not made by the Governors of the Hospital: nor can it be readily explained how the nomination passed out of their hands on this occasion.' William Haig Brown, *Charterhouse Past and Present* (Godalming: H. Stedman, 1879), 117–18; see also 106.

5 THE VULGAR HISTORY OF THE ORDER OF THE GARTER

1. In an illustrated pamphlet on *The Most Noble Order of the Garter: Its History and Ceremonial*, Peter Begent, the Order's modern historian, describes it as 'the oldest surviving order of Chivalry in the world'. Begent extols the continuity of the Order from medieval times, and its capacity to hold those traditions in suspension with the claims of modernity. He describes the 'magnificent and moving blend of ceremony, *medieval and modern*, sacred and secular which annually reminds us of the continuing tradition and ideals of the Most Noble

Order of the Garter [my emphasis]'. Peter J. Begent, *The Most Noble Order of the Garter: Its History and Ceremonial* (Windsor: n.d., n.p.).

2. See the discussion of these earliest records in Richard Barber, *The Black Prince* (1978; Phoenix Mill, Sutton Publishing, 2003), 83–4; and Hugh E. L. Collins, *The Order of the Garter 1348–1461: Chivalry and Politics in Late Medieval England* (Oxford: Clarendon Press, 2000), 9–14.

3. Peter J. Begent and Hubert Chesshyre, *The Most Noble Order of the Garter: 650 Years. With a Foreword by His Royal Highness the Duke of Edinburgh KG; and a Chapter on the Statutes of the Order by Dr Lisa Jefferson* (London: Spink, 1999), 15 (p. 357, n. 70).

4. See *Wynnere and Wastoure*, ed. Stephanie Trigg, EETS 297 (Oxford: Oxford University Press, 1990), line 68. There is a long tradition of dating this poem quite precisely in 1352–53, but see my 'Israel Gollancz's *Wynnere and Wastoure*: Political Satire or Editorial Politics', in Gregory Kratzmann and James Simpson (eds.), *Medieval English Religious and Ethical Literature: Essays in Honour of G. H. Russell* (Cambridge: Boydell and Brewer, 1986), 115–27.

5. Recent work on the poem has opened up the question of the poem's date and its possible patron: see W. G. Cooke and D'A. J. D. Boulton, '*Sir Gawain and the Green Knight*: A Poem for Henry of Grosmont', *Medium Aevum* 68 (1999): 42–54; and Leo Carruthers, 'The Duke of Clarence and the Earls of March: Garter Knights and *Sir Gawain and the Green Knight*', *Medium Aevum* 70 (2001): 66–79.

6. Lisa Jefferson, 'MS Arundel 48 and the Earliest Statutes of the Order of the Garter', *English Historical Review* 109 (1994): 356–85.

7. Joanot Martorell and Martí Joan de Galba, *Tirant lo Blanc*, trans. David H. Rosenthal (1984; London: Pan Books, 1985), xxviii. Rosenthal also reports that much of the Tirant dedication was shown by Martí de Riquer to have been plagiarised from the dedication to Don Enrique de Villena's *Los doce trabajos de Hércules* (Burgos, 1499), a work that remains unpublished as the only known version is in possession of a bibliophile who refuses to permit its publication.

8. *Tirant lo Blanc*, translator's foreword, x–xii.

9. *Tirant lo Blanc*, LXXXIV, 117.

10. *Ibid.*, LXXXV, 121.

11. The role of women in the Order is a complex issue, beyond the scope of this essay. It is worth noting, however, that there are two fifteenth-century effigies of women wearing the Garter around their upper or lower arm, in the parish churches of Ewelme and Stanton Harcourt in Oxfordshire.

12. Jean le Bel tells the story of Edward raping the Countess, in the *Chronique de Jean le Bel*, ed. J. Viard and E. Déprez, 2 vols. (Paris, 1904–05), 30–4, though le Bel makes only brief mention of the Order. See also Michael Packe, *King Edward III*, ed. L. C. B. Seaman (London: Routledge & Kegan Paul, 1983), 170–4, for speculation that the episode may allude to Alice Montagu and Alice Perrers. Leo Carruthers summarises many of the early stories in '*Honi soit qui mal y pense*: The Countess of Salisbury and the "Slipt Garter"', in Colette Stevanovitch and René Tixier (eds.), *Surface et profondeur: Mélanges offerts à Guy Bourquin à l'occasion de son 75ᵉ anniversaire* (Nancy: AMAES (collection

GRENDEL, no. 7), 2003), 227–33. Carruthers untangles the confusing marital history of Joan of Kent, who became Lady Holland, then Countess of Salisbury, and finally the Princess of Wales, and suggests the story about the garter and the implied affair between king and countess may have been invented, or at least, enthusiastically disseminated by Henry IV and his Lancastrian successors to discredit the mother of Richard II (233).

13. Susan Crane, *The Performance of Self: Ritual, Clothing and Identity During the Hundred Years War* (Philadelphia: University of Pennsylvania Press, 2002), 139.

14. C. Stephen Jaeger, 'L'Amour des rois: Structure sociale d'une forme de sensibilité aristocratique', *Annales: Economies, Sociétés, Civilisations* 46 (1991): 547–71. 'L'aura du corps du roi dessine un cercle magique. Le fait de pénétrer dans ce cercle, comme celui de se retrouver en présence d'un dieu et de participer soudain de la divinité, a un effet d'enchantement' (553). The Garter is one such example, where private and intimate acts lose their power to embarrass, once they are re-written as deeds of ennobling chivalric import. The king puts the Garter 'comme par magie dans la sphère de l'invulnérabilité qui lui est réservée, où le vulgaire, l'obscène et l'illicite ne sont qu'illusions et où tout est noble et digne de vénération; du même coup, il les sauve' (563).

15. According to Denys Hay, *Polydore Vergil: Renaissance Historian and Man of Letters* (Oxford: Clarendon Press, 1952), 79, Vergil wrote his first manuscript around 1512–13. The first published edition of 1534 covered events up to 1509, and the third edition of 1555 went up to 1538.

16. Barber, *The Black Prince*, 85, translating *Polydori Vergili Historiae anglicanae . . .* (Basle, 1555; rpt. Menston, 1972), 379.

17. Hay, *Polydore Vergil*, 100. Vergil may be drawing on the same tradition that gave rise to Mondonus Belvaleti's *Tractatus ordinis serinissimi domini regis Angliae vulgariter dicti la Gerretiere*, written in 1463 (Cologne, 1631), BL Harl. MS 5415. Belvaleti says 'many assert that this order took its beginning from the feminine sex, from a lewd and forbidden affection', but does not elaborate. Belvaleti's treatise played little part in the early discussion of origins. See Barber, *The Black Prince*, 86.

18. *Holinshed's Chronicles of England, Scotland and Ireland*, intro. Vernon F. Snow, 6 vols. (1807–08; New York: AMS Press, 1965, 1976).

19. George Peele, *The Honour of the Garter* (London, 1593).

20. [William] Segar, *The Booke of Honor and Armes* (London, 1590), The Fifth Book, 15–16.

21. William Segar, *Honor Military and Ciuill* (London, 1602), 66.

22. Peter Heylyn, *Cosmographie* (1652; 2nd edn, London, 1657), 321–2.

23. Elias Ashmole, *The Institution, Laws and Ceremonies of the Most Noble Order of the Garter* (London, 1672), 180.

24. *Ibid.*, 180.

25. *Ibid.*, 182.

26. *Register of the Most Noble Order of the Garter*, intro. John Anstis, 2 vols. (London, 1724), 1: 62. Anstis is equally dismissive of several other putative narratives of origin of the Order.

27. Begent and Chesshyre, *The Most Noble Order of the Garter*, 15, quoting Anstis, *Register*, 181.
28. Begent and Chesshyre, *The Most Noble Order of the Garter*, 15.
29. Collins, *The Order of the Garter*, 12.
30. Begent, *St George's Chapel*, pamphlet, 1. See also Barber, *The Black Prince*, 87; and Begent and Chesshyre, *The Most Noble Order of the Garter*, 16, citing J. L. Nevinson, 'The Earliest Dress and Insignia of the Knights of the Garter', *Apollo* 47 (1948): 80–3 (80–1).
31. The word 'honi', or 'honni' as it appears more often in French, was never common and soon became obsolete in French. While the English historians regularly translated this as 'Shamed', the French commentators often give a stronger reading, as 'cursed', 'vituperé, laidangé'. In 1694, it has become a 'Vieux mot François qui n'est plus en usage qu'en raillerie' (*Dictionnaire de l'Academie française*, 570).
32. So, for example, Ashmole, *The Institution*, 184.
33. It has also been suggested that Edward modelled the Garter on the Castilian Order of the Sash. See Barber, *The Black Prince*, 87; Cooke and Boulton, '*Sir Gawain and the Green Knight*', 48.
34. Leo Carruthers similarly emphasises 'the literary influence of chivalric romance on England's first order of chivalry', 'Honi soit', 223.
35. *The Cronicle of Polydore Virgil*, BL MS Royal 18.c.viii, ix, my transcription. Parts of this translation were edited by Henry Ellis for the Camden Society in 1845 and 1846, but not the sections covering the reign of Edward III. The British Library Catalogue describes 'the minute hands of the third quarter of the sixteenth century'. See also the slightly different transcription in Sir Nicholas Harris Nicolas, 'Observations on the Institution of the Most Noble Order of the Garter', *Archaeologia* 31 (1846): 1–163 (131).
36. 'Dautant qu'Edoüard estant feru de l'Amour de la Belle Alix Comtesse de Sarisbery, un Jour devisant avec elle, la Iartiere Gauche (de Soye Bleuë) de ceste Dame estant tombee sur son Patin, Edoüard prompt à servir sa Dame & la relever, leva quant & quant la Chemise si haut, que les Courtisans l'ayans veuë, ne se peurent tenir de rire.' André Favyn, *Le Theatre d'Honneur et de Chevalerie ou L'Histoire des Ordres Militaires . . .* (Paris, 1620), 1039–40. Favyn's account is taken almost verbatim from his earlier work, *Histoire de Navarre, Contenant l'Origine, les Vies & conquestes de ses Roys, depuis leur commencement iusques a present* (Paris, 1612), 463.
37. Andrew Favin, *The Theatre of Honour and Knighthood* (London, 1623). Favyn compares the story of the Golden Fleece: Duke Philip of Burgundy kept a mistress from Bruges, who had in her chamber a fleece of wool on her couch, a most uncourtly (even mercantile) textile. In reproof of the laughing courtiers, Philip vows to form an Order that will become as honoured as the fleece is now shamed. Favin, Book IV, 14. Ashmole also cites this story.
38. Richard Johnson, 'A Gallant Song of the Garter of England', in *The Golden Garland of Princely Pleasures and Delicate Delights* (London, 1620).
39. Peter Heylyn, *The History of That Most Famous Saynt and Souldier of Christ Jesus St George of Cappadocia* (London, 1633), part 3, chapter 2, 323–4.

40. *The Progresses, Processions, and Magnificent Festivities, of King James the First*, ed. John Nichols, 4 vols. (London, 1828).
41. John Selden, *Titles of Honour*, 2nd edn (London, 1631), part 2, chapter 5, section 40, 793.
42. Charles Allen, *The Battailes of Crescey and Poictiers* (London, 1631).
43. Michael Drayton, *Poly-Olbion, being the Fourth Volume of his Works*, ed. J. William Hebel (1933; corrected edn, Oxford: Shakespeare Head Press, Basil Blackwell, 1961).
44. Less concerned with the Garter, but captivated by the idea of Edward's infatuation for the Countess of Salisbury, is the French novel of that name by D'Argences, translated by Ferrand Spence in 1683, and one of the main sources for Alexandre Dumas's novel of 1839.
45. Begent and Chesshyre, *The Most Noble Order of the Garter*, 68–9.
46. Diarmaid MacCulloch, *Tudor Church Militant: Edward VI and the Protestant Reformation* (London: Allen Lane, 1999), 32.

6 MYTHS OF ORIGIN AND THE STRUGGLE OVER NATIONHOOD IN MEDIEVAL AND EARLY MODERN ENGLAND

I would like to thank Ruth Evans, John Ganim, David Matthews and Gordon McMullan for comments, suggestions and interesting conversations about foundation myths.

1. Geraldine Heng, *Empire of Magic: Medieval Romance and the Politics of Cultural Fantasy* (New York: Columbia University Press, 2003), 17.
2. *Ibid.*, 18. Contemporary doubters of Geoffrey included Alfred of Beverly, *Aluredi Beverlacensis Annales*; Giraldus Cambrensis, *Itinerarium Cambriae*; William of Newburgh, *Historia Rerum Anglicarum*. As Heng points out, there are 217 extant manuscripts of the *Historia* (18).
3. *Polydore Vergil's English History*, vol. 1, ed. Henry Ellis (London, 1846), 29. In his translation of the *Historia*, Lewis Thorpe notes that 'In essence the story of Brutus is taken from §10 of the *Historia Brittonum* of Nennius, where the birth of the hero is described; and §15, which gives the journey westwards' (*Geoffrey of Monmouth: The History of the Kings of Britain*, trans. and intro. Lewis Thorpe (Harmondsworth: Penguin, 1966), 55, n. 1).
4. See James P. Carley and Julia Crick, 'Constructing Albion's Past: An Annotated Edition of *De origine gigantum*', in James P. Carley and Felicity Riddy (eds.), *Arthurian Literature XIII* (Cambridge: D. S. Brewer, 1995), 41–91 (45, n. 14): 'By the early sixteenth century the tale had fallen into disrepute and John Major referred to it as nonsense and the stuff of dreams.' However, as Gordon McMullan suggests in chapter 7 of this volume, the Albina myth does not disappear, but finds an afterlife in early modern theatre (see 131–8). See also Laurie A. Finke and Martin B. Shichtman, *King Arthur and the Myth of History* (Gainesville: University Press of Florida, 2004), esp. 146–49.

5. Carley and Crick, 'Constructing Albion's Past', 44 n. 14, drawing on Susan Reynolds, 'Medieval *Origines Gentium* and the Community of the Realm', *History* 68 (1983): 375–90.

6. *Polychronicon Ranulphi Higden Monachi Cestrensis; together with the English Translations of John Trevisa and of an Unknown Writer of the Fifteenth Century*, 9 vols., ed. Churchill Babington and J. Rawson Lumby, Rolls Series 41 (London: Longmans, Green, and Co., 1865–86), II (1869): lib. I, 5.

7. See Carley and Crick, 'Constructing Albion's Past', 48 n. 26.

8. Jeffrey Jerome Cohen, 'The Tradition of the Giant in Early England: A Study of the Monstrous in Folklore, Theology, History and Literature' (Ph.D. dissertation, Harvard University, 1992), 197.

9. Carley and Crick, 'Constructing Albion's Past', 45. See also Tamar Drukker, 'Thirty-Three Murderous Sisters: A Pre-Trojan Foundation Myth in the Middle English *Brut* Chronicle', *The Review of English Studies*, New Series, 54.216 (2003): 449–63; Julia Marvin, 'Albine and Isabelle: Regicidal Queens and the Historical Imagination of the Anglo-Norman Prose *Brut* Chronicles', *Arthurian Literature*, 18.1 (2001): 143–92.

10. For more on this, see *Ibid.*, esp. 45.

11. Lesley Johnson, 'Return to Albion', in Carley and Riddy (eds.), *Arthurian Literature XIII*, 19–40 (21–2 n. 7). There are two versions of this story, the 'Greek' and the 'Syrian'. In the former, the parents of the Greek sisters are unnamed; in the latter we are told that they are the daughters of the Syrian King Diodicias and his queen, Labana. While in the Greek version the youngest daughter reveals the plot to her husband, who prevents the killings, in the Syrian version the sisters stick together and succeed in murdering their sleeping spouses. The number of sisters also varies, and we are told that they mate either with invisible demons, with demons in the shape of men, or with the devil himself, or even that they impregnate themselves through their own heated and excessively lecherous imagination (on this last point, see chapter 7, 132). The version which became most widely known in English, the Syrian one, is the one I refer to here. Carley and Crick state that it was used as a preface to the Middle English Prose *Brut* from the fourteenth century, and survives in more than 170 manuscripts. It was first published by Caxton in 1480 as *The Chronicles of England*. See Carley and Crick, 'Constructing Albion's Past', 48.

12. See, for instance, the Auchinleck version in *An Anonymous Short English Metrical Chronicle*, ed. Ewald Zettl, EETS os 196 (London: Oxford University Press, 1935), 46, lines 7–22.

13. See, for example, *Castleford's Chronicle or The Boke of Brut*, 2 vols., ed. Caroline D. Eckhardt, EETS 305–6 (Oxford: Oxford University Press, 1996), vol. I, lines 207–14:

> Qwene þe Deuyll persauyd all thys,
> He went be many dyuers contres,
> And toke body of the ayre he had,
> And liking natures of men schad,
> And come to the land of Albyon,
> And lay be þo women, all and some,
> And they consentyt to þe same.

In Richard Grafton's 1543 edition of Hardyng's *Chronicle*, it is the imagination of the women itself that creates the spirits who impregnate them. Hardyng tells us that their desire is '[s]o hote that spyrites in mannes forme / Laye by theim their desyres to performe'; John Hardyng, *The Chronicle . . . from the firste begynnyng of Englande* (London, 1543), fol. viii v.

14. See *Geoffrey of Monmouth*, trans. Lewis Thorpe, 62–5.
15. *Ibid.*, 72.
16. *Ibid.*
17. Kathleen Davis, 'National Writing in the Ninth Century: A Reminder for Postcolonial Thinking about the Nation', *JMEMS* 28 (Fall 1998): 611–37 (626).
18. W. Matthews, 'The Egyptians in Scotland: the Political History of a Myth', *Viator* 1 (1970): 289–306 (295).
19. John Gillingham, *The English in the Twelfth Century: Imperialism, National Identity and Political Values* (Woodbridge: Boydell, 2000), 9.
20. Gillingham, *The English in the Twelfth Century*, 10. For the three characteristics as outlined by Gillingham, see 10–11.
21. Cited in *ibid.*, 11. Here Gillingham is quoting Richard of Hexham's (*c.* 1140) 'description of a Scottish attack on Northumbria in 1138' as an example. Richard of Hexham concludes that the fate of those captured was slavery, either with the Scots or with 'other barbarians'.
22. See also Matthews, 'Egyptians in Scotland', esp. 249.
23. As Carley and Crick point out, 'By the thirteenth century, Scottish and English circles were nurturing competing traditions about the historical foundations of their respective kingdoms' ('Constructing Albion's Past', 55).
24. On the Scota legend in general, see E. J. Cowan, 'Myth and Identity in Early Medieval Scotland', *The Scottish Historical Review* 63 (1984): 111–35, esp. 120–4; R. James Goldstein, *The Matter of Scotland: Historical Narrative in Medieval Scotland*, Regents Studies in Medieval Culture (Lincoln: University of Nebraska Press, 1993), 104–32; Matthews, 'Egyptians in Scotland'; Reynolds, 'Medieval *Origines Gentium*'. On medieval accounts in English of the Scottish wars for independence see R. A. Albano, *Middle English Historiography* (New York: Peter Lang, 1993).
25. See Matthews, 'Egyptians in Scotland', 293–4. As Matthews points out, 'the earliest extended version of their migration from Egypt can be dated to 1280 and is inserted into the account of Edward I's campaigns in [Sir Thomas] Gray's *Scalacronica*' (295).
26. Carley and Crick, 'Constructing Albion's Past', 43.
27. Matthews, 'Egyptians in Scotland', 296. See also E. L. G. Stones (ed. and trans.), *Anglo-Scottish Relations, 1174–1328: Some Selected Documents* (London: Thomas Nelson and Sons, 1965) and Hugh A. MacDougall, *Racial Myth in English History: Trojans, Teutons, and Anglo-Saxons* (Montreal: Harvest House; Hanover: University Press of New England, 1982).
28. William F. Skene (ed.), *Chronicles of the Picts, Chronicles of the Scots, and Other Early Memorials of Scottish History* (Edinburgh, 1867), ix.

29. *The Historians of Scotland, Vol. IV: John of Fordun's Chronicle of the Scottish Nation*, trans. Felix J. H. Skene, ed. William F. Skene (Edinburgh: Edmonston and Douglas, 1872), 6–7.

30. Matthews suggests that it is 'a variant of an Irish migration myth' which had reached Scotland by the tenth century ('Egyptians in Scotland', 293–4).

31. *Ibid.*, 294–5.

32. *Ibid.*, 293 n. 6.

33. Richard Grafton, 'Dedication', in Hardyng, *The Chronicle*, part 1, fols. ii–v (Dedication ii r).

34. For more on this see Jeffrey Jerome Cohen, *Of Giants: Sex, Monsters, and the Middle Ages*, Medieval Cultures 17 (Minneapolis: University of Minnesota Press, 1999).

35. Victor I. Scherb, 'Assimilating Giants: The Appropriation of Gog and Magog in Medieval and Early Modern England', *JMEMS* 32 (Winter 2002): 59–84 (59).

36. *Ibid.*, 59; see further 60–1.

37. In MS F (CUL Ff.v.48); see *An Anonymous Short English Metrical Chronicle*, ed. Zettl, 55, lines 115–20.

38. As W. R. J. Barron, Françoise Le Saux and Lesley Johnson point out, this text sees Hengist as 'an exemplary king and conqueror of "Jnglond Wales & Scotland" who rules for 250 years, plays the most important role in organizing the government and civilizing the whole land'. They also note that Hengist's conquest of France is characterised by an 'extraordinary technological approach' and concludes that 'he seems designed to offer a idealised "historical" role model for the contemporary king of England, Edward III'. W. R. J. Barron, Françoise Le Saux and Lesley Johnson, 'Dynastic Chronicles', in W. R. J. Barron (ed.), *Arthurian Literature in the Middle Ages II: The Arthur of the English: The Arthurian Legend in Medieval English Life and Literature* (Cardiff: University of Wales Press, 1999), 11–46 (42–3). See also Thorlac Turville-Petre, *England the Nation: Language, Literature, and National Identity, 1290–1340* (Oxford: Clarendon Press, 1993), 109–10.

39. Edmund Spenser, *The Faerie Queene*, 2 vols. (London, 1590), ii.x.8.

40. Matthews shows that some Scottish historians accept the Trojan origin but discount the Albina story. John Major, in his *Majoris Britanniae historia* (1521), 'grants the truth of the Trojan settlement of Britain . . . [but] declares that the legend related by Caxton that Albion was originally settled by Albina and her ladies was fabulous and absurd . . . And as for the Scottish story of Gathelus, he counted it a fable: the Scots and the Irish were both descended from migrants from Spain, but since "their English enemies had learned to boast of an origin from the Trojans, so the Scots claimed an original descent from the Greeks who had subdued the Trojans, and then bettered it with this about the illustrious kingdom of Egypt' ('Egyptians in Scotland', 302). Origin myths, undoubtedly potent, were also always at the centre of both political and historiographical conflict.

41. Jodi Mikalachki, *The Legacy of Boadicea: Gender and Nation in Early Modern England* (London: Routledge, 1998), 124.

42. *Ibid.*, 120.

43. See Raphael Holinshed, *The Historie of England* (London, 1587), chapter 10.

44. Mikalachki, *The Legacy of Boadicea*, 115.

45. Cohen, *Of Giants*, 48.

46. Cited in Matthews, 'Egyptians in Scotland', 292.

47. Holinshed, *Historie of England*, chapter 11.

48. John Hardyng, for example, believed that English women were so headstrong and difficult because of Albina's heritage.

49. Gillingham, *The English in the Twelfth Century*, 10.

50. Holinshed, *Historie of England*, chapter 11

51. Ellis (ed.), *Polydore Vergil's English History*, 1: 30.

52. For a fascinating account of the orientalism inherent in medieval and early modern foundation myths, especially also the Albina, Scota and Brutus myths, see John M. Ganim, *Medievalism and Orientalism* (New York: Palgrave Macmillan, 2005), esp. chapter 2, 'The Middle Ages as Genealogy, or, the White Orient'.

53. Cited in Barbara Fuchs, 'Conquering Islands: Contextualizing *The Tempest*', *Shakespeare Quarterly* 48 (1997): 45–62 (52). On English national identity, colonisation and decolonisation in relation to Ireland in the fourteenth century, see, for instance, Claire Sponsler, 'The Captivity of Henry Chrystede: Froissart's *Chroniques*, Ireland, and Fourteenth-Century Nationalism', in Kathy Lavezzo (ed.), *Imagining a Medieval English Nation*, Medieval Cultures 37 (Minneapolis: University of Minnesota Press, 2004), 304–39.

54. Barbara Fuchs, 'Imperium Studies: Theorizing Early Modern Expansion', in Patricia Clare Ingham and Michelle R. Warren (eds.), *Postcolonial Moves: Medieval Through Modern* (New York: Palgrave Macmillan, 2003), 71–90.

55. *Ibid.*, 73. While Fuchs discusses the use of the trope in relation to the sixteenth century, she ignores its earlier uses.

56. Ganim, *Medievalism and Orientalism*, 61.

57. Stephen Nichols, *Giants in Those Days* (Lincoln and London: University of Nebraska Press, 1989), 72–3.

58. The ambiguities also persist in the Scota and Gathelos legend. As Ganim points out, 'the Scottish narrative from its legendary inception was beset with contradictions that continued to play themselves out through its history' (*Medievalism and Orientalism*, 61).

59. Jeffrey Jerome Cohen, *Monster Theory: Reading Culture* (Minneapolis: University of Minnesota Press, 1996), 6–7.

60. Nichols, *Giants in Those Days*, 63.

61. Allen J. Frantzen, *Desire for Origins: New Language, Old English, and Teaching the Tradition* (New Brunswick: Rutgers University Press, 1990), 143.

62. Holinshed, *The Historie of England*, chapter 11.

7 THE COLONISATION OF EARLY BRITAIN ON THE JACOBEAN STAGE

I would like to thank Anke Bernau, Matthew Dimmock, Ruth Evans, Paulina Kewes, Carolyn Lyle, David Matthews, Lucy Munro, Richard Proudfoot, Tiffany Stern, and Valerie Wayne, each of whom contributed in different ways, all much appreciated, to the construction of this essay.

1. See, for example, Mary Floyd-Wilson, 'Delving to the Root: *Cymbeline*, Scotland, and the English Race', in David Baker and Willy Maley (eds.), *British Identities and English Renaissance Literature* (Cambridge: Cambridge University Press, 2002), 101–15, reworked as chapter 7 of *English Ethnicity and Race in Early Modern Drama* (Cambridge: Cambridge University Press, 2003), 161–83.

2. William Camden, *Britain, Or a Chorographical Description* (London, 1610), F2r.

3. Valerie Wayne, from '*Cymbeline*, Colonialism, and the Ancient Britons', an as yet unpublished paper. I am very grateful to Professor Wayne for sharing with me material from her forthcoming Arden edition of *Cymbeline*.

4. Emrys Jones, 'Stuart *Cymbeline*', *EiC* 11 (1961): 84–99.

5. Leah Scragg, 'Saxons versus Danes: The Anonymous *Edmund Ironside*', in Donald Scragg and Carole Weinberg (eds.), *Literary Appropriations of the Anglo-Saxons from the Thirteenth to the Twentieth Century* (Cambridge: Cambridge University Press, 2000), 93–106; Griffin, *Playing the Past*, appendix A.

6. There is, of course, disjunction as well as continuity, the most obvious general pattern being the fading of interest in Brutish and Arthurian history after Elizabeth's death when the role of Geoffrey of Monmouth's British kings in the construction of the Tudor myth became of less interest.

7. Gary Taylor and Michael Warren (eds.), *The Division of the Kingdoms: Shakespeare's Two Versions of* King Lear (Oxford: Clarendon Press, 1983), vi.

8. J. G. A. Pocock, 'The Limits and Divisions of British History: In Search of the Unknown Subject', *American Historical Review* 87 (1982): 311–36 (318). For a helpful account of the limitations of critics' understanding of the relationship between nationhood and colonialism in early modern Europe, see Fuchs, 'Imperium Studies'.

9. Helgerson, *Forms of Nationhood*; John Speed, *The Theatre of the Empire of Great Britain* (London, 1611); Michael Drayton, *Poly-Olbion* (London, 1612). See chapter 3, 'The Land Speaks', in Helgerson, *Forms of Nationhood*, 105–47, esp. 108–24; Claire McEachern also addresses the *Poly-Olbion* frontispiece, reading it provocatively as the product of collaboration, in her fine book *The Poetics of English Nationhood*, esp. 167–8.

10. Helgerson, *Forms of Nationhood*, 120.

11. Randall Martin outlines the case for the date and location of first performance of *The Love-Sick King* as 1617 and Newcastle. When I gave an early version of this paper at the University of Sussex, Matthew Dimmock observed that the action of the play, including the fortification of Newcastle and the changing

fortunes of the lands between Tweed and Tyne, might echo the events of the Bishops' Wars of 1638–40. The fact that the extant text of the play was not published until 1655 leaves open the possibility that it might have been written or revised as late as 1640, though this seems unlikely; still, the play is, at the very least, remarkably prescient of the future King Charles's struggles with the Scots. See Martin (ed.), *'Edmond Ironside' and Anthony Brewer's 'The Love-sick King'* (New York: Garland, 1991), 200–17, drawing on Frederick Gard Fleay, *A Biographical Chronicle of the English Drama 1559–1642*, 2 vols. (London: Reeves and Turner, 1891), I: 34, and Madeleine Hope Dodds, *'Edmund Ironside* and *The Love-sick King'*, *MLR* 19 (1924): 158–68; on the wars, see Mark Charles Fissel, *The Bishops' Wars: Charles I's Campaigns against Scotland, 1638–1640* (Cambridge: Cambridge University Press, 1994).

12. On the sources of *The Love-Sick King*, see Martin (ed.), *'Edmond Ironside' and Anthony Brewer's 'The Love-sick King'*, 171–89.

13. Anthony Brewer, *The Love-sick King, An English Tragical History: With The Life and Death of Cartesmunda, the fair Nun of Winchester* (London, 1655), B2r–v.

14. William Shakespeare, *Cymbeline*, in Stanley Wells, Gary Taylor, John Jowett and William Montgomery (eds.), *William Shakespeare: The Complete Works* (Oxford: Clarendon Press, 1988), 5.6.481–2.

15. Dodds, *'Edmund Ironside* and *The Love-sick King'*, 159. For Swaen, the play is not is not just naïve pseudo-history, it is also negligible as literature: '[a]esthetic value', he points out crisply, 'it has none'; see A. E. H. Swaen (ed.), *'Anthony Brewer's* The Love-Sick King', in W. Bang (gen. ed.), *Materialen zur Kunde des älteren Englischen Dramas* 18 (Louvain: Uystpruyst, 1907), ix–xiii, xiv.

16. See Robert W. Dent, *'The Love-Sick King*: Turk Turned Dane', *MLR* 56 (1961): 555–7.

17. Martin (ed.), *'Edmond Ironside' and Anthony Brewer's 'The Love-sick King'*, 178.

18. Robert Daborne, *A Christian Turn'd Turk* (*c.* 1610); Philip Massinger, *The Renegado* (1624).

19. R[ichard] V[erstegan], *A Restitution of Decayed Intelligence In Antiquities. Concerning the most noble and renowned English nation* (Antwerp, 1605), A1r.

20. William Camden, *Remaines Concerning Britaine* (London, 1636), C2v–C3r.

21. Floyd-Wilson, *Ethnicity*, 164.

22. Thomas Middleton, *Hengist, King of Kent; Or The Mayor of Queenborough*, ed. R. C. Bald (New York: Scribner, 1938), 2.2.39–44.

23. On *Hengist* and the Counter-Reformation, see Margot Heinemann, *Puritanism and Theatre: Thomas Middleton and Opposition Drama under the Early Stuarts* (Cambridge: Cambridge University Press, 1980), 134–50, esp. 141; Julia Briggs, 'Middleton's Forgotten Tragedy, *Hengist King of Kent*', *Review of English Studies* 41 (1990): 479–95; Swapan Chakravorty, *Society and Politics in the Plays of Thomas Middleton* (Oxford: Clarendon Press, 1996), 120–6.

24. Anthony Munday, *The Triumphs of Reunited Britannia*, in Richard Dutton (ed.), *Jacobean Civic Pageants*, Ryburn Renaissance Texts and Studies (Keele: Ryburn/Keele University Press, 1995), 121, 123. For Brewer's reference to

Munday see Martin (ed.), '*Edmond Ironside' and Anthony Brewer's 'The Love-sick King*', 190.

25. Bernau, 107 above; see also Lesley Johnson, 'Return to Albion' and James P. Carley and Julia Crick, 'Constructing Albion's Past: An Annotated Edition of *De Origine Gigantum*', in Carley and Felicity Riddy (eds.), *Arthurian Literature XIII* (Cambridge: D. S. Brewer, 1995), 19–40, 41–114, and Ruth Evans, 'The Devil in Disguise: Perverse Female Origins of the Nation', in Liz Herbert McAvoy and Teresa Walters (eds.), *Consuming Narratives: Gender and Monstrous Appetite in the Middle Ages and the Renaissance* (Cardiff: University of Wales Press, 2002), 182–95.

26. See Bernau, 250 above, n. 11.

27. Jodi Mikalachki, 'The Masculine Romance of Roman Britain: *Cymbeline* and Early Modern English Nationalism', *Shakespeare Quarterly* 46 (1995): 301–22.

28. On Boudica, see Bernau, 113–14 above.

29. On the relevance of the Albina myth to *The Tempest*, see Lynn Forest-Hill, 'Giants and Enemies of God: The Relationship of Caliban and Prospero from the Perspective of Insular Literary Tradition', forthcoming in *Shakespeare Survey*. I am grateful to Dr Forest-Hill for sending me her essay, which arrived just as this volume was going to press.

30. John Fletcher and Philip Massinger, *The Sea Voyage*, ed. Cyrus Hoy, in Fredson Bowers (gen. ed.), *The Dramatic Works in the Beaumont and Fletcher Canon*, vol. IX (Cambridge: Cambridge University Press, 1994), 2.2.54–8.

31. Gordon McMullan, *The Politics of Unease in the Plays of John Fletcher* (Amherst: University of Massachusetts Press, 1994), 235–54; see also Anthony Parr (ed.), *Three Renaissance Travel Plays*, Revels Plays Companion Library (Manchester: Manchester University Press, 1995), esp. 20–31. For recent readings of *The Sea Voyage* which address the play's intersections with discourses of gender and colonialism, see Claire Jowitt, *Gender Politics and Voyage Drama 1589–1642: Real and Imagined Worlds* (Manchester: Manchester University Press, 2002), 191–213, and Teresa Walters, '"Such stowage as these trinkets": Trading and Tasting Women in Fletcher and Massinger's *The Sea Voyage* (1622)', in McAvoy and Walters (eds.), *Consuming Narratives*, 67–80.

32. On the relationship between *Syrinx* and *The Sea Voyage*, see Gustav Adolf Jacobi, 'Zur Quellenfrage von Fletchers "The Sea-Voyage"', *Anglia* 33 (1910): 332–43.

33. William Warner, *Syrinx, or A Sevenfold History* (London, 1597), BIV.

34. John Hardyng, *The Chronicle . . . from the firste begynnyng of Englande* (London, 1543), fol. vii r.

35. Belief in the possibility of impregnation by spirits or by self-induced arousal continued into the mid-seventeenth century: '[T]hat the *Genii* or Spirits which Antiquity called Gods, might impregnate Women so, that they might bring forth children without the help of a man, seems not to me to be at all incredible . . . [T]he Pagan Gods, when they would have to doe with women, needed no such *ambages* as ordinarily men imagine, viz. first to play the *Succubi*, & then the *Incubi*, that is, first to receive the Seed of man, having transformed

themselves into the shape of a woman, & then to transfuse the Seed into the womb of a woman, after they had changed themselves into the form of a man. For it is not the Matter of the Seed, but a grateful contact or motion fermenting or spiriting the place of conception, that makes the Female fruitfull' (Henry More, *An Explanation of the Grand Mystery of Godliness* (London, 1660), 15v, 16v). I am grateful to Carolyn Lyle for this reference.

36. William Warner, *Albions England: A Continued Historie of the same Kingdome from the Originals of the first Inhabitants thereof* (London, 1589), G4r.

37. Raphael Holinshed, William Harrison et al., *The First and second volumes of Chronicles* (London, 1586), 'The First Booke', A3v.

38. On *The Island Princess* and English hopes for the Moluccas, see Shankar Raman, 'Imaginary Islands: Staging the East', *Renaissance Drama* 26 (1995): 131–61 and Michael Neill, '"Material Flames": The Space of Mercantile Fantasy in John Fletcher's *The Island Princess*', in Neill, *Putting History to the Question: Power, Politics and Society in English Renaissance Drama* (New York: Columbia University Press, 2000), 311–38; see also McMullan, *The Politics of Unease*, 222–35.

39. Theodor de Bry, *America* (1590), E1r; see also Andrew Hadfield, 'Bruited Abroad: John White and Thomas Harriot's Colonial Representations of Ancient Britain', in Baker and Maley (eds.), *British Identities and English Renaissance Literature*, 159–77, esp. 166.

40. William Shakespeare and John Fletcher, *Henry VIII (All is True)*, ed. Gordon McMullan (London: Arden, 2000), 5.4.52. The prophecy scene is, according to authorship analysts, a Fletcher scene. It is perhaps also worth mentioning that around this time Fletcher explored the other principal instance of early British female rule in his play *Bonduca*.

8 *TAMBURLAINE*, SACRED SPACE, AND THE HERITAGE OF MEDIEVAL CARTOGRAPHY

1. This is the classification used in J. B. Harley and David Woodward (eds.), *The History of Cartography, Volume One: Cartography in Prehistoric, Ancient, and Medieval Europe and the Mediterranean* (Chicago: University of Chicago Press, 1987), part 3 (on medieval cartography), 281–501.

2. See P. D. A. Harvey, 'Medieval Maps: An Introduction', in Harley and Woodward (eds.), *History of Cartography*, 283–5 (283).

3. In my attempt to deal with these issues, I silently draw on recent critical work on space and spatiality, most notably on Henri Lefebvre, *The Production of Space*, trans. Donald Nicolson-Smith (French original 1974; Oxford: Blackwell, 1991).

4. *1 Tamburlaine*, 4.4.81–2. All *Tamburlaine* quotations are taken from Christopher Marlowe, *The Complete Plays*, ed. J. B. Steane (Harmondsworth: Penguin, 1969).

5. See Richard Helgerson, 'The Folly of Maps and Modernity', in Andrew Gordon and Bernhard Klein (eds.), *Literature, Mapping, and the Politics of Space in Early Modern Britain* (Cambridge: Cambridge University Press, 2001), 241–62.

6. See *Durkheim on Religion*, ed. W. S. F. Pickering (London and Boston: Routledge and Kegan Paul, 1975).

7. See Rudolf Otto, *The Idea of the Holy: An Inquiry into the Non-rational Factor in the Idea of the Divine and Its Relation to the Rational*, trans. John W. Harvey, 2nd edn (German original 1917; Oxford and New York: Oxford University Press, 1950).

8. See Richard Knolles, *The Generall Historie of the Turkes* (London: Adam Islip, 1610), 297. Marlowe could not have seen this book in print, as it was first published in 1603, but we can assume that he had access to the manuscript when he was writing the *Tamburlaine* plays. See David Fuller, 'Introduction', *The Complete Works of Christopher Marlowe. Vol. v: Tamburlaine the Great, Parts 1 and 2*, ed. Fuller (Oxford: Clarendon Press, 1998), xvii–liii (xxiv).

9. Alan Sinfield, 'Legitimating Tamburlaine', in Richard Wilson (ed.), *Christopher Marlowe*, Longman Critical Readers (Harlow: Longman, 1999), 111–19 (115).

10. For a recent attempt at an inclusive and comparative approach to the analysis of sacred space, coming out of the *One World Archaeology* movement, see David L. Carmichael et al. (eds.), *Sacred Sites, Sacred Places* (London and New York: Routledge, 1994).

11. J. S. Cunningham, 'Introduction', Christopher Marlowe, *Tamburlaine the Great*, ed. Cunningham, The Revels Plays (Manchester: Manchester University Press, 1981), 1–105 (14); internal quotation from Eric Voegelin, 'Machiavelli's Prince: Background and Formation', *Review of Politics* 13 (1951): 142–68 (165).

12. George Whetstone, *The English Myrror* (London: I. Windet for G. Seton, 1586); Petrus Perondinus, *Magni Tamerlanis Scythiarum Imperatoris Vita* (Florence, 1553). The pioneering survey of Marlowe's sources can be found in Una Ellis-Fermor's edition of the play: *Tamburlaine the Great* (London: Methuen, 1930). For recent overviews see the editions by Cunningham (1981) and Fuller (1998).

13. John Gillies, 'Marlowe, the *Timur* Myth, and the Motives of Geography', in John Gillies and Virginia Mason Vaughan (eds.), *Playing the Globe: Genre and Geography in English Renaissance Drama* (Madison: Fairleigh Dickinson University Press, 1998), 203–29 (209).

14. The terms are Cunningham's. See his 'Introduction', 47.

15. *Ibid.*, 59.

16. I take this idea from John Gillies, *Shakespeare and the Geography of Difference* (Cambridge: Cambridge University Press, 1994), 57.

17. See Ethel Seaton, 'Marlowe's Map' [1924], in Clifford Leech (ed.), *Marlowe: A Collection of Critical Essays*, Twentieth-Century Views (New Jersey: Prentice Hall, 1964), 36–56.

18. For a historically specific survey of the forms and uses of the *mappaemundi*, see David Woodward, 'Medieval *Mappaemundi*', in Harley and Woodward (eds.), *History of Cartography*, 286–370.

19. John Gillies, 'The Body and Geography', *Shakespeare Studies* 29 (2001): 57–62 (58).

20. Of course, the idea – implicit in this thinking – of a single community laying claim to a particular sacred place is looking increasingly problematic in a pluralised world. Jerusalem is only the most obvious example of this.
21. See Gillies, 'The Body and Geography', 58–9.
22. On the atlas as theatre, see Gillies, *Shakespeare and the Geography of Difference*, 70–5. For some contemporary attitudes to cartography, see chapter 4 of my *Maps and the Writing of Space in Early Modern England and Ireland* (Basingstoke: Palgrave, 2001).
23. See Catherine Delano-Smith and Elizabeth Morley Ingram, *Maps in Bibles, 1500–1600: An Illustrated Catalogue* (Geneva: Droz, 1991).
24. Quoted here from the title-page of the 1619 English edition: Heinrich Bünting, *Itinerarium totius sacrae scripturae* (London: Adam Islip, 1619). This edition comes without maps.
25. *Ibid.*, title-page.
26. 'Das aber ist dagegen vnser trost / das Dauid in obgenandten 39. Psalm / sich nicht allein einen Pilgerim / sondern auch einen Bürger vnsers HERRN Gottes nennet / damit anzuzeigen / das / ob wir wol hie auff Erden keine bleibende stat haben / so sein wir doch gleichwol Bürger und *Haußgenossen* vnsers lieben Gottes.' Bünting, *Itinerarium totius sacrae scripturae* [German edn] (Magdeburg: Paul Donat, 1585), iij v (my italics).
27. 'Die eigentliche vnd warhafftige gestalt der Erden vnd des Meers.' Bünting, *Itinerarium*, German edn, 8.
28. Arthur M. Hind, *Engraving in England in the Sixteenth and Seventeenth Centuries*, 3 vols. (Cambridge: Cambridge University Press, 1952), I: 176.
29. See Helgerson, 'The Folly of Maps and Modernity'.
30. On this pictorial convention see my 'Randfiguren. Othello, Oroonoko und die kartographische Repräsentation Afrikas', in Ina Schabert and Michaela Boenke (eds.), *Imaginationen des Anderen im 16. und 17. Jahrhundert* (Wiesbaden: Harrassowitz Verlag, 2002), 185–216.
31. See J. B. Harley, 'Silences and Secrecy: the Hidden Agenda of Cartography in Early Modern Europe', *Imago Mundi* 40 (1988): 57–76.
32. My implicit reference here is to the work of Michel de Certeau on everyday life. See his *The Practice of Everyday Life*, trans. Steven Rendall (French original 1974; Berkeley and Los Angeles: University of California Press, 1988).
33. See, for instance, Denis Wood, *The Power of Maps* (London: Routledge, 1993).

9 LELAND'S *ITINERARY* AND THE REMAINS OF THE MEDIEVAL PAST

I am grateful to readers who helped me develop this essay from earlier incarnations; particularly Christopher Ivic, Walter Mignolo, Paula Moya and Simon Firth. This essay is dedicated to the memory of Mike Firth.

1. Building on the work of Richard Helgerson, recent work on Renaissance geography includes Garrett A. Sullivan, Jr., *The Drama of Landscape, Land, Property,*

and Social Relations in the Early Modern Stage (Stanford: Stanford University Press, 1998); Bernhard Klein, *Maps and the Writing of Space in Early Modern England and Ireland* (New York: Palgrave, 2001); Andrew Gordon and Bernhard Klein (eds.), *Literature, Mapping, and the Politics of Space in Early Modern England* (Cambridge: Cambridge University Press, 2001); and Rhonda Lemke Sanford, *Maps and Memory in Early Modern England: A Sense of Place* (New York: Palgrave, 2002).

2. John Leland and John Bale, *The laborious journey and serche of Johan Leylande, for Englandes antiquitees, geven of hym as a new yeares gyfte to Kynge Henry the viii* (London, 1549), reprinted in *The Itinerary of John Leland*, ed. Lucy Toulmin Smith, 5 vols. (Carbondale: Southern Illinois University Press, 1964), 1: xli. All citations from Leland, unless otherwise noted, are from this edition, with volume and page numbers marked in parentheses.

3. Thomas Hearne; also William Dunn Macray, *Annals of the Bodleian Library Oxford with a notice of the earlier library of the university*, 2nd edn (Oxford: Clarendon Press, 1890, repr. 1984). 76.

4. F. J. Levy, *Tudor Historical Thought* (San Marino: Huntington Library Publications, 1967), 158. Similarly, Robin Flower notes that Leland's mapping and recording project 'served as a draft instruction for the labours of all the antiquaries of the Tudor times'. See Robin Flower, 'Lawrence Nowell and the Discovery of England in Tudor Times', *Proceedings of the British Academy* 21 (1935): 47–73 (49).

5. William Camden, *Britannia*, trans. Philemon Holland (1610), ed. Robert Mayhew, 2 vols. (Bristol: Thoemmes Press, 2003), 1: 4. All translations from Camden, unless otherwise noted, are from this edition, with volume and page numbers noted parenthetically.

6. Thus Stan Mendyk asserts that 'Leland lacked the capacity to realize fully the potentialities of archaeological remains as evidence for the reconstruction of the past . . . [but indiscriminately] drew past and present together'. 'Early British Chorography', *Sixteenth Century Journal* 4 (1986): 468. For a persuasive critique of early modernist readings of Leland, see William Rockett, 'Historical Topography and British History in Camden's Britannia', *Renaissance and Reformation / Renaissance et Reforme* 14 (1990): 71–80.

7. See Flower, 'Lawrence Nowell and the Discovery of England'; John Chandler, *John Leland's Itinerary: Travels in Tudor England* (Dover: Allan Sutton, 1993), xxi–xxii; A. L. Rowse, *The England of Elizabeth* (London: Macmillan, 1964), 32.

8. See Walter D. Mignolo, *The Darker Side of the Renaissance: Literacy, Territoriality, and Colonization* (Ann Arbor: University of Michigan Press, 1995).

9. This is the argument of Foxe's *Acts and Monuments*: see Thomas Betteridge, *Tudor Histories of the English Reformations, 1530–83* (Aldershot: Ashgate, 1999), chapter 4: 'John Foxe and the Writing of History'.

10. On *The laboryouse journey* and its representation of Leland's double historical role, see James Simpson, 'The Melancholy of John Leland and the Beginnings of English Literary History,' in *Reform and Cultural Revolution*, 15, and David

Lawton, 'The Surveying Subject and the "Whole World" of Belief: Three Case Studies', *New Medieval Literatures* 4 (2001): 9–37. See also Wallace, *Premodern Places*, which offers a trenchant model of the 'mental mapping' of places across historical time.

11. See Duffy, *Stripping of the Altars* and David Aers's review, 'Altars of Power: Reflections on Eamon Duffy's *The Stripping of the Altars: Traditional Religion in England 1400–1580*, *Literature and History*, 3rd series 3 (1994): 90–105, for a debate on the Reformation that highlights the various meanings and uses of these terms.

12. On this point, see the analyses of medieval geography by Lawton, 'The Surveying Subject'; Daniel Birkholz, 'The Vernacular Map: Re-Charting English Literary History', *New Medieval Literatures* 6 (2003): 11–77; John Howe, 'Creating Symbolic Landscapes: Medieval Development of Sacred Space', in Howe and Michael Wolfe (eds.), *Inventing Medieval Landscapes* (Gainesville: University of Florida Press, 2002). I am grateful to Catherine Sanok for sharing with me her work in progress on pre-modern sanctity, landscape, and national identity.

13. Lesley Johnson and Jocelyn Wogan-Browne, 'National, World and Women's History: Writers and Readers of English in Post-Conquest England', in David Wallace (ed.), *The Cambridge History of Medieval English Literature* (Cambridge: Cambridge University Press, 1999), 106.

14. William Worcestre, *Itineraries*, ed. John H. Harvey (Oxford: Clarendon Press, 1969). All references to Worcester's work will be to this edition, with the page numbers noted in parentheses.

15. Harvey, Introduction, *Itineraries*, xix. The manuscript is now Corpus Christi College Cambridge MS 210.

16. Howe, 'Creating Symbolic Landscapes', 210.

17. So, for example, in the post-Reformation Injunctions for the Clergy (1536), readers are warned against 'workes devysed by mens phanthasyes, besydes scripture, as in wandering to pilgrimage . . . as thynges tendyng to ydolatrye and supersticyon'.

18. *The Oxford Dictionary of Saints*, 2nd edn, ed. David Hugh Farmer (Oxford: Oxford University Press, 1987), 336.

19. De Certeau, *Practice of Everyday Life*, 119.

20. Helgerson, *Forms of Nationhood*, 132.

21. Wyman H. Herendeen, *From Landscape to Literature: The River and the Myth of Geography* (Pittsburgh: Duquesne University Press, 1986), 196.

22. John Scattergood, 'John Leland's Itinerary and the Identity of England', in A. J. Piesse (ed.), *Sixteenth-Century Identities* (Manchester: Manchester University Press, 2000), 58–74 (67).

23. Thus Herendeen observes, 'the river sets off Leland's view of history' (192). For an analysis of 'the stream of time' as a model of linear history, see David Lawton, '1453 and the Stream of Time', forthcoming in the *Journal of Medieval and Early Modern Studies*.

24. See Simpson, *Reform and Cultural Revolution*, 51.

25. Victor Watts, 'English Place-Names in the Sixteenth Century: The Search for Identity', in A. J. Piesse (ed.), *Sixteenth-Century Identities* (Manchester: Manchester University Press, 2001), 34–57 (51).

26. Wallace T. MacCaffrey, *Exeter, 1540–1640: The Growth of an English Country Town*, 2nd edn (Cambridge, Mass.: Harvard University Press, 1975), 182.

27. On these grants, see Joyce Youings (ed.), *Devon Monastic Lands: Calendar of Particulars for Grants, 1536–1558* (Torquay: Devon and Cornwall Record Society, 1955), 4–5, 12.

28. MacCaffrey, *Exeter*, 189, 205–6; see also W. G. Hoskins, *Two Thousand Years in Exeter* (1960; Chichester: Phillimore and Company, 1974), 57–8.

29. Similarly in Malmesbury he notes 'The hole longginges of thabbay be now longging to one Stumpe, an exceding riche clothier that boute them of the king . . . At this present tyme every corner of the vaste houses of office that belongid to thabbay be fulle of lumbes [i.e., looms] to weve clooth yn . . .'

30. A plan of Tichfield House appears in Joyce Youings (ed.), *The Dissolution of the Monasteries* (New York: Barnes and Noble, 1971), 247.

31. Letter to Thomas Wriothesley, 2 January 1538, from John Crayford, clerk, and Roland Latham, the king's commissioners for the dissolution of Titchfield Abbey, reprinted in Youings (ed.), *Dissolution of the Monasteries*, 248.

32. As de Certeau observes, 'the map . . . colonizes space . . . [It] pushes away into its prehistory or into its posterity, as if into the wings, the operations of which it is the result or the necessary condition' (*Practice of Everyday Life*, 121).

33. Arthur F. Kinney asserts that Norden aimed to produce a work 'that would combine the history of Camden and the chorography of Saxton', 'Imagining England: The Chorographical Glass', in Peter E. Medine and Joseph Wittreich (eds.), *Soundings of Things Done: Essays in Early Modern Literature in Honor of S. K. Heninger, Jr.* (Newark: University of Delaware Press, 1997), 181–214 (195). On Norden's Key, see J. B. Harley, 'Meaning and Ambiguity in Tudor Cartography', in Sarah Tyacke (ed.), *English Map-Making, 1500–1650: Historical Essays* (London: The British Library, 1983), 22–45.

34. Bernhard Klein observes of Camden's *Britannia*, 'even when the description follows a county's rivers, these are shown to be flowing exclusively around stately mansions, ancient castles and private parks', asserting that Camden 'employ[s] the land itself as the central element of historical stability'. At the same time, in Camden's descriptions of places like Tichfield, which is traversed by a 'little river' that joins the 'Solente . . . in which the tides at set houres [rush] with great violence out of the Ocean at both ends' (1: 267), the river takes on the violence implicit in the property's Reformation transfer; see Klein, 'Imaginary Journeys: Spenser, Drayton, and the Poetics of National Space', in *Literature, Mapping, and the Politics of Space in Early Modern Britain* (Cambridge: Cambridge University Press, 2001), 209.

35. *OED*, s.v. 'main stream'.

36. See Mayhew, Introduction, *Britannia*, 1: xviii–xix.

37. De Certeau, *Practice of Everyday Life*, 120; Helgerson, *Forms of Nationhood*; Klein, 'Imaginary Journeys'. See also Howard Marchitello, 'Political Maps: The Production of Cartography and Chorography in Early Modern England', in Margaret J. M. Ezell and Katherine O'Brien O'Keeffe (eds.), *Cultural Artifacts and the Production of Meaning* (Ann Arbor: University of Michigan Press, 1994), 13–40.
38. On the relationship between Speed, Leland and Camden, see Levy, *Tudor Historical Thought*, 196–7; and on the relationship between Speed's maps and Norden's, see Stan A. E. Mendyk, *'Speculum Britanniae': Regional Study, Antiquarianism and Science in Britain to 1700* (Toronto: University of Toronto Press, 1989), 78–9.
39. Mendyk, *'Speculum Britanniae'*, 78.
40. John Davies, 'To the right well deserving Mr IOHN SPEED the Author of the worke', John Speed, *Theatre of the Empire of Great Britaine* (London, 1611), n.p.
41. J. B. Harley, 'Silences and Secrecy: The Hidden Agenda of Cartography in Early Modern Europe', *Imago Mundi* 40 (1988): 57–76 (66). On the empty spaces in early modern maps, see also Mignolo, *The Darker Side of the Renaissance*, 305–9.
42. On this point, see Kathleen Biddick, 'Decolonizing the English Past: Readings in Medieval Archaeology and History', *Journal of British Studies* 32 (1993): 1–23 (4).
43. Speed to Cotton (n.d.) in *Original letters of eminent literary men*, ed. Sir Henry Ellis, Camden Society No. 23 (London, 1843), 110. On the relationship between Cotton and Speed, see Graham Parry, *The Trophies of Time: English Antiquarians and the Seventeenth Century* (Oxford: Oxford University Press, 1995), 75.
44. David Aers critiques Eamon Duffy's use of similarly agent-less metaphors to describe the Reformation as '"a relentless torrent" which swept away "the landmarks of a thousand years"' ('Altars of Power', 100).
45. Roland Greene, 'Island Logic', in Peter Hulme and William H. Sherman (eds.), *The Tempest and its Travels* (London: Reaktion Books, 2000), 144.
46. On this passage in Harriot, see Stephen Greenblatt, *Marvelous Possessions: The Wonder of the New World* (Chicago: University of Chicago Press, 1991), 8.
47. Christopher Ivic, 'Mapping British Identities', in Baker and Maley (eds.), *British Identities and English Renaissance Literature*, 145, 144.
48. This point might be compared to Andrew Hadfield's argument that the literature of colonisation also unwittingly reveals and enables critique of the violence implicit in the very colonising process it documents; see *Literature, Travel and Colonial Writing in the English Renaissance, 1545–1625* (Oxford: Clarendon Press, 1998), esp. 70–3. On connections between 'medieval' and 'colonial' spaces, see Bruce Holsinger, 'Medieval Studies, Postcolonial Studies, and the Genealogies of Critique', *Speculum* 77 (2002): 1195–1227, as well as the essays collected in the recent special issue of *JMEMS*: 30 (2000), 'Decolonizing the Middle Ages', edited by John Dagenais and Margaret R. Greer.

10 JOHN BALE AND RECONFIGURING THE 'MEDIEVAL' IN REFORMATION ENGLAND

1. Simpson, *Reform and Cultural Revolution*, chapter 1; John Bale, *The laboryouse Iourney of Johan Leylande, for Englandes antiquitees, geuen of hym as a new yeares gyfte to Kynge Henry viii. in the xxxvii. yeare of his reygne, with declaracyons enlarged: by Johan Bale* (London, 1549), B7v.

2. John Bale, *A brefe Chronicle concerynynge the Examinacyon and death of the blessed martyr of Christ syr Iohan Oldecastell the lorde Cobham* (Antwerp, 1544), 9v.

3. *Gods Promyses* was possibly written after 1536, as it does not appear in the list of fourteen plays in Bale's *Anglorum Heliades* which Bale produced for John Leland *circa* 1536; the title page of the printed edition (Wesel, *c.* 1547–48) says the play was 'compyled . . . Anno Domini 1538', but this date may refer to the revision of the play, not its composition. See Peter Happé, *John Bale* (New York: Twayne, 1996), 5–6, 9; Jesse W. Harris, *John Bale: A Study in the Minor Literature of the Reformation*, Illinois Studies in Language and Literature, 25 (Urbana: University of Illinois Press, 1940), 72–3.

4. John Leland, *Commentarii de Scriptoribus Britannicis*, ed. Anthony Hall, 2 vols. (Oxford, 1709), II: 415.

5. John Leland, 'Ad Richardum Hirtium', cited in James Carley, 'John Leland in Paris: The Evidence of his Poetry', *Studies in Philology* 83 (1986): 1–50 (26).

6. Henry Stalbrydge (i.e. John Bale), *The epistle exhortatorye of an Englyshe Christyane vnto his derely beloued co[n]treye of Englande / against the pompouse popyshe Bysshopes therof / as yet the true members of theyr fylthye father the great Antichryst of Rome* (Antwerp, 1544?), 3r.

7. John Harison (i.e. John Bale), *Yet a Course at the Romyshe foxe* (Antwerp, 1543), 2r.

8. Simpson, *Reform and Cultural Revolution*, 19.

9. Bale, *Laboryouse Iourney*, A5r. For the Plague of Darkness, see Exodus 10:21.

10. John Bale, *Scriptorum illustrium maioris Britanniae, Catalogus*, 2 vols. (Basle, 1557, 1559), II: 450. Cf. Revelation 22:16.

11. John Bale, *The first examinacyon of Anne Askewe, lately martyred in Smythfelde, by the Romysh popes vpholders, with the Elucydacyon of Johan Bale* (Wesel, 1546), 6r.

12. *Ibid.*, 1r.

13. Diarmaid MacCulloch, *Thomas Cranmer* (New Haven: Yale University Press, 1996), 27.

14. Bale, *Chronycle concerynynge . . . Oldecastell*, 3r.

15. Bale, *Laboryouse Iourney*, A4r.

16. For interest in continuities between 'medieval' and 'early modern', cf. the essay by Patricia Badir in this collection, 205–19 above.

17. For examples of this generic range, see John Bale, *An excellent and right learned meditacion, compiled in two prayers, most frutefull and necessary to be vsed and said of all true English men, in these daungerous daies of affliction, for the comfort*

and better stay of the christen co[n]science (London?, 1554); Bale (as Stalbrydge), *Epistle exhortatorye*; John Bale, *A dialogue or communycacyon to be had at a table betwene two chyldren, gathered out of the holy scripture, by Johan Bale, for his .ii. yonge sonnes Iohan and Paule* (London, 1549); *A Comedy concernynge thre lawes, of nature, Moses, & Christ, corrupted by the sodomites. Pharysees and Papystes* (Wesel, 1548?); Bale, *Catalogus*; Bale, *Chronycle concernynge . . . Oldecastell*; John Bale, *The vocyacyon of Ioha[n] Bale to the bishoprick of Ossorie in Irela[n]de his persecucio[n]s in [th]e same / & finall delyueraunce* (Wesel?, 1553).

18. Philip Schwyzer, 'The Beauties of the Land: Bale's Books, Aske's Abbeys, and the Aesthetics of Nationhood', *Renaissance Quarterly* 57 (2004): 99–125, esp. 111–22.

19. Barnabe Googe, *Eglogs, epitaphes and Sonettes* (London, 1563), A7r–v.

20. Bale, *Thre lawes*, G2r; John Bale, *Illustrium Maioris Britanniae scriptorum, hoc est, Angliae, Cambriae, ac Scotiae summariu[m]* (Wesel, 1548): this portrait does not appear in all copies of the *Summarium*; see Thora Blatt, *The Plays of John Bale* (Copenhagen, 1968), insert between 7 and 8. The portrait in *Thre Lawes* shows Bale face-on, again in academic dress, with a book in his right hand.

21. Bale, *Vocacyon*, 8v; Bale, *First examinacyon*, ♣1r; John Bale, *The latter examinacyon of Anne Askewe, lately martyred in Smythfelde, by the wicked Synagoge of Antichrist, with the Elucydacyon of Johan Bale* (Wesel, 1547), A1r.

22. Cited in MacCulloch, *Tudor Church Militant*, 53 (my emphasis).

23. John Bale, *King Johan*, in Peter Happé (ed.), *The Complete Plays of John Bale*, 2 vols. (Cambridge: D. S. Brewer, 1985–86), I: line 1119.

24. See, for example, titles in n. 17 above.

25. Cited in *OED*, 'compile', sense 3.

26. See, for example, the dispute between Satan and Christ in John Bale, *A Brefe Comedy or Enterlude Concernynge the Temptacyon of our Lorde and Saver Jesus Christ by Sathan in the Desart*, in Happé (ed.), *Complete Plays of John Bale*, II: lines 208–41.

27. MacCulloch, *Tudor Church Militant*, 138.

28. Bale, *Laboryouse Iourney*, A7v.

29. Leslie P. Fairfield, *John Bale: Mythmaker for the English Reformation* (West Lafayette, Indiana: Purdue University Press, 1976), 90. For Foxe on the printing press, see John Foxe, *Actes and Monuments* (London, 1563): 'The lord began to work for his Church not with sword and target to subdue his exalted adversary, but with printing, writing, and reading . . . so that either the pope must abolish knowledge and printing or printing must at length root him out', cited in Elizabeth L. Eisenstein, *The Printing Press as an Agent of Change: Communications and Cultural Transformations in Early Modern Europe* (Cambridge: Cambridge University Press, 1979), 151.

30. Bale, *Laboryouse Iourney*, A7v. For the importance of print to the Reformation imagination, see Badir, 212–14 above.

31. For the early modern assimilation of the past, see the essay by Summit in this collection, 000–00 above.

32. Bale, *Laboryouse Iourney*, C2r.

33. For Bale on idolatry, see John Bale, *The Tragedy or Enterlude Manyfestyng the Chefe Promyses of God vnto Man by All Ages in the Olde Lawe from the Fall of Adam to the Incarnacyon of the Lorde Jesus Christ*, in Happé (ed.), *Complete Plays*, vol. II:

> PATER COELESTIS I can nat abyde the vyce of idolatrye,
> Tho I should suffer all other vyllanye.   (lines 584–5)

34. Blatt, *Plays of John Bale*; E. S. Miller, 'The Antiphons in Bale's Cycle of Christ', *Studies in Philology* 48 (1951): 629–38; Happé, *Bale*, ix. Of the twenty-one plays which Bale lists as his own in *Anglorum Heliades* and *Summarium*, five survive: *Gods Promyses*, *Johan Baptystes Preachynge*, *The Temptacyon*, *Thre Lawes* and *King Johan*.

35. One play, the Grocers' Play of Adam and Eve, survives from a mystery cycle performed at Norwich, where Bale was sent aged twelve to join the Carmelite friars; see John C. Coldewey, 'The Non-Cycle Plays and the East Anglian Tradition', in Richard Beadle (ed.), *The Cambridge Companion to Medieval English Theatre* (Cambridge: Cambridge University Press, 1994), 189–210 (201). The 'N-Town cycle' of forty-three plays is also strongly associated with East Anglia; see Alan J. Fletcher, 'The N-Town Plays' in the same volume, 163–88.

36. Rainer Pineas, 'The English Morality Play as a Weapon of Religious Controversy', *Studies in English Literature 1500–1900* 2. 2 (1962): 157–8; cf. Pineas, *Tudor and Early Stuart Anti-Catholic Drama* (Nieuwkoop: De Graaf, 1972).

37. Bale, *Chronycle concernygne... Oldecastell*, IIr. Cf. the depiction of the 'popyshe Byshhoppes' in Bale, *Epistle exhortatorye*, passim.

38. Bale's appearance, book in hand, is here reminiscent of the woodcut-portraits in *Thre Lawes* and the *Summarium*, and of his representation as 'Baleus Prolocutor' in *Johan Baptystes Preachynge*, where he appears for the epilogue holding the Bible, referred to in his speech as 'thys gospell' (John Bale, *A Brefe Comedy or Enterlude of Johan Baptystes Preachynge in the Wyldernesse, Openynge the Craftye Assaultes of the Hypocrytes, with the Gloryouse Baptyme of the Lorde Jesus Christ*, in Happé (ed.), *Complete Plays*, II: line 462).

39. Blatt, *Plays of John Bale*, 95.

40. Simpson, *Reform and Cultural Revolution*, 532.

41. Peter Happé, '"Erazed in the booke": The Mystery Cycles and Reform', paper delivered at 'Writing and Reform in Sixteenth-Century England', 3rd International Conference of the Tudor Symposium, University of Newcastle-upon-Tyne, 5–7 September 2002.

42. *Johan Baptystes Preachynge* was originally published as companion text to *The Temptacyon*, with continuous page signatures, but was lost when the Harley library was distributed in the eighteenth century. The text only survives today because it was reprinted for the *Harleian Miscellany* (1744), which is the authority for the text. See Happé, *Bale*, 109.

43. Happé, *Bale*, 5. Of the five extant dramas, only *King Johan* and *Thre Lawes* are included in Bale's list of fourteen plays in *Anglorum Heliades* (c. 1536); the other three appear only in the list in the *Summarium* (1548).

44. Cited in Harris, *Bale*, 100.
45. Happé, *Bale*, 10. Cromwell's accounts record both his authorisation of such payments, and his presence at the plays: for example, 'Bale & his Fellowes The last of Ianuary (1539) given to him & his ffelowes for playing before my lorde–xxxˢ', cited in Harris, *Bale*, 102, n. 14. For evidence of the likelihood that 'Bale and his Felowes' were 'Lord Cromwell's Players', see White, *Theatre and Reformation*, 12–27.
46. G. R. Elton, *Policy and Police: The Enforcement of the Reformation in the Age of Thomas Cromwell* (1972; Cambridge: Cambridge University Press, 1985), esp. 171–216.
47. Harris, *Bale*, 65–6.
48. *Ibid.*, 101, n. 11.
49. MacCulloch, *Cranmer*, 227; for list of plays, see Happé, *Bale*, 5–6.
50. Pineas, 'English Morality Play', 172; cf. Richard Rex, 'The Crisis of Obedience: God's Word and Henry's Reformation', *The Historical Journal* 39.4 (1996): 863–94 (883) on the importance of obedience in *King Johan*; and Andrew B. Chrichton, '*Kyng Johan* and the *Ludus de Antichristo* as Moralities of the State', *Sixteenth Century Journal* 4.2 (1973): 61–76.
51. For further discussion of how 'papists' were blamed for the West Country uprising, see Stewart James Mottram, 'Reforming Nationhood: England in the Literature of the Tudor Imperial Age, 1509–1553' (Ph.D. dissertation, University of Leeds, 2005), 199–202.
52. The 1546 and 1560 editions of *The actes of Englysh votaryes* do not have illustrations on the title pages.
53. Margaret Aston, *The King's Bedpost: Reformation and Iconography in a Tudor Group Portrait* (Cambridge: Cambridge University Press, 1993), 82–8.
54. 'Where by divers sundry old authentic histories and chronicles it is manifestly declared and expressed that this realm of England is an empire, and so hath been accepted in the world, governed by one supreme head and king having the dignity and royal estate of the imperial crown of the same . . . he also being institute and furnished by the goodness and sufferance of Almighty God with plenary, whole and entire power, pre-eminence, authority, prerogative and jurisdiction to render and yield justice and final determination to all manner of folk resiants or subjects within this realm, in all causes, matters, debates and contentions happening to occur, insurge or begin within the limits thereof, without restraint or provocation to any foreign princes or potentates of the world', Act in Restraint of Appeals, in G. R. Elton (ed.), *The Tudor Constitution: Documents and Commentary*, 2nd edn (Cambridge: Cambridge University Press, 1982), 353–8 (353).
55. For a discussion of this tension, see Evelyn B. Tribble, *Margins and Marginality: The Printed Page in Early Modern England* (Charlottesville: University Press of Virginia, 1993), 11–56. Cf. Kimberley Anne Coles, 'The Death of the Author (and the Appropriation of her Text): The Case of Anne Askew's "Examinations"', *Modern Philology* 99.4 (2002): 515–39 (530–1).
56. Cited in Coles, 'Death of the Author', 531.

57. Baleus Prolocutor appears in four of Bale's five extant plays; in the fifth, *King Johan*, this role is taken on by 'The Interpretour'.

58. Bale, *First examinacyon*, 5r; Bale, *Chronycle concernynge . . . Oldecastell*, 3v (emphasis added).

59. Bale, *Epistle exhortatorye*, 3r.

60. Françoise Waquet, *Latin, or the Empire of a Sign from the Sixteenth to the Twentieth Centuries*, trans. John Howe (London: Verso, 2001), 125. Cf. James W. Binns, *Intellectual Culture in Elizabethan and Jacobean England: The Latin Writing of the Age* (Leeds: Francis Cairns, 1990), 297–306. For vernacular arts of rhetoric, see Leonard Cox, *The arte or crafte of Rhetoryke* (1524), Richard Sherry, *A treatise of schemes & tropes* (1550), and Thomas Wilson, *The Arte of Rhetorique* (1553).

11 MEDIEVAL PENANCE, REFORMATION REPENTANCE AND *MEASURE FOR MEASURE*

I thank the Medieval Reading Group at the University of Michigan at Ann Arbor for a very stimulating response to and discussion of this essay. I would also like to thank the anonymous readers of this volume, and the National Humanities Institute at Ann Arbor for the award of the Nicholas Frehling fellowship which allowed me to complete work on this essay.

1. All quotations from J. W. Lever's Arden edition of *Measure for Measure* (London and New York: Methuen, 1965).

2. Frederick J. Furnivall (ed.), *Handlyng Synne*, EETS, os 119 (London: K. Paul, Trench, Trübner, 1901). The manual was translated by Robert Mannyng of Brunne from William of Waddington's *Manuel des Pechiez*.

3. See, in particular, Stephen Greenblatt, *Hamlet in Purgatory* (Princeton: Princeton University Press, 2001).

4. For a recent exception, see Brian Cummings, *The Literary Culture of the Reformation: Grammar and Grace* (Oxford: Oxford University Press, 2002), esp. chapter 8.

5. Stephen Greenblatt, *Shakespearean Negotiations: The Circulation of Social Energy in Renaissance England* (Berkeley: University of California Press, 1988) and Louis Adrian Montrose, *The Purpose of Playing: The Cultural Politics of Elizabethan Theater* (Chicago: University of Chicago Press, 1996).

6. G. Wilson Knight, '*Measure for Measure* and the Gospels' in *The Wheel of Fire* (1930; London: Routledge Classics, 2001), is the best example. See also Roy Battenhouse, '*Measure for Measure* and the Christian Doctrine of Atonement', *PMLA* 61 (1946): 1029–59.

7. For example, in his long debate on church government with John Whitgift, Thomas Cartwright calls the archbishop's court a 'filthy quave-mire and poisoned plash of all the abominations that do infect the whole realm'; quoted in *The Defence of the Answer to the Admonition, against the Reply of T[homas] C[artwright]* in Revd John Ayre (ed.), *The Works of John Whitgift*, 3 vols. (Cambridge: Parker Society, 1851–53), vol. 1.

8. Brian Tierney, 'Canon Law and Institutions', in Peter Linehan (ed.), *Proceedings of the Seventh International Congress of Medieval Canon Law* (Città del Vaticano: Bibliotheca Apostolica Vaticana, 1988), 49–69 (67). Tierney argues that 'canonists had invented a form of marriage which of its nature could not be proved' (67).

9. Yet R. M. Helmholz, the foremost authority on canon law in England, suggests that this did not end all study of canon law at Oxford and Cambridge. See Helmholz, *Roman Canon Law in Reformation England* (Cambridge: Cambridge University Press, 1990), 152.

10. Legislation both in 1536 and subsequently in 1544 authorised a commission to reform canon law but it was not until Edward VI's first parliament that canon law revision began. The resulting *Reformatio* was published by John Foxe in 1571 but it was never enacted in parliament despite several abortive attempts. The document and the attempts to legislate it are given in Gerald Bray, *Tudor Church Reform: The Henrician Canons of 1535 and the Reformatio Legum Ecclesiasticarum*, Church of England Record Society 8 (Woodbridge: Boydell, 2000).

11. For a brilliant reading of the incoherence of these categories as they are explored in Chaucer's *Pardoner's Tale*, see Elizabeth Fowler, *Literary Character: The Human Figure in Early English Writing* (Ithaca and London: Cornell University Press, 2003), chapter 1.

12. See Helmholz, *Roman Canon Law*, 113: 'Conduct that had once been sorted out privately now gave rise to public controversy.'

13. E. H. Weatherley (ed.), *Speculum Sacerdotale*, EETS, os 200 (London: Oxford University Press, 1936), 79.

14. The *Order of Communion* later included in the first Edwardian prayer book (1549) is marked by a sense of the altogether different speech acts of individual and general confession and makes allowances that 'suche as shalbe satisfied with a generall confession, not to be offended with them that doe use, to their further satisfiyng, the auriculer and secret confession to the Priest: nor those also whiche thinke nedeful or conuenient, for the quietnes of their awne co[n]sciences, particuliarly to open their sinnes to the Priest: to bee offended with them that are satisfied, with their humble confession to GOD, and the generall confession to the churche'. *The First and Second Prayer-Books of King Edward VI* (London: Dent, 1910), 217. In the Elizabethan Prayerbook of 1559 something of the unfinished matter of the reform of church government enters the language introducing the 'commination' with its regret for the practice of open penance and the anticipation of a future 'restoration' of 'the said discipline'.

15. See James Sharpe, '"Last Dying Speeches": Religion, Ideology and Public Execution in Seventeenth Century England', *Past and Present* 107 (1985): 144–67, and Michael Questier and Peter Lake's chapters 6 and 7 in Lake's marvellous book, *The Anti-Christ's Lewd Hat: Protestants, Papists, and Players in Post-Reformation England* (New Haven and London: Yale University Press, 2002).

16. Patrick Collinson, 'Shepherds, Sheepdogs, and Hirelings: The Pastoral Ministry in Post-Reformation England', in W. Sheils and Diana Wood (eds.), *The Ministry*, Studies in Church History (Oxford: Blackwell, 1989), 216.

17. The Sermon on the Mount is Jesus' radicalisation of the Torah and is thus intimately concerned with the relation between law and gospel that is such a vital component of Angelo's central debates with Isabella in the second act of the play. This is also of course a foundational concern for Reformation theology. Jesus' demands in the Sermon are impossibly demanding; they represent not so much 'a program of human fulfillment as a measure of all Christian existence'; Luke Timothy Johnson, *The Writings of the New Testament: An Interpretation* (Philadelphia: Fortress Press, 1986), 186. What Jesus demands is the perfect coincidence of inner heart and outward action. In his commentary on the Sermon, Luther fulminated about the misapprehensions and obfuscations of previous exegesis on the Sermon. How ludicrous it would be if this sermon were misunderstood to mean that 'it forbade any criticism or judgment at all'. No, this sermon was delivered only to Christ's disciples; it was not meant for any in authority – for parents, princes or judges. It was all too liable to give rise to errors for those who failed to appreciate the proper distinction between the secular and the spiritual. Insofar as he is addressing all Christians his injunctions are about a purely spiritual existence, '[h]e is telling them to live and behave before God and in the world with their heart dependent upon God and uninterested in things like secular rule or government, power or punishment, anger or revenge'; see Jaroslav Pelikan (ed.), *The Sermon on the Mount (Sermons) and The Magnificat*, Luther's Works vol. xxi (St Louis: Concordia, 1958), 210, 108, on Matthew 7:1 and Matthew 5:38–42. Luther's splitting between secular and spiritual and between the an inner realm of spirit and an outer realm of government might then seem to work against precisely the kind of conformity of thought, mind, heart, and spirit to action demanded by the teachings.

18. Thomas Aquinas, *Summa Theologiae*, ed. Thomas Gilby et al., 61 vols. (London: Blackfriars in conjunction with Eyre & Spottiswoode, 1964–81), vol. xvii (1966): i–ii, 19.6, 67. In the *Summa*, Thomas defines the law as 'a kind of direction and measure for human activity, through which a person is led to do something or held back . . .' (1a 2ae 90.1). Calvin is much more likely to model images of the law that render it diagnostic, purgative and restraining. I mention this, though I have not the proper space to pursue it here, because *Measure for Measure* gives us a variety of *pictures* of sin and law and if Thomas gives us the genealogy of law as measure, so Calvin gives us the genealogy of law as bridle and bit. I pursue some of these pictures more fully in my essay 'The Play of Voice: Acknowledgement, Knowledge, and Self-Knowledge in *Measure for Measure*', in Robert E. Stillman (ed.), *Spectacle and Public Performance in the Late Middle Ages and the Renaissance* (Leiden: Brill, 2006), 121–44.

19. Debora Kuller Shuger, *Political Theologies in Shakespeare's England: The Sacred and the State in* Measure for Measure (Basingstoke: Palgrave, 2001), 60; see also 36, 48.

20. For an analysis of the relation between sexual ethics and constitutional thought, see Elizabeth Fowler, 'Chaucer's Hard Cases', in Barbara Hanawalt and David Wallace (eds.), *Medieval Crime and Social Control* (Minneapolis: University of Minnesota Press, 1999), 124–42, esp. 127ff. See also Wallace, *Chaucerian Polity.*

21. Ernst Kantorowicz, *The King's Two Bodies: A Study in Mediaeval Political Theology* (Princeton: Princeton University Press, 1957).

22. If we were meant to respond to the impropriety of the Duke's disguise, Shuger thinks, one of the other characters would have commented on it (*Political Theologies*, 5). The 'ethics of the bed-trick' and the silence of Isabella at the end of the play are similarly dismissed as unworthy of comment because in the play no character in the play comments on them. She sees such commentary as a necessity in theatre where 'meanings must be apprehensible at first blush'. This is to vastly over-play the role of the text in theatre at the exclusion of the silent language of movement and gesture, and to under-play the role of convention which does not obviate a writer's intention in including it. Besides, there are no 'ethics' to the bed-trick unless, that is, we see no difference between a human act which implies agency, will and intention, and a trick in which participation is unwitting.

23. See chapter 7, 'Theaters of Signs and Disguises', in Sarah Beckwith, *Signifying God: Social Relation and Symbolic Act in the York Corpus Christi Plays* (Chicago: University of Chicago Press, 2001). *King Johan* may be found in Happé (ed.), *Complete Plays of John Bale*, vol. 1.

24. The most complex and illuminating commentary on these issues is William Langland's *Piers Plowman* where the failure of the friars in their office as confessors brings on the apocalyptic ending of the poem.

25. See Gordon Kipling, *Enter the King: Theatre, Liturgy, and Ritual in the Medieval Civic Triumph* (Oxford: Clarendon Press, 1998).

26. The speech is printed in Charles Howard McIlwain (ed.), *The Political Works of James I* (Cambridge, Mass: Harvard University Press, 1918), 272.

27. Rowan Williams, *Lost Icons: Reflections on Cultural Bereavement* (Edinburgh: T. & T. Clark, 2000).

12 MEDIEVAL POETICS AND PROTESTANT MAGDALENES

1. Elaine Scarry, 'On Vivacity: The Difference Between Daydreaming and Imagining-Under-Authorial-Instruction', *Representations* 52 (1995): 1–26 (13).

2. Aemilia Lanyer, *Salve Deus Rex Judaeorum*, from Suzanne Woods (ed.), *The Poems of Aemilia Lanyer* (Oxford: Oxford University Press, 1993), 107.

3. See Ceri Sullivan, 'The Physiology of Penitence in 1590s Weeping Texts', *Cahiers Elizabethains* 57 (2000): 31–47.

4. Patricia Phillippy, *Women, Death and Literature in Post-Reformation England* (Cambridge: Cambridge University Press, 2002), 30–9.

5. John 20:10–18.

6. Julian of Norwich, *A Revelation of Love*, ed. Marion Glasscoe (Exeter: University of Exeter, 1976), 2.
7. Michal Kobialka, *This Is My Body: Representational Practices in the Early Middle Ages* (Ann Arbor: University of Michigan Press, 1999), viii, 32–3, 35–9, 77–9, 198, 217–18.
8. Beckwith, *Signifying God*, 31, 73–4.
9. *Ibid.*, 121–35.
10. Richard Hooker, *Of the Lawes of Ecclesiastical Politie Eight Bookes by Richard Hooker* (1611). The engraving was designed to appeal to James I, pictured in the top left corner. The state (the edifice) descends from God (the Tetragrammaton). Power comes from God to the King as well as to a woman (the prototypical Protestant penitent) holding a book (the Scriptures) and to the Church (a Cathedral). The State itself is supported by two women – Charity and Justice.
11. Debora Shuger, *The Renaissance Bible: Scholarship, Sacrifice, and Subjectivity* (Berkeley: University of California Press, 1998), 168, 173–5, 187–8, 190–1.
12. I discuss the Anglo-Catholic Magdalene tradition at length in my forthcoming book, *The Maudlin Impression: Mary Magdalene and Religious Poetry 1570–1700*.
13. Desiderius Erasmus, *The First tome or volume of the paraphrase of Erasmus upon the Newe Testamente* (1548), ppp7r–v.
14. Herbert Kessler, *Spiritual Seeing: Picturing God's Invisibility in Medieval Art* (Philadelphia: University of Pennsylvania Press, 2000), 118, 136. Beckwith connects the form of sight made possible at the sepulchre with Lollard anticlericalism by citing Wycliffite sermons in which the guarding of Christ's body in the tomb 'is made analogous to the retention of Christ as word'. (*Signifying God*, 78–80). Specifically relevant to the Magdalene literature is Barbara Lewalski's articulation of 'Sanctification', a part of the Protestant understanding of Justification, involving 'the actual but gradual repairing of the defaced image of God in the soul, whereby it enjoys a "new life"'. The perfect restoration of the image of God, therefore, begins in this life but is fully attained only after death (*Protestant Poetics and the Seventeenth-Century Religious Lyric* (Princeton: Princeton University Press, 1979), 8).
15. Theresa Coletti, *Mary Magdalene and the Drama of the Saints: Theater, Gender, and Religion in Late Medieval England* (Philadelphia: University of Pennsylvania Press, 2004), 278–83.
16. *Ibid.*, 84–97.
17. The authorship of the text is uncertain. It was initially assumed to be Chaucerian because it was included in sixteenth-century printings of Chaucer's *House of Fame*. The text cited here is from the volume published by Richard Pynson entitled *Here begynneth the boke of Fame, made by Geffray Chaucer: with dyuers other of his workes* (1526) in which one finds 'The Complaynt of Mary Magdaleyne'. The British Library Catalogue entry comments that the text is 'from Origen' and possibly by Lydgate. The text also appears in Wynkyn de Worde's printing of *The Complaynte of the louer of Cryst Saynt Mary Magdaleyn* (1520?). Charles Edward Tame's edition (*Our Lady's Lament and the Lamentation of St.*

Mary Magdalene (London: 1871)) attributes the poem to Lydgate. Bertha Skeat further discusses the authorship question in her edition, *The Lamentatyon of Mary Magdaleyne* (Cambridge: Fabb and Tylor, 1897). The passage cited here is found on E6r.

18. Susan Stewart, *Poetry and the Fate of the Senses* (Chicago: Chicago University Press, 2002), 194.

19. Gregory writes that the Magdalene's eyes that once gazed upon worldly objects would henceforth be cast upon the feet of the Lord; her hair, the crowning ornament upon her vainglorious figure, would now modestly dry the Lord's blessed feet; the lips that once spoke words of pride would also kiss those feet and the oil that once perfumed her body would anoint them (*Homily 33, Homiliarum in evangelia*, Lib. II, in *PL*, vol. LXXVI, 1240. See also Susan Haskins, *Mary Magdalene: Myth and Metaphor* (New York: Harcourt Brace, 1993), 153).

20. Sarah Beckwith, *Christ's Body: Identity, Culture and Society in Late Medieval Writings* (London: Routledge, 1993), 88–91.

21. The sculpture dates to 1511. See Arthur Granville Peter, *The Story of the Church of St. Mary Magdalene Launceston* (Gloucester: British Publishing Company Ltd, 1936), 15.

22. Pierre Bersuire (Petrus Berchorius), for example, argues that 'Christ is a sort of book written into the skin of the Virgin . . . that book was spoken in the disposition of the Father, written in the conception of the mother, exposited in the clarification of the nativity, corrected in the passion, erased in the flagellation, punctuated in the imprint of the wounds, adorned in the crucifixion above the pulpit, illuminated in the outpouring of the blood, bound in the resurrection, and examined in the ascension.' Cited in Jesse M. Gellrich's *The Idea of the Book in the Middle Ages: Language Theory, Mythology, and Fiction* (Ithaca: Cornell University Press, 1985), 17. For further discussion of medieval paintings of reading women see the essays collected in Lesley Smith and Jane H. M. Taylor (eds.), *Women and the Book: Assessing the Visual Evidence* (London and Toronto: The British Library and University of Toronto Press, 1996).

23. 'The Complaynt of Mary Magdaleyne', E6r.

24. *Ibid.*, E6v, FIV.

25. Peter Meredith (ed.), *The Passion Play from the N. Town Manuscript* (London: Longman, 1990), 162.

26. Katherine Jansen, *The Making of the Magdalene: Preaching and Popular Devotion in the Later Middle Ages* (Princeton: Princeton University Press, 2000). In particular, see Part I in which Jansen looks at the mendicant friars' identification with the Magdalene and their use of her as a symbol of both the active and the contemplative life.

27. Richard Beadle (ed.), *The York Plays* (London: Edward Arnold, 1982), 358.

28. Gervase Markham's 'Mary Magdalenes lamentations for the losse of her master Iesus' (1601), Thomas Walkington's sermon *Rabboni; Mary Magdalenes teares, of sorrow, solace* (1620), the Magdalene sermons of Lancelot Andrewes, as well as the Magdalene poems of Herbert, Herrick, Marvell and Vaughan, are other possible examples.

29. Nicholas Breton, *Mary Magdalens loue* (1595), D8v–E11. See also *Auspiciante Jehoua: Maries exercise* (1597).
30. Breton dedicated *Pilgrimage to Paradise, ioyned with the Countess of Penbrookes Love* (1592), *Auspicante Jehoua. Maries exercise* (London, 1597) and *The passions of the spirit* (otherwise known as *The Countess of Pembroke's passion*, (London, 1599)) to the Countess.
31. Nicholas Breton, 'The Blessed Weeper' in *A Diuine poeme, diuided into two partes: The rauisht soule and the blessed weeper. Compiled by Nichals Breton, gentle-man* (London, 1601), A2r.
32. Breton follows in the tradition of Southwell and the pseudo-Origenist homily here.
33. Breton, 'Weeper', F1r.
34. *Ibid*, F4r.
35. *Ibid*, F4r.
36. Literary historians are at odds on the subject of Breton's religious sympathies and thus the authorship of some of his religious writing remains disputed. The *DNB* entry remarks, for example, that Breton's 'enthusiasm for the Virgin Mary . . . has led to the belief that the poet was an ardent Catholic. But it is almost certain . . . that the undoubtedly Catholic poems ascribed to Breton were by another hand; his long intimacy with Pembroke, which probably rested mainly on common religious sentiments, the direct attacks on Romanism which figure in many of Breton's prose tracts, and his sympathetic references to the practices of the English reformed church, point in quite the opposite direction.' His habitual comparison of his own spiritual condition to that of Mary Magdalene merely illustrates according to this source 'the strength of his religious fervour'. Michael G. Brennan's entry in the *ODNB* makes no such claims, confirming only that the poet had an interest in cultivating the Countess's patronage.
37. Breton, 'Weeper', F4r.
38. Nicholas Breton, 'The Countesse of Penbrookes loue' (1592) and *The Passions of the Spirit* (1599).
39. The problem of propriety between author and patron is differently resolved by Suzanne Trill, who notes that in 'The Countesse of Penbrooke's loue' as well as in other Breton texts dedicated to the Countess, Pembroke achieves the same 'loss of subjecthood' that Irigaray sees as the 'core of mysticism'. See 'Engendering Penitence: Nicholas Breton and "the Countesse of Penbrooke"', in Kate Chedgzoy, Melanie Hansen and Suzanne Trill (eds.), *Voicing Women: Gender and Sexuality in Early Modern Writing* (Liverpool: Liverpool University Press, 1998), 25–44 (40).
40. Breton, 'Weeper', D4v.
41. Stewart, *Poetry and the Fate of the Senses*, 194.
42. Breton, 'Weeper', F4r.
43. W. J. T. Mitchell, *Iconology: Image, Text, Ideology* (Chicago: University Press of Chicago, 1986), 42.
44. *Ibid.*, 43.

45. Breton, 'Weeper', D4r.
46. Lanyer, *Salve Deus*, 139. For further discussion of the relationship between dream, prophecy and female authority, see Elizabeth M. A. Hodgson, 'Prophecy and Gendered Mourning in Lanyer's *Salve Deus Rex Judaeorum*', *Studies in English Literature 1500–1900* 43 (2003): 101–16.
47. Scarry, 'On Vivacity', 13. The correlation between my reading of Lanyer's and Breton's Magdalene poetry and Mary Sidney's self-fashioning as the reader and memorialiser of Phillip Sidney is very apropos here. See Wendy Wall, 'Our Bodies/Our Texts?: Renaissance Women and the Trials of Authorship', in Carol J. Singley and Susan Elizabeth Sweeney (eds.), *Anxious Power: Reading, Writing, and Ambivalence in Narrative by Women* (Albany: State University of New York Press, 1993), 131–59 and Hodgson, 'Prophecy and Gendered Mourning', 111–12.
48. Badir, *The Maudlin Impression*.

Select bibliography

Aers, David. *Community, Gender and Individual Identity: English Writing 1360–1430* (London: Routledge, 1988).

'A Whisper in the Ear of Early Modernists; or, Reflections on Literary Critics Writing the "History of the Subject"'. In David Aers (ed.), *Culture and History 1350–1600* (New York: Harvester Wheatsheaf, 1992), 177–202.

Aers, David, and Lynn Staley. *The Powers of the Holy: Religion, Politics and Gender in Late Medieval English Culture* (University Park, Penn.: Pennsylvania State University Press, 1996).

Aston, Margaret. *England's Iconoclasts*, vol. 1: *Laws Against Images* (Oxford: Clarendon Press, 1988).

Baker, David, and Willy Maley (eds.). *British Identities and English Renaissance Literature* (Cambridge: Cambridge University Press, 2002).

Beckwith, Sarah. *Signifying God: Social Relations and Symbolic Act in the York Corpus Christi Plays* (Chicago: University of Chicago Press, 2001).

Benson, Larry D. (gen. ed.). *The Riverside Chaucer* (Boston: Houghton Mifflin, 1987).

Betteridge, Tom. *Literature and Politics in the English Reformation* (Manchester: Manchester University Press, 2004).

Burckhardt, Jacob. *Die Kultur der Renaissance in Italien* (1860). Trans. S. G. C. Middlemore, *The Civilisation of the Renaissance in Italy* (1878).

Burrow, J. A. 'Should We Leave Medieval Literature to the Medievalists?'. *EiC* 53 (2003): 278–83.

Collinson, Patrick. *The Birthpangs of Protestant England: Religious and Cultural Change in the Sixteenth and Seventeenth Centuries* (London: Macmillan, 1988).

Cooper, Helen. *The English Romance in Time: Transforming Motifs from Geoffrey of Monmouth to the Death of Shakespeare* (Oxford: Oxford University Press, 2002).

Cox, John, and David Scott Kastan (eds.). *A New History of Early English Drama* (New York: Columbia University Press, 1997).

Cummings, Brian. *The Literary Culture of the Reformation: Grammar and Grace* (Oxford: Oxford University Press, 2002).

Daston, Lorraine. 'The Nature of Nature in Early Modern Europe'. *Configurations* 6 (1998): 149–72.

De Certeau, Michel. *The Practice of Everyday Life*, trans. Steven Rendall (French original 1974; Berkeley and Los Angeles: University of California Press, 1988).

Dimmick, Jeremy, James Simpson and Nicolette Zeeman (eds.). *Images, Idolatry and Iconoclasm in Late Medieval England*. (Oxford: Oxford University Press, 2002).

Duffy, Eamon. *The Stripping of the Altars: Traditional Religion in England, 1400–1580* (New Haven: Yale University Press, 1992).

Elton, G. R. *Policy and Police: The Enforcement of the Reformation in the Age of Thomas Cromwell* (1972; Cambridge: Cambridge University Press, 1985).

Evans, Blakemore, *et al.* (eds.). *The Riverside Shakespeare* (Boston: Houghton Mifflin, 1974).

Ferguson, Wallace K. *The Renaissance in Historical Thought: Five Centuries of Interpretation* (Boston: Houghton Mifflin, 1948).

Gadd, Ian, and Alexandra Gillespie (eds.). *John Stow (1525–1605) and the Making of the English Past* (London: British Library, 2004).

Ganim, John M., *Medievalism and Orientalism* (New York: Palgrave Macmillan, 2005).

Gertz, SunHee Kim. *Chaucer to Shakespeare, 1337–1580* (Basingstoke: Palgrave, 2001).

Gordon, Andrew, and Bernhard Klein (eds.). *Literature, Mapping, and the Politics of Space in Early Modern Britain* (Cambridge: Cambridge University Press, 2001).

Gordon, G. S. 'Medium Aevum and the Middle Age'. Society for Pure English Tract no. 19 (Oxford: Clarendon Press, 1925), 1–25.

Grafton, Anthony. *Defenders of the Text: The Traditions of Scholarship in an Age of Science, 1450–1800* (Cambridge, Mass.: Harvard University Press, 1991).

Greenblatt, Stephen. *Hamlet in Purgatory* (Princeton: Princeton University Press, 2001).

Gregory, Brad S. *Salvation at Stake: Christian Martyrdom in Early Modern Europe* (Cambridge, Mass.: Harvard University Press, 1999).

Griffin, Benjamin. *Playing the Past: Approaches to English Historical Drama, 1385–1600* (Woodbridge: D. S. Brewer, 2001).

Hadfield, Andrew. *Literature, Politics and National Identity: Reformation to Renaissance* (Cambridge: Cambridge University Press, 1994).

Hamm, Berndt. *The Reformation of Faith in the Context of Late Medieval Theology and Piety: Essays by Berndt Hamm*. Ed. Robert J. Bast (Leiden: Brill, 2004).

Happé, Peter (ed.). *The Complete Plays of John Bale*, 2 vols. (Cambridge: D. S. Brewer, 1985–6).

Hay, Denys. *Polydore Vergil: Renaissance Historian and Man of Letters* (Oxford: Clarendon Press, 1952).

Helgerson, Richard. *Forms of Nationhood: The Elizabethan Writing of England* (Chicago: University of Chicago Press, 1992).

Howard, Jean. *The Stage and Social Struggle in Early Modern England* (London: Routledge, 1994).

Hudson, Winthrop S. *The Cambridge Connection and the Elizabethan Settlement of 1559* (Durham, NC: Duke University Press, 1980).

Ingham, Patricia Clare, and Michelle R. Warren (eds.). *Postcolonial Moves: Medieval Through Modern* (New York: Palgrave Macmillan, 2003).

James, Heather. *Shakespeare's Troy: Drama, Politics, and the Translation of Empire* (Cambridge: Cambridge University Press, 1997).

Johnston, Arthur. *Enchanted Ground: The Study of Medieval Romance in the Eighteenth Century* (London: Athlone Press, 1964).

Kabir, Ananya Jahanara, and Deanne Williams (eds.). *Postcolonial Approaches to the European Middle Ages: Translating Cultures* (Cambridge: Cambridge University Press, 2005).

Kastan, David Scott. *Shakespeare and the Book* (Cambridge: Cambridge University Press, 2001).

Kemp, Anthony. *The Estrangement of the Past: A Study in the Origins of Modern Historical Consciousness* (New York and Oxford: Oxford University Press, 1991).

Krier, Theresa (ed.). *Refiguring Chaucer in the Renaissance* (Gainesville: University of Florida Press, 1998).

Jed, Stephanie. *Chaste Thinking: The Rape of Lucretia and the Birth of Humanism* (Bloomington: Indiana University Press, 1988).

Lake, Peter. *The Anti-Christ's Lewd Hat: Protestants, Papists, and Players in Post-Reformation England* (New Haven and London: Yale University Press, 2002).

Lavezzo, Kathy (ed.). *Imagining a Medieval English Nation*. Medieval Cultures 37 (Minneapolis: University of Minnesota Press, 2004).

Le Goff, Jacques. 'For an Extended Middle Ages'. In *The Medieval Imagination*, trans. Arthur Goldhammer (Chicago: University of Chicago Press, 1988).

Lerer, Seth. *Chaucer and His Readers: Imagining the Author in Late Medieval England* (Princeton: Princeton University Press, 1993).

Courtly Letters in the Age of Henry VIII: Literary Culture and the Arts of Deceit (Cambridge: Cambridge University Press, 1997).

Levy, F. J. *Tudor Historical Thought* (San Marino, Calif.: Huntington Library Publications, 1967).

MacCulloch, Diarmaid. *Tudor Church Militant: Edward VI and the Protestant Reformation* (London: Allen Lane, 1999).

MacDougall, Hugh A. *Racial Myth in English History: Trojans, Teutons, and Anglo-Saxons* (Montreal: Harvest House; Hanover, NH: University Press of New England, 1982).

McEachern, Clare. *The Poetics of English Nationhood, 1590–1612* (Cambridge: Cambridge University Press, 1996).

McMillin, Scott, and Sally-Beth MacLean. *The Queen's Men and their Plays* (Cambridge: Cambridge University Press, 1998).

McMullan, Gordon. *The Politics of Unease in the Plays of John Fletcher* (Amherst: University of Massachusetts Press, 1994).

Machan, Tim William. *Textual Criticism and Middle English Texts* (Charlottesville: University Press of Virginia, 1994).

Matthews, David. *The Making of Middle English, 1765–1910* (Minneapolis: University of Minnesota Press, 1999).

Mendyk, Stan A. E. *'Speculum Britanniae': Regional Study, Antiquarianism and Science in Britain to 1700* (Toronto: University of Toronto Press, 1989).

Mignolo, Walter D. *The Darker Side of the Renaissance: Literacy, Territoriality, and Colonization* (Ann Arbor: University of Michigan Press, 1995).

Miskimin, Alice. *The Renaissance Chaucer* (New Haven: Yale University Press, 1975).

Nelson, Marilyn. *The Cachoeira Tales and Other Poems* (Baton Rouge: Louisiana State University Press, 2005).

Parry, Graham. *The Trophies of Time: English Antiquarians and the Seventeenth Century* (Oxford: Oxford University Press, 1995).

Patterson, Lee. *Negotiating the Past: The Historical Understanding of Medieval Literature* (Madison: University of Wisconsin Press, 1987).

   'On the Margin: Postmodernism, Ironic History, and Medieval Studies'. *Speculum* 65 (1990): 87–108.

Pearsall, Derek. *Chaucer to Spenser: An Anthology of Writing in English, 1375–1575* (Oxford: Blackwell, 1999).

   Pearsall, Derek, and Duncan Wu. *Poetry from Chaucer to Spenser* (Oxford: Blackwell, 2002).

Phillippy, Patricia. *Women, Death and Literature in Post-Reformation England* (Cambridge: Cambridge University Press, 2002).

Prendergast, Thomas A. *Chaucer's Dead Body: From Corpse to Corpus* (New York and London: Routledge, 2003).

Rackin, Phyllis. *Stages of History: Shakespeare's English Chronicles* (Ithaca and New York: Cornell University Press, 1990).

Ruggiers, Paul G. (ed.). *Editing Chaucer: The Great Tradition* (Norman: Pilgrim Books, 1984).

Schwyzer, Philip. *Literature, Nationalism, and Memory in Early Modern England and Wales* (Cambridge: Cambridge University Press, 2004).

Scragg, Donald, and Carole Weinberg (eds.). *Literary Appropriations of the Anglo-Saxons from the Thirteenth to the Twentieth Century* (Cambridge: Cambridge University Press, 2000).

Simpson, James. *Reform and Cultural Revolution. The Oxford English Literary History,* gen. ed. Jonathan Bate, 13 vols. Vol. II (1350–1547) (Oxford: Oxford University Press, 2002).

   'Chaucer's Presence and Absence, 1400–1550'. In Jill Mann and Piero Boitani (eds.), *A Chaucer Companion,* 2nd edn (Cambridge: Cambridge University Press, 2003), 251–69.

Shrank, Cathy. *Writing the Nation: Literature, Humanism and English Identities, 1530–1580* (Oxford: Oxford University Press, 2004).

Sluhovsky, Moshe. 'Discernment of Difference, the Introspective Subject, and the Birth of Modernity'. *JMEMS* 36 (2006): 169–99.

Starn, Randolph. 'The Early Modern Muddle'. *Journal of Early Modern History* 6.3 (2002): 296–307.

Stock, Brian. 'The Middle Ages as Subject and Object'. *New Literary History* 5 (1974): 527–47.

Summit, Jennifer. *Lost Property: The Woman Writer and English Literary History, c. 1380–1589* (Chicago: University of Chicago Press, 2000).

Targoff, Ramie. *Common Prayer: The Language of Public Devotion in Early Modern England* (Chicago: University of Chicago Press, 2001).

Thomas, Keith. *Religion and the Decline of Magic: Studies in Popular Beliefs in Sixteenth and Seventeenth Century England* (Oxford: Oxford University Press, 1970).

Thompson, Ann. *Shakespeare's Chaucer: A Study in Literary Origins* (Liverpool: Liverpool University Press, 1978).

Tribble, Evelyn B. *Margins and Marginality: The Printed Page in Early Modern England* (Charlottesville: University Press of Virginia, 1993).

Trigg, Stephanie. *Congenial Souls: Reading Chaucer from Medieval to Postmodern* (Minneapolis: University of Minnesota Press, 2002).

Walker, Greg. *Plays of Persuasion: Drama and Politics at the Court of Henry VIII* (Cambridge: Cambridge University Press, 1991).

Persuasive Fictions: Faction, Faith and Political Culture in the Reign of Henry VIII (Aldershot: Scolar, 1995).

Wall, Wendy. *The Imprint of Gender: Authorship and Publication in the English Renaissance* (Ithaca and London: Cornell University Press, 1993).

Wallace, David. *Chaucerian Polity: Absolutist Lineages and Associational Forms in England and Italy* (Stanford: Stanford University Press, 1997).

Premodern Places: Calais to Surinam, Chaucer to Aphra Behn (Oxford: Blackwell, 2004).

Wallace, David (ed.). *The Cambridge History of Medieval English Literature* (Cambridge: Cambridge University Press, 1999).

Walzer, Michael. *The Revolution of the Saints: A Study in the Origins of Radical Politics* (London: Weidenfeld and Nicholson, 1966).

White, Paul Whitfield. *Theatre and Reformation: Protestantism, Patronage, and Playing in Tudor England* (Cambridge: Cambridge University Press, 1992).

Williams, Deanne. *The French Fetish from Chaucer to Shakespeare* (Cambridge: Cambridge University Press, 2004).

Youings, Joyce (ed.). *The Dissolution of the Monasteries* (New York: Barnes and Noble, 1971).

Index